Published by Employment Law Services Limited, Unit 3, Chequers Farm, Chequers Lane, Watford, Hertfordshire WD25 0LG

I978-1-913925-03-1

THE EMPLOYMENT LAW LIBRARY

1. Employee Investigations

2. GDPR for HR Professionals

3. Preventing and Defending Employee Stress Claims

4. Employment Tribunal Time Limits

5. Deconstructing TUPE

6. Changing Terms & Conditions

7. Constructive Dismissal

8. Resolving Grievances

9. HR Hazards

10. Employment Status

CONTENTS

ACAS EARLY CONCILIATION

ANDREW SHORT QC, OUTER TEMPLE CHAMBERS

Daniel Barnett

I'm joined this afternoon by Andrew Short from Outer Temple Chambers for this webinar on ACAS early conciliation.

Andrew, good afternoon. To get started, there are a couple of questions that I'd like to ask you. Do you think the early conciliation legislation is working well?

Andrew Short

Well, in one sense, it's certainly working well. I think that the latest figures released by ACAS, which had been fairly standard over the last three years, show that about 130,000 cases are notified to them each year. And of those, 70% - or 90,000 - one way or another don't proceed to an ET1. And if you take one of the purposes of early conciliation as being to avoid unnecessary claims, certainly to avoid claims that need and proceed with conciliation of some sort, then they're really successful. That doesn't mean that all of the 90,000, all of the 70%, that don't proceed are settled. But I think the figures show about 10% - that's 13,000 or so a year - of the notifications to ACAS end up being settled within that period on a COT3. Doubtless, others are settled either informally or because the parties reach some kind of resolution or a potential claimant realises they don't have a claim. So in terms of the numbers, I think it's working pretty well.

In another sense, it hasn't been working as intended, because one of the purposes of this regime was to avoid the satellite litigation that bedevilled the Statutory Disciplinary and Grievance Procedure ranging from 2004. And one of the problems there was that that legislation used very open-textured language, so what was a grievance was an issue and how much information had to be given. And there was an immense amount of appellate litigation before the Court of Appeal really sorted it all out. Now, this legislation sought to avoid that by using much more tightly drawn concepts with a series of requirements that were hoped, more or less, to provide yes and no answers. Despite that - I think, as the EAT has commented - this has still resulted in quite a lot of satellite litigation. And it's a testament to human ingenuity that they can find lots of things to argue about in relation to a piece of legislation that's meant to be very straightforward.

Daniel Barnett

Do you think the legislation as it stands was well designed?

Andrew Short

Well, I think the legislation was certainly well-intentioned, but I don't think I'd necessarily describe it as being well-drafted. There is an irony, certainly, at the heart of this which is that legislation that's been construed as meaning a claim will be automatically rejected where there's a typographical error in an EC number when it's put onto the claim form contains a series of errors. So there are typos in the Queen's Printers' copy of these statutory instruments. There are two mistakes in the EC regulations. They're both erroneous cross-references, so they refer to regulation 4(a) and 4(a) when it should be regulation 4.1(a) and 4.1(b). There are mistakes in the rules of procedure, dealing with the EC regulations - I was going say dealing with the 2014 regulations - that's really the problem because the rules of procedure in at least one place, refer to the 2013 EC regulations when the regulations are 2014. There's an infelicity of language in the prescribed form of the ET1 which doesn't cater well for some situations when people have an exemption, particularly in multiple claims. And there's really not been very much examination of how the rules work in relation to multiple claims.

Finally - and it's almost heretical to say this - there's a typo in the Butterworths Employment Law handbook. Rule 10(c) gives a list of the things that have to go into a claim form for it to be valid. The list is the EC number, confirmation that the proceedings don't include relevant proceedings where you need to go through EC, or confirmation that one of the exemptions applies. Butterworths says the claim form must contain ALL of the following, rather than ONE of the following. So, there's a difference. It's obvious in context and it's clear from the regulations that you only need one of the following. Obviously, you only need either the EC number or confirmation. That error has followed its way through into some of the decisions and who's to say whether it's had any material impact or not.

I do think there's an irony when claimants have been told that a typo brings an end to their claim that this is an area that's particularly strewn with mistakes. But perhaps more important than that is the use of these tightly drawn definitions. Inviting a mechanistic application of the rules has resulted in many claims being rejected, sometimes once and for all, in circumstances that certainly don't further the purpose of the underlying legislation because the claimants have gone through EC. Now that mechanism has been steadily relaxed in subsequent amendments. But there are still

problems where those specific relaxations don't apply.

Daniel Barnett
Final question from me: what are the recent developments in ACAS early conciliation?

Andrew Short
The recent amendments to the EC Rules of Procedure have also brought about changes to both the EC regs themselves and the references to early conciliation in the Rules of Procedure. The EC regs have changed because there's now an express power for ACAS to go back to the claimant during the conciliation period to either correct errors or obtain missing information in the form. It's quite important. As well as that, you had this very difficult notion of a conciliation period being 28 days but could be extended for 14 days, which just cause confusion. And that's now being extended, so the conciliation period is now six weeks.

The changes to the rules may well have more impact on the sorts of problems that we've seen with the application of these rules in practice. The first is there's now a specific provision dealing with cases where the EC number on the certificate doesn't match the EC number on the claim form. It was probably already covered in some of the provisions. This is typically where someone misses a number off the end or transposes two numbers in the form. But the real reason for the introduction of that possible ground for rejection as an express ground is that it's introduced in parallel with a provision whereby the employment judge need not reject the form if they are satisfied that the claimant made an error, and it's not in the interest of justice to reject the claim form. The first amendments to this regime gave tribunals the discretion not to reject where there was a minor error, in the name or address that the claimant used for themselves or for the respondent. That's been changed. So now, rather than having to show it's a minor error, you just need to show it's an error and it's in the interest of justice. So sadly, we're all going to be denied the opportunity to argue about whether an error was a minor error or not. And the explanatory notes to the regulations make clear that these are being done because the purpose was to allow tribunals to engage in dispute resolution rather than allow parties to litigate upon technical matters.

Now, one feature I should mention about these amendments is that there's a slight quirk in the transitional provisions because most of the changes in the recent amendments apply generally to all cases. But the changes to the EC regulations only apply where the notification to ACAS is made on or after 1 December 2020. Now, that only applies to the changes to the EC regulations, i.e. the six-week period, and the option for ACAS to go back and correct errors. It doesn't apply, on my reading of the transition provisions, to the EC-related amendments to the rules. So, if you like, fat-fingered typists who put in the wrong number can take the benefits of the new discretion even though that error was made in relation to a notification before 1 December last year. So they're the changes.

I've talked a lot about ACAS. Obviously, this is dependent on the work that ACAS do. And I should, I think, apologise to ACAS - this is something to get off my chest - because when I was a student, in 1986, there were some demonstrations complaining about the Department of Employment's Policy. There was an occupation of the Department of Employment offices that I may or may not have been part of. We went to the offices, someone knocked on the door. They were very polite and someone said, "We don't mind you being here at all, but you should know that this is ACAS and the Department of Employment offices are next door". So, we had to leave ACAS apologising for any inconvenience, and then quietly into the corridor and do the same thing over there. Very good, because they didn't phone ahead and when we depart, so I apologise for that.

Victoria Duff
What types of claims are exempt from ACAS early conciliation?

Andrew Short
Realistically, almost no proceedings that we deal with on a regular basis are exempt. There are a tiny number - I must say, I can't actually remember the list off the top of my head - of unusual ones. Some of the proceedings depend on the respondent. So those people who have claims against the security service, the special intelligence service the Government Communications Headquarters (GCHQ) don't need to bring claims. There are also certain claims under part 10 of the Employment Rights Act, various trade union-related claims, but it's a very small, very finite list.

Daniel Barnett
I think the most important one is probably applications for interim relief because you can't be expected to get your ET1 in within seven days if you're going to spend six weeks chatting to a cast first.

Andrew Short
That's right. That's the main one if it's accompanied by an interim relief application.

Gillian Howard
What are the discrete circumstances that can render a COT3 agreement - that's an ACAS settlement agreement - void after the parties have entered into the settlement agreement with an ACAS conciliation officer?

Andrew Short
I saw that question when it came up earlier. I do wonder if there's a moral hazard in offering a prize for the most questions read out in any week, particularly as that goes slightly beyond EC. There are very few circumstances where you can reopen what's effectively a binding contract. I'd imagine fraud is one because fraud unravels everything. But other than that, I'm not sure what will unravel what would otherwise be a binding agreement. There's fraud and misrepresentation, but other

than that sort of serious wrongdoing that would unravel any agreement, I think they're likely to be the matters.

Victoria Duff

Is it wise to have raised a grievance with your employer before telling ACAS? And will a tribunal expect you to have raised a grievance with your employer before instituting ACAS EC?

Andrew Short

There are two questions there. The EC conciliation is about one thing: access to the tribunal. You have to do it in order to get access to the tribunal. It's a positive thing because it will, in some cases, result in a conciliation and agreement. The question envisaged an ongoing employment relationship. If you have an ongoing employment relationship - many of these issues are things about existing employees - I think it would be unwise from an industrial relations perspective not to raise these matters with your employer before going to ACAS because you can resolve things internally. But it might well be fact-specific and it might be that it will be difficult to deal with it in terms of very small employers. You might want ACAS to be involved, and this is one way in which ACAS can get involved. More generally, I think tribunals will expect you to have raised matters with your employer before you begin a relatively formal approach. But of course, that's not always possible and not always sensible.

Christopher Temmink

If a claimant refuses to engage in conciliation, either meaningfully or at all, should they still be issued with a certificate?

Andrew Short

The answer to that from a legal point of view is definitely yes. And in fact, one of the things that a claimant can do having contacted ACAS is say that they're not interested in conciliation, at which point the conciliation period will come to an end and ACAS will send out a form.

So this is not about the quality of conciliation and that has to be the case. Quite a lot of the cases where conciliation isn't successful and which become ET1s, are claims in these large multiples - large equal pay multiples, for example. And there, it really is just a technical step that has to be taken. So if a large chain of one sort or another has 10,000 live claims, claimant 10,001 isn't going to have their issue meaningfully conciliated by either party. And so the most sensible option is for the claimant to go through the step and then say they're not interested in conciliation and then they get a certificate.

It would, in my view, be a terrible step if there had to be a willingness to consider conciliate meaningfully because then we would have exactly the same problem that we had in 2004. People said, well, they didn't conciliate meaningfully. What that really means, in many cases, is "they didn't agree with me". And the Court of Appeal recently considered the extension of time limits where someone had misunderstood early conciliation. In fact, that was the other way round. That was where the claimant thought that an earlier attempt at early conciliation shouldn't have counted because the employer wouldn't engage meaningfully. So it really is just looking at whether the technical requirements have been satisfied, rather than examining the quality of engagement by either party.

Katie Milne

What's your view on whether it's worth - as an employer - providing a detailed response to issues raised by a claimant at the ACAS early conciliation stage? Should you keep your powder dry or spill the beans?

Andrew Short

It really depends on what you're seeking to achieve here. There will be cases that are capable of settlement. If someone has genuinely misunderstood, it may be that you can explain things to them and that will produce a resolution. Some of the 90,000 cases that don't proceed to an ET1 after going through EC don't proceed because the employer has told the employee why something has happened. Then either through taking advice or speaking to ACAS or reflecting, the prospective claimant has thought, you know what, that's right, or that's okay, or I understand. If there's a possibility of that happening, you could save an awful lot of money. If you're thinking about its impact on litigation, it's not going to be of any use to you at all. In many cases, you'll know whether it's something that might be effective or whether it's something that definitely won't be effective. It will improve your prospects of a conciliation rather than improving your prospects in litigation. Actually, it won't always improve your prospects of conciliation because if you give someone lots of detail, they might find lots of things to disagree about, even if the areas of disagreement aren't actually relevant to the claim itself. So you always have to be a little bit careful. Giving too much detail can be a disadvantage generally. But other than that, it's always worth having a think about what you're trying to achieve.

Lara Scott Ellis

We reach agreements with about one employee a month for them to leave our employment. We'd like to use a COT3 because we don't want them to see a solicitor, but ACAS won't get involved because early conciliation hasn't formally been started. What can we do?

Andrew Short

Employers can ask ACAS to engage in early conciliation.

Daniel Barnett

I'm actually wondering whether the real issue here is that ACAS don't like being used as a rubber stamp for a deal that's already been reached.

Andrew Short

That may be true because you can invite early conciliation even if you're an employer.

My experience with ACAS over the years is that that has changed somewhat. In the past, certainly on occasions, ACAS were willing to become involved where deals had largely been done. But maybe the practical solution to this issue is to try and engage by contacting ACAS with a view to commencing early conciliation before you have reached a final agreement.

Daniel Barnett

Lara Scott-Evans is commenting that that's their experience. ACAS don't assist with rubber stamping. Tracey Munro says ACAS won't entertain it if it's a done deal. Sam Proffitt comments that it massively depends on which conciliator you get. So I think that broadly reflects your experience, Andrew.

Andrew Short

I have definitely been aware of cases where ACAS have become involved when a lot of the legwork has already been done.

Daniel Barnett

Of course, there could always be a furious dispute between the parties, which they simply can't resolve without the help of ACAS over whether payment should be made within 14 days or 28 days, and you desperately need ACAS's help to resolve that one.

Diana Eguizabal

Where you have discrimination claims against both an employer and an individual, do you need an ACAS early conciliation certificate number for the ET1 for the employer as well as the individual?

Andrew Short

With multiple respondents, you need an ACAS number for each respondent.

Anonymous

Given the volume of backlog of employment tribunal claims, do you think ACAS should have greater authoritative powers to triage and refuse to allow cases to proceed to a tribunal if ACAS think there's no realistic prospect of a successful claim?

Andrew Short

No. To develop that, the Court of Appeal doesn't really do that; it lets people explain their case before making a decision, and we have tribunals making decisions. I think it would be very difficult to transfer that decision-making power to ACAS, particularly within the six-week period. But it would be a completely different thing. ACAS would cease to be a conciliating body and would become an adjudicating body. I suppose they can arbitrate, but this definitely wouldn't be arbitration. They'd need another 'A' in the name.

A Tovey

How important is the word 'limited' in a respondent's name on the ACAS form?

Moira Kinnear

If you mistakenly identify a group subsidiary company, rather than the actual employer, does that invalidate the early conciliation and any subsequent tribunals?

Andrew Short

That brings back some very difficult memories for me. When I was very junior, I had to return from a senior member of my chambers and I went to the Chancery Division to argue that there's no such thing as Barclays Bank, because that was the name of the claimant trying to repossess my client's house. There may have been a Barclays Bank PLC, but they hadn't issued the claim. I think I came in the top two on that one.

Here, the answer is yes in the sense that 'limited' or identifying the wrong corporate body is a mistake and it can mean, for example, if the EC certificate says 'limited', and the claim form doesn't or vice versa, you haven't complied strictly with the Rules of Procedure rather than the substantive rules. But the first set of amendments to the regulations introduced this power, this discretion, so that an employment judge could waive that error, where there had been a minor error in names

and the interest of justice didn't require the claim to be struck out. That remains and it's been broadened so that it no longer needs to be a minor error. So in cases where it's genuinely an error, I think it is something where one would have some expectation that a tribunal will exercise their discretion to allow the claim to proceed. If it's more than that, though, if you have identified the wrong body and it has made a difference - and there will be cases on the facts where that happens - then you cannot count on that because they are different bodies. But if it's just a technical mistake as to names, then that will be fine. I mean, there are cases where tribunals have become very critical of employers taking very dry points on that, but again, it's going to depend on the facts, whether it's an opportunist attempt to avoid a claim or whether it's a more substantive objection, if, for example, some prejudice has been caused because it's been dealt with by the wrong body. evidence has been lost that kind of thing.

Laura Sheridan

If a claimant chooses to simply be provided with a certificate rather than go through conciliation, is the employer told about this?

Andrew Short

If the employer is subsequently a respondent on an ET1, they will be told on the ET1 whether there's an EC number or whether an exemption applied. And in those circumstances, if that's the case, in effect, they will be told that the employee went to ACAS and said they're not interested in conciliation. If however, they go to ACAS and they say they're not interested in conciliation but they then decide not to issue a claim, then I don't think the employer will be told. And I think ACAS will only contact the employer with the consent of the individual.

Daniel Barnett

That was certainly the case when the rules came in. I have a funny feeling I've read somewhere that that changed a couple of years ago, and ACAS now send out the form to employers. I might be wrong. I know we've got people from ACAS on this call. If you're from ACAS and you know the answer to this, if you pop it in the chat I'll read it out.

Anonymous
Could I be missing calls from ACAS while I'm working from home?

Daniel Barnett
I'm not sure Andrew Short will know the answer to that. Could our anonymous attendee be missing calls from ACAS while working from home?

Andrew Short
Yes. I mean, he could be missing them, but he's at work. I don't know. I don't always have my phone on me, but I'm not sure that's the gist of the question. In practical terms, yes. In terms of timing, that's not so much a problem. In terms of the certificate, the certificate is sent by email or by post. So as a claimant, you're not told that the conciliation process is finished without getting something in writing. So you can't miss that phone call in a material way.

Daniel Barnett
A number of ACAS conciliators have been in touch on the chat. An employer is not sent a copy of the ACAS certificate unless the claimant has authorised a copy be sent to them. So an employee who just does the rubber-stamping job but doesn't want the employer to know anything means that the employer won't get the certificate.

Hema Mistry
Who's responsible for drafting the COT3? Is it ACAS or is it the employer?

Andrew Short
I'm not sure that there's a clear legal obligation that makes one person or another do that. It would be a surprise if there was a statutory obligation that placed the burden on the employer. I think sometimes ACAS will drive it and sometimes the parties will drive it. it's really going to depend. It's quite different if you have

a very small, very informal employer and an unrepresented employee. If lawyers are involved, they'll tend to make it more tricky, generally. But I think it's gonna depend on the circumstances.

Peter
Should ACAS promote a final early conciliation deal that's not necessarily in the best interests of an aggrieved employee?

Daniel Barnett
So, does ACAS have a duty to make sure the settlement is fair?

Andrew Short
I think ACAS have a duty to ensure there's a settlement where appropriate. I don't think ACAS can really decide whether something's fair or not because they would need to consider so many things. And it really would step beyond what's possible in this kind of period. Think how long are some hearings on quantum are. You'd need to know the respective merits of the case and ACAS can't possibly do that.

JP Choi
Realistically, how enforceable are confidentiality provisions in COP3s?

Andrew Short
My general response is they're really difficult, and I don't know how often they have been enforced. And it reminds me that my friend Michael Lamb did a case where they settled, more or less, and then the employer at the last minute said they insist - as an absolute deal-breaker - on confidentiality. Mike was already taking instructions and then 15 minutes later, the solicitor on the other side phoned back and said there's no need to worry about confidentiality. Michael asked the solicitor what had changed, and he said, well, mostly what's changed is that your client's being carried around the factory, shoulder high, by a group of people chanting, "£30,000".

Daniel Barnett
Andrew Short QC from Outer Temple, thank you very much.

CHANGING TERMS AND CONDITIONS

LYDIA SEYMOUR, OUTER TEMPLE CHAMBERS

Daniel Barnett

I'm joined today by Lydia Seymour from Outer Temple Chambers, and she'll be speaking on changing terms of conditions.

Lydia, Good morning. I'm going to throw a few questions at you first, if I may. First of all, Boris Johnson's roadmap means that we're all hopefully going to be heading back to work soon. Can an employer rely on a specific flexibility clause to insist that employees work from home indefinitely in the future?

Lydia Seymour

I'll start with a general health warning for all contract issues that we might cover today, which is that obviously all contractual clauses need to be looked at individually and in context. But there are general principles that we can apply.

In relation to flexibility clauses and homeworking, there's quite a wide spectrum of situations that we might be thinking about. At one end, there may be recently drafted contracts which say in terms that employees can be expected to work entirely from home, either as a default option or as one of a set of specified options. There is nothing objectionable about that - obviously an employer and employee are entitled to agree home working.

At the other end of the spectrum - and I think these are the sorts of cases we're likely to be needing to look at over the next few months - are clauses that didn't specifically anticipate the current situation, but which allow for some degree of flexibility. An example of a general flexibility clause would be something like:

> *"the employee shall perform their duties at Outer Temple Chambers, or such other place within the UK as the company may require from time to time"*

An employer could try and argue that a clause of that nature is enough to impose indefinite homeworking, on the basis that the employees' home is such other place in the UK as the company may require. But I would expect courts and tribunals to take a fairly close look at any attempted use of flexibility clauses in that way. If you're arguing on behalf of an employee, you can say that an employer who wanted to impose home working could have done it perfectly easily by means of actually saying so. And that such-other-place-within-the-UK-type clauses are simply not enough to allow an employer to do something quite as fundamental as make a shift to permanent home working. That is particularly the case given that the reality of a shift to indefinite home working is a shift of cost from the employer, who no longer has to provide an office, to the employee.

So broadly speaking, my view would be that employers should be cautious about trying to use a standard, general, flexibility clause to impose indefinite homeworking.

I should perhaps add to that the second general health warning in relation to all contractual changes issues, which is that it's not just the common law situation that you have to think about – i.e. whether the clause is sufficiently broad to give you the power to make the change - but also all the various overlaid statutory duties, implied duties, that limit the power of employers in this area. So in any individual case, you'll also have to think about those.

Daniel Barnett
If I was cross-examining you, Lydia, I'd point out you hadn't answered the question.

Lydia Seymour
Well, that's because the answer to the question is that it's all very fact-specific! But my general view is that courts and tribunals are going to be really cautious about allowing changes that occurred during the pandemic to become permanent, particularly in circumstances in which they are to the financial benefit of the employer, but not to the financial benefit of the employee.

And the reality is that contractual drafting - in the case of employment contracts – has long been a process of trying to get the absolute broadest power for the employer in all circumstances. The pandemic has led to changes in working practices that are beyond even that very broad drafting, and I would expect courts and tribunals to want to try to return us as best as possible to a more restrictive approach to the power of the employer. Something like indefinite homeworking strikes me as precisely the sort of area in which a restrictive approach is likely to be taken. So the answer to your question is that my view is that employers will only be able to rely on general flexibility clauses to impose indefinite homeworking if the clause has the clearest and most unambiguous meaning.

Su Apps
Can you obtain agreement to change the terms and conditions by sending a letter to an employee stating the changes and saying, if you haven't objected by three weeks hence, then you're deemed to have agreed to the changes?

Lydia Seymour
Well sticking with the cross-examination approach of answering the question directly, the answer to that is you can try! But if you are concerned to ensure that the change is effective, that's not a brilliant way forward. The reason for that is that if you provide a fresh contract which the employee doesn't sign – whether because it contains a 'if you haven't objected by such a date' we will take it that you have agreed provision, or whether you send out the contract but don't actually make sure that people have signed it, and people leave it in their desk drawer, or whatever - the terms will only actually be effective if the court or tribunal takes the view that what the employee has done is "only referable" to an acceptance of the terms. That's a case called Solectron v Roper *(Solectron Scotland Ltd v Roper [2004] IRLR 4)* from 2004. So what the court will say is that unless the way the employee has behaved is "only referable" to acceptance – i.e. the only reasonable explanation for it is that they have accepted the terms, then simply sending them a letter saying that unless they object they are deemed to have agreed is not enough.

There are situations in which a person can be taken to have agreed without signing the contract or specifically saying yes to it. There was a case called Farnsworth v Lacey *(FW Farnsworth Ltd v Lacy [2012] EWHC 2830 (Ch))*, where a new contract was introduced which included a new right to private healthcare. The individual concerned left the contract in his drawer at work, but later did make use of the private health care. He later tried to argue that he shouldn't be bound by the other terms of the new contract because he hadn't agreed it, but he lost. By taking the private healthcare - so taking advantage of the new contract - he took on all of the terms of that contract.

But going back to the question, no, you can't reliably obtain agreement by saying if the employee is silent, they will be deemed to have agreed.

Daniel Barnett
I think there's another case called System Floors v Daniel *(System Floors (UK) Ltd v Daniel [1982] ICR 54 EAT)* which is about the more important the changes to the employee, the less likely they are to have been taken to have agreed it.

Lydia Seymour
Absolutely. And I suppose the more unusual as well. One of the other things that the court will take into account is whether the impact of the change on the employee is immediate. For example, seeking to make a change to pension entitlements, which will not actually hit the employee until they are of retirement age, is less likely to be taken to be taken as agreed than something which impacts on them on a day-to-day basis and immediately, like their immediate pay, for example.

Steven Eckett
What's the best way, from your experience, to implement any necessary changes to staff terms and conditions with minimum legal risk?

Daniel Barnett
There's a wide question for you.

Lydia Seymour
Well, absolutely! I suppose the first question is where you start from. So obviously, starting from the point of view of having got all of your terms conditions in good order, and preferably starting from a place in which the majority of your staff are on the same or similar terms and conditions. Because one of the first things you want to identify is whether you're acting fairly and consistently, as between your various staff. So I'm going to assume that we're starting from a good place and that we're starting from

a position in which we're acting fairly and consistently.

The next point that you need to bear in mind, I suppose, is just that, broadly speaking, carrot is going to be better and easier and less risky than stick. It's not a coincidence that companies tend to introduce changes to terms and conditions at the point of pay rises. A company is entitled to make a pay rise conditional on a change to terms and conditions and, broadly speaking, that is likely to be your best bet. Once you've made a decision as to what carrot you're going to use and the changes that you're going to introduce in relation to it, it's obviously best practice to consult and to ensure that once the consultation has occurred, you are keeping good records and dealing appropriately with the changes on an administrative level moving forwards.

That's a broad and general answer to a broad and general question - I don't know whether there are any specific aspects of it that might be helpful to look at.

Lucy Greatorex
When going down the fire and rehire route for employers who are willing to accept changes, what advice would you give to an employer as best practice?

Daniel Barnett
Of course, 'best practice' is really a euphemism for being as nice as you can be. In being as pro employees you can be. What I suspect Lucy is really asking but doesn't want to say is: what can you do to get away with it as an employer?

Lydia Seymour
At the moment - again, sticking with the cross-examination approach - best practice, I would take to mean least risk of subsequent claims. And when you're going down the fire and rehire route, the first thing to bear in mind is, how serious is what you're doing? Is it actually proportionate for you to fire and rehire in relation to the particular changes

that you're trying to make? Going back to the previous question, you hope that with sufficient consultation, with a bit of carrot as well as a bit of stick, you can actually carry everybody along with you.

So again, in terms of being in the best position from the start, you want to be in a position whereby you've acted reasonably; it's a reasonable and necessary change to be making; you have consulted widely, but you're stuck with, perhaps, a rump of individuals who simply will not accept.

At the moment, the reality is the fire and rehire is politically sensitive. There's a concern at the moment that large companies are using fire and rehire to bully employees to make changes. That means that employers have to be particularly careful at the moment to be able to establish that they have the best possible reason, that dismissal truly is necessary in the circumstances. A Tribunal is going to take a lot of convincing at the moment that it was truly necessary to dismiss and rehire and my feeling at the moment is that employers need to be particularly careful.

Daniel Barnett
I remember a case called Catamaran Cruisers (Catamaran Cruisers Ltd v Williams & Ors [1994] IRLR 384) that says that the legal test for fire and rehire is that the employer has to demonstrate a 'sound good business reason', as well as going through consultation. I remember that case because I've always thought the phrase 'sound good business reason' has the adjectives the wrong way around and it should be 'good sound business reason'.

Lydia Seymour
It's also largely meaningless, particularly in the context of a tribunal system in which tribunal judges are wary of placing themselves into the position of the employer. 'Sound good business reason' is a very subjective test and the true ability of a third-party judge or anyone to determine whether a particular business has

put forward a 'sound good business reason' strikes me as really rather limited. It is not going to be a million miles away from a reasonableness test albeit wrapped up as something else.

Su Apps
If an employer is introducing a change to terms and conditions for more than 20 employees, do they have to start collective consultation straight away? Or is the duty only triggered when it becomes clear that 20 or more may not agree to the changes?

Daniel Barnett
So this all turns on the meaning of the phrase 'proposing to dismiss' in s188 Trade Union and Labour Relations (Consolidation) Act.

Lydia Seymour
That's right, because the definition of redundancy for the purpose of TULRA is broader than it is for the standard unfair dismissal provisions - so that a person is redundant for the purposes of TULRA - and consultation obligations are triggered - even if they are fired and rehired so would not count as redundant in the normal sense.

The answer is going to be a question of fact and degree. At the outset, when you are proposing the changes to terms and conditions, you are clearly not proposing to dismiss, but there may come a point where it is clear that there is a rump of people are not going to agree, and at the point that fire and re-hire becomes a realistic possibility you are at risk of a Tribunal finding that you were proposing to dismiss them. But it's going be a question of facts and degree in each case.

Daniel Barnett
The real test on whether a judge is going to say that you started consulting early enough is whether the judge likes you or not as an employer.

Lydia Seymour
I thought it was 'sound good business reasons'?

Daniel Barnett
That's the one.

Anonymous
When updating contracts of employment, should employers reissue contracts to existing employees, and what's the best way to do that?

Lydia Seymour
Yes is the answer to that. Assuming for the moment that the contract is changed in respect of one or more of the items set out in s1 of the Employment Rights Act, i.e. the aspects of the contract that have to be provided in the form of written particulars, then when there is a change, the employer must provide a new contract (under s4 ERA). I'm not completely sure of the best way to do this in practical terms, in terms of sending them out. I think that perhaps goes back to our point about people who put their contract in a drawer or whatever. Obviously, the best way to provide a contract is to provide it to the individual and ensure that there's a robust system of following up in practice to make sure that they've been signed. I'm not sure how far the practical question goes or whether that's more of an HR issue.

Daniel Barnett
Under s1, is the obligation to send out a completely fresh contract or is it to send out a statement of variation to the existing contract?

Lydia Seymour
The question of how substantial a change has to be to make it worthwhile to send a whole contract rather than simply saying, you've got a pay rise, is again a question of facts and degree. Also, of how long it is since you last made a change. So if you've made repeated small changes, after a few years it's going to be wise to reissue a completely fresh contract, not least because it's tedious to have to keep checking lots of different documents, and it's a good idea to have everybody's contractual entitlement all in one place.

Kirsty Stokes
What's the most common step people miss when changing terms conditions?

Daniel Barnett
I think for me, it's probably failing to get evidence of the employees' agreement, either by way of their signature or by way of, at the very minimum, them ticking a box on some sort of form on the internet.

Lydia Seymour
That's interesting. I was thinking it's checking they are entitled do it in the first place. Perhaps that just reflects the sorts of cases that tend to come our way. I think this is a problem particularly when you end up with complex situations of different employees on different contracts and you are trying to harmonise. It is frequently the case that an assumption is made as to the ability to change terms and conditions without careful thought about whether this is something the employer has the power to do in the particular case. You can do everything to make sure that it's all done procedurally correctly, but find at the end of it you weren't entitled to do it at all.

Another thing that comes up quite often is the assumption that because it's not much of a change, it will be alright. Although the extent of the change, and in particular, the extent to the impact on the employee can be relevant, the reality of contracts is that they are legal documents, and it doesn't matter whether the employer or employee thinks it's important; the question is what the contract says. I think sometimes people can fall into traps. I did a case quite recently involving a change from weekly pay to monthly pay, that the employer thought of as being a very minor change, but the employees didn't. A trip to the employment tribunal and nearly getting to the EAT later, quite a lot of trouble was caused.

Gillian Howard
What compelling evidence would satisfy a tribunal that terminating the current contract

and offering a new contract wouldn't be an unfair dismissal?

Daniel Barnett
I think the answer's in the question here: 'compelling' evidence.

Lydia Seymour
The question of what is compelling leads to the greatest mis-step that parties make in litigation - failing to realise that the question of what is compelling evidence to a Tribunal may not be the same as what constitutes compelling evidence for you and the party that you're representing at the time.

I think, perhaps the way to look at this is to consider the question from the point of view of the other side. If you are, for example, advising the employer in this case, rather than thinking about what compelling evidence would satisfy the tribunal that your client was entitled to do this, think about whether the other side might have compelling reasons why it shouldn't happen. Contracts are bilateral agreements, and if you want to unilaterally amend them (and fire and rehire is, at the end of the day, just a mechanism for unilateral amendment) when you get to a court or tribunal, they are going to be looking at it from an objective viewpoint. That isn't whether your side found the reason compelling, but whether it was objectively compelling, taking account of both sides.

I read something the other day about negotiation generally, which is that it's a negotiation tactic and it's a litigation tactic, too, to say that things are impossible. So, for example, saying on behalf of an employer that it is 'impossible' to continue to provide particular terms and conditions. When people say 'impossible' in these circumstances, what they really mean is 'unappealing'.

So I think perhaps thinking about a situation from the point of view of the other side, and from the point of view of an objective judge or tribunal, makes you think about whether your

evidence really is as compelling as all that; whether it really was impossible to continue with the existing T&Cs for example, or whether it was merely unappealing, or perhaps somewhere in between. Of course in most cases it is the last of these.

Yuri
If an employer imposes new terms without an agreement and the employee carries on working without raising objections, how long has to pass before the employee is considered to have impliedly agreed to the change?

Lydia Seymour
Solectron and Roper that we talked about earlier are examples of decisions on that point. It will depend in part upon the nature of the change. In broad terms, if I continue to work, if I continue to take my pay, and if I know about the change that's being made, then the question of when/whether I have accepted a change will depend on the nature of the term that's been changed. There is always, therefore, going to be a risk. No one would start from the position that this is the best way to try to impose new terms: i.e. impose the terms, hope that no one objects and then wait and see. But if you find yourself in this position, provided that the term is one which 'bit' immediately - say pay or something which relates to somebody's day-to-day terms and conditions - I would assume that within a few months of working without objection it is likely to be found to have been accepted as impliedly by conduct.

But going back to one of the points that I think we raised earlier, be careful about terms which don't bite immediately - terms relating to pension or terms relating to something like a death in service benefit or something - a court or Tribunal might take a much more sympathetic approach to an employee who hasn't objected and who had worked on if they can say that they didn't realise what the impact of the term would be. So the length of time is relevant, but it will depend on the type of the clause.

Victoria Duff
What's the best way of introducing a written statement of employment where only a verbal contract exists, especially where you've got different terms amongst different employees?

Lydia Seymour
I am assuming that we are imagining a situation in which the employer has multiple employees, each of whom has a distinct oral contract entitling them to different terms. I'm not sure that, as such, the legal principles that relate to the introduction of a written statement of employment here differ from those which apply if you were trying to introduce a harmonised written statement of employment conditions in a situation where everybody had previously had written statements.

Saying that, of course, on a practical level it could be very different because you start from the awkward position that (a) you're in breach of your statutory duty to provide written terms of employment, and (b) the main difficulty with verbal contracts, which is that you may have disputes as to what people are entitled to.

There are two realistic ways forward, one of which is a great deal more trouble than the other. The first way forward would be to try to identify in writing what everybody's existing contractual terms are and then undertake a harmonisation programme. Or secondly you could cross your fingers and simply introduce written terms and conditions as the first step, ideally along with a pay rise and then deal on a bespoke basis, with anybody who came along to say they, for example, that were entitled to more sick pay than that, or whatever it might be.

Mike Clyne
Can an employer change terms and conditions to prevent homeworking from another country to prevent a tax or employment law risk in another jurisdiction?

Daniel Barnett
That's a very specific question.

Lydia Seymour
This question assumes what I think would be quite an unusual situation, in which there are terms and conditions which currently and specifically allow for homeworking in another country, but the employer wishes to say, no, you may not work from home in a foreign country. The tax and National Insurance complications that relate to people homeworking from another country are quite significant, and as a matter of general principle, I would expect an employer to be entitled to say that anything which changes the tax and National Insurance situation that is currently in place, i.e. a situation in which the employees both taxed and pays National Insurance in the UK in respect of all of their work, is something which an employer is properly entitled to refuse.

I hesitate only slightly because there are conceivably situations in which, if you've thought to introduce that now, and somebody had been doing it in the past, you might have an issue of trust and confidence. Equally, it is just about conceivable that it could raise an indirect or even perhaps direct discrimination claim, but I think they're rather to the edges of this. Broadly speaking, I think the answer is yes, an employer can provide that the employee not be entitled to do work from another country if that raises a tax or employment law risk.

Jamie Anderson
Why do you think Jones v Associated Tunnelling *(Jones v Associated Tunnelling Co. Ltd [1981] IRLR 477)* isn't relied on more by employees, and if it is relied on, what's the best way for the employer to get around it?

Jones is where a variation has occurred a while back, but the employee has not affirmed the contract because the variation didn't immediately bite. So it's where a variation occurs, but the effect of the variation is a future event.

Lydia Seymour
I think this goes back to the point that we were making about when changes 'bite'. Jones is an example of a case in which you might say an old-school and a formal approach was taken to variation. I've seen it relied on a few times, so I'm not sure I would necessarily agree that it isn't relied upon, but that may be because it tends to come up particularly in pension cases. Pensions are perhaps the absolute acme of this sort of situation - in which a change is made today but the employee doesn't realise the impact until much later. I think it takes us back to the fact that it's a brave employer who relies on silence, in any circumstances, to obtain an implied agreement. The reality is that nobody would do that deliberately from the outset and attempts to get an agreement implied by silence are always a question of trying to cobble something together when someone finds themselves in an awkward situation.

Natalie White
How long can an unwritten practice be in place before it becomes an implied contractual term?

Daniel Barnett
Have we answered that one?

Lydia Seymour
Not in these precise terms, which I think go to the woolliness of the law when it comes to incorporation by custom and practice (which everyone will be excited to hear very much depends on the facts of the individual case). In terms of when something becomes an implied contractual term I don't think it's necessarily a question of how long an unwritten practice has been in place, although that may be part of the determination.

There are a set of things that you have to think about - they're very clearly set out in a case called Albion Automotive v Walker (*Albion*

Automotive Ltd v Walker [2002] EWCA Civ 946), which is a 2002 case in the Court of Appeal: Has it been drawn to the attention of employees? Has it been followed without exemption for a substantial period? Has it been followed lots of times? Was the nature of the communication about the policy such that people thought that it was going to be a contractual promise? Was adopted by agreement? Was it set out in writing? And did the employees have a reasonable expectation that it would continue? So those are the sorts of things that the court will think about when trying to work out the legal headache of whether a term has been become a contractual term by custom and practice. Length of time is one of the issues, but there are quite a few others.

Daniel Barnett
Albion Automotive was about redundancy terms, wasn't it?

Lydia Seymour
Exactly. Was the employer in that circumstance obliged to continue to make what had been, frankly, eye-wateringly generous redundancy payouts into the future as well as having done so in the past.

Daniel Barnett
Is an employment contract that's changed and e-signed, rather than having a wet signature, considered to be valid?

Lydia Seymour
I haven't looked at this specific point yet, but I cannot think of any reason why it wouldn't be. There's no magic to employment contracts to say that they even need to be in writing. In various other situations, contracts relating to the sale of land and so on, there are formalities that have to be complied with. But employment contracts are just a record of an agreement between the parties. There is a requirement in the Employment Rights Act for written particulars to be provided and there is a requirement for agreement. But I would have thought that any

robust and reasonable evidence of agreement should be good enough. I can't see why e-signing as evidence of agreement should be less good than any other.

Daniel Barnett
In the same way that verbal agreement is good enough.

Lydia Seymour
A verbal agreement absolutely is good enough. And of course, an e-signature has all the advantages of actually knowing what it is that's been agreed.

Tracy Adam
If an employee has been employed for many years - more than 10 years - but neither we nor they can find their employment contract, and they don't want our current contract, what's the best way to agree a contract?

Lydia Seymour
Well, obviously, it rather depends on what aspect of the current contract they don't want. One assumes it's not the whole thing, it's some specific term or smallish groups of terms. The underlying question here is what are the current terms upon which that employee is employed and a specific written contract for an individual isn't the only way in which you could answer that question. For example, if you have got evidence that everybody was sent a contract of a particular type at the time that this person joined the company, that is evidence, and in the absence of any evidence either way, that might be sufficient evidence to establish on the balance of probabilities that the employment contract that they were working under was, in fact, the one that you want to impose.

Assuming that you've got nothing, and there's no evidence at all of any sort - which seems quite unlikely, but let's assume that maybe because it's been more than 10 years, we've got no evidence at all - that means that in theory, at least, the question of that employee's terms and conditions, as they currently stand is at large. They could allege, if they went to

an employment tribunal that the terms are X when the company believes them to be Y. Ultimately, the only way that that dispute could be resolved, if no agreement could be reached, is via a tribunal or a court. That said, a bit like any change to terms and conditions, if you as the employer decide that it's not worth the candle to get involved in a dispute about this, you could implicitly accept from the employee that their terms and conditions currently say X, and then try to change the contract so that in provides for Y, trying a pay rise, and the various other techniques that you might use to try to get them to agree.

Daniel Barnett
It used to be a thing 20 plus years ago - I haven't seen it done much recently - that where the terms were lost in the mists of history and couldn't be agreed, the employer and the union would go jointly to an employment tribunal and seek a declaration as to what the terms and conditions were. But that's not really done much anymore, is it?

Lydia Seymour
No. Obviously, there are lots of cases in which employees go to a tribunal for a declaration as to what their terms and conditions are, but it's usually done in a rather more adversarial manner than the one that you're suggesting.

Robert
May an employer change terms to require employees to wear PPE - personal protective equipment - outside of work? This relates to the employer's reputation or image in the wider community.

Daniel Barnett
It would be useful if Robert could add in the chat what sector this refers to. As a general rule, would it be a sound a good business reason for an employer to say we expect you to wear masks out of work?

Lydia Seymour
I think there are two potential types of situations there. Is the idea that we've got

somebody who's not mask-exempt, and are talking about something outside work – e.g. you work for my company and I want to make sure that every time you go to the supermarket you comply with the law and guidance, which says that you wear a mask, because failing to comply with that law could impact on my reputation? So here it isn't so much wearing PPE as such, but complying with the law. Otherwise I'm struggling to think of a scenario in which an employer would be entitled to require the wearing of workplace PPE outside work.

Daniel Barnett
Robert has put in the chat that it relates to food selling. The employer caters to a specific product, and the customers tend to be the same. I'm not sure that takes the question much further, though. I wonder if when he says 'outside work', he is referring to an outdoor market or something of that nature?

Lydia Seymour
Broadly speaking, an employer is going to be entitled to impose the wearing of reasonable PPE in the workplace. It is always possible that would be subject to exemptions, but they're going to be individual exemptions.

But if the question you are asking here is whether an employer can say to an employee who is not mask-exempt that they are making the employer look dreadful, because when they go to the supermarket, they don't want to wear a mask, say for a political reason, I would imagine that would be seen with quite some sympathy by a tribunal.

Daniel Barnett
Sympathy to the employer or sympathy to the employee?

Lydia Seymour
Sympathy to the employer, just like any failure by employees to comply with a legal or reputationally important moral obligation. More broadly, there's quite an interesting question about whether being a mask sceptic or a lockdown sceptic could constitute a *Grainger*-compliant political or philosophical belief. I suspect that that will be tested in the Tribunals pretty shortly.

Daniel Barnett
Lydia Seymour from Outer Temple, thank you very much.

COMPENSATION ISSUES

GAVIN MANSFIELD QC, LITTLETON CHAMBERS

Daniel Barnett

I'm joined today by Gavin Mansfield QC from Littleton Chambers and he's going to be answering your questions on compensation issues.

Gavin Mansfield, good morning. If you don't mind, I'm going to throw a few questions at you. In an unfair dismissal case, can an employee receive notice pay in addition to the maximum compensatory award?

Gavin Mansfield

Well, the short answer to that direct question is no, but then there's a 'but'. The 'no' is that the cap on unfair dismissal compensatory award applies, as you would expect, to the whole compensation. So you can't get round that by saying the unfair dismissal compensation should be the capped amount plus the notice monies.

The 'but' is that you have got another way of claiming that money because you can claim the notice pay as a breach of contract claim, either in the tribunal or in the civil courts. What you've got to bear in mind is that there is a different cap. In the employment tribunal, the breach of contract claim is subject to a £25,000 cap, but that's a separate cap and a separate claim to the unfair dismissal compensation.

Assuming your numbers fit within these caps, you can claim the capped amount of compensation for unfair dismissal for compensatory award and, of course, your basic award, and separately, up to £25,000 worth of breach of contract damages. If your notice claim is more than £25,000, then you're going to have to claim that in the civil courts. That's an area that people listening in will know to be very careful about but I'll just flag it. You've really got to be very careful not to end up being precluded from claiming your breach of contract loss in the civil courts because you've included it in your tribunal claim, even if it's not being pursued. So something you see a lot in claim forms is people distancing themselves expressly saying they're not claiming their breach of contract loss and reserving the right to claim it elsewhere.

Daniel Barnett

If I dredge my memory banks correctly, that's a case called Harper v Virgin Net *(Harper v Virgin Net Ltd [2004] IRLR 390)* that says if you claim it in the EAT, you're capped.

Gavin Mansfield

There's also a case called Fraser v HLMAD *(Fraser v HLMAD Ltd [2006] IRLR 687)* in the Court of Appeal, which was the case where a claimant had claimed it in the tribunal up to £25,000 and then had a go at trying to claim the balance over £25,000 in the civil courts over the cap. And the court said no, you only get one crack at it.

Daniel Barnett

And the £25,000 cap in the employment tribunal that was brought in some years ago, I think, in the mid-1990s.

Gavin Mansfield

Yes. It was brought in in the early 1990s and it has not been adjusted at all since then. And despite the fact that a number of EAT presidents and judges have said from time to time that it really needs to be looked at in terms of the limit, nothing has been done about it.

Daniel Barnett

Changing the subject completely, how is future loss calculated if employment hasn't ended by the time of a remedy hearing?

Gavin Mansfield

That's a good question. Let's assume that we're talking about an unfair dismissal claim or a discrimination claim. I know that there are differences in the statutory rules for those but for these purposes, let's focus on a discrimination claim so that we're only looking at one set of rules. The principles are broadly the same.

I'll just quickly take a step back and look at what we are trying to do when we're assessing any loss. Of course, we are looking to put the claimant in the position that they would have been in if the unlawful act had not occurred. That's true across the whole range of torts, but particularly in unfair dismissal and discrimination. What that tells us is that we're involved in an exercise of comparison between what has happened and what would have happened but for the unlawful action.

If we go back to the Dunnachie v Kingston Council case *(Kingston Upon Hull City Council v Dunnachie [2003] UKEAT/706/02)*, not as it went on to the House of Lords, but in the EAT, Mr Justice Michael Burton talked about old job facts and new job facts. In other words, comparing what would have happened in the old job and what has happened now in whatever the new job is or isn't. You see that language used quite a bit. Personally, I prefer a comparison between the 'actual world', what has happened, actually, and the 'but for

world', what would have happened but for the breach.

Any of that assessment involves an assessment of facts, of what has happened; and counterfactuals, what might have happened in a different world. So when we're assessing, the starting point is to look at what our losses are to the date of the hearing because that's going to set a lot of the landscape for loss. What job has the claimant found? Are their earnings the same as or less than they would have been? What would have happened with the old job? And that's quite tricky. When we're looking at future loss, we've got an even trickier exercise because we're now crystal ball gazing about what's going to happen in the future.

So, if you take a current loss of earnings - let's assume that the claimant has not found alternative employment by the date of the remedies hearing - you've got an actual loss per month at the date of the hearing. You're then looking forward to what that loss is going to be over time. That involves assessment of a number of factors that might reduce that loss. One is when the claimant is going to find alternative work to replace their earnings. That could be an 'anyone's guess' issue, but a tribunal has got to try and work out how long that loss will run for. And on the other side of the equation, would the earnings that we are seeking to replace have continued in any event? Would the claimant have continued in employment in the long term? Say, for instance, if at the date of the remedy hearing, you've got a situation where a respondent is on its last legs and likely to go bust because of the pandemic, well, you're looking to replace earnings that would have stopped anyway because the workforce would have been made redundant when the business closed down. So there are a lot of hypotheticals to consider.

What tribunals don't like doing is what we do in a personal injury case, which is to look at what your current run rate of loss is and multiply that by a multiplier to reflect rest of career earnings. I mean, that's pretty rare in the tribunal because there are far more variables. The prospect of a fit claimant who has been discriminated against finding replacement earnings is likely to be much higher. So the tribunal has got to take a broader brush assessment of what the replacement earnings are likely to be.

You do sometimes see full career loss and Chagger v Abbey National (*Chagger v Abbey National Plc [2010] IRLR 47*) is the case that sticks in everyone's mind from about 10 years ago. But they tend to be employees who are perhaps older and closer to what would have been their retirement age. Or they're cases where you've got a substantial overlay of psychiatric injury or personal injury on top of the particular facts that mean that you can have more confidence they will not replace their earnings. But in a normal case, it tends to be much shorter.

Daniel Barnett

One more question for me. Do any special issues arise if an employee is a shareholder in the employer company?

Gavin Mansfield

In terms of assessing their compensation, there are several issues that might arise. So forgive me if I just worked through what some of the options are. Let's assume we're dealing with a dismissal case, be it unfair or discriminatory. The first thing to work out is the impact of that unlawful termination on the shares. So for example, it may be that the employee's ownership of the shares is wholly unconditional, that's a property right of their own. Whatever unlawful action has happened is not going to make any difference to that employee's entitlement to keep their shares and benefit from their capital value and the dividends. In that case, no issues arise. You just keep the shares, say thank you very much and carry on receiving your dividends.

Another route (and not one that's going to help you in the employment tribunal -you might have to go to the civil courts for) is to look at whether there's a way of seeking to retain those shares or get compensation for the value of them in the courts. Usually, the reason for forfeiture of the shares is that the scheme rules for the shares will have said they fall to be forfeit in the circumstances of the particular termination. Usually, these schemes will have good leaver and bad leaver definitions. If you're a good leaver, you keep the shares, or at least some of them. If you're a bad leaver, you forfeit the shares.

The potential loss arises where ownership of the shares is conditional, so think share option schemes, or any of the whole range of restricted stock-type schemes, or phantom share arrangements that are conditional, usually on continued employment in some way. And in that situation, it will be quite common for the shares or the right to accrue those shares to be forfeit in consequence of the dismissal. So, in principle, there are a number of ways that you might claim in relation to that. The first is if you lose the shares because of the discriminatory dismissal, potentially, you can claim for the loss of the value of those shares because that's a benefit that you've lost that you would have had, or been likely to have had but for the dismissal. Quantifying that is always going to be very difficult. One approach might be to question what the dividend return, the income, from those shares would have been. But in most share option schemes, you're not getting shares that are paying out a dividend anyway. They're classes of shares that don't have a dividend. So it's often going to be that if there's value in this, you're going to need some expert evidence to look at what the value of those shares would be.

The scenario where you're claiming the shares is probably going to be where the company treats you as a bad leaver because of your dismissal. But you need to think about whether the fact that you've been unfairly dismissed or dismissed in a discriminatory way means that the company was right to treat you as a bad leaver or not. It's a rare scheme that will say expressly that you are a bad leaver and therefore surrender your shares even if we discriminate against you or unfairly dismiss you. It's a common scheme that doesn't address that question expressly. Here is a principle that is helpful for us, a question of construction, that the courts will try as much as is possible to construe a contract so as not to allow a wrongdoer to take advantage of their own wrongdoing. There's a late 90s case that's helpful on share options called Levett v Biotrace (Levett v Biotrace International Plc [1999] IRLR 375) that says just that.

There's often an argument that says that you know this scheme looks like you're a bad leaver if the employer has dismissed you and your employment is at an end. But that shouldn't apply to a situation where the employer has dismissed you in an unlawful way. So the employer is not taking advantage of their own wrongdoing. So those arguments might give you a route to a claim for breach of contract in relation to the shares that has two advantages. One, potentially, it allows you to keep the shares or get them retransferred back to you. So you don't have to have a big argument about valuation of the shares. Two, obviously, it gets round the issue of the cap in an unfair dismissal claim.

Just one last point on shares, there are some cases around inclusion of dividends on shares in compensation for unfair dismissal that say, in principle, if you've lost a right to dividends because of the unfair dismissal, you can claim that as compensation. But certainly at employment tribunal level, though I don't think in the EAT, there's a suggestion that for calculation of the 52-week cap for unfair dismissal, the cap on compensatory awards, dividend payments are not included in a week's pay because they're not remuneration. So if you've got an earner who's up at the cap for unfair dismissal, then they may not be able to claim back, for cap reasons, the lost dividends from the shares.

Jamie Anderson
What factors are most persuasive in successfully getting an order for reinstatement or re-engagement?

Gavin Mansfield
Being cynical, not many factors are persuasive, I don't think, in getting orders for reinstatement or re-engagement, by which I mean tribunals don't order them very often. In most cases, it's not really going to be practical. The key issue is going to be around persuading the tribunal, first of all, that trust and confidence survive the dismissal and, therefore, the employee is able to go back into the workforce, either in the same role or in a different role under re-engagement. In a matter that has been subject to hot litigation, it's going to be very difficult to persuade tribunals that trust and confidence can be maintained. Where we see it at all, it's likely to be in cases of relatively large workforces, where the claimant can slot back into the job without necessarily needing to come into contact with those who are responsible for the particular unlawful matters that are being complained of.

I think it's really difficult. You've got to focus on reasons why trust and confidence can be re-established, you've really got to look at the role that the claimant can go back into and why that is not going to be problematic for them or for the respondent in trust and confidence terms.

My experience is that the only times that reinstatement and re-engagement applications have really been successful are in big, big companies - it just doesn't work in small companies - and, typically, where the manager who did the dismissal has moved on to another role, and so there are fresh people dealing with each other.

Anonymous
What are your top tips for drafting schedules or counter schedules of loss?

Daniel Barnett

There's a nice wide question for you.

Gavin Mansfield

I know there's a certain way of doing schedules if you look at proformas that are around and that are often submitted. And you get this incredible granularity about certain facts at the beginning of it around gross pay, net pay, notice period and continuous service. All of that helps you work out your basic award and gives you the start for your compensatory award.

Then, whether you're acting for claimants or respondents, the further you get through the schedule, the more you tend to get 'TBC' as the answer to almost all of the boxes. I can understand exactly why you do that early. My first tip is to try and fill in as much of it as possible. When I was talking about assessing future loss a few minutes ago, I was saying that it's a question of assessment of the counterfactuals, of what would have happened in the 'but for' world. I favour something you don't tend to see that much, which is a narrative section setting out the assumptions that you're working on fairly early in the schedule, so what's actually been lost - the earnings from the employment - your counterfactual assumptions as to what would have happened to those earnings if you'd remained in employment (i.e. promotion, bonus, etc.) and then your actual replacement earnings and your counterfactual replacement earnings as to whether you're suffering any particular ongoing difficulty in replacing your earnings. For instance, because you were discriminated against, you've suffered a personal injury that means that you're not going to be able to look for alternative work until X. Often in a schedule there are just the numbers in a grid, you've got to try and deduce what the underlying assumptions are. The exercise of drafting out a narrative set of assumptions of the basis on which you're claiming loss is really clarifying for your own thinking in what you're claiming. It's also very

helpful for the other side, in terms of them understanding what the claim is based on and counter schedule.

If you flip it round, it works in just the same way. As a respondent, you want to be setting out your challenge to those assumptions. For example, no, employment wouldn't have continued because they would have been made redundant by X. Or no, they would never have got a bonus because the performance of the business was X. And so on.

Daniel Barnett

When you're crafting a schedule, keep it reasonable. No respondent is ever going to be impressed by a ridiculously inflated schedule, because they'll know it's ridiculously inflated. All you'll do is irritate the respondent and probably cause them to spend more money on better lawyers than they otherwise would have done. You'll just irritate the judge as well. Keep it realistic.

And if you're acting for an employer, set out the counterfactuals but remember to deal with every possible argument you might run. So factor in Polkey (*Polkey v AE Dayton Services Ltd [1987] UKHL 8*) and factor in contributory fault because these are things that affect the numbers and when it's written out in a Word document or an Excel spreadsheet, it makes it much easier for the employee to realise the impact that Polkey or contributory fault arguments might have on what they'll eventually recover. A final tip is to never forget grossing up, because so many people forget grossing up.

Gavin Mansfield

That's very true. I deprecated the use of 'TBCs' in schedules, but I would tend to leave the grossing up calculation to be done at the end because it's a bit of a pain to do and there's no point doing it until you've got the numbers settled on. But definitely, you'll want to flag it up in the schedule that you are going to be grossing up.

Su Apps
If a settlement for compensation is agreed between the parties, can a tribunal make a consent order confirming this? If so, is this, for the purposes of a claim to the Redundancy Payments Service, considered to be a judgment?

Daniel Barnett
The answer to the first part is yes. But it's the second part of the question that I think the important one. Is the Redundancy Payments Service bound by a tribunal order where the judge has filled in the figures that have been agreed by the parties?

Gavin Mansfield
I'm going to say yes, on that, although I can't point to either a statute or an authority that says so. But by analogy with other cases that have looked at the effect of a judgment, whether that judgment is reached after substantive argument or by consent or otherwise, a judgment is a judgment. I think the rules in relation to claims to the Redundancy Payments Service bite on sums ordered by a judgment. I don't think there's anything that governs how that judgment came to be made. I'm happy to be proved wrong about that, but that's my approach to it.

Daniel Barnett
The only thing that I'm thinking about is if a director of a company agrees with the company that they should get a redundancy payment of £17 million and for some bizarre reason, a busy employment judge rubber stamps that. Is that binding on the Redundancy Payments Service?

Gavin Mansfield
I mean, you raise a good hypothetical. The answer to that is that the employment judge should never approve that order in the first place. I mean, rubber stamping is not what judges are supposed to do, nor do they

ordinarily do. In those situations, there might be grounds to unwind that judgment because of the collusive way in which it had been reached between the company in the director it controls.

Daniel Barnett
As a rule, absolutely, yes. It's binding on the Redundancy Payments Service.

Gillian Howard
What considerations and reasons should an employment judge give when exercising their discretion in making a finding of no reduction in compensation for contributory fault?

Gavin Mansfield
That's a pretty fact-dependent question. It depends upon the nature of the contributory fault allegation. It's an issue that needs to be considered with the same care as the other issues in the case. So if there's a credible reason raised for a contributory fault reduction, then the tribunal is going to have to make findings of fact about it and set out its reasons as to (1) whether or not there was fault, (2) whether it, in fact, contributed to the dismissal, and (3) what the appropriate level of reduction should be. That last point is a rather more broad-brush point in terms of the percentage reduction. There are some EAT cases that take broad brands of kind of 25%, 50%, 75% or 100%, but that's not binding. It's really a question of factual assessment for the tribunal. So it's difficult to say without more specific facts.

Mark Irlam
Would you disclose to ACAS a draft schedule at the beginning of a claim to negotiate a settlement?

Daniel Barnett
I'll rephrase that. Is there a reason not to send ACAS a draft schedule?

Gavin Mansfield
Well, if you've not got one - if you're at a stage where you've not really properly worked

out your loss - then you might not do so. If it's a low-value case that doesn't warrant the time and effort of compiling one, you might not do. Otherwise, I see no real downside. If it's a case that's worth the effort and you're trying to map out what your losses are, then I think there's a value in ACAS seeing it for the purposes of knowing what it is that you're looking for. You can caveat it on the basis that it's early or provisional or conditional on disclosure of full financial information or whatever. In principle, I'd see no problem with that.

Laura Sheridan

Is there any particular guidance or key cases that are helpful when working out compensation for injury to feelings according to the Vento bands *(Vento v Chief Constable of West Yorkshire Police [2002] EWCA Civ 1871)*? The definitions for each band aren't very specific and it's sometimes difficult to know whether someone would fall within the upper or lower part of each band.

Daniel Barnett

Can you just explain what the Vento bands are as you answer that question?

Gavin Mansfield

The Vento bands are three bands of different levels of compensation for the injury to feelings component in a discrimination award. So as we know, in contrast to unfair dismissal, you can recover non-financial loss in discrimination cases for injury to feelings. And that's a distinct head of loss and different to general damages for personal injury, which is possibly recoverable as a separate head. So we're looking at the injury to feelings that has been caused by the discriminatory conduct.

Vento set three bands, going from the lower band all the way up to the imaginatively named upper band. These are subject to inflation over time. From April last year onwards, the lower band is £900 to £9,000, the mid band is £9,000 to £27,000 and the upper band is £27,000 to £45,000. Bear

in mind that the cases say that the top of the upper band is not a limit. It is possible in an extreme case to go above £45,000.

Laura's question is whether there's any particular guidance or key cases in deciding where your case goes within the bands. I think Vento itself is helpful. There's De Souza *(De Souza v Vinci Construction (UK) Ltd [2017] IRLR 844)* and Da'Bell *(Da'Bell v NSPCC [2010] IRLR 19)* that are helpful. There's presidential guidance on the levels which is also helpful. But ultimately, it's a question of factual assessment for the tribunal on the particular blend of facts in the cases, bearing in mind that what is an issue is compensation, not punishment. We're looking at the severity of injury to the claimant, not the culpability or egregiousness of the respondent's behaviour.

I'm not sure there's much to be gained from trawling through cases and looking at the levels of awards in particular cases because the fact patterns are so different. The tribunals are always going to say that they've always got to look at the particular facts of how the particular claimant was injured.

Daniel Barnett

I totally agree. IDS Brief contains many, many examples of different injury to feelings awards in different cases. You can get it from Practical Law. There are lots of cases where awards in the upper band, middle band and so on, have been given and they're all set out there. But if you try to put those before an employment judge, the employment judge is going to laugh at you and say that the facts of this case are different to the facts of that case. Why should they be bothered by what another tribunal judge thought? I don't think I've ever shown a judge examples of first instance judgments from other judges to try to say you should find this or that.

Broadly speaking, it's enough of a challenge to try to get the judge to go to the band that you want them to go to. By trying to ask them to find a particular spot within that band you're on hiding to nothing. The biggest struggle I find is with dismissals. There's always an argument over whether dismissals should be lower band, middle band or upper band in the more extreme dismissal cases, and the judge is going to do what they want. They're never going to listen to the advocate.

Gavin Mansfield
I find that generally true in all my cases, but maybe that's just me. The judges never listen to the advocate.

Mark Irlam
What issues do you find are most common when dealing with compensation cases?

Gavin Mansfield
Failure to mitigate - I can say a bit more about that in due course, if helpful - and assessment of period of loss. Also in the more complex cases with pre-dismissal detriments leading to a dismissal, issues around untangling the losses caused by the detriments and losses caused by the dismissal and the extent to which the loss of earnings is attributable to the particular unlawful act. Those are probably my headline points.

Nigel Forsyth
What sort of out-of-pocket expenses or losses can an employee claim as part of the compensatory award? For example, can they claim the additional cost of mortgage repayments because they've had to take a mortgage holiday?

Gavin Mansfield
Well, that's a good question. I don't think I've ever seen that in a case, actually.

Daniel Barnett
it raises that old bugbear of whether a claimant can recover losses flowing from their own impecuniosity.

Gavin Mansfield
We're helped in this whole area in a discrimination case by Essa v Laing (Laing Ltd

v Essa [2004] IRLR 313), which is a case that draws a distinction from the ordinary course of tortious compensation. So, the ordinary approach to tortious loss is that your losses need to be reasonably foreseeable and are conditioned by questions of remoteness of damage. In Essa v Laing, at least in a case of a deliberate harassment-type discrimination case, the court says that they're not concerned with remoteness of loss, they're concerned with the direct losses flowing from the unlawful action. That makes life a little bit easier.

Ordinarily, one's looking at replacement of the direct loss flowing (i.e. the loss of earnings and benefits and the like), not particular expenses that were caused by not having the earnings that you've lost. I can't think of a case that addresses that question.

Anonymous
How should an employee prepare their schedule of loss? If a claimant earns £32,000 per annum and has one year of losses, should they only gross up the final £2,000?

Gavin Mansfield
Well, my glib answer to that is, as I said earlier, just put in the concept of grossing up but leave it to be worked out at the end of the day. And the non-glib answer is that you can only do the grossing up when all of the losses have actually been determined. So you don't really want it on the schedule. But the approach to be taken is as per Shove v Downs (Shove v Downs Surgical plc [1984] ICR 532) in that you work out what the overall net compensation would be, then you deduct the £30,000 and then you gross up at the marginal rate after that. It's a fool's errand to try and explain the Shove calculation off the top of my head without either a diagram or a note. But that's the gist of it. Don't try and do it too early is my main tip.

Derian Kymes
Are all elements of Universal Credit subject to recoupment?

Daniel Barnett
This is a question I'm betting you don't know the answer to on the basis that this is a question that all solicitors know the answer to and barristers don't. I certainly don't know the answer.

Gavin Mansfield
I think I do know the answer to that. In its narrow form, the answer is no, they are not all subject to recoupment. If you ask me which components are and which components aren't, then I would have to say that I can't remember which bits are and which aren't. Pre Universal Credit it was certainly the case that some but not all benefits were subject to recoupment. Universal Credit covers a range of those benefits, so I believe the position is that there are components of that that aren't subject to recoupment. But I would certainly go straight to the Recoupment Regulations and read them carefully before offering anyone advice in relation to that question. So that's a fantastically unhelpful answer to the question, but that's as good as you get, I'm afraid.

Mike Clyne
Do you foresee any changes to the cap on compensation awards?

Gavin Mansfield
No.

Daniel Barnett
You don't think there's any prospect of having a cap on discrimination awards? That's actually not quite the question that was asked.

Gavin Mansfield
That's not quite the question that was asked. Just one qualification: the existing cap, of course, you will have noticed that over the last week, the new rates are out for the inflation on cap. But will there be a change? Will there be an introduction of a cap on compensation and discrimination cases now that we're in the sunny uplands of the post-Brexit world? I don't think so. I mean, I'll just take a different view. But I really don't think that there is likely to be

the political will to fight and succeed on that particular issue. You call me a foolish optimist in a year's time when we look at this again.

Michael Foster
Can you claim losses if you receive the same salary in a new job, but you have to work extra hours to get that same salary?

Gavin Mansfield
That's a good question. I've never seen that done. But why not? In principle, I suppose the answer to my own question is that you haven't actually suffered any loss. Conceptually, I like the idea. It's ingenious. But the problem is that it opens up the tribunal to a much wider set of considerations as to the overall benefits and burdens and amenity of the new job you've got into. I suspect as well that nobody's ever going to want to get involved in that. If we remind ourselves that compensation as a whole in an unfair dismissal case is that which is just and equitable, and although a discrimination compensation is assessed on tortious principles, it's got to be just and equitable to make an award in the first place. Something tells me you're not likely to succeed using that approach. Daniel? Do you have a different view?

Daniel Barnett
I do take a different view, although, I agree it's not clear and it's arguable either way. I think if somebody is effectively having their wage reduced from £14 an hour to £11 an hour, that's a loss that under the just and equitable jurisdiction, there should be some recognition for. I think another tricky aspect of that question is what happens if somebody gets a new job on the same salary and has to travel for three hours rather than one hour to get there? That is a very real non-financial loss that might not be capable of being met in a compensatory award but might be in a discrimination award.

Gavin Mansfield
What if for the new job you've got to get a different bus and there's always a longer

queue to get on the bus, and that's all a bit of a drag? Or what if the food in the canteen isn't as good? I do take your point that if the circumstances are such that the hourly rate of pay works out as being different, then I see the force of that. But a general comparison of old jobs and new jobs, benefits and burdens, is an unattractive exercise for a tribunal to get into.

Anonymous
Is it reasonable to include losses where the delay and backlog of a hearing date is because of the impact of COVID-19?

Daniel Barnett
So if it's two years to a tribunal date rather than one year, is it reasonable to award two years' loss of pay?

Gavin Mansfield
Yes. It's not the claimant's fault that they've been delayed in obtaining their loss, subject, of course, to the cap because the cap is going to apply however long. In a funny way, although there are huge disadvantages to a claimant in the delays that are happening to cases, a later assessment of damages may often be to a claimant's advantage. What I mean by that is that with a claimant who has not replaced their earnings by the time of the hearing, because the burden is on the respondent to prove failure to mitigate - and tribunals tend to think that many claimants have not just been lying around eating biscuits but have genuinely been trying to find earnings - tribunals are often pretty hard on respondents on failure to mitigate. So getting losses to date of hearing may not be so hard.

Tribunals are much more optimistic when they're looking at questions of future loss about the prospect of the claimant finding alternative employment. So in a sense, if you shift the balance of your loss from future to past, you might get more out of it. There is no principal reason why an employer should get the benefit of the fact that the case has been later to be

heard than otherwise would have been the case.

Su Apps
What evidence should an employer prepare and produce to counter a schedule of loss and, in particular, demonstrate there's been a failure to mitigate?

Gavin Mansfield
Well, that is a good question because it's often overlooked by respondents. They often overlook two things. First of all, the burden is on the employer to prove failure to mitigate. That's actually a pretty granular exercise. There's a decision of Brian Langstaff's, Cooper Contracting v Lindsey (*Cooper Contracting Ltd v Lindsey [2016] ICR D3*), where he says it's an exercise of, first of all, looking at what the employee should have done to find mitigating employment and then making an assessment of how much that would have paid and when it would have started from so you can then make the deduction. So it's pretty granular exercise.

To translate that into reality, I think it's always worth advising respondent clients to start gathering job vacancies for a claimant pretty much as soon as the claim has been intimated because when you get to a hearing, you're going to need to show specific examples of what you say the claimant should have done in order to find alternative employment. So you want to be able to say that there are this many jobs that the claimant could have applied for within a week or two weeks of the dismissal. You're never going to be able to prove, as a matter of fact, what would have happened, but it's an assessment of likelihood. So gather the evidence. In a high-value case, you might look at employment consultants to give expert evidence as to what should have happened, but I've always found those to be pretty unsatisfactory in terms of the quality of the evidence. It's no substitute for real-life examples of what should have happened.

The other thing for the respondent is to be realistic about what it is you say a claimant should have done. That cuts both ways. If you've got someone who has been dismissed from a job in a restaurant, say, where they were a waiter or working in the kitchens, there's no point saying they should have been applied to be the chef patron of a three-star Michelin restaurant if they've not got the skills and experience to do it. Equally, if you've got someone who is in that sort of senior position, you're not going to get much favour in saying that they should have applied for a job as a kitchen porter at Nando's having been fired from the three-star Michelin restaurant. Over time, tribunals will expect claimants to broaden the net of what are acceptable, reasonable or replacement earnings. But try and stay within the realms of reality.

I generally find that although employers don't like doing this - most ignore my advice because it can be a double-edged sword - it's a good idea to send the claimant bunches of potential vacancies in the post or by email every week or two. It achieves two things. First of all, it irritates the pants off them. Second of all, it means that when you come to cross-examine the claimant about why they haven't applied for all these dozens and dozens and dozens of jobs, they cannot reply - or at least if they do, they'll have no credibility - I didn't know about that vacancy or I didn't know that magazine had vacancies in my field or I didn't know about that website, because you've handed the vacancies to them on a plate.

Daniel Barnett
It is a slightly double-edged sword, of course, because they might apply for all of them and not get any job at all, which takes away the failure to mitigate argument. But with any luck, they might apply for those jobs and actually get one of them, in which case compensation stops.

Gavin Mansfield
I agree with that.

Siobhan
If someone's claiming backdated holiday pay, does the two-year backdating apply from when the claim is brought - the date of the ET1 - or when the hearing takes place?

Gavin Mansfield
It's from when the claim is brought, isn't it?

Daniel Barnett
I thought that was easy because I've done a case on that recently. Maybe it wasn't as easy as I thought. It's from the date the ET1 goes in.

Henry
Does a tribunal apply contributory fault reductions in an ordinary unfair dismissal case to the total financial loss or the capped financial loss?

Gavin Mansfield
The cap is the last thing. So you apply it to the total loss and then apply the cap after that.

Mark Irlam
Would you say a personal injury claim is better dealt with in an employment tribunal or in the county court for stress and depression?

Daniel Barnett
Presumably, it's a discrimination claim. Let's ignore the liability aspects and just deal with quantum. Does it make a difference where you bring the claim? You mentioned Essa and Laing before.

Gavin Mansfield
The drivers on that are going to be liability issues. So we're often not going to have the luxury of choosing where the best place for remedy is. And I say that first because your cause of action is often going to be personal injury flowing from the discrimination. Stress at work claims are incredibly difficult on liability because the Sutherland v Hatton (Sutherland v Hatton [2002] IRLR 263) principles for establishing liability set a pretty high threshold.

I have to say that my own personal experience suggests to me that the judges in the courts have a better experience of assessing damages for personal injury, due to the range of PI cases that they deal with than in the tribunal where it is a less common issue in the run-of-the-mill tribunal claim. So given a free choice (i.e. liability issues, other limitation issues and other issues that are equal), if I can bring the same claim in either forum, then I might get a more rigorous assessment in the county court. But that's an impressionistic issue. Your other big factor, of course, is what risk you want to take in relation to costs and what your funding availability issues might be in terms of what people might do on a conditional fee or otherwise in either forum.

Daniel Barnett
Gavin Mansfield from Littleton Chambers, thank you very much. What's the best way for someone to get in touch with you if they want to instruct you on a case?

Gavin Mansfield
Email gmansfield@littletonchambers.co.uk. Please get in touch if you want to follow up on anything we've talked about.

Daniel, thank you very much for having me. This has been a fantastic series of seminars, and you've done a brilliant job in raising money for FRU. As all of us in employment law know, it's a really vital service. This last year, given the difficulties everyone's faced with the pandemic, it's been even more vital and you've made a huge contribution to their ability to carry on providing their services. So, thank you from all of us.

Daniel Barnett
Thank you.

CONSTRUCTIVE DISMISSAL
SEAN JONES QC, 11KBW

Daniel Barnett
I'm joined today by Sean Jones QC from 11KBW. He's going to be answering all of your questions on constructive dismissal. Many of you will know that Sean was one of the barristers involved in the Tomlinson-Blake v Mencap case *(Royal Mencap Society v Tomlinson-Blake [2021] UKSC 8)*. He represented Ms Tomlinson-Blake. The Supreme Court handed down judgment this morning.

He's the general editor of Tolleys. He's a grateful senior trustee of the Free Representation Unit and he is a Twitter buff. What's your Twitter handle, Sean?

Sean Jones
@seanjonesqc

Daniel Barnett
Sean Jones, good afternoon. First of all, a couple of questions from me. What is constructive dismissal? What's so constructive about being dismissed?

Sean Jones
I feel terribly sorry for constructive dismissal because it's much misunderstood. I'm going to answer immediately one of the questions in the chat. Someone has asked what the difference is between constructive dismissal and constructive unfair dismissal, and that's something you hear a lot in the tribunal. Constructive just means 'judges pretend it is a'. So, judges pretend it is a dismissal. You're dealing with resignation situations, which the law and judges will treat as if the employee

has been dismissed. So, a constructive unfair dismissal is just an unfair dismissal case which is based on a resignation. And a constructive wrongful dismissal case is a wrongful dismissal case which is based on a resignation. But that's all it means. Despite what the ET1 form appears to suggest, it isn't a discrete form of action.

So, translating it, what it comes down to is that there will be a dismissal in circumstances where an employee has resigned in response to what the law calls a repudiatory breach, and that's a principle of contract law. And one of the most exciting things about this area for me, being sad, is that underneath all of this statutory law is this tiny surviving nugget of pure contract law. But both the Employment Rights Act 1996 and the Equality Act 2010 have their own statutory definitions of the circumstances in which a resignation can amount to a dismissal. There's some debate about whether they're materially different to the contract law position, but broadly, it's understood that they're not.

Daniel Barnett
What is a repudiatory breach - the sort of breach you have to have to give rise to constructive dismissal?

Sean Jones
This is where it all gets a bit poetic. The definition is circular. A repudiatory breach is one which is bad enough that it allows you to resign in response to it without having to give your own period of notice, etc. It kind of self-

defines, and because it's that kind of definition, when you read through the legal authorities, they're full of the most fabulous language.

Reputiatory breach means a breach which, in essence, is one party to the contract behaving in a way which suggests they no longer intend to treat themselves as bound by the terms and conditions that they've agreed. But you'll also see it referred to as a fundamental breach, and you'll hear it referred to as a breach which goes to the root of the contract. What does all that mean? Well, it's really aimed at a notion of seriousness. But the takeaway message for employment lawyers and people working in HR is that not every breach of contract will count as a reputiatory breach. In fact, most won't. The whole idea is that you're setting it at a high level.

Take a case like Adams v Charles Zub Associates *(Adams v Charles Zub Associates Ltd [1978] IRLR 55)*, for instance. There's late payment of salary which is a breach of contract but it doesn't rise to the level of entitling someone to resign. Other things do. Also, because it's Contract law, it's uncomfortable for us as employment lawyers because it's not all about reasonableness. Breach of contract is strict. If you breach a contract term, you've breached the contract term. It doesn't matter whether you intended to breach the contract term. It doesn't matter whether it was reasonable for you to breach it because of the circumstances of your business, etc. Broadly speaking, if you've got a contractual obligation as an employer and you don't keep it, you're in breach. The only question is whether it's serious enough to amount in those circumstances to repudiation.

You can have breaches of express terms and breaches of implied terms. And let me spend about a minute on that. So far as express terms are concerned, the one which really consistently triggers trips to the employment tribunal is attempts unilaterally to vary contracts. In a sense, that's an obvious

repudiation. As an employer, you're saying that you no longer want to be bound by the existing terms and conditions, that you want new ones. So you want to impose new duties or cut pay or change the way in which the employee is paid. You're not going to invite the employee to agree it, you're just going to insist that these are the new terms. That is ordinarily a plain repudiation.

At the other end of the scale, there are some real employer frightening cases. One of my favourites is Pedersen v Camden *(Pedersen v London Borough of Camden [1981] IRLR 173)*, which was a case in which someone's job was 'bar manager/kitchen assistant'. And they changed his job to 'kitchen assistant/bar manager.' So it was effectively the same job, but with a slightly different emphasis. And the court said that was a reputiatory breach. His job role is an express contractual entitlement, and the employer had changed it. Even though most people probably wouldn't be capable of noticing the difference, it was something which really mattered to the employee. It was a matter of real importance. In those circumstances, you've got a repudiation. So employers need to be really careful where they are consciously trying to vary any express aspect of contract of employment.

The mother of all reputiatory breaches, the one that really takes up 99% of tribunal cases is a breach of the implied term of trust and confidence. So you're almost always, in practice, dealing with a breach of that specific implied term. Because of a really excellent decision in the EAT in a case called Morrow v Safeway Stores *(Morrow v Safeway Stores plc [2002] IRLR 9)*, we know that any breach of the implied trust and confidence duty is, by definition, reputiatory. So if you can show there is such a breach, that is it. You have succeeded in establishing repudiation and you can, on the face of it, resign. But be a little careful because it seems to me that what's really being said in Morrow is that it's not every unreasonable act - just as

Lord Denning said in Western Excavating (Western Excavating v Sharp [1978] ICR 221) - it's not just a kind of general obligation to be reasonable, it's got to be something very serious, something which goes to the root of the employment relationship. I should conclude by saying that it can be built up by a cumulative series of acts - what we call the last straw doctrine. Someone has asked what the minimum number of breaches in the last straw is, and the answer is two.

So you can have more than one matter about which you're complaining. Each matter may not itself amount to a breach of contract or repudiatory breach, but taken together they do. And it has this magic power which is that it can revive old breaches. So there may have been a breach which you put up with as an employee and, therefore, you're taken to have affirmed the contract and or waived that breach, and yet it can spring back into life as a result of later unreasonable conduct added together with the chain of events and last straw, you can treat yourself as having had your contract repudiated.

Daniel Barnett

I love that one of your favourite cases is one I've never heard of before. My favourite cases tend to fall firmly into the category of those with funny names, like Hogg v Dover college (Hogg v Dover College [1990] ICR 39) or Baggs v Fudge (Baggs v Fudge ET/1400114/05). I would never ever have a case that's a favourite one unless it's got a silly name.

Melanie Bonas

Do you need to resign without notice to have a constructive dismissal, or are you allowed to resign on notice?

Sean Jones

So can we start with bringing an unfair dismissal claim? If you're bringing an unfair dismissal claim, when you look at s95, what you'll find is that their statutory definition of

a resignation transformed into a dismissal expressly allows you to resign on notice. So far as unfair dismissals are concerned, that's not a problem at all. If you look at 95(1)(c), the employee terminates the contract under which they're employed with or without notice.

It's more complicated in contract cases, if you're running a wrongful dismissal claim, because you need to avoid affirming the contract. So the idea is, just to simplify it, that the employer does something completely intolerable, and you say that the contract no longer applies to you, you're not bound by any of its terms and you resign. If you say here is the notice to which your employer is contractually entitled under the contract, that tends to create the impression that you are affirming the contract. But the courts have been relatively generous in determining the circumstances in which someone might be taken to have affirmed. So, for instance, you would have thought it would be very, very obvious that if what you do is invoke a contractual grievance procedure, it must follow that you're affirming the contract. But the courts have said not necessarily. And they will look sympathetically upon employees who, for instance, don't immediately jump into a resignation. Sometimes because they're ill, sometimes because they need the work and they need to obtain alternative employment before they go.

It's not infinitely extensible, and you can get the wrong tribunal where they might take a very dim view, but broadly speaking, if you've given notice and been clear from the outset that you're treating the employer as having repudiated the contract, you're certainly okay for unfair dismissal. And in many cases, I think you can persuade a tribunal to make sure you're okay for a wrongful dismissal purpose. The same will also be true of discrimination claims because it's a very similar provision to the provision in the Employment Rights Act.

Anonymous

How long is too long after the breach before the employee resigns in response to the breach if there's been no process such as a grievance process delaying matters?

Daniel Barnett
So how long does an employee have to resign in order to not be taken to have affirmed the contract?

Sean Jones
In an amazing coincidence, it's exactly the same as the length of a piece of string. But what the authorities are pretty good at is saying that it's not really the time, it's the conduct. So you can lose your right to resign by saying, in effect, that you're not resigning. So that's a nice clear affirmation. You can say to an employer that they're in breach but you're calling on them to have another go to perform and you're prepared to give them their chance. That's an affirmation.

Where it gets tricky is where you're seeking to imply affirmation out of conduct. So that's where the question really bites. How long can you effectively do nothing? It depends on what you're doing. If you're working and complaining, you're likely to get more indulgence from a tribunal than if you're working and not complaining about it. But even then, to take a case like Jones v Associated Tunnelling (*Jones v Associated Tunnelling Co Ltd [1981] IRLR 477*, where there was a unilateral variation of contract and there was an issue about whether you could imply consent from lack of objection, the court took the position that because the impact wasn't immediate, the complaint didn't have to be immediate. So this is all a very long way of saying that, ultimately, it turns on the individual circumstances of the case.

If the employee wants to buy time for themselves, being clear that what has happened is not appropriate, that you don't accept it and that you're taking your time to think about it is important. But each time a pay cheque is cashed and no resignation appears, the risk of a finding that you have affirmed the contract begins to rise exponentially. I think it's one of the reasons why - and I'm sure none of you would ever advise this - there's a really strong correlation between people facing potential repudiation and them suddenly going away sick with a stress-related disorder. Because at that point, that's another factor that can be taken into account in terms of whether someone could be said, unequivocally, to have either accepted a repudiation or to have affirmed the contract.

Daniel Barnett
I'll pick up that gauntlet. When should an employee resign and when shouldn't they resign? What factors should they think about?

Sean Jones
I think this is about the most difficult question in employment law. So put aside all of the TUPE questions. Someone comes to see you and says, "Should I resign now?" And I have an overarching philosophy of employment law derived from my deep Catholic upbringing, which is always, always be passive-aggressive. So if what you say to the employee is, "here's a clear breach. Jump!", what's the consequence of that? Well, from an employer's point of view, assuming the employer wanted to be rid of this employee and has made their life hell, that's pretty good news. At that point, the employer has all of the money in their bank account, they have achieved their aim of bringing an end to the employment relationship, and the only way in which any of that money is leaving their bank account and finding its way to the employee is if they undertake the expense of commencing proceedings.

So in many a case, you might have quite a clear ground for resignation, you may have made that clear and raised the crisis, but if you jump, all you do is really put a smile on the employer's face. At least for a period, I think that it's worth, in practical terms, trying to use that as leverage to persuade the employer that it's worth compromising with you. If you're content that the relationship has come to an end, let them buy you out rather than jump.

Some of the really unhappy outcomes in cases are people who have walked off and decided that there's a resignation. And then when they come to the tribunal, it's for them to prove that they've been dismissed. It's their burden of establishing that there's been a repudiatory breach. And they don't always hit that burden. What felt really terrible for them at that time may prove not to be sufficient.

My answer to it is to be slow to jump out of the door. Take the other measures, make it clear that you object and why, and that there's a crisis and that trust and confidence is being undermined, etc. Demand that it be put right. Suggest that you are actively considering resignation. But you should, generally speaking, on a without prejudice basis, be trying to make sure that all of that happens with you leaving with money in your pocket.

Amir Gill
If an employee has worked successfully from home for over a year during the COVID-19 pandemic, can the employer insist they must return to work against their will? And if the employer persists and the employee resigns, could this be a constructive dismissal?

Sean Jones
Well, the first question is whether there's an express term. So, most contracts of employment will have a clause along the lines of 'your place of work is X or such other place as the employer may reasonably require you to work'. The easiest case is a case in which you are expressly engaged on the basis that you're going to be working at home. So you say, for instance, that your work-life balance is such that all you want to do is work from your home office and that you're not taking the job unless that's the deal. And that's fine. You're recruited at the start of the COVID crisis, that works for the employer and at the end of it, they want you in. Well, in those circumstances,

that might well be a repudiation if they've expressly agreed home as a place of work and then changed their minds. If they haven't, if they have the ordinary express term, which says you work in the office or some other place and they've made a temporary arrangement with you, there's a possibility that that might amount to a kind of permanent variation of your contractual terms, but I think a remote one. So it's extremely unlikely that just having you work from home during the COVID crisis would be understood to be a permanent change to your place of work. So again, that's not looking promising.

Where does that leave you? It leaves you where most people are, which is with a trust and confidence issue. So it wouldn't be enough, I think, simply to say to an employer that you really like working at home and it's great for your home life so you're not going back. Ultimately, is for your employer to decide where it is you work and where you perform your duties. And there are all sorts of issues about supervision and training, etc, which are harder to do at home. So that's ultimately going to be a matter of your employer's discretion.

There might be cases, for instance, where you have a very particular set of circumstances which apply to you. You might be living with someone who's shielding and vulnerable and coming into work might mean exposing you to a risk of infection, which you would then carry home and place your loved one in jeopardy. You can see that in those circumstances it might be considered that this does begin to feel like the kind of circumstance in which you wouldn't be expecting a reasonable employer to be issuing this instruction and that that might amount to repudiation.

So the answer, as with all legal questions, is that it depends. But I think it's going to be an incredibly rare case in which you're going to be able to run a constructive dismissal claim simply because you're required to go back to your previous habitual place of work at the end of the COVID crisis.

Daniel Barnett
Is there also the argument on behalf of the employer that the employee is really trying to use an implied term to oust an express term, and that's a bit naughty?

Sean Jones
Yes, although sometimes they do that. All of the express terms are effectively claused around by the trust and confidence terms. So we know from cases like United Bank v Akhtar *(United Bank Ltd v Akhtar [1989] IRLR 507)* that you might have a clause that says you'll work from any office they want you to. But if they say you start in Glasgow on Monday, then that's not going to be a reasonable exercise of your employer's discretion. So, yes, you can't overrule an express term. But insofar as it confers a discretion, that discretion is going to be limited at the outer ring by the trust and confidence term.

Paula Early
Does an employee need to state the reason for their departure in their resignation letter?

Sean Jones
Nope. It's absolutely better that you should do, but you don't specifically have to. The tribunal will simply ask itself as a matter of fact, what caused the termination. And it works the other way too. So if you say that the reason you're resigning is definitely X, but they decide it isn't X, that won't help you. So you do occasionally get cases in where what someone really wants to do is go away and work for another employer or at a much larger salary but there are questions about restrictive covenants. So it's in their interest to say they've identified a breach which has entitles them to treat themselves as constructively dismissed and that they do so now. And they can be absolutely clear in their resignation letter that the reason they are going is the employer being naughty and not because they have a much better-

paid job with the employer's direct competitor waiting for them. It's then open to courts and tribunals to say that they just don't buy that. They will listen to evidence on the facts. The resignation letter is an important source of evidence, but it is not in any way an estoppel. It doesn't prevent you from turning up to a tribunal and telling them what the real reason was.

Sarah Matthews
If an employee walks out a few days before they reach two years' continuous service, will their continuity be extended under the 1996 Act so that they can claim unfair constructive dismissal?

Daniel Barnett
So this is all about the rules allowing you to extend the statutory minimum notice period to hit your two years.

Sean Jones
That's a good question. I'm not entirely sure, actually. So far as the qualifying period of service is concerned, in circumstances where you're terminated with no notice, your EDT is treated as being the date on which the statutory minimum notice would have expired. That's added on to what they call in s97 the material date. And the material date means the date when notice of termination was given by the employer, or if no notice is given, the date when the contract of employment was terminated by the employer.

So you could read that one of two ways. You could either say it's terminated by the employer - a resignation is not a termination by the employer - or you might try and read it constructively and ask why it should make a difference whether or not the employer has summarily terminated your employment or you have summarily terminated the contract in response to the repudiatory breach. So I'm afraid I'm just going to have to say that I don't know. It seems to me to be a very interesting question and there's almost certainly an answer, but I don't know.

Anonymous

What's the most minor of fundamental breaches which is likely to result in a claimant successfully claiming for constructive dismissal?

Daniel Barnett

I suppose the question is predicated on what's the difference between a breach and a fundamental breach?

Sean Jones

Whenever I answer any question, can we just assume I said 'it depends' at the start of the sentence? We'll get more questions in. So, my wife is a family lawyer. Nothing keeps you more honest than being married to a divorce lawyer, let me tell you. But every night when she's updating the affidavit that she will eventually present to the court, she reminds me that they have a concept of unreasonable behaviour. She always says that there is no marriage which, if properly spun, could not produce sufficient unreasonable behaviour to justify divorce. So there's a sense in which there is no behaviour which, on the face of it, is too minor not to be strung together with other elements of minor behaviour so as to amount to, cumulatively at least, a kind of last straw repudiatory breach. It depends how it is presented.

If you had a single incident, if someone said they got their pay this week and it was two pence down on where it should be, you've plainly breached an express term. It's plain that that's one side of the line. If every week for a year they were underpaid by two pence, they complained and nothing was done about it, then it starts to feel like an issue of trust and confidence. What you're not doing is resolving their complaint about your consistent practice of underpaying them.

It's going to be impossible for there to be a bright line. There shouldn't be a bright line. The reason why there shouldn't be a bright line

is that firstly, employers would then all adapt their behaviour to make sure that they never crossed it, but they'd be breaching contracts left, right and centre in a way which was understood to fall just the right side of the line, and secondly, because of the way in which employment judges' minds work.

You're dealing, effectively, with a jurisdictional issue. Unless the employee can establish that they've been constructively dismissed, the tribunal doesn't get to hear the case. So judges will want a broad discretion as to how to look at a particular set of circumstances in order to determine whether or not they're going to allow the claim to go forward and to consider the fairness or the wrongfulness of it. So what you're asking for will never happen. No one is ever going to give you that answer, partly because it would be impossible to catalogue it and partly because it's in no one's interest that it should be.

Alex Jones

Can a constructive dismissal ever be automatically unfair?

Daniel Barnett

I don't think the question is talking about the Morrow and Safeway Stores type of automatically unfair. It's talking more about the no statutory cap and no qualification period required type of automatically unfair. He gives the example of a protected disclosure where the employer refuses to deal with it, presumably, on the grounds of the disclosure, and the employee resigns.

Sean Jones

Yes, it definitely can. All a constructive dismissal decides is that you've been dismissed. And if you have been dismissed because you have made a protected disclosure, then s103A is going to apply. Just to give you a very straightforward set of circumstances, you've got two employees and they both raise the same protected disclosure. In relation to one, the employer says they're sacked. In relation to the other, the employer says they are reducing the employee's pay to 10 pence a year so that there's a repudiatory breach and the employee resigns. There's no reason, as a matter of policy, why those two sets of circumstances should be treated in any way differently. The tribunal wouldn't and the statute doesn't.

Steve Hall
Does a failure to make a reasonable adjustment constitute a repudiatory breach?

Sean Jones
It can do. There's the silent 'it depends'. So there are a couple of weird things about constructive dismissal. Firstly, not every constructive dismissal is unfair, which always surprises me. There's a case called Savoia v Chiltern Herb Farms *(Savoia v Chiltern Herb Farms Ltd [1982] IRLR 166)* which establishes that. Tribunals do occasionally get spanked for not going through the additional piece of reasoning about whether or not it was unfair.

Not every act of discrimination amounts to a constructive dismissal - and there's a case called Shaw *(Shaw v CCL Ltd [2008] IRLR 284)* that says that - but many will. You can entirely see why, if your practices are ones which place people with disability at a substantial disadvantage and there is something that you can reasonably do about it and you don't, that might well be the kind of thing which would have an impact on trust and confidence.

I think as a rule of thumb if you are confident that there has been a resignation which has been caused by an act which the tribunal is effectively certain to determine is an act of discrimination, it's going to be a very unusual case in which the tribunal decides that you weren't justified in resigning. There must be, logically, some terribly trivial act of discrimination that should trigger liability and yet not amount to a fundamental breach. But in the overwhelming majority of cases, including reasonable adjustment cases, it seems to

me that a clear breach of the Equality Act is likely to found a constructive dismissal claim if you've resigned.

Mark Irlam
If an employee would have a constructive dismissal claim but has negotiated an exit package with the employer and after weeks of negotiation, the employer refuses to sign on the dotted line, has the passage of time amounted to an acceptance of the repudiatory breach?

Sean Jones
I doubt it. So again, that principle is not time, but conduct. So what will happen is the employer will say that they breached it on the first of April and the employee didn't resign until 31 of May. And the tribunal will say that that sounds bad and ask if that means that the employee has affirmed the contract. And the employee would say that they can't tell the tribunal what the specific contents of negotiations were, but that they were in negotiation. I think in those circumstances, it's unlikely the tribunal will say that the employee has affirmed the contract.

If it goes on for a year or more, it does begin to get a little harder to buy. But I think a period of time in which the employee is effectively negotiating the terms of a termination is unlikely to prevent the employee from treating themselves as constructively dismissed.

If you're advising someone in those circumstances, you want them to be sending open letters saying that they're negotiating and that progress isn't being made at anything like the pace or with the constructive attitude they'd hoped for. They should remind that the employer is in repudiatory breach and that it is, at present, their intention to resign unless some other arrangement can be reached. So you want it papered, effectively.

Gillian Howard
Would Futty v Brekkes *(Futty v D and D Brekkes Ltd [1974] IRLR 130)* be decided the same way now as it was in 1974?

Daniel Barnett

Futty and Brekkes is yet another case which is one of my favourites because it's got a very silly name. And just to remind people, Futty v Brekkes is one of those cases you learn about in university where a fish filleter in Hull was rebuked by his supervisor and told, "If you don't like the job, fuck off". And the tribunal held that that wasn't a dismissal given the general level of profane language on the fish filleting floor at the time that Futty said 'fuck'. Would it be decided the same way today?

Sean Jones

Wow. It's not a case I'm particularly familiar with. But it sounds like it's addressed to a different point. That's a question about whether or not the words used were clear and unambiguous words on dismissal. So it's not a resignation case by the sound of it. It's whether or not the words 'fuck off' are effectively words which terminate the contract. I wouldn't have thought they would amount to words which terminate the contract even today, although surrounded by other words they might form part of the effective dismissal.

Could it amount, effectively, to grounds to run a constructive dismissal on the basis of trust and confidence? I think that's going to depend very much on the environment. So without wanting to break any hearts or ruin any impressions, the language one hears around chambers means that I suspect a rude word muttered in someone's presence, or indeed at someone, probably wouldn't terminate an employment in chambers just because it's the level of language and interaction that one expects. If anything, that language is a lot less shocking to modern ears than it was back in 1974. But if said with sufficient aggression and often enough, it begins to feel like bullying and harassment, and that would be a rich source of an argument that there'd been a constructive dismissal.

Emma Reid

If pay is protected, can demotion amount to a constructive dismissal?

Sean Jones

Yes. Pedersen and Camden. This is why this case is so great. It's been a long time since I've done any, but there used to be lots of cases like this, where people were saying that their jobs had been altered and their employer had taken away the bit of it that they really cared about.

It quite often arises in cases in which there's been a management restructure. Your title remains the same, your pay remains the same but you used to have 20 people reporting to you now you have two people reporting to you. And you say that yes, you're still a manager; yes, you still get paid; yes, you've kept your title. But you used to have responsibility for a much larger number of people and the job just isn't the same anymore. It feels different and, in practice, it's a demotion.

Another way in which that can sometimes arise is where you might have a reporting line that goes directly to a board member. And the employer inserts a layer of management between you and the board so that you're now reporting to someone who then reports to a member of the board. And yes, your title is still the same and you get the same pay. The structure below you is the same, but it's different above you. And you now feel more junior because you used to have direct influence on board matters and now you don't. So it's always possible, I think someone could say that this apparently minor change which hasn't affected title and pay, etc. nevertheless has sufficiently fundamentally altered the nature of what they do. It's removed the bits of it that they really value, meaning that it amounts to a constructive dismissal.

Anonymous

I've never won an unfair dismissal claim. I used to get depressed about it until a fairly senior barrister, now a judge, told me he'd never won one either. How are you supposed to win one?

Sean Jones

Which side are you on? It's going to make a material difference. Someone's always winning in an unfair dismissal claim. So assuming you're for a claimant, I wouldn't have thought it was all that difficult to win one. I mean, it's quite hard to win one substantively. It's rare that an employer hasn't done something that you can criticise in terms of the procedural approach to a matter. But, you know, Polkey reductions are common for a reason, which is that tribunals often find some unfairness but no ultimate substantive difference to the financial position of a claimant.

From a respondent's point of view, it ought to be easy to win them, in the sense that if you've got an appropriate policy and you follow it to the latter, and you adopt the Sean Jones patented passive-aggressive approach to dealing with your employees - what would YOU like to happen? Who do YOU think should represent you? How do YOU say we should deal with it? - before each stage, then you ought to be able to go into a tribunal and persuade them that you've been reasonable.

Weirdly, my feeling, rather bitterly after 13 years at the Bar, is that employers get themselves into trouble often by trying to do the right thing. But no good deed goes unpunished. Local authorities suffer from having the most baroque imaginable disciplinary procedures with 1400 stages of appeal. It's almost impossible to get from point A to point Z without going wrong somewhere. Or they decide to amend the procedure in order to enable what feels like a fair outcome or a fair development at that point of the process, only later to find that the person they thought they were helping then criticises them and says that the local authority departed from what was the agreed process and that that shows that the authority approached the matter in a biased way because it ultimately resulted in the employee's termination.

So there's a sense in which you are well advised, I think, to cleave hard to any policies that you have. In really contentious cases, it often helps to get someone independent in. There's a big-growth industry now in HR advisors and lawyers conducting investigations or being asked to give advice, as it were, on the record - in circumstances where the employees can see it - about whether or not alleged acts of conduct are capable of amounting to gross misconduct or conduct sufficient to justify termination. And the more you push matters towards independent decision making, the safer you're likely to be as an employer.

Daniel Barnett

Sean Jones, thank you very much.

COVID ISSUES IN THE WORKPLACE

CASPAR GLYN QC, CLOISTERS

Daniel Barnett

I'm joined today by Caspar Glyn from Cloisters and we are going to be answering your questions on Covid-19 in the workplace.

Caspar Glyn, good morning. I'd like to start by asking you a few questions of my own. First of all, can an employer impose a no jab, no job policy on new recruits?

Caspar Glyn

I'm going to come to the question, but just before I do, I want to say this whole webinar is about COVID. And it's about the legal consequences of COVID. And I think sometimes we can forget about what COVID has done, how it's killed over 100,000 people. When we're talking about issues in the workplace, it's about businesses trying to survive, trying to get back on their feet and trying to provide a safe service to others. It's about individuals who are fearful - fearful of going to work, or fearful of having a vaccine, or fearful of other issues. And it's these real human problems that were asked to advise on. It's important to realise that what we're talking about today in the webinar are general principles of law. There will be specific facts and evidence in each and every case that you'll need to address. I don't address them, nor can we address them on this call.

Let me turn to the no jab, no job policy for new recruits? Well, firstly, it's a matter of contract: can you impose a no jab, no job policy? Yes. You're not imposing a policy that they need to get the job in the sense that you're forcing

them to get the job, they just can't have a job. So in our view, it would be as a matter of contract law an obligation that a contract could contain. Secondly would a court enforce it? When looking at whether a court would enforce that type of term, we would look at human rights. We know it would be article eight, and maybe article 14 of the convention that would be engaged. And we know from Strasbourg that forced medical treatment is, of course, an interference with your bodily integrity and therefore falls under the jurisdiction of article eight and it comes down to a simple justification question.

You'll be delighted to know that Strasbourg will provide the answer in the summer of 2021. And it's considering two cases, Mr Vavřička, (*Pavel Vavřička and others v Czech Republic (Application no. 47621/13)*) which was a Czech man who refused to have his children vaccinated for polio and tetanus and was fined, and Miss Novotny (*Novotny v The Czech Republic (Application no. 16314/13)*), whose children were excluded from court because they didn't have the MMR. And they've both taken their case to Strasbourg. It was due to be held in December, but it was then released to the grand chamber in December, so it's coming up in the summer. There is Strasbourg authority that forced tests are appropriate and can be justified. There's also good Strasbourg authority that in times of pandemic and emergency, there's a wide margin of appreciation, certainly to states. So depending on the circumstances of your case, there may be a justification of Article eight rights and insisting that someone have a vaccination before they work with you.

Which leads us to the final of three. So that deals with the contractual issue, the human rights issue and then the final issue, which may be the thorniest issue, which is one of discrimination. And at this stage - because I know we'll get into more detail - all we can say is that it does engage a number of issues in terms of discrimination, whether that be direct discrimination; indirect discrimination, which is justifiable; harassment, which I think people need to think about more than they have done because it's not justifiable, although, for instance, it doesn't cover some protected characteristics such as pregnancy; and finally, religion and belief. And those I think we'll get more granular with. But those are the types of balancing acts it applies to. And subject to someone not having a protected characteristic and subject to being able to justify it, then yes, I think you can impose a no jab, no job policy on new recruits.

Daniel Barnett
Is there a difference if an employer wants to introduce a 'you've got to have a jab' policy for existing employees?

Caspar Glyn
Let's start again at looking at our analysis of it. Firstly, for someone who's in work, we need to have a look at the contractual mechanism. Let's say there's no express term. And if you look at any number of articles on the internet, you'll see that everyone's talking about is it a reasonable order? Is that a reasonable instruction for an employer to give to an employee? And another way of looking at that is there an implied term? What would the officious bystanders say if standing beside someone who it was insisted that they have a jab in order to keep their job? And here it would be informed by matters like s2 and s3 of the Health and Safety at Work Act, the employer's criminal duty to keep the

workplace as safe as reasonably practicable. It would be informed by the employer's duty under s7 of the Health and Safety at Work Act to take reasonable care for other people's safety at work. It would be informed by other implied duties, such as taking reasonable care, negligence, tort. And there may be - depending on the evidence - a mechanism where it would be a reasonable order. So depending on the facts, that could be a reasonable order.

Secondly, looking if someone refuses to have the jab, then what one would do is either dismiss them - and I'll come to that - or suspend them. And for suspension, it's a question of is the pay under an unlawful deductions claim? Is the pay properly due? And that'll depend on the contractual analysis, which I've just talked about.

Thirdly, the issue of unfair dismissal. We've all read the case of the masked driver *(Deimantas Kubilius v Kent Foods Ltd (England and Wales: Unfair Dismissal) [2021] UKET 3201960/2020)*, who was dismissed for not wearing a mask in the cab of his truck, and that was a misconduct dismissal. But in this circumstance, I think we'd be looking more at some other substantial reason. And here, it's important to realise that it's whether the employer was acting reasonably, in treating that as a reason for the dismissal. Now, ladies and gentlemen, the word 'reasonably': Is it fair or not? I have made a 30-year career out of the word 'reasonably', and so have most other lawyers. And it will be fact dependent on each circumstance.

And then finally, if we're looking at discrimination - as long as it's not direct discrimination - we'll be looking at whether there's a justification, whether there's a legitimate aim, and whether what you're doing is proportionate. Could you redeploy someone elsewhere? Could they be given other duties? Subject to those issues - again, depending on the evidence - in my view, it could be lawful to impose a no jab, no job policy on current employees.

Daniel Barnett
Do the new more transmissible variants affect COVID-secure workplaces?

Caspar Glyn
It's really important. I've read any number of articles where lawyers say this and lawyers say that about the new transmissible variant. But we must remember what we are: we're lawyers. We're not epidemiologists - although many of us, I'm sure, have become armchair epidemiologists. We're not bacteriologists or virologists. So we have to look at what the evidence leads up to. Now, in terms of evidence, if it's right that the Kent version, the UK version of the coronavirus as it's called, is more transmissible through air, then I think what I would just do is simply stress the government's workplace guidance and one particular part of it that I don't think has been given enough coverage.

We know that effectively having a COVID-secure workplace involves three things. Firstly, keeping the infectious factors out of the workplace. That means ensuring that people are tested and or self-isolate if they have symptoms. Secondly, it's hygiene. Hygiene is washing of hands. Thirdly, it's social distancing. Now, social distancing is one part of it. But one should also look at ventilation. Because if you keep people socially distance - say two meters apart - in a room with no ventilation for eight hours, that simply isn't going to provide any protection. So I think something that we should all focus on in COVID-secure workplaces - and something I've encouraged employers to focus on - is ventilation. And I think as the evidence grows about this being an airborne virus and airborne transmissible, as the evidence seems to suggest, ventilation is more and more important.

Julie
If we have a COVID-secure working environment but a member of staff is refusing to return to work, saying it's causing them anxiety, can we take disciplinary action against that member of staff if they refuse to return to work?

Caspar Glyn
It depends. I mean, if they simply assert that it is anxiety-making - and let's not forget that COVID is; it makes us all anxious about the risks that we face - obviously, the best way to deal with this is by consultation engagement with the employee, showing them what you've done, showing them the evidence and taking a slow and measured approach. Ultimately, if you're satisfied that the workplace is safe and if you're satisfied that they're not suffering from a disability - that the anxiety doesn't amount to a disability - then you can make it a reasonable instruction, if it is reasonable in all the circumstances, to attend work. So yes, you can discipline them at the end of the road.

Gillian Howard
What good arguments can an employee put forward if they wish to continue working from home - as they've been doing during the pandemic - but their employer is now saying that in accordance with Boris Johnson's roadmap, they must come back to work at their normal place of work?

Caspar Glyn
I think there are a number of things an employee can do. Firstly, in terms of the roadmap, it's not that clear, necessarily, that those who do not need to should not work out of the home at any stage during the roadmap. So one has to look carefully at that. Secondly, I think it's a matter of engagement with the employee in terms of health and safety and COVID risks. Are they vaccinated? If they fall within a vaccinated population, they may have less good arguments. Are they vulnerable? There may be arguments as to vulnerability and arguments as to productivity. I don't

think it's a matter of being able to stand on a contract and launch. I think these matters are matters of negotiation and good sense between the employee and the employer.

Anonymous
An 'anti-vaxxer' brings a complaint that an employer's no jab, no job policy is indirect discrimination on grounds of their belief - their belief being rabid anti-vaccination beliefs - is that belief worthy of respect in a democratic society?

Caspar Glyn
Well, I'm just going to break that down. Do they get that far? If we look at the test for a belief. Firstly, is it genuinely held? Let's say it is. Secondly, is it a belief, not an opinion or a viewpoint? And what I mean by that, is that this anti-vaxxer is not just looking at something and saying, actually, this vaccine's only 60% effective; I'm not going to have it. That isn't a belief, that's a view on the medical science. Is it about a weighty and substantial aspect of human life? Probably. And then maybe this strong anti-vaxxer: does their belief have a level of cogency, seriousness, cohesion and importance?

Here, one might look at anti-vaxxers - and I think it's important not to lump everyone in the same boat - but certain people believe against vaccination. There's a whole multitude of beliefs about that. A bit like the case of vegetarianism, where veganism was a protected belief, but vegetarianism wasn't because it had so many different strands to it. Is anti-vaxxing like that? And there are cases such as the intelligence analyst who when working for the police believed that in 9/11 and other conspiracy theories there were false flag operations run by the British and US governments. And he said his belief was protected. And the tribunal said, well, no, it isn't. It isn't because it just doesn't come to a level of cogency. So does anti-vax fall at that hurdle?

And then finally, is it worthy of respect in a democratic society? And here, what we've seen with tribunals is beliefs that don't affect other people, i.e. a belief that you hold, can often be worthy of respect in a democratic society. For instance, have a look at Employment Judge Taylor's recent judgment *(Forstater v CGD Europe & Others [2019] UKET 2200909/2019)*, that where a belief is expressed that affects other people, it is, in his view, effectively denigrating other people and would not be worthy of respect. Alternatively, look at militant Trotskyism, for instance - which is a militant state overthrow - again, that isn't worthy of respect as a democratic belief, a tribunal found *(Unison v Kelly & Ors UKEAT/0188/11/SM)*. So on the fact it may be that an anti-vaxxer, by creating a risk that others, may not hold a view that is worthy of respect in a democratic society. But there are other arguments to be made, such as why should they have this vaccine that hasn't been fully tested in their view? So it's a difficult question. It's going to be fact dependent, and you need to test the belief.

Leszek Werenowski
In a suspected 'COVID outbreak at work' scenario, can an employer demand employees take a COVID test as an alternative to self-isolation?

Daniel Barnett
I suppose the first question is whether there's a legal obligation, because they've been contacted by track and trace, for the employee to stay at home. In which case, if they're legally obliged to stay at home, they can't be asked by the employer to take a COVID test at work. But let's assume that's not the case, and assume they haven't been tested by track and trace.

Caspar Glyn
The problem here is what type of test? You've got the LFD lateral flow device, which they say, misses 50% of positive cases. So if you're relying on that, it could be a reasonable step.

You'd have to manage the data that comes out of that - it's special category data. It depends on the circumstance. If there's a widespread outbreak at work, and they are a close contact who needs to isolate, they need to follow the law. If they are not in close contact and they do not need to isolate - and it may be a good employer who says why not take an LFD test just to see if you need a PCR test? But firstly, you'd have to look at the legal obligations as to whether or not they're at close contact. I think in the right kind of circumstance an employer could insist on the test.

Hannah Thomas

How will tribunals balance competing interests between keeping all workers safe, and allowing disabled workers who can't comply fully with safety requirements to work? As an example, a severe asthmatic who can't wear a mask and gets sent home on long term sick. Is sending that severe asthmatic home a detriment? Or is it a reasonable way of balancing competing rights and responsibilities?

Daniel Barnett

I suppose it could be both.

Caspar Glyn

Daniel, you've hit the nail on the head. it is a Shamoon detriment. Would a reasonable employee think that that's a detriment? Yes, it is a detriment to be sent home. On the example you've given, it's probably not direct discrimination if the employer would do it to someone else who equally couldn't wear a face covering and created danger. So it'd probably be disability-related discrimination, and that would be subject to having a legitimate aim and balancing it. So we'd want to look at proportionality. Wearing a face covering is just one way in which to protect other people. Can they be reallocated to jobs? Can better ventilation be supplied? Can they effectively work 'down flow' so that their breath is taken away by ventilation? Are there other issues? Are there other ways we can redeploy them?

And again, what I would seek to do - and this may be strange; I'm a litigator - is in these difficult times when employers are trying to provide safety and employees are anxious, there needs to be a dialogue in order to solve issues. And obviously, if there can't be, they need to be litigated.

Daxa Patel

What options are available for an employer, where the employee returning from maternity leave says she doesn't want to put her baby in a nursery, and that the employer should put her on furlough, as she wants to keep her baby safe? The employee can work from home, and the employer is willing to allow the employee to work from home, but not while the baby is at home also.

Daniel Barnett

I think summing that up, the question is can an employee compel an employer to place her on furlough? And on the facts of this case, is there any discrimination involved because the reason for furlough is maternity?

Caspar Glyn

An employee cannot compel, in my view, an employer to put them on furlough. Again, this is a matter of dialogue and understanding different positions. It looks to me like it's not a case of direct discrimination, but this would probably be indirect discrimination. And again, it would come down to is there a legitimate aim and are the steps the employer is taking a proportionate means of achieving that legitimate aim? And in the end, an employee agrees to work for an employer.

Ed Jenneson

Can you force employees to have a COVID test? What happens if the employee says no?

Caspar Glyn

Well, a COVID test is, effectively, a relatively invasive placing of a swab in the nasal canals and a wipe at the back of the throat. Can you force someone to do it? Absolutely not. There's no specific performance. Can you make it a term of the employment? Can you make it a condition? Again, you'd go back to my analysis of vax at the beginning. I don't think it would be as strong for an employee to resist the test as to vaccination, because the test is arguably less invasive. Can you make it a term? If you can properly justify why LFD tests have to be taken, potentially, Yes, you could.

Mike Clyne

Should employers allow employees who travel abroad and then get caught out with unexpected isolation demands on return to be paid in full?

Daniel Barnett

There may be a distinction here between employees travelling for work and employees travelling for leisure.

Caspar Glyn

This is a matter for tribunal and evidence. It was different last year when quarantine was new, and the need to self-isolate at home was imposed. But now we understand that at any stage quarantine could be imposed. So is it really unexpected? I think the employee, if they're going abroad for their own holiday, will be in difficulties. But again, can the employee work from home? Is there useful stuff that they can do? Is there a way round this? It's important for us all not to stand on our rights too quickly, but to negotiate and consult.

Elish Kennedy

Do you think employers could withhold company sick pay for an employee who's ill with COVID after that employee refuses the vaccine?

Caspar Glyn

It's an interesting question. There's potential if one gives enough time one consults and one makes the policy clear. And clearly what one is doing is saying it's a matter of necessity or a reasonable order to have the vaccine and then your failure to have the vaccine has materially increased your risk. Again, it depends on the

evidence. I don't see a reason why not in the appropriate case, depending on the evidence.

Anonymous

What's your advice regarding the effects of long COVID? And what would you suggest to manage the long-term effects of long COVID?

Caspar Glyn

It's a medical matter. But what I can say is several of my friends and a member in chambers have suffered from the post-viral syndrome. And as I understand it, they're being advised to rest. Get your medical tests because COVID can have infected internal organs. Speak to your doctor, not lawyers.

Daniel Barnett

Can an employer discipline an employee who refuses to wear a mask at work? Does it make a difference if that employee is client-facing? And we'll assume there's no medical condition preventing them wearing a mask.

Caspar Glyn

Well, there are certainly people for whom there's legal obligation to wear face coverings at work. And those are people who work in various sectors, such as, for instance, retail, and that if they don't wear a face covering, it becomes a conduct issue. But again, the question is can we discipline? What we should all be looking to do is speak with each other and find ways out. Explain why the face covering is so important, and why we need it. But ultimately, in the right case on the facts, it seems to me that yes, disciplinary action could follow.

Steven Eckett

Can Pimlico Plumbers lawfully change terms and conditions of employment for their workers to make sure that Pimlico Plumbers has a 100% vaccinated workforce?

Caspar Glyn

I'm not going to answer a question which is directed at one employer. I think I've answered earlier that depending on the evidence, such as does the virus reduce transmissibility? Do workers work together? Do workers work with vulnerable people? Is there a risk of COVID transmission in the workplace? All those questions will go into the evidential considerations that I set out right at the beginning of this talk as to whether or not an employer can impose a no jab, no job policy on people who are already working for it.

Daniel Barnett
And presumably, case law on amending terms or conditions of employment would apply. So the employer has to establish a sound good business reason and there has to be an element of balancing the competing rights of the employer and employee when a tribunal decides whether any consequent dismissal is fair. I appreciate that's fairness rather than contractual provisions.

Caspar Glyn
I think so, but I think it might be better to analyse not whether actually terms of conditions are being changed, but whether or not there's, for instance, an ability to give the lawful instruction within the employer's current panoply of powers, or whether indeed, it might arise out of implied terms giving business efficacy to the contract. So I think the approach of can you amend terms and conditions is perhaps a fallback for an employer, but they would first look at those two factors: implied term and lawful order.

Natalie
How regularly should we update a COVID-19 risk assessment for the workplace, given how often the advice and knowledge around COVID-19 changes?

Caspar Glyn
I think you'd want to keep up to date with the government's COVID-secure workplace guidance. I think that whilst if you comply with it, it isn't conclusive evidence of not being negligent, I think it's very good evidence of discharging your duties. I think you want to

keep abreast and look at things but at the same time, you shouldn't necessarily react to everything you read in the Daily Mail. But one should be careful in terms of leaping on the basis of one article or one piece of evidence that one sees. These are careful matters; the hierarchy of controls. So, hygiene, keeping infected people out, space, ventilation, face masks. These are the keys and they're important. However, people are vaccinated, you need to keep and enforce the hierarchy of controls.

Andrina
Are there any reasons why we can't keep a list of staff who have had a COVID vaccination? Literally just the name of the staff member - no details of which job. Our chief executive is keen to have a list to help us plan any eventual return to the office.

Caspar Glyn
The Information Commissioner has brought out a very good piece on testing, not on vaccination. But there's a good piece on testing and the data in terms of keeping that data. As I said earlier, this is special category data. An employer needs to be careful that just because someone's an employee, that isn't a proper reason for consent. There's probably one of the other reasons for processing this under GDPR, such as health and safety operations of the employer. You need particular GDPR advice to make sure that you are complying with your obligations and duties. But before you do that, I would suggest you read the ICO publication on testing (https://ico.org.uk/global/data-protection-and-coronavirus-information-hub/coronavirus-recovery-data-protection-advice-for-organisations/testing/). It's not the same as vaccination, but it will give you an idea of the type of matters that you want to be thinking about before you make that list, how you keep that list and how securely you restricted that list to only certain people.

Ruth Christy
If an employer knows that a member of staff is very keen not to work closely with somebody

who hasn't had the vaccine, what duty does an employer have, if any, to tell that member of staff that the person at the next door workstation has refused a vaccine?

Caspar Glyn
It's interesting, isn't it? Because vaccinations are happening at the moment, the vaccine has become everything. And we must remember that to have a COVID-secure workplace, you need to implement the hierarchy of control. And that's keeping infected people out of the workplace, washing your hands, social distancing and ventilation, and managing exits, entrance and passing. Now, vaccination is an added way in which to reduce the ability of transfer. In my view, on the facts you've given me, the employer would be in gross breach of the GDPR if it had found - through its lawful processing mechanisms - and it had thought it justified to keep a record - of sharing that record with an employee that another employee was not vaccinated. So I don't believe there's any proper mechanism for that other employee to find out about the vaccine status or fellow employees.

Hannah Thomas
Regarding age discrimination, would a failure to consider age as a risk factor for COVID when implementing a furlough scheme give rise to a risk of indirect discrimination?

Daniel Barnett
I'm actually going to turn that on its head and ask that if an employer takes age into account when deciding who to furlough, could younger workers sue for indirect discrimination?

Caspar Glyn
Potentially. Again, I don't think that there's any way in which to force an employer's hand to put you on furlough. But if a protected characteristic is made a factor in which you're making furlough decisions, then there may be direct discrimination. In the case of age that would obviously be subject to the legitimate aim and proportionate means of

achieving that aim. So if you employed two lighthouse keepers, for instance, who worked by themselves, age wouldn't seem to be an appropriate consideration to furlough them, because their safety isn't affected. If you employed two members of the Welsh scrum, who weren't having testing, who work in necessarily close contact in a scrum together, then age may be a reason to follow. I can only re-emphasise how important the facts of individual cases are in terms of arriving at conclusions.

Jim Jaffri
For employees suffering with the vast array of long COVID symptoms, could these symptoms lead to a capability dismissal in the long term?

Daniel Barnett
I'm going to rephrase that very slightly. When dealing with long-term sickness dismissals, should an employer treat somebody with long COVID differently from the way it treats other people on long-term sick?

Caspar Glyn
No. The same issues arise. Is that person disabled? Could that condition last for longer than a year? Are they unable to do day-to-day activities? Then looking at disability, you have to go through your reasons for a disability-related reason and you have to be able to justify it. Again, it's emerging evidence, but no, there's no difference. The fact that COVID is the source does not affect the way in which the employer acts.

Beth Bearder
What is your view on the Kubilius and Kent Foods case?

Daniel Barnett
Just to remind people, that's the case that was decided about two weeks ago. It's an employment tribunal decision only. It's the case where a delivery driver was dismissed for refusing to wear a face mask when he delivered items to a client's premises. The client said they would not have the person on their premises

again, and there was no way to redeploy that particular delivery driver. The case was decided on the basis of the range of reasonable responses test. The tribunal said it fell within the range of reasonable responses for the employer to dismiss in those circumstances.

Caspar Glyn
It reminds me of two things. Firstly, in the 1970s - if you look at the Industrial Relations Law Reports, they are full of Employment Tribunals' - or as was Industrial Tribunals' - decisions, because there weren't any other things around and that's what people relied upon. Now, one just wouldn't rely upon industrial tribunal or employment tribunal authority. Each case is determined by its own facts. So be careful. In this thirst for knowledge, we're looking at ET decisions that are wholly factually dependent. I would not be taking too great a message out of each individual case. So be careful. And then secondly, it's a range of reasonable responses, that wide range, that margin of appreciation which tribunals afford to employ as in such situations. So I think that the important takeaway from that case is that isn't actually that much to take away from it.

Anonymous
Can we issue an instruction to employees not to discuss whether they've had the jab in the workplace, in order to prevent heated discussions when there are different viewpoints?

Caspar Glyn
I think it's a difficult order. It might be against article 11. But for workplace cohesion, you might say, well, let's not discuss this and encourage that. You might encourage your employees for that reason not to do so. Whether you'd go to the extent of disciplining someone for actually just discussing it would be very much more difficult. If someone became violent and abusive, or something like that. That, of course, transcends to a disciplinary measure. But it may be a sensible thing for an employer to do, to encourage its employees not to discuss those types of difficult issues. It may be.

Anonymous
Can an employer discipline an employee for failing to follow social distancing rules outside of work, because that leads on to risk to people within work?

Caspar Glyn
There's the potential that where an employee's behaviour away from work affects safety, then it may do. You'd want to have a decent evidential basis before you looked to act. You'd want to know what the breach was and how egregious it was. With a simple one-off breach it would be difficult. And of course, these are what people describe as draconian rules. Potentially, in the right circumstances, yes, you can see that affecting the workplace and entitling an employer to act. But you'd want to have a look very carefully at the evidence and that it wasn't just a quick breach, walking past someone, and it didn't have any real effect. But potentially, depending on the egregiousness of the breach, yes, it could.

Anonymous
Can employees walk off the job if they believe the workplace is not COVID-secure?

Caspar Glyn
Yes. Under s44 of the Employment Rights Act, yes, they can.

Daniel Barnett
Are there any qualifications for that?

Caspar Glyn
It's whether they reasonably believe it poses an immediate danger to them under s44. And if it does, then they can. They're protected against detriment. And it affects not only employers, but now, as a result of a judicial review, it also affects workers.

Daniel Barnett
I believe it's not just a risk of serious and imminent danger to them, it can also cover risk

of serious and imminent danger to those they care for and love.

Caspar Glyn
Certainly to other people. For instance, a restaurant chef was able to claim that the food he cooked could pose a risk to other people. So it does include other people, that's right. There's authority on that.

Daniel Barnett
Caspar Glyn, thank you so much for your time.

CROSS-BORDER AND JURISDICTION

SARAH CROWTHER QC, OUTER TEMPLE CHAMBERS

Daniel Barnett

I'm joined today by Sarah Crowther QC of Outer Temple Chambers, who's going to be answering your questions on territorial issues and cross-border jurisdiction.

Sarah Crowther, good afternoon. I'm going to ask you a couple of questions but by way of apology to anybody here in Scotland or Northern Ireland, when we're talking about jurisdiction and civil courts, the civil court system is based around England and Wales. So for that purpose, to an extent, Scotland is regarded as a different territory, a different jurisdiction. In employment tribunals, as you know, Scotland is the same law, the same jurisdiction, but you've got to issue your claim or have your claim heard in the correct constituent part of the UK. So if your respondent is based in London, for example, you can't normally get the case heard in Scotland and vice versa. So that's just to explain why sometimes Sarah's going to draw a distinction between Scotland and England or Wales.

A question from me: if a contract of employment says that it's governed by the law of England and Wales but the employee works in a different country, including Scotland, how do we know what law actually applies to the employment contract?

Sarah Crowther

Obviously, if you've got a contract, then your starting point is going to be what the terms of it say in terms of the governing law. But in an employment contract, the rules are derived in English law from the Rome I and the Rome II regulations. Those continue to apply, notwithstanding the fact of Brexit, because they are retained and now incorporated as English law.

There are special rules in respect of contracts of employment when you're looking at the governing law. The basic rule is that the parties can choose their applicable law. But there are specific protective measures that are also in place for the employee's benefit in order to mitigate the effect of the imbalance of bargaining power. So there is, therefore, for example, in article three of the Rome I regulation, a rule which prevents the parties to an employment contract from contracting out of any mandatory rules. And importantly, in article eight, even if you have a choice of law in an employment contract, that can't have the effect of depriving the employee of the protection of provisions which would otherwise apply, apart from the choice of law rules. So, for example, you can't contract out of the whistleblowing protection. There is a statutory floor of rights for which the employee would be able to have the benefit regardless.

I suppose that gives rise to the question of why you would ever choose the law in an employment contract, in that case. There can be very good reasons for that, particularly if you're thinking about issues other than employee protection because of course, it can be material for things like injunctions, team moves, post-termination contractual issues and the like. And of course, it creates significant certainty to have the question of choice of law resolved.

If you don't choose it, and the contract is silent, which can happen, then Rome I has default rules. The first is that it's the law of the country where the employee habitually carries out their work. And if you can't get within that rule, there are others. The next rule down the hierarchy is that you look at the place of the employer's seat from which the employee was engaged, and the law of that country will apply. All of this is subject to what European law is calling an escape clause, which means that if there's a closer connection to a different country, in fact, then those rules can be displaced in favour of that country. So, ultimately, if you've not taken the care to choose in your contract, or it hasn't been chosen for the employee for them, then it's a bit of a 'depends' answer.

Natalie White

If an employer introduces a homeworking policy post-COVID-19 and an employee under an existing UK contract wants to move back to their home country to be with their family and work from there, will there be any impact on their statutory employment rights?

Sarah Crowther

The first part of that question is about where the employee is going to be working from because there isn't necessarily a right of an employee to say that they're going to be home working and therefore, it doesn't matter where in the world their home is. There could be legitimate business reasons for an employer to say that actually, you can't go to New Zealand, because everybody there is asleep when we're all awake, and you're a member of a team and we need you to be working with us. So it doesn't necessarily follow that the employee can choose where they wish to work. Unless the contract is particularly generous to

the employee, I would have thought that that's something that would need to be negotiated.

Assuming that an employer has now said, yes, you can go and work from Greece or Finland or I don't know where, then the question would arise, say, for example, in the case of an unfair dismissal situation, of what the power of an English employment tribunal would be to hear and determine a claim, and that would depend on the jurisdiction rules. Once you've got through those jurisdiction rules, then there would be a separate question of the territorial extent of the protective statute on which the employee wishes to rely.

In respect of the jurisdiction question, I suspect that under this example, it would be quite straightforward because if you had an English-based employer who was resident here, then the jurisdiction of the tribunal would be very easily established. So perhaps more interesting in this scenario is whether the territorial extent to the Employment Rights Act 1996 would cover this particular situation.

We know from the well-established principles in Lawson v Serco *(Lawson v Serco Ltd [2006] IRLR 289)* that we've got three categories of employee. We've got the standard case of somebody who works in England and Wales. We've then got what they call the peripatetic category of workers who move around, which wouldn't apply here. Then you'd have to look on a case-by-case basis as to whether you could establish what the courts have called a sufficiently close connection, which has had different labels over the years. Sometimes people talk about 'enclaves', which is a word with wonderfully colonial connotations, and people also talk about 'posted workers'.

In essence, all the cases have tried to do the same thing. You can see this in the case of Hamam and British Embassy in Cairo *(Hamam v British Embassy in Cairo and Foreign and Commonwealth OfficeUKEAT/0123/19/ JOJ)*, which was decided last year on these principles. What you're looking at is a factual test to establish whether the employee's employment has a sufficiently close connection.

So after that very long walkabout, I think the answer is probably yes, the statutory provisions would still apply. But hopefully, I've explained why that would be the case and you'll be able to work out from there if there are situations where it was perhaps different. But it is very fact-sensitive.

Daniel Barnett
A few people are asking questions about immigration and international tax. Unless you tell me otherwise, I'm going to take an executive decision not to ask you those.

Sarah Crowther
I'm afraid I couldn't possibly begin to opine on tax issues.

Ben
If an employee's contract of employment requires that they work from home in the UK, but unknown to the employer and without permission they work from abroad, could the employee successfully assert rights under the laws of the foreign jurisdiction?

Sarah Crowther
Broadly speaking, no. The reason for that is that on the working assumption that in the example given the law governing the contract of employment here is English law, what Rome I provides is that either there's a choice of law in the contract, in which case choice of location isn't going to change that at all, or, perhaps more likely, if there isn't a choice of law in the contract, even a temporary removal of the employee to work in a different place doesn't change the habitual place of their employment. So if they're habitually to work in England, if they temporarily remove themselves - perhaps during the pandemic - to a different place, that isn't going to change the governing law.

Insofar as you then say, well, there might be foreign protective statutes that would apply,

the answer to that is, well, good luck getting an English court to apply those in the teeth of the English law applying. I mean, I never say never. If you want to instruct me with the exceptional case, I'll always look at it, but I think that's a tough one.

Sanya
In a situation where an employer and/or an employee is based abroad and you feel there might be a question around jurisdiction, can you sign off a settlement agreement, which is governed by the law of England and Wales, even if the law of England and Wales doesn't actually apply to the employment relationship?

Sarah Crowther
Yes, is the short answer. As we all know, a compromise or settlement agreement is a contract in its own right, and therefore it can have its own governing law clause and it can have its own choice of forum clause. So you can choose the courts where any dispute arising out of it might be settled. So that is completely independent of any previous contractual relationship between the parties. So, in principle, yes.

Having given that broad answer, there are a couple of things that you would want to be alive to as an issue in that particular situation. If a subsequent dispute were to arise, then there have been cases - and I think the most famous one in England was called Yukos (Yukos Oil Company v Dardana Ltd [2001] EWCA Civ 1077). In that case, there was a Dutch law settlement agreement following on from a Dutch law contract of employment. Subsequently, the Dutch employer discovered what it considered to be breaches of the contract, which wish to sue the employee for and wanted to bring proceedings in England. The question arose then of whether it was being pursued under the settlement agreement of the termination of employment or whether it was under the original contract of employment and thus captured by the asymmetrical, protective position in what was then Brussels

I Recast. The Court of Appeal said, no, this is all arising out of the original employment relationship.

So although there was a choice of law clause in that settlement agreement, it was effectively bypassed. I would always say it's worthwhile putting one in, but I think you just need to be alive to the fact that if there are previous agreements with different jurisdiction choices, then, in the end, the settlement agreement clause may not actually have teeth because the court might still decide that any subsequent disagreements actually arise out of the original relationship.

Natalie White

What are the relevant factors that a tribunal will think about when assessing whether an employee has a sufficiently close connection to the UK to claim employment protections, and are some factors more important than others?

Sarah Crowther

They're going to look at the context of the whole relationship. In cases I've dealt with, I've tended to see evidence about tax domicile and tax relationship because that can be very closely related to employment relationship. You can also look at peripheral benefits and the terms of the contract and where that's linked to. Obviously, you can look at the history of the working relationship and, perhaps, the length of the posting - whether it's a fixed-term or a permanent contract. In particular, I find that the tax relationships and the other financial relationships between the parties tend to carry more weight than some of the other factors.

Natalie White

How effective is an express clause in the employment contract that governs the choice of law and jurisdiction?

Sarah Crowther

One of the big changes that have happened in the last 12 months since the end of the transition period for leaving the European Union is that the choice of jurisdiction clauses

in the employment contract has potentially assumed a much bigger role. Under the Brussels regime, it was very difficult to choose the jurisdiction because article 23 effectively limited such choice to situations where the dispute had arisen already and the employee agreed with the employer in writing to choose a jurisdiction other than the one set out in the Brussels regulation.

Now, that's all been swept away, leaving a lower floor of rights and jurisdictional terms for employees and greater freedom for employers to have effective jurisdiction clauses. And although the UK has now ratified the Hague Convention on choice of court - which certainly in a wider contractual context has quite a great impact - even that doesn't really bite on individual contracts of employment because they are expressly excluded from its ambit. So one falls back on to the common law and then it becomes a pure contractual issue. Generally speaking, the English courts have proved themselves to be very much in favour of upholding a party's agreement in respect of a choice of forum.

My only caveat to that is that I'm not aware of a case yet where it's actually been tested in the employment contract post-Brexit. It remains to be seen whether we're looking at an employment situation. Even the English court might be persuaded to have a balance of bargaining power in its mind when considering whether to enforce a choice of forum clause in an employment situation. But if one went from the basic commercial cases, it certainly would.

I talked about choice of law clauses before. I think, again, Rome I applies there, so, obviously, there are limitations on what one can do with a choice of law clause. But I would still advocate having one from an employer's perspective because it can be very costly to have a row about the choice of law and even to negotiate on it. So having clarity in the contract, even if it's subject to the basic protections and the exceptions in Rome I, is, in my view, still worthwhile.

Daniel Barnett
A couple of people have commented that they're not entirely familiar with Rome I. Could you give us a 30-second summary of what it is?

Sarah Crowther
Absolutely. Rome I is the latest in a succession of European provisions that started with the Rome convention in 1990. It provides rules about the choice of law in contractual situations in civil and commercial matters. The basic framework is that it sets out a scope of the material law and then it sets out rules for choosing that law. And the general rule in article four is that the parties choose the law in a contractual context. There are then special rules for employment contracts, which are contained in article eight, which limit the choice and also, as I said earlier, provide a kind of protective floor. So article eight says that even if an employer or an employee have chosen a law of a country, they can't contract out of statutory provisions or protective measures that would protect the employee. So there is a scope for choosing law in an employment contract, but it is limited, always, by reference to the protective rights, which the employee would enjoy at all times anyway.

GGM
How does Rome I differ from Brussels Recast?

Sarah Crowther
Brussels Recast was - and still is - the European scheme for allocating jurisdiction of courts between the member states of the European Union. And until 31 December and respective proceedings were commenced before then, it applied in England and Wales. It no longer applies and as at today's date, it hasn't been replaced by anything, although there is discussion about whether the UK might accede to the Lugano Convention, which is, in many ways, similar to Brussels I. So Brussels I Recast deals with jurisdiction, which is whether the courts have power to hear and determine the claim, and Rome I and Rome II then look at what law the court is going to use to determine the dispute before it.

Su Apps
How do you resolve the situation where an employee works on a boat which is under the flag of one country, sails around the seas of another country, docks in a third country, the employer is based in a fourth country, and they're paid in yet another currency?

Sarah Crowther
Well, I usually start by getting a big towel, putting it in cold water and wrapping it around my head! That is definitely a master's degree kind of question on conflicts of laws. The answer, usually, is to start with the contract always. If there's a choice of law or jurisdiction in the contract, then it makes one's life immensely easier.

If you haven't got a choice of either law or jurisdiction in a situation like that, then starting with jurisdiction, first of all, you need to be looking at - particularly the employer and their domicile - you need to be looking at what the causes of action are that you're trying to assert and to see whether you can come with any of the common law gateways. Then, in any case, now, the English courts would have a discretion and a forum non conveniens, as to whether to accept a case or not. So you need to have regard to whether England is actually the natural forum for the dispute.

Having said all of that, the high seas are literally a law unto themselves. In conflicts terms, there always used to be a category called the law of the high seas, which always worked on the wonderful presumption that everybody adopted English law because obviously English law is the best, or something like that. Certainly, in maritime cases, there was always a presumption that the law of the ship would be the same as English law unless anybody asserted otherwise. I know great many of the older cases proceed on that assumption.

So, yes, that would be very fact-sensitive and it would completely depend on what your causes of action are, whether you're looking at confidential information or conspiracy or wrongful dismissal or fiduciary duties. You'd have to look at each one on its merits, I'm afraid.

Melanie Bonas

If I were to work in my home country, which the UK, for nine months of the year, and I then work from abroad for the remaining three months of the year - carrying out the same work on behalf of the same UK clients - are there any implications?

Sarah Crowther

I can see that she says that she's the director of the company as well as an employee. As I touched on in my last answer, you need to always bear in mind the different types of obligations. Although, generally speaking, fiduciary duties in the context of someone who has an employment contract, usually walk hand in hand. The fiduciary duties are not always categorised as contractual, so you have to be a little bit careful about that. But the short answer to your point is that it is entirely possible in applicable law terms to have more than one place where you habitually carry out your work. European law sees no difficulty with someone having more than one habitual residence or more than one habitual pace of work.

It looks to me under that particular example, particularly if it was a fixed routine of nine months of one and three months of the other, that it would be arguable that there were two seats of habitual work for the employee. So there'd be two choices of law, effectively, which would throw you onto the escape clause. Then you'd have to look at all of the circumstances and say where your closest connection is, and in the round, that looks like England and Wales, doesn't it? So I think in broad terms,

the applicable law looks like English law. In terms of jurisdiction, then we're back to the gateway rules as to looking at who we're suing and what the causes of action are. Happily, it doesn't sound like you've got a dispute yet.

Su Apps

Can an employee be subject to one country's jurisdiction for statutory purposes but the contract be subject to another country's laws?

Sarah Crowther

Absolutely. That's the kind of case that I end up engaged with quite often. It is entirely plausible, and the commercial courts regularly apply the laws of another country. And what I would add about that is that obviously, an English judge doesn't know what the laws of another country are and so in that situation, as a litigant, you have a choice. Either you get some evidence and you set out what the laws are and why they're different from English law and how you rely on them - and you'll need to call an expert witness to prove it - or you do what many litigants do, which is simply behave as if the foreign law was materially identical to the English law, at which point English law adopts a marvellous fiction that that is the truth and everybody carries on regardless.

So it might be that you would need to look carefully at whether it was really worth your while to assert what those country's laws are, whether it's actually going to make a difference to you. And in many cases, the parties conclude that it's disproportionate to go through that exercise and that it isn't going to make sufficient difference to their dispute to do so.

Anonymous

If an employee in an organisation in Great Britain is required to work at home due to the current situation and their place of home is Northern Ireland, does the employer need to be careful to make sure they're complying with the Employment Rights Order in Northern Ireland as opposed to the English Employment Rights Act?

Daniel Barnett

Working from first principles again, I would expect that you've got an English law clause in your contract and if you don't, the default choice is going to be English law. If their usual place of work is outside Northern Ireland, then I would expect it to be an Employment Rights Act case. But you can tell from my slight hesitancy that I'm just slightly wondering whether it would be possible for them to bring a claim in the Northern Irish tribunal and what law the Northern Irish tribunal would apply at that point. I'm just slightly outside my comfort zone because I'm not a Northern Irish-qualified lawyer. They might give you a slightly different answer if the claim were brought there. Certainly, insofar as a claim brought in an English tribunal is concerned, I'm pretty confident that it'll be the ERA, but I wouldn't necessarily know what the Northern Irish tribunal would do with that.

Sat Gill

What are the key cross-border jurisdictions to be considered if an employee to - and their employer can agree to - being partly based in an overseas location and partly in the UK? This is a hot topic as we come to the latter part of lockdown.

Daniel Barnett

I think we've answered that one already.

Sarah Crowther

I suppose the other considerations that I didn't touch on before are largely the practical ones; they may not really be legal issues at all. Obviously, most contracts of employment have clauses about place of work and obligations and expectations. The whole thing would need to be varied in order to reflect the changing obligations. There are also tax implications because in order to be tax domiciled in the UK, if somebody's going to be paid on a PAYE basis, then you would need to be sure about that as well. I'm far from the tax expert, but I would have thought that most of the ramifications of that kind of arrangement are practical ones, apart from the choice of jurisdiction clauses.

Amanda Davies

Are there any pitfalls that employers should be aware of during a TUPE situation if the transferring employees are based in Scotland but the employer is based in England?

Sarah Crowther

I'm not totally sure that there is a cross-border dispute there. Certainly if there were dispute arising under TUPE, it seems to me that those employees potentially would have a choice whether to bring their claim in the employment tribunals in Scotland or the employment tribunals in England and Wales. But it wouldn't make any difference substantively, so I'm not quite sure why they would necessarily want to come to England.

It might be that I've not completely understood the question. At the moment, I can't see how the fact that the parties have got their habitual residence or domicile in different countries impacts on the actual legal relations. But if I've missed something, please do come back to me on that.

Anonymous

Can an employment solicitor based in England advise an employee based in Scotland, if Scottish laws are applicable?

Sarah Crowther

The answer is that Scottish law is as foreign to English laws as the law of any other country. If you don't hold a practising certificate to practice in Scotland, then I'd say it's intrinsically dangerous to be advising on a law that's not that of England and Wales.

Daniel Barnett

Even if it's just statutory employment rights?

Sarah Crowther

If it's just statutory employment rights - where it's identical because they apply across the whole of Great Britain - then, in principle, there's no problem with that, because you're perfectly qualified to advise on those rules. I wouldn't necessarily want to give detailed advice about the rules of procedure in the Scottish tribunals. I don't get to go there very much anymore. I think the last time I did, I raised a lot of eyebrows as being proper London counsel and having come all the way up from England.

I think as long as you stay within the four corners of those parts of law where it's identical, then it's no problem. Just as a matter of interest, I do sometimes advise people who are in Scotland in respect to choice of law issues, because Rome I and Rome II are identical in Scotland because it's it's derived from the European law. So there are areas where the law is identical and that's not a problem.

Sonia Wilson
What changes might there be in questions of cross border and territory jurisdictional in the future?

Sarah Crowther
Well, as I touched upon earlier, I think one of the big hopes that those of us who were believers in the European approach to a bit more protectionism in this area in favour of weaker parties, including employees, is that the UK will become a signatory to and ratify the Lugano convention. That would replace, in large part, what has been lost as a result of the loss of Brussels I Recast and it can't be done without reciprocity. We do need the other signatories to allow that to happen.

The latest I've heard is that the European Union is unhappy with the idea that the UK might become a signatory to Lugano although the other EFTA countries who are the signatories have all indicated that they're perfectly happy so far as they're concerned. So I can only imagine that it's going to become a bargaining chip in future relationship deals. But the sooner that that

happens, in my personal view, the better. I guess the other thing that might happen is that somebody might grasp the nettle of sorting out our common law jurisdiction rules. But that might just be a conflict lawyer's dream than a realistic prospect.

Anonymous
How do you decide if an employee is entitled to claim s188 collective redundancy rights if they work abroad in a smaller team in Singapore but the rest of the team is based in the UK?

Sarah Crowther
You're back to the Lawson and Serco three-step categorisation. You would have to look at all of the circumstances of that individual based in Singapore to say whether they've got a sufficiently close connection with England and Wales that it can properly be said that Parliament would have intended for the rights to extend to them. Not knowing a huge amount about it, obviously, I can't give you a concluded view. But if that employee had integral links to, say, a London-based team and was working harmoniously with them from a UK employer, then I can see the beginnings of a case saying that actually, they're part of a kind of sub-undertaking or sub-organisation that did have a sufficiently close connection. But that's just a sniff test rather than a firm view on that. You'd have to look at that quite closely, I think.

Natalie White
Is there another argument that could be run here as well, which is that if you've got a single person or a small group of people in Singapore, then the employer is not making more than 20 people redundant in that one establishment because the Singapore establishment won't be the same as the London establishment, so they wouldn't actually meet the threshold of 20 to engage s188 rights? Is that a question to address before you come to cross-border issues?

Sarah Crowther
Actually, yes, that might also be a way through it

Anonymous
What's the territorial scope of the Equality Act?

Sarah Crowther
We're back to Lawson and Serco again, and there are other cases like Ravat v Halliburton (*Ravat v Halliburton Manufacturing and Services Limited [2012] UKSC 1*), which particularly look at the Equality Act provisions. But fundamentally, if you've got somebody who's based here and works here, then no problem. If you've got someone who's peripatetic and therefore doesn't really work anywhere, then again, not really a problem. If you've got someone who's got a more permanent base in a specific location outside England and Wales, then you're into that test of whether there is a sufficiently close connection between their actual work and England and Wales for it to be right for those rights to apply in much the same way as the unfair dismissal rules and looking at all those factors I've mentioned already in a very similar fashion.

Anonymous
Do employment tribunals in England and Wales have jurisdiction to hear claims of unfair dismissal from offshore employees living on an oil rig?

Daniel Barnett
My very small amount of knowledge on this tells me there are special rules about this, but I can't remember what they are.

Sarah Crowther
There are special regulations that govern workers on oil rigs and offshore installations. My personal experience is that when these cases come up, they tend to have Scottish jurisdiction clauses in their contracts. Most of them work, effectively, out of Aberdeen. I suppose it's possible that some of them don't. If you had an English employer or an England and Wales-governed contract, then you could get jurisdiction that way and you could start your claim. But I would imagine most of them will end up in Scotland.

Daniel Barnett
Sarah Crowther QC from Outer Temple Chambers. Thank you very much.

DIRECTORS

DANIEL TATTON BROWN QC, LITTLETON CHAMBERS

Daniel Barnett

I'm joined by Dan Tatton Brown from Littleton Chambers. Dan has very kindly stepped in for this Q&A on directors' duties because the speaker who was advertised for this talk is unfortunately unwell. Dan specialises in employment competition cases in the high court and high-value or complex discrimination claims. He appeared in the well-known case of CLFIS v Reynolds *(CLFIS (UK) Ltd v Reynolds [2015] IRLR 562)* which established the need to focus on the mental processes of the person responsible for an alleged act of discrimination rather than other employees whose prior decisions might have influenced the ultimate decision-maker. We might ask him a little bit later on how that case reconciles with Jhuti *(Royal Mail Group Ltd v Jhuti [2019] UKSC 55)*, the Supreme Court case that came a little bit later. He recently appeared for the successful corporate defendant in Quilter Private Client Advisers v Falconer *(Quilter Private Client Advisers Ltd v Falconer [2020] EWHC 3294 (QB))* in the High Court, where Judge Mr Justice Culver held that all three covenants relied on by the claimant - non-competition, non-solicitation and non-dealing - were all unenforceable.

Dan Tatton Brown, good afternoon. A couple of questions for me first. Are non-executive directors considered to be workers?

Daniel Tatton Brown

The answer to that question is that it all depends on whether their terms of engagement mean that they fall within the statutory definition of workers. As we all know, post the Supreme Court decision in Uber *(Uber BV and others v Aslam and others [2021] UKSC 5)* that the key starting point is a statutory language. The language of 'limb (b) workers' will be well known to many of you. In essence, does the individual work under a contract of employment, i.e. as an employee, or another contract whereby an individual has undertaken to provide work or services whose status to that contract is neither a client nor a customer of any professional undertaking carried on by the individual? So most non-executives will be undertaking to provide their services personally, and most non executives won't, vis-a-vis the company, be treating the company as a client or customer. So the critical question will be whether or not there's a contract between the non-executive and the company and if there is, then they're likely to be a worker.

Daniel Barnett

And if they're a worker, what rights does that give them?

Daniel Tatton Brown

That would give them the conventional rights, for example, rights to National Minimum Wage, rights under the working time regulations, those sorts of rights. Rights, importantly, to bring a claim for a whistleblowing detriment under the Employment Rights Act.

Daniel Barnett

That, presumably, would then mean that some non-executive directors who are working on an unremunerated basis would technically be entitled to a tiny bit of money, given that non-executives don't spend very long working for a company.

Daniel Tatton Brown

Obviously, any claim for injury to feelings would be independent of any lost remuneration. But if, for example, the non-executive was booted out for having made a protected disclosure, then you're absolutely right that the lion's share of compensation for any substantial whistleblowing claim will be loss of remuneration, whether consequent upon dismissal or detriment from losing the consultancy arrangement or whatever it is. And clearly, if the remuneration is minimal then the loss will be minimal. City non-executives seem to earn an awful lot of money for doing very little, so they would perhaps be well placed to reap rich financial rewards.

Daniel Barnett

If anybody is looking for a non-executive director, do contact me or Dan because we do have an hour spare every Friday afternoon to be able to help out with the very demanding non-executive role.

Just carrying on from that, if a non-executive director or indeed any director of a company can claim holiday because of their status as a worker, if the company goes bust, can they bring a claim for unpaid holiday?

Daniel Tatton Brown

The answer to that is that it depends on whether or not they are also an employee. So as many of you will know, employees of limited companies have rights to claim monies owed to them - or arrays of wages, holiday pay, notice pay or redundancy pay - from the Insolvency Service Redundancy Payments Office, the RPO, if the employer has gone into insolvent liquidation. So the question is whether they are an employee. And the usual rules in terms of determining employment status apply. Most of the cases, concern directors who are directors of companies that they own or control. And the critical question is whether or not in those circumstances the worker has a genuine contract with the putative employer, the limited company, and whether or not they can be said to be subject to the requisite degree of control for there to be employment status. The problem being, of course, that if it's a one-person company owned by Mr Smith, and Mr Smith claims he is also an employee of that company, there may well not be anyone, in reality, exercising special control over Mr Smith to render him an employee.

Daniel Barnett

If you have a director of a company who is also an employee of that company, can the individual be removed from their directorship whilst being retained as an employee? Is that considered a demotion that might give rise to a constructive dismissal claim?

Daniel Tatton Brown

Can an employee director be removed as a director? I think that was the first part of the question. The answer is yes. The circumstances in which a director can be removed as a director are set out amongst other matters in the Companies Act 2006. s168 provides that by normal resolution of the company, shareholders can remove a director so that happens whether or not the director happens to be an employee.

The significance of them the director being an employee, obviously, is that having been removed as a director, they may have employment-related claims. And they will have rights qua employee whether or not they're a director. So whether the removal of the office of director amounts to a detriment, it may well amount to a detriment, and if, for example, that was done on prescribed grounds and contrary to the Equality Act, or because the director had blown the whistle, that would be a detriment for the purposes of the statutory employment legislation about which they could complain. The employee may or may not be dismissed as a result of the directorship being removed. As a general proposition, removing someone from the office of director doesn't amount to a dismissal, which involves termination of a contract of employment. But it may be that the nature of that employment is such that being a director is an integral part. So if you're employed as a managing director, and, as such, you're reporting to the board, and it's integral to performing that role that you are a director, there's clearly a strong argument to say that your removal as director amounts to dismissal for the purposes of the Employment Rights Act as well.

Mike Clyne

In your experience, what are the key contractual elements that are forgotten when hiring directors?

Daniel Tatton Brown

That's a good question. I think that the broad answer is that the question of the director's status is very important, as we've just discussed. If they are an employee, then they have a number of rights qua employee. If they are a worker, they have a number of rights qua worker. And I think the key thing is to set out, as you would with an employee, an appropriate contractual document setting out what the director's role and responsibilities are so that the issue of their status as employee or worker is clear and there's no ambiguity between the parties.

Just to pick up on the point of the right to holiday pay, if the director is a worker, they will have a right to a holiday. That may typically be missed in an agreement simply specifying that the director will attend for X days per month for Y fees. So I think the starting point probably is to consider whether or not it's intended that they should be an employee or a worker, and if they are, to make sure that there's a document that accurately records their rights and respect to those matters that are relevant to an employee or worker. So if, for example, any employees have an

entitlement to avail themselves of the company disciplinary procedure or grievance procedure, then it seems to me as well to set that out in writing so that every party knows where they stand.

Mike Clyne

Are there any obligations that directors have that don't sit well with employment law?

Daniel Tatton Brown

There are none that immediately springs to mind. The overarching or defining characteristic of fiduciary duty - and, of course, all directors owe fiduciary duties to their company - is one of undivided loyalty. And that is an obligation that is more onerous than a mere employee will owe. So a mere employee will be subject to an implied duty of fidelity. And the language is very similar. There will be an implied duty to act in good faith and loyally on behalf of the company. But it's very clear law that the undivided obligation of loyalty that is characteristic of the fiduciary relationship is not typically characteristic of the employment relationship. So there are no obligations that immediately springs to mind. The legal obligations to which a director is subject are obviously more onerous than those of a typical employee. But that, it seems to me, doesn't mean that they're inconsistent or difficult to reconcile with employment obligations.

Daniel Barnett

Could it be argued that, for example, the director's duty to act in the best interests of the company or its shareholders is inconsistent with employment law because the obligation to act in the best interest of the company or shareholders might require a director to sack poorly performing employees ruthlessly, whereas employment law requires a process?

Daniel Tatton Brown

Well, first of all, the primary fiduciary obligation is to the company as opposed to the shareholders. So the obligation is to act in the best interest of the company. And there may be situations where those interests diverge or the interests of some class of shareholders differs from the interests of the company as a whole. So the obligation is owed to the company, but the company will have an interest, obviously, in avoiding behaving in a way that will attract liability. So booting out the underperforming employee in disregard of their rights is likely to result in potential legal liability, which won't be acting in the best interests of the company.

The other point, I think, is that there's a broader obligation to act in the interests of the company, having regard to certain stakeholders including employees. And in the long term, a company that abides by good employment practice is probably acting in its own interests.

Then the final point I'd make is that it's in the interests of the company, or at least you can scarcely say it's not in the interest of the company, to abide by the law. And one of the laws that companies are subject to is the law not to unfairly dismiss employees. So my answer would be that acting in the best interests of the company would certainly require the director to take into account relevant employment legislation. And unless there's some compelling reason to the contrary, there may be some situation of emergency, I think the obligation would require the director certainly to have regard to and probably to abide by whatever good employment practice would demand.

Anonymous

How does a TUPE transfer affect a director's status and shareholding?

Daniel Tatton Brown

Let's start with TUPE. There's an undertaking which is a business or part of an undertaking situated in the UK, and that undertaking or the economic activity associated with it is transferred to the transferee. So that's a TUPE transfer. And as many of us will know, a

change in share ownership does not amount to a TUPE transfer. The primary effect of a TUPE transfer is to protect the rights of those employees working in the undertaking or assigned to the undertaking that has been transferred. The key concept that underlies the TUPE regulations is the idea that there will be a statutory novation of those employees' contracts by the transferee. So instead of losing their employment and losing existing employment rights, those employees will continue their employment with the transferee on their pre-existing terms and rights. So, from that perspective, a TUPE transfer won't have any effect on a director's shareholding and nor will it in itself affect a director's office.

In a transfer from Company A to Company B, the director of Company A will remain a director of Company A even though the entity or an undertaking is transferred to Company B. What may provide a degree of complexity is if the director is an employee of Company A and their contract is transferred over to Company B under the regulations because then, obviously, they will be a director of Company A but employed by Company B. And going back to one of the earlier questions, it may be that the nature of their role requires them to be a director in order to perform it, in which case the logical solution ought to be that they become a director of Company B. But it certainly doesn't, it seems to me, have any impact on shareholding and it doesn't have any direct impact on directorships.

Becky Boston

Is there a difference between a director's service agreement and a director's contract of employment?

Daniel Tatton Brown

The answer is no. 'Service agreement' and 'contract of employment' are just two different ways of describing the same thing, and 'employment contract' is the third way of describing what we're talking about. Any employee, by definition, will be employed under a contract of employment or a service agreement. That may be expressed, it may be implied, it may be written or it may be oral, but they're all the same thing.

Clare Chappell

If two director-employees have equal shareholdings or are equal along with smaller minority shareholders, how does one director dismiss the other? Assume there's no written shareholders' agreement.

Daniel Tatton Brown

The answer is it that can be quite complicated. I think a starting point is to look at the articles of association that may confer particular rights or priority of one director over the other. The two directors may not be the only directors; there may be a board of directors. It may be that the constitution of the company or the terms on which particular directors are engaged means that the board as a whole has a right to terminate the contract of one of the individual directors even though they are a 50% shareholder of the company. So I think you need to look at the articles of association, the terms on which the various directors are engaged, and derive your answer from those key starting points.

Mark Irlam

How should a company deal with a director who's making defamatory comments about his company when he's left as an employee but not left as a director?

Daniel Tatton Brown

The answer is that they continue as a director and so continue to be subject to fiduciary duties owed to the company, and those duties include the duty to act in the best interest of the company. So to make defamatory, which I assume implies untrue, reputational damaging comments - and 'untrue' is important because if they're making truthful allegations exposing wrongdoing or so, they may be whistleblowers - but assuming that the comments are damaging and unjustified, the immediate

recourse, potentially, would be to seek an injunction against them. The circumstances in which you can get such an injunction depend, obviously, on the facts. There's always an issue in seeking an injunction preventing someone from communicating freely. But assuming that the comments that have been made are unjustified, particularly if it can be shown that they're malicious, they will be examples of acts done in breach of that director's fiduciary duties, so there's a legal basis for seeking an injunction. The other obvious step would be to remove the director as a director. They have already left as an employee, so pass a resolution to remove them as director.

David Reid

Would the removal of an employed director's directorship by the shareholders usually be a breach of the employer's duty to maintain trust and confidence in the employment relationship?

Daniel Tatton Brown

That's a good question. I think the answer, as to many of these questions, is that it all depends. The implied duty of trust and competence, as you all know, is an implied duty without reasonable and proper cause, which are very important qualifying words, not to act in a manner that is likely to destroy or seriously damage the relationship of trust and confidence. So is the removal of a directorship likely to destroy or damage trust and confidence? Well, probably is the answer. The critical question will be whether or not doing that was without reasonable and proper cause. And that's all going to depend on facts. So if under the constitution, there's a right to remove a director, and they are removed for a reason that's legitimate, then my answer is no. But if, for example, the director was removed, for the sake of argument, because of some antipathy towards their race or gender, that plainly would be a breach of implied duty and also clearly give rise to consequential employment-related claims.

Alan Lewis

What right does a director have if they aren't invited to a board meeting that has been called specifically to discuss the termination of that director's employment?

Daniel Tatton Brown

It's a good question. Again, I think the starting point is to look at the articles of association and look at the rights that the director has to attend board meetings. There may be provisions in the articles catering for this precise circumstance. So there may be, depending on the constitution of the company, and this also applies in particular in the context of members agreements and the LLP agreement. So in solicitors firms, can you dismiss or remove a member of the LLP? And what rights does he or she have to attend and separately to make representations and thirdly, to vote on the proposed resolution? So I think you need to look at the articles and see what they say in terms of what rights there are to attend, to make representations or to be notified of the board meeting because those are different things. Then, if there are no express rights, there are arguments or there will be arguments about whether or not there's an implied right to be heard - a natural justice right - before any decision to remove is made. But generally speaking, articles of association will give a steer on what rights the minority director will have to be heard.

Liz Burley

Are generous change of control and golden parachute clauses, which are included by owner-managers in their own director's service contracts, likely to be worth the paper they're written on?

Daniel Barnett

So in other words, clauses that say if ownership of the business changes, the existing owner will get a million pounds.

Daniel Tatton Brown

I'm hesitant about answering that in the abstract, to be honest. I think it all depends.

There may well be very good commercial reasons why there's a golden parachute provision. If it's been entered into with full disclosure and it's been agreed by the shareholders of the business, I'm not sure on what basis it could fairly be challenged, to be honest. So I think in principle, yes, is my answer.

Anonymous

Are there any claims that directors are at risk of employees bringing against them?

Daniel Tatton Brown

The short answer is yes. The two most obvious ones that spring to mind are whistleblowing claims and discrimination claims. So the way the statutes work is that the primary respondent to an employment claim for discrimination in the employment context is typically the corporate employer. The reason for that is that the employer will be liable for the acts of the employees. The individual employee - in this case, the director - may also be liable because they are a person who actually does the act of discrimination, I'm assuming. The way that the legislation is structured, they will be deemed to have aided the act that was performed by the employee, even though the director was the person who was primarily responsible.

So the upshot of that is that the victim of the wrongdoing can bring a claim, both against the employer and the individual. And that's obviously particularly important in the context of insolvent companies. The well-known decision of Osipov *(Timis v Osipov [2019] IRLR 52)*, which is a whistleblowing case, was a case in which the company was insolvent but the claimant brought a very valuable claim against non-executive directors complaining of whistleblowing detriments, including the detriment of dismissal, and that was held in law to be a valid approach. So, yes, the individual director acting as agent of the company might be liable in that way.

Gillian Howard

What are the essential elements of fiduciary duties of directors and how do they differ from the implied terms such as trust and confidence or fidelity?

Daniel Tatton Brown

The essence of a fiduciary is that the fiduciary has been given powers to act on behalf of the principal. In this context, the director has powers to act on behalf of the company. And the quid pro quo, as it were, for the individual having those powers is that they will act with exclusive loyalty to the principal. So the powers that they have been subject to the obligation to act exclusively in the best interests of the principal.

In addition to that core fiduciary obligation, company directors have a number of statutory obligations that are set out in the Companies Act, and they include the duty to act within powers. So the director must act within whatever powers they have been given under the articles of association or otherwise. They have a duty to promote the success of the company. They have a duty to exercise independent judgment to act in what they, in good faith, believe to be the best interest of the company. They have a duty to avoid conflicts of interest. They have a duty not to accept benefits from third parties. They have a duty to declare an interest in a proposed transaction or arrangement. So those are all very clear statutory duties that any company director owes.

The core concept behind fiduciary duties is one of undivided loyalty. So that is to be contrasted with the position of an employee, which is primarily a contractual relationship. So the duties that the employee owes are to be discerned from the terms of their service agreement or employment contract. And in sophisticated employment contracts, there will often be contractual obligations very similar to those that I've just described. Many service agreements will include provisions requiring the employee to act in the best interests of the company at all times. The difference is that as an officeholder and as a director of

a company, any director will owe the duties I've just described and they will own fiduciary duties. They may or may not as an employee owed such duties, and typically they won't. To give one example, because of this obligation of undivided loyalty, a fiduciary will typically be subject to an obligation to report misconduct, including their own misconduct, and that's quite an important obligation, particularly for example, in an application for springboard relief in the context of employee competition. A mere employee is an employee who isn't a fiduciary and isn't a director may well not have such an obligation.

Lorna Clark

Is there a conflict between a director's duty to act in the best interests of a company and their right as an employee to raise a grievance?

Daniel Tatton Brown

That's a good question. I think the answer is that assuming the grievance is raised in good faith, I don't see any conflict. The reason is that it's an integral part of an employment relationship that an employee is entitled to raise a grievance and has some means of raising the grievance. The expectation is that the employer will treat that grievance seriously and deal with it appropriately. So availing yourself of that right, it seems to me, is your entitlement as an individual employee. Does that conflict with an obligation to act in the best interest of the company? I don't see how it does, assuming that the grievance is raised in good faith.

If in good faith you believe that you have a matter about which you can legitimately complain in the workplace, it's in the interests of the company for that matter to be addressed and resolved. And one of the ways to do that is to raise a grievance. Raising a grievance not in good faith, obviously, would conflict with that fiduciary obligation. So if you're raising a grievance in order to tee up a potential claim for victimisation, for example, or to establish a position from which to negotiate some sort of enhanced terms for your departure, then I can see a basis for arguing that that isn't consistent with the duty to act in good faith in the interest of the company.

Daniel Barnett
What would the damages be in that situation, other than having to return any monies that you may have extorted by way of a settlement agreement if you raise a grievance in bad faith to bolster your position in termination negotiations?

Daniel Tatton Brown
Well, it's going to be a difficult claim for the company to pursue against the departing director because the assumption is that the company has entered into the settlement agreement. And it's going to be quite difficult to then turn around and say that they were only faced with that scenario, because of the director's bad faith in raising a grievance. I think a court would say that in such a case the company should dismiss the grievance as they're not obliged to enter into a consensual settlement agreement.

It's difficult to see how the loss flows from the alleged lack of bad faith. I guess it would be slightly different if the grievance was raised, the company took it seriously and, believing it to be raised in good faith, entered into a compromise agreement and then discovered afterwards some newly discovered fact that showed that the premise of the grievance was entirely fabricated. And then it seems to me there wouldn't be a basis for arguing. I'm ignoring for the moment the terms of the settlement agreement, which often, as everyone will know, will include a warranty that there hasn't been any act of misconduct to act that would justify summary dismissal or anything of that sort. But then the claim would be for breach of fiduciary duty and the loss would be the sums paid out under the settlement agreement. And the outcome would be that the company would never have sustained that loss

but for the bad faith and breach of fiduciary actions of the departing director.

Chris Davis
Will a director have any right to retain documents when leaving a company to show the company had been trading in a lawful and solvent manner up to that point or can the board insist that all company documents are returned?

Daniel Tatton Brown
Again, I think you need to look at the terms of any service agreement. Often the service agreement will include a provision requiring the return of documents. This is a knotty area and employment lawyers listening will know that there's case law addressing whether, for example, it's a breach of confidence for an employee who believes that they need to retain documents in order to formulate a claim against their employer, who then emails those confidential documents for that sole purpose. That is likely to amount to a breach of confidence. And the general rule is that the employee is expected not to retain documents. They should trust the system, as it were, for the documents to be produced by way of disclosure in due course.

I think that the general principle would apply to a director retaining post-directorship confidential documents belonging to the company. So particularly if they've been demanded to be returned or there's a contractual obligation to return them, I think the safer course would be to return them but to request the right to retain them, explaining the reason for doing so. And it may be that if no such right is agreed that some sort of application could be made to court if it was sufficiently serious to warrant it. But I think just to retain them and hope that the explanation you've given provides sufficient justification would be foolhardy.

Daniel Barnett
Gillian Howard has pointed out in the chat that the case you were referring to was Brandeaux

v Chadwick *(Brandeaux (Advisers) UK Limited & Ors v Chadwick [2011] IRLR 224).*

If somebody wants to get in touch with you to instruct you on a director's dispute, what's the best way to do so.

Daniel Tatton Brown
Contact my excellent clerks at Littleton Chambers and I'd be delighted to work with you.

Daniel Barnett
Dan Tatton Brown, thank you so much, particularly for stepping in at such short notice.

DISABILITY DISCRIMINATION
KAREN JACKSON, DIDLAW

Daniel Barnett

I'm joined today by Karen Jackson from didlaw who is going to answer your questions on disability discrimination.

Karen Jackson, good morning. I'm going to exercise my normal chair's privilege and ask you a couple of questions of my own. How does a discrimination arising from disability claim work - so discrimination arising from disability, not direct discrimination - where there are multiple disabilities?

Karen Jackson

There's a pretty simple answer to that one, actually, because s15 Equality Act 2010, discrimination arising in consequence of disability, kicks in when there's a disability. It doesn't really make any difference whether there's one disability or three disabilities. It's two different parts of the Act. s6 of the Act says, Is this person a disabled person for the purposes of the Act? Do they meet that test? If so, the provisions around disability kick in. When it comes to s15, remember, this is quite a loose test and all that is required is for the employee to show that there is a connection between their disability and the unfavourable treatment. It's not because of their disability that they are being treated in the way that they've been treated. So the short answer is, it doesn't make any difference. As long as there is one disability, you're home and dry. Well, you're not home and dry, because you've got to get through the various hoops around knowledge and justification, but this

section will kick in whether there's one or more disabilities. It's the same test.

Daniel Barnett

Where an employee doesn't disclose their disability to an employer in an application form - so they conceal the fact of a disability - is there any form of reduction of compensation that you can argue for if you're acting for the employer? Is it akin to contributory fault in a disability discrimination claim?

Karen Jackson

I don't think so. And I think that's a very unattractive argument to run. I have seen it run a number of times, and actually, quite often, an employer will seek to show that even the person who is claiming disability discrimination didn't believe that they qualified for the protections because, on their application form for the job, they didn't tick the box that said, 'Do you have a disability?' And I think the issue with this in practice is that, particularly with invisible disabilities, people are unlikely to disclose them on an application form or during a recruitment process because it might mean that they don't get the job. And there was actually a case on this in the county court about 20 years ago - I'm afraid I don't remember the name of it - where a local authority tried to rely on the fact that a councillor had not declared her long-standing issue with depression. And giving judgment for the councillor, the judge said, you can totally understand why she would not have declared that on her application form, and it would be unfair to use that against her in the context of a discrimination claim. So no, I don't think there's any scope there at all.

Daniel Barnett
Can a disabled employee argue that continuing with performance management against them is a failure to make reasonable adjustments?

Karen Jackson
I think they absolutely can, and I see this a lot in practice. Remember that the whole thrust of reasonable adjustments is to level the playing field for employees who have disabilities, and to remove barriers. If you take a classic example - somebody who suffers from depression, let's say. Performance starts to tail off a bit at work. The manager notices and says, is anything wrong because you're not quite your usual self and your output's not fantastic - is anything going on? And the employee says, no, I'm fine. Fast forward a few weeks, and the person needs to take time off. They take some time off to get better and come back to work. Is it going to help that person come back to work and get back up to speed and get back up to performance if they're immediately put on a performance improvement plan and have the manager breathing down their neck? Absolutely not. I see this happen all the time. I quite often will say to an employer, as a reasonable adjustment, to get this person back on track, to get this person back into the workplace and avoid another absence, can you just please hold this process in abeyance until they've had an opportunity to improve? Because I think that sometimes - not always - where there's a connection between the performance issue and the illness, it's not really reasonable to insist on performance management at that stage. And I would argue that that is absolutely what reasonable adjustments are all about. I don't recall seeing a case on that to prove the point, but I would run that argument.

Anonymous
Following a dismissal for long-term sickness, how much evidence will a tribunal expect

to see when considering an employer's objective justification defence for a s15 claim - discrimination arising from a disability? For example, if a retailer said they needed to dismiss to ensure deployment of staff met customer needs in the run-up to a peak period of trading, would a manager's oral evidence suffice? Or would a tribunal expect to see financial figures, staff costs, et cetera?

Karen Jackson
I think the answer is always the same when you're talking about tribunals. And it is that tribunals like evidence - fact. You're going to want a maximum amount of written evidence. You need to be able to justify the decision. There will have been meetings between management, there will have been discussions with the employee. It's absolutely vital that you document the reasons because otherwise, a tribunal is going to look at it and say, there's absolutely no evidence here that this has been considered carefully and that all the right decisions have been made. I'm always saying to my clients: you might not think it's important, but make attendance notes and record a conversation that you've had with somebody in an email afterwards - just follow up on the chat that we had today, etc. You want the maximum amount of paper if you're going to go in front of a tribunal and try to justify your position.

Gillian Howard
Would you explain the recent judgment of the Court of Justice of the European Union in the VL case *(VL v Szpital Kliniczny im. dra J. Babińskiego, Samodzielny Publiczny Zakład Opieki Zdrowotnej w Krakowie (Case C-16/19) EU:C:2020:479))*, which held that it can be direct disability discrimination for one group of disabled workers to compare themselves to another group of disabled workers, and do you think the employment tribunals in the UK will follow this judgment?

Karen Jackson
I'd like to think the employment tribunals will follow this judgment. I wish we'd had this

judgment when I was running the Williams case [Williams v The Trustees of Swansea University Pension & Assurance Scheme & Anor [2018] UKSC 65] in the Supreme Court because we were comparing Mr Williams to somebody else who had a disability but a different disability to his, and it would have proved quite useful. On the face of it, I think it's a good decision, a reasonable decision and I'd like to see the tribunals follow it.

Anonymous

When an employer fails in its duty to make reasonable adjustments, does the three-month trigger for an employment tribunal claim reset every day on the basis that it's a continuation and the duty to make reasonable adjustments never ends?

Karen Jackson

Yes and no. The time limit becomes slightly more complex with tribunal claims because with something like reasonable adjustments, each day the adjustment isn't made - that's an ongoing failure. So you can argue that there is an ongoing course of conduct. It's unlikely that you're going to issue a claim the first time there is a refusal to make that adjustment because you'd have to keep issuing or amending claims every time something subsequent happened.

Karen Jackson

So what you ordinarily see - as was the case in a case I dealt with last year - is a string of reasonable adjustment failures going back two years or so. And I don't think it really matters when it comes to the time limits because as long as your most recent act is within the three-month minus a day, time limit, you're always going to be able to bring the reasonable adjustments claim. And it's up to the tribunal to decide whether it considers those other reasonable adjustments failures are within time or out of time. But it doesn't really matter in the circumstance where you've got one claim that it that is within the time limits. This is quite usual with reasonable adjustments.

Karen Jackson

In a similar situation, I had a case recently where there were lots of reasonable adjustments failures. The reasonable adjustments were put in place and the claim was withdrawn from the employment tribunal. But now we have new reasonable adjustments failures. So it's an ongoing thing. Just because some previous ones have been settled doesn't mean that we haven't got a whole lot more. You don't have to be quite as nervous about time limits with something where there is going to be a series of acts or failures or omissions.

Anonymous

What's the shortest period of sickness absence that's justified a fair capability dismissal?

Daniel Barnett

That's presumably for a person with a disability.

Karen Jackson

Up until 2013, I think I'd read all of the judgments that had come out under disability discrimination law. Up until 2013. Since then, I haven't. I don't remember seeing any capability dismissal where the period wasn't around 18 months to two years. And certainly, if I'm advising somebody on a capability dismissal, I will say you're way too soon to be able to look at it. But it's one of those things that depends on circumstances. If one person is off sick long term in an organisation that has three people, that's going to have a massive impact on the organisation and you may very well be justified in having a much shorter time period. If it's a multinational conglomerate where there are 3000 staff, they probably are going to be able to tolerate an absence for quite a bit longer. And in a situation like that, I would expect it to be something like two years, potentially. That's always bearing in mind, of course, that if there's anything else that comes into play, like permanent health insurance, that impacts the ability of the employer to terminate anyway.

Karen Jackson

It's really difficult. you just have to look at the circumstances. Certainly, you need to look at reasonable adjustments and you need to consider alternatives to dismissal. But unfortunately, there will often be a situation where the absence just can't be tolerated any longer. You've done everything you can and then you just have to bite the bullet. But obviously, you'll need to be able to justify the decisions that you've made, and have documented them so that you have some safety if you're presented with a tribunal claim.

Natalie White

To what extent can an employer justify requiring good communication skills and good teamwork for a position where a requirement for good communication skills and good teamwork may be discriminatory for some, such as those with autism?

Karen Jackson

This is a perennial problem but when an employer advertises a job or seeks to fill a role, They are asking that a person meets certain requirements. So it might be that you need a degree; it might be you need to know how to do engineering; it might be you need to be an architect. Where there is a role that requires a certain level of communication and forward-facing interaction, I would have thought it was unusual for somebody who maybe has communication difficulties to want to be in that role anyway. But what you have to remember is that an employer does have a right to say, that a person needs to fulfil the essential requirements of the job to be able to do it. It's a banal analogy, but it's a bit like hiring a window cleaner who has vertigo; you're just not going to do it because the two things are incompatible. And so if the role essentially requires a function that cannot be fulfilled because of a disability, I think that the employer will have some justification for that. It's unfortunate that it might impact a certain category of employee, but I don't think it's necessarily discriminatory.

Anonymous

An individual's been dismissed for gross misconduct as part of the appeal, they allege a pre-existing medical condition, which wasn't known of before. What can we do? He doesn't have two years to qualify for unfair dismissal rights.

Karen Jackson

Well, this is where the knowledge defence comes in, which applies across lots of different parts of the disability discrimination provisions. But if at the time of making the decision the employer didn't know that there was any condition, then there cannot be any criticism that the decision been made on the basis of disability. Now if in the context of an appeal, the person says they wouldn't have done any of that, anyway, if they had not had their disability, which impacted their ability to do that work. And then I think an employer has to look and ask whether it would have made any difference. And I certainly think that an employer needs to consider whether it would have made any difference. But whether that will get the person out of trouble. I'm not entirely sure. And it's something we see quite often in the context of performance management and disciplinary issues where somebody will suddenly raise a flag about a health issue. I think a key point in relation to the appeal that we're discussing here is that the first thing is to get medical evidence. You can't take it at face value. You need to delve a little bit more and find out if there is something that could impact the situation in the way that's being suggested. But I think you'd be on shaky ground if you just dismissed it out of hand and didn't consider it in the appeal.

Daniel Barnett

I'm being asked in the chat if the following details would alter your answer to the question about the individual dismissed for gross misconduct who then, at the appeal stage, raises medical conditions. The reason for dismissal was that he posted about Adolf Hitler on social media - that doesn't really mean much without knowing whether he said something positive or negative about Adolf Hitler - and claimed car allowance fraudulently. Does that affect your answer?

Karen Jackson

Well, claiming car allowance fraudulently possibly does affect my answer. Having a disability is not a shield to a conduct issue. I dealt with a case years ago where a salesman who was unfortunately terminally ill was taking bribes from customers. He tried to use the fact that he was terminally ill as an excuse for taking bribes. At a certain point, you just have to say, well, that has no connection whatsoever to your disability. That's misconduct and has to be treated as such. Disability is not a shield to bad behaviour. Yes, there are lots of very important protections for people with disabilities but they're not going to get you off the hook if you are categorically misbehaving and doing things that are unacceptable in the workplace for anybody else that didn't have a disability. It's not going to help you.

Rachel Hancock

Can you provide guidance on how to decline reasonable adjustments?

Karen Jackson

I think the first thing I want to say about that - and it's not answering the question but I will answer the question - I'm a big fan of trialling reasonable adjustments because if you can say to a tribunal that a person asked for an adjustment, you trialled it for four weeks and it didn't make any difference, you can then say to the tribunal that it didn't alleviate the substantial disadvantage that the person was suffering. You tried it, it wasn't operationally sustainable for you to do it and therefore it's not a reasonable adjustments failure.

I'm often a little frustrated that people don't trial things, to placate the employee but more than anything to give yourself evidence for the tribunal that you've tried it and it didn't work. The thing about reasonable adjustments that I

see quite commonly is that an employee says they want something and that it's a reasonable adjustment. Well, you don't have to take it at face value. You can go back to the employee and ask how the thing they've asked for is going to help them, what the disadvantage is that's being caused, and how that particular thing will help them.

Karen Jackson

I dealt with a case years and years ago where somebody wanted their office painted a different colour. How could that possibly alleviate any kind of issue that you're suffering? it might do for somebody on an autistic spectrum; I don't know. Just ask the questions and probe. I'm always frustrated that people don't look at the Equality and Human Rights Commission code (https://www.equalityhumanrights.com/sites/default/files/employercode.pdf). Get a copy of it if you haven't got one because it's got loads and loads of examples in it about the kinds of adjustments that might be reasonable and how to go about it. It's everybody's desktop friend.

Karen Jackson

I dealt with a case where somebody, during the course of their employment, had become paraplegic. They were in a sales role and insisted on travelling by first class plane. I was acting for the employer and we basically said you are provided with somebody to travel with you. You have assistance getting to the airport. What actual difference did it make to they whether they travel business class or first class? It didn't. It didn't remove any further disadvantage that they had, and therefore that wasn't reasonable.

I think there's a tendency among some employers when a reasonable adjustment is requested to say that as someone has asked for a reasonable adjustment, they've got to make it or else they're going to be in trouble and face a tribunal claim. Well no, actually, you're allowed to ask what it's for and how it will help. You can ask a few more questions. Just be a little bit bolder. Obviously, you should do so in a sensitive manner because dealing with people insensitively is always going to get you into trouble regardless of whether they've got a valid claim or not. But it is okay to ask those questions.

Daniel Barnett
I remember back in the day when the Disability Discrimination Act first came in that there was actually a defence to reasonable adjustments, which was you could run a justification defence to a failure to make reasonable adjustments. It never made any sense to me because if you had a good reason for not doing something, it wouldn't be reasonable in the first place. But they abolished that defence in the 2010 Equality Act, probably because someone realised it didn't make any sense.

Karen Jackson
Exactly. Basically, if an adjustment is reasonable, then you have to make it and that's the beginning and end of it. But it's that big word: 'reasonable'. What is reasonable in law? On the face of it, you can often spot things that are reasonable and things that are wildly unreasonable. But again, you know, just listen, probe and ask the right questions. There might very well be a good reason why somebody wants something that you think is quite peculiar.

It is the mainstay of the disability provisions, and before s15, pretty much all of the case law was about reasonable adjustments. We don't see quite as much of it now, which is a shame. But I also think that's because employers are much better at dealing with common or garden adjustments. It's all about full and effective participation for people with disabilities. What can you do? There was a case a few years ago, where Lloyds Bank had to remove internal screens which were see-through glass because they were really impacting people with visual issues. So in terms of physical reasonable adjustments, I don't deal with that many cases where employers are unable to make those

adjustments. It tends to be more around the mental health side of things where employers don't always think that what's being asked for is reasonable.

I just want to say one more thing about the code. You can download the whole thing online, completely free. So put it in your favourites. If the only chapter you ever read is the one on reasonable adjustments, you'll be really happy that you've got it.

Paul
An employee has a customer-facing role. They say they're exempt from wearing a face covering and they've downloaded a badge to say they're exempt from wearing a face covering on grounds of disability. The employer has no reason to believe that the employee has a genuine medical condition to support an exemption. The employer thinks the employee is faking. If the dialogue results in a stand-off, can the employer discipline for a refusal to obey a reasonable management instruction and defend any discrimination claim that may arise on the basis that protecting the safety of colleagues and customers is a proportionate means of achieving a legitimate aim?

Karen Jackson
Well, that is a big question. I think that this is something we're going to see coming up again, and again and again. The first thing that I thought on hearing that question is that you're going to have to investigate the medical position first and foremost. You're not going to take somebody's word for it that there is an exemption; you're going to have to have a look at it. But I think that where they're in a front-facing role dealing with the public, the employer is going to have to balance the impact on the person who's saying they can't wear a mask, because they've got an exemption because they have a disability and the employers other duties - protecting other workers and protecting customers. There's going to be this ongoing issue around health

and safety generally. There was a recent case, it's only a first instance decision, about a lorry driver who was dismissed for not wearing a face mask, and that was found to be a fair dismissal, and I agree with that decision. That invokes the question of, failure to abide by a reasonable order.

I think the first thing I would be doing in relation to that employee would be saying, well, maybe as a reasonable adjustment, so that we can keep this person in work, we're going to move him or her into another role right now. If they can't wear a mask, and the employer requires a mask, I don't think a tribunal would be critical of an employer who made that decision. And I don't think the employee would be able to say that it was discriminatory to remove them from a front-facing role because of the failure to wear a mask because the employer has got to protect other people too. I actually think that following that decision in East London, recently, that tribunals potentially will be quite bold around these issues concerning face masks. We know that that may have an adverse effect on particular groups of disabled people, but it may just be one of those situations where public safety is involved and there just isn't an alternative way of dealing with matters other than to have that person wear a mask. I think that ultimately, if that gets in the way of them being able to do a job, then it very well may be open to the employer to legitimately dismiss - having been through all the hoops, of course.

Joanne Morton
What should an employer think about when an employee is absent from work due to workplace stress and anxiety?

Karen Jackson
I have quite a lot to say about this, but I'll keep it brief. The first thing to do is when somebody goes off with stress and anxiety, do not ignore them. Get somebody to contact that person. Now, it might not be a manager, it might not be an HR person. Get a colleague

to touch base with that person and say, "Hi, Jane. I'm sorry to hear that you're not well. Is everything, okay?" What you don't want is that person to retreat and go into a bunker and refuse to communicate with anybody because that's the beginning of a breakdown in a relationship. And what you want, ideally, to do is to establish a contact and to say, "We don't know what's going on. We're not prying, but what can we do to help you? Have you seen a doctor?" And where appropriate, say, "Can we refer you to Occupational Health?"

Karen Jackson
I think that there's a very marked difference between how people are treated when they go off work with stress than how they are treated if they go off work with cancer, or for a hip operation. That's what gets people upset, and that's what makes them ring people like me, because they feel pushed out and alienated. There's also a tremendous amount of self-stigma that goes with anxiety and with stress. Somebody's gone off work, they're worried about their job, they're worried about what everybody's saying about them and they're thinking that they're less of a person because they've got stress. What you don't want to do is perpetuate that issue. Now, sometimes employers - for the want of trying - can't raise somebody who's gone off sick with stress, and I acknowledge that that, too, can be quite a problem.

I think the other thing I would say is ask the questions, be proactive, don't let them go to ground and if there is anything outstanding in relation to a work issue, any kind of grievance - it doesn't have to be, "I am raising a grievance because of..." - if somebody's flagged an issue, listen to them, make sure that they know they are being heard, and that that will be addressed. I can't tell you how many people go off sick and get very, very upset because there is an issue in the workplace that they've flagged and nobody's doing anything about it. So deal with things promptly and keep communications going.

Daniel Barnett
By an astonishing coincidence, there happens to be an excellent book on stress (https://amzn.to/3sLqiYE). I don't know who wrote it, but it's always worth looking it up.

Su Apps
What would an employee need to do to show that an employer had constructive knowledge of a mental health-based disability?

Karen Jackson
I like that question because it's a bit of a bugbear of mine. When I have tried to run a constructive or imputed knowledge claim in the tribunals, I have never had any success. Even though my favourite blue book, the code, flags the point that employers can be imputed to know. I think that it's all about signs in the workplace. It's a bit of an aside, but if you look at some of the really big stress at work cases, you can see the kinds of behaviours that are exhibited, which would make you believe that there was something wrong with somebody. So you have somebody who's a good worker and who comes in happy and cheerful, who is suddenly really grumpy, emotionally labile and bursts into tears at the drop of a hat. There's got to be more than just your average having a bad day, for an employer to be held to have constructive knowledge. And that's just based on my experience in the tribunals. An employer can't be expected to see everything and to be on the pulse of what everybody's feeling. There would need to be some fairly clear signs, and I think it is things like a bad temper and turning up late. Crying as a big one. Now, you might have some employees who cry all the time, and you might not notice particularly. But you'll have others who just are just not like that at all. I think the short answer is you've got to go quite a long way to land an employer with imputed knowledge for it to succeed.

Neil Coombes
If there are several examples of unlawful harassment such as name-calling or sending

someone to Coventry, is it worth pleading direct discrimination in the alternative? Or should you just leave everything as a harassment claim?

Daniel Barnett
I suppose the question is: does direct discrimination add anything to harassment?

Karen Jackson
There are two schools of thought here. One is plead everything as several different kinds of discrimination and one of them might land. That's not going to make you popular with the employment tribunal judge, I don't think. You really should look at what your best claim is. I would be minded to think that if if you're talking about harassment, I think you're going to really struggle with direct discrimination. I would just stick with harassment. With direct you've got so many more hurdles to go through - the whole comparator exercise, for example. It's so much harder to prove direct discrimination than harassment, so I would stick with harassment.

Andy Crisp
To what extent can employers ask about the health of a job applicant?

Karen Jackson
This is another major bugbear. Basically, the rule is that you can't ask anything until you've made a job offer, other than in the context of making adjustments for an application process. So it's okay to say do you need us to make any adjustments for the application? And that might be even more important if you've got a written test or some kind of assessment. But basically, no, you shouldn't ask anything until you've made the offer. Of course, you then get into difficulty if you've made an offer and you rescind an offer on learning that somebody has a disability. Although, that is not the most easy claim to action anyway. Just don't do it.

Mark Irlam
What are the best tips you can give for pleading a disability discrimination claim?

Daniel Barnett
I'm assuming Mark's asking from the perspective of the employee.

Karen Jackson
I'll tell you how I do it - I'm giving away my secrets now. I start with a piece of A4. and I hash it into eight little grids. I start with s13, s15, s19, s21. I look at every single thing that's happened and I ask, is that direct discrimination? Yes? No? Is it indirect? is it harassment?

You really do want to pick out very carefully which head of claim you're going to plead under because otherwise, you'll end up with a 'kitchen sink' approach and that'll just go down really badly with the employment tribunal. One of the major things to think about - with disability discrimination in particular - is that because you have the knowledge defence and you have the justification defence across some of the strands, you need to think about that as well. For example, if you've got an issue with knowledge, you probably do want to look at indirect discrimination as a head of claim. I normally wouldn't look at that because s15 is so much easier. But if you haven't got knowledge then you're not going to do very well on s15 because the employer will just say, well, we couldn't have discriminated, because we didn't know. So you've got to be thinking, from the beginning about knowledge and also about justification and just be really vigorous in looking at it. There are some where there naturally will be some overlap - particularly with s15 and harassment - because s15, unfavourable treatment, is so broad and harassment is quite specific. I think it's okay to plead some in the alternative, but for the most part, you want to try and pin your colours.

JP Choi
What are your tips on dealing with associative discrimination, such as an employee who's unable to do a shift because of a partner's disability and their caring obligations to their partner?

Anna Denton-Jones
Can you give any examples of successful associative discrimination other than the Coleman case (EBR Attridge Law LLP & Anor v Coleman UKEAT/0071/09?

Karen Jackson
I can't give you any concrete examples of associative discrimination cases. I have dealt with a few that haven't that have settled rather than going to tribunal. A classic example might be, an executive who wasn't promoted to the next level because he had caring responsibilities for a disabled wife. But in terms of associative discrimination, I think the key thing to remember is that there's no requirement for an employer to make reasonable adjustments in relation to somebody who has caring responsibilities for a disabled person. So there's no formal requirement to make reasonable adjustments. A nice employer might be able to swing things just to help somebody out if they're a good employee, but there's no legal obligation. We haven't seen as many associative discrimination claims as I would have liked. I'm always on the lookout for them. So if anyone's got a good one, think of me.

Charlotte
Is the menopause capable of amounting to a disability?

Karen Jackson
I think it is. I've only seen one case and it was in Scotland. It was about a woman who worked on a factory floor and she kept having to go to the bathroom a lot because she had very, very heavy bleeding. This was getting in the way of her productivity. I haven't seen any other cases. It's going to come back down to the s6 definition. Is it substantial? Is it long term? Does it have an adverse effect on all day-to-day activities? We know that it's not enough just to have an impairment. Any woman who has been or is in the menopause will tell you that it absolutely can be an impairment because it can cause brain fog and

moods and it can cause depression. So, yes, it is capable of being a disability, but it's not going to apply in every single case. It's going to come down to that functional test of how far does it impact your day-to-day activities? You're going to have to go through those hoops.

Anonymous
What adjustments would be reasonable for somebody with a hearing impairment?

Karen Jackson
I don't feel qualified to answer that question, because I think you should ask somebody who has a hearing impairment. But I do know from dealing with clients that have hearing impairments and a classic one is open-plan offices - not that anybody is in them at the moment. Open-plan offices are a nightmare for people with hearing impairments because even if they've got an implant, background noise will really affect the effectiveness of that. So it would be perfectly reasonable to ask to be in a separate private office, if possible because that would just stop the issue altogether. I can't think of another. We need to ask somebody with a hearing impairment that question.

Can a respondent's unreasonable refusal to concede a disability during proceedings be a factor that increases an injury to feelings award?

Karen Jackson
I'm not sure as a matter of law that it would necessarily mean that a higher injury to feelings award is appropriate. I would have thought it would be more appropriately dealt with under aggravated damages. I've dealt with cases where in a preliminary hearing where I'm for the claimant and the judge

has turned to the oppo and said you're not seriously going to dispute disability with this extent of medical evidence. Most sensible respondents will withdraw at that point. It's just not an attractive argument to run when the evidence is really in favour. So I don't think it should have an impact on injured feelings, no. But I would be prepared to look at it in terms of aggravated damages.

Daniel Barnett
The case on that is Zaiwalla & Co v Walia (*Zaiwalla & Co v Walia [2002] IRLR 697*). It's a fairly old case of the EAT where a firm of solicitors behaved appallingly in the way it defended a discrimination claim. The EAT held that it was proper - and indeed desirable - to award aggravated damages because of the way they acted in defending the claim.

We've had a few suggestions for what adjustments can be made for those with hearing impairments. I'm just going to read out a few of them. Clear masks for lip reading, suggests KLS. Penny Douglass suggests speakers for computers that are separate from the in-built speakers. Judith Alexander points out that the RNID has good advice sheets on this. Lucy Maxwell Scott says a client of hers arranged for the person with a hearing impairment to have a signing companion at work. Sue Dover says don't talk behind their back - they can't hear and feel excluded from banter. That word, Sue, we don't like that word in an employment and discrimination context. Melanie Bonas says make sure you use their name when you're speaking with them so they know you're talking to them. KLS says use quiet music if working in a shop.

Karen Jackson from didlaw, thank you so much for your time.

EMPLOYEE DATA, MONITORING AND PRIVACY

JEREMY SCOTT-JOYNT, OUTER TEMPLE CHAMBERS

Daniel Barnett

I'm joined today by Jeremy Scott-Joynt from Outer Temple Chambers who is going to be speaking on employee data, monitoring and privacy. Jeremy is one of the co-authors of the Employment Law Handbook (http://www.employmentlawhandbook.co.uk) published in 2020.

Jeremy Scott-Joynt, good morning. A couple of questions from me, if I may. First of all, since lockdown last March, we've seen a massive, massive increase in the numbers of online meetings such as Zoom, Microsoft Teams, et cetera. If an employer's got recordings of those meetings, are the classified as personal data under the GDPR and so the recordings have to be disclosed as part of a subject access request?

Jeremy Scott-Joynt

Well, the definition of personal data is immensely broad. Really anything that is to do with - it's not quite the words of the legislation, but it helps you understand it - to do with an identifiable individual or points towards an identifiable individual is going to be their personal data. There are two important things to consider when you're talking about these recordings. And by the way, if you're recording people's meetings, even within an organisation, for goodness sake make sure that's clear. Don't try and do it covertly or simply forget. People need to know that they're being recorded. Otherwise, you're going to get into some very sticky ground indeed.

Generally speaking, the caveat to the simple answer, yes - if someone's mentioned in something or they feature in it, then yes, it's personal data - is going to be this: firstly, when you get a subject access request, what's being asked for is information, not necessarily documents, so you don't necessarily have to weigh someone down with a whole bunch of recordings. The second point, of course - and I guess this is going to come up several times today because it's quite an important one - is when someone asks for their own personal data, that doesn't entitle them to everybody else's personal data as well. By the way for the statute nerds among us, this is in schedule two paragraph 16 of the Data Protection Act 2018. There's a balancing act that has to be undertaken when you're trying to work out whether somebody else's privacy rights need to be respected over the data protection rights of the person making the request. It's a tricky balancing act, but it is one you always have to bear in mind. Then again - final point on this because I don't want to go on for too long - ultimately, if what someone's asking for is relatively innocuous, there's nothing confidential or otherwise generally problematic in it, then you might have to consider whether it's actually much of an issue at all.

Daniel Barnett

If an employee is bringing some sort of claim, such as unfair dismissal or discrimination, and they say that there's data held on a colleague's phone about them - say, for example, a colleague has been making discriminatory comments in text messages or WhatsApp messages to other people in the organisation - is the personal data held on a colleague's mobile phone something that has to be disclosed as part of a subject access request?

Jeremy Scott-Joynt
This is actually quite a tricky one for a similar kind of reason. I notice you said the colleague's 'own' mobile phone, because the situation is likely to be different if it's a work mobile, for instance, one that your company owns, and they've given you, and particularly if you've been sensible enough to draw up a bunch of rules about the use of that device for personal purposes. So if it's a company mobile device and you've got proper policies in place, then disclosing the stuff on there, as long as it's about the person - and taking into account what we've said already about the balancing act of disclosing other people's data - what the GDPR beautifully calls the rights and freedoms of others - is probably going to be something you have to do.

Where it's a colleague's own mobile phone, what you're talking about is their personal communications, say between them and friends, or them and colleagues. The company is not going to be the controller of that data, the individual is going to be the controller of that data. So in my view, it's going to be a real struggle for a data subject to make any kind of real case why they should get their data, unless - there's always an unless - it's, for instance, in work-related communication, say, a Bring Your Own Device Policy that so many companies have these days, where they don't give you a mobile phone. Instead, they say, use your own and we'll agree a policy to cover that. That's where it's going get a little more sticky because then there may well be a live question as to who actually controls the data. There were a couple of interesting cases on this recently - I'm not going to spend a lot of time on this; otherwise, we won't have time for other questions - but if you want to look up a case called Pipia (Pipia v BGEO Group Ltd [2020]

1 WLR 2582), that deals with the whole question - particularly for senior employees - of what the circumstances are under which the company actually controls the data or not when it's the individuals own device.

Daniel Barnett
Last question from me. Let's imagine there's an ongoing disciplinary investigation going on and the employee thinks to himself, I want to see what the employers got on me. Can they put in a subject access request to find out what's going on in an ongoing investigation?

Jeremy Scott-Joynt
Oh, you had to ask me that one, didn't you? I've fallen foul of this in the past. Back when I ran investigations for Standard Chartered Bank, one of the first investigations I did for them was a large matter where, essentially, a relatively senior employee was being accused of colluding with a client, pretty much to defraud the bank. Myself and someone else inside the organisation were communicating over email quite a lot, and the other person said some pretty rude things about the subject of the investigation. Those communications were not privileged. Neither of us were lawyers at that point. And sure enough, later in the investigation, a subject access request came in and yes, those communications were disclosed.

The simple fact is that there's nothing in the law that prevents non-privileged documents or those that, for instance, might fall into the exemption that covers the prevention and detection of crime or the prosecution and conviction of offenders, which is somewhere in schedule one of the DPA. There's nothing inherently in the law that stops investigative information being shared. Now, again - and we come back to paragraph 16 of schedule two - if, for instance, part of that information involves a whistleblower, another person to whom you owe a duty of confidence, then the chances are you can make a case that you're not going to have to share that stuff,

(a) because that person is not going to give consent in a million years, although you should probably ask them, and (b) because it's a balancing act and there's a really wide margin of appreciation. But generally speaking, yes, I learned the hard way that if you're engaged in an investigation of an individual, unless things are genuinely privileged, keep it professional.

Daniel Barnett
I know that some HR people think that as long as they use a code name for an employee - so they refer to the employee as 'Big Bear' rather than Jeremy Scott-Joynt - then it's not going to be disclosable under a subject access request. Is there any truth in that?

Jeremy Scott-Joynt
The simple answer is no. The point is that personal data is a legal construct. And frankly, the fact that you're calling someone Big Bear is in itself personal data about that individual. So if you're going to use a code name, again, make it a sensible one, otherwise, you'll pay the price later. I'll leave it to the audience's imaginations to work out what kind of embarrassing code names might be came up with, although Big Bear itself is, is terrifying me slightly. If it's about that person, if it could be linked to them through jigsaw identification - and obviously, it can - the fact that you're calling them 'Little Turnip' or something really doesn't make any difference. It's personal data. This kind of slightly squirrely attempt is not going to get you anywhere. As I said, it's probably a better idea just to be professional about it in the first place.

Anonymous
Can an employee make a subject access request to ask for emails between their boss and HR in relation to their investigation and dismissal?

Jeremy Scott-Joynt
We've sort of covered half of that already in some ways, haven't we? On the face of it, I don't think there's anything to stop it. I

mean, again, we come back to the point that technically speaking, personal data is not in a document, it's the information that's held in a document. So in theory, a company could go through a whole exercise of rewriting emails and extracting information from them. Of course, if you did that, in order to cover stuff up, then that will be problematic for and you might end up getting taken to the Information Commissioner.

The simple fact is that unless there's privilege involved, or unless one of the other exemptions applies - for instance, to do with references, because information shared as part of a job reference is covered, at least to the extent that's proportionate by another exemption in the Data Protection Act - ultimately, if it's not privileged, it's about you. It's your personal data. It can be shared, subject to the whole third-party business. But in a circumstance like this, again, the general rule is don't write about in an email, something that is non-factual, rude or dismissive - something that you wouldn't ultimately like to be shared. People would say, that that limits what they can do and that's going to tie their hands. And I'd always ask the question: Why? What the hell were you thinking of writing in this email that's going to get you into trouble? If someone's performance is substandard, then their performance is substandard. If you use that as an excuse to call them a whinging layabout, then frankly, you've only got yourself to blame.

Daniel Barnett
You mentioned that if the information isn't privileged, of course, it often comes as a shock to HR professionals to realise that communications between them and the managers - including if they're outsourced HR professionals - are not privileged. And there's clear case law on that, New Victoria Hospital v Ryan (*New Victoria Hospital and Ryan [1993] ICR 201*) for example. I've recently been doing a disclosure application against an employer, which was represented by a large well-known employment consultancy based

out of the Northwest, and they're still taking the argument that their communications are privileged. It's just absolute nonsense. They use it every time.

Jeremy Scott-Joynt
Are they lawyers?

Daniel Barnett
No.

Jeremy Scott-Joynt
Okay. Isn't that the end of the conversation?

Daniel Barnett
It totally is, but it doesn't stop them arguing it.

Jeremy Scott-Joynt
Good luck to them.

Victoria Duff
Can an employer monitor your work productivity while working at home through some kind of monitoring software, and if so, does the employee have to consent first?

Jeremy Scott-Joynt
This one's topical, isn't it? I guess partly, it depends on what's being monitored. A general rule, of course, and this isn't so much a rule of law as it is a rule of sense, one should never ever do anything to an employee that involves looking over their shoulder without telling them first, unless we're dealing with covert surveillance as part of an investigation where it's absolutely necessary. So for goodness sake, make sure you're clear and transparent about these things. And also, just as a practical point, nobody likes to feel someone staring over their shoulder unless it's absolutely necessary. So if you don't need to, don't do it. Ultimately, there's a part of me that always comes back to the principle that if your employees are only going to do their jobs if you're standing behind them with a big stick, then you've probably got the wrong employees or the wrong management. But that's not a legal point.

As for consent, well, again, you're going to have to think about what you're collecting. Is it personal data? Is it identifiable to an individual? It probably is. But then there are other bases on which you could do it. You could seek their consent, but let's remember that in the employment context, consent is almost always vitiated. There's good case law that says that employees cannot give free and informed consent, or only under very, very rare cases. It would be far better to do it on a basis of legitimate interest, although legitimate interest is usually a pretty weak source. And that means, obviously, that you're going to have to think about what you need to monitor and how. Do the minimum. Don't look on it as an excuse to stare over someone's shoulder every hour of every day.

Daniel Barnett
Sam Proffitt has sent a message in the chat commenting that litigation privilege might be invoked in a situation where an employer is having a chat with HR. That's absolutely right. But there's case law that says that until you're actually at the point of litigation, then litigation isn't the dominant purpose of the correspondence. Dismissal is the dominant purpose of the correspondence.

Anonymous
Where an employer is shown seriously inappropriate messages, such as racist messages, between employees on the employees' private phones, can these messages be used for disciplinary purposes?

Daniel Barnett
I don't see why not.

Jeremy Scott-Joynt
No, me neither. I'm going to interpret this as where the employee is the person who is the victim of the problem comes to their employer and says, "Look, this is what someone's just sent me. This is horrific. This is that guy on the desk, three desks down." Ultimately, what you have there is evidence of discriminatory

behaviour. The fact that it's on the employee's private mobile phone and may have been sent from the other employee's private mobile phone, I don't see as here or there, really. It's there; it's in front of you. I don't see any reason why you can't act on it - properly, of course.

Su Apps

To what extent do you need to redact employee data in tribunal proceedings where the personal data relates to employers who aren't party to the claim?

Jeremy Scott-Joynt

The point is, it's the bit that deals with third-party rights. The important thing to remember is that, aside from anything else, we're talking here about tribunal proceedings rather than subject access requests. If the tribunal needs to see the information, then ultimately, the tribunal is going to want to see the information. So it's a different question here from a subject access request. The real question is going to be what the sensitivity of the information is.

Generally speaking, I would say that you wouldn't redact stuff that's going to go before a tribunal. If you need to redact - in other words, if you need to keep this information from the other side, as well as from the tribunal - then I would suggest, for safety's sake, that it's probably a good idea to apply to the tribunal to do so. If you're putting information in that's got huge black blobs all over it, bluntly, if I'm on the other side, I'm going to want to know what's under there. I'm probably going to ask the tribunal what is under that, and so you're going to have an argument about whether that redaction is actually proper or not. I would generally keep redaction to a minimum. Again, ask yourself why you are blocking it out. Are you just blocking it out because it might be somebody else's personal data? Or are you blocking it out because there's something genuinely confidential or sensitive in there? You're going to have the argument if you produce redacted stuff, so be ready for it.

Daniel Barnett

Penny Douglass has put in the chat that she had the same problem as I've had with the same HR consultancy. The fought privilege, she says, then eventually disclosed and redacted everything except the claimant's name. It's now gone to the Information Commissioner's Office.

Gillian Howard

Is the use of covert recordings - CCTV covert recordings by employers - compatible with employees' rights and protections under the GDPR?

Jeremy Scott-Joynt

Let's think about the word 'covert' here because CCTV isn't necessarily covert. In fact, most of the time, it's not. In the olden days, it was a huge flipping great camera. These days, it's usually a teeny tiny little dome stuck in the ceiling somewhere or up in a corner. But nonetheless, if you're using closed-circuit television to record your employees, then you should have told them about it already, most of the time, except in those vanishingly rare circumstances where you've put in a camera especially to deal with a particular investigation. So, as a general rule, if it's not covert, then in any case, you should be telling your employees it's happening, explaining the circumstances under which it's going to be used, and obeying the regulations. There are statutory steps you need to take and most of them revolve around being absolutely crystal clear in advance about what you're actually doing.

If it's covert recording, on the other hand, it can be compatible, but you're going to have to tread very carefully. You're going to have to think extremely carefully about why that rather than any other means of investigation is necessary, i.e. you needed to do the job, and proportionate, i.e. there's no other less intrusive way of doing it. If you can't justify that level of pretty significant intrusion, then I think you do run some significant risk. I'm not saying don't do it, but always, always, always, if you're going to be using any kind of covert recording or investigation, make sure you've clearly thought through and written down why that's the only option that's going to work for you.

Dom KS

If an employer wants to take control of an employee's email account for business continuity while the employee is off sick, does the employer have to tell the employee and does the employer have to automatically leave that account when the employee returns?

Jeremy Scott-Joynt

No, but - it's always either 'yes, but' or 'no, but,' isn't it? - if we're talking about a business email account, so, say Daniel works for Acme Incorporated, so danielbarnett@acmeinc.com, if that is an account that Daniel has been given for work purposes - and this is the 'but' - and you've made sure there are clear rules about what Daniel should be using that account for, and you don't live in Germany, I'll come to why that's important in a minute, then, on the whole, it's probably not going to be an issue. After all, it's a work account; it's used for work purposes. And if you've got a decent policy that explains what Daniel can do with that account for personal reasons, and the employer's rights to look at it, then contractually speaking and legally speaking, you're probably going to be fine. That's always the 'but'. It's the old joke, you know, when you ask, how do I get to point X? And they reply, well, if you want to get to point X, you shouldn't start from here. The answer is, the 'shouldn't start from here' is having the right policy in place to start with. The gag about Germany - and this again, goes back to my investigation days - is that Germany in particular has incredibly tight rules about the use of work email. Really, you have to ban people from using it for personal purposes at all; otherwise, your ability as an employer to look into it is going to be severely constrained. We're not there yet here. But in any case, get it straight, get the rules straight to start with, and

you shouldn't have too many problems. There's no real reason why you have to announce that you've stopped, although again, why would you not tell them? I can't think of a reason.

Daniel Barnett

I think the question was more, are you obliged to stop? But again, the answer is obvious: why would you stick in?

Jeremy Scott-Joynt

Exactly.

Rebecca

What's the biggest pitfall employers fall into when capturing data?

Jeremy Scott-Joynt

You know what? It all comes down to the same fundamental thing in my view: not putting yourselves in the shoes of your employees and forgetting, in the process of doing so, the biggest change that GDPR made. GDPR comes in for a lot of stick, and in some cases, rightly. It's rigid, it's civil law-based and for us common law nutters it can feel awfully restrictive. But what it did, critically, was make absolutely clear that personal data is mine and yours. My data is mine. Daniel's data is his. That was a step change and a radical change. And what employers always get wrong is that they forget that that's the starting point. You don't own this stuff - they own this stuff. If you start your planning for how to handle employees' personal data on the basis that their personal data is theirs, on the whole, you'll get it right. If you forget that, you'll get it wrong.

Mike Clyne

What issues can you foresee, with companies holding records about COVID vaccination status?

Jeremy Scott-Joynt

This goes to what's called special category data. Now, article nine of what's now UK GDPR, since there are now two different versions - our one and the EU's version - deals with special category data. That's everything to do with belief and ethnicity, but particularly health status and issues of health. You cannot process special category data including health data unless you satisfy a narrower range of restrictions, which you can find in article nine. One of them is for employment purposes, so that covers it. But then there's a further list of rules in the back of the Data Protection Act that narrow what you can do with this stuff. The simplest way of putting it is this: why do you need it? Make it really clear why you need it. If you can make a case for why you need it, make sure you hold it really securely and can prove that you hold it really securely. Think about whether you need to disclose it to anybody because you're going to have to step very, very carefully on that and document all of this. Critically, for any special category data, if you think you can make a case for why you need it, why you need to hold it, what you need to do with it and how you're going to protect it, make sure you've written all of that down in an explicit policy. Because for almost all special category data under the Data Protection Act, a condition of processing is that you specifically deal with how you're going to look after it and why you needed it. If you don't do that, you can't hold it at all.

Natalie White

What issues are there with recording online training so that other people can be sent the video if participants' names and sometimes faces are on show? Should we ask permission from every participant, or rely on legitimate interests, or both?

Daniel Barnett

I think I can say for these webinars, just in case anybody's wondering, every one of you signed up to terms of conditions that said, if you put your name in the chatbox or Q&A box, it will appear on a recording and a transcript.

Jeremy Scott-Joynt

This is why, of course, you cover it in advance. So much of this stuff is thinking about what the problems are going to be later and try and deal with them upfront. And I know that's a trite answer, because, you know, the problems that really hurt are the ones you didn't think of or couldn't have thought of. But nonetheless, for the obvious stuff like this, if you're going to record something, of course, it's going to be people's personal data. At the point where people sign up to that, ask their permission to share it or say to them, if you don't want to appear, don't ask questions.

Consent is great, although consent, again, within an employment context - if it's in a training session within a company - we're back to the point that employees can't consent. So yes, you may have to fall back on legitimate interests. I really don't like legitimate interests. I'm not going to waggle my mouth too much about this, but one thing that's really annoying me at the moment is that every time you go onto a website these days, they now ask you not only to tick the boxes to whether they can use cookies but ask you to confirm that their legitimate interests trump yours. That annoys me because it's just not how the law works. It's meaningless, and it's wasting my time. A lot of the time, legitimate interests are problematic because, on the whole, your legitimate interests may well not trump those of the individual. But if you've got someone who's taking part in a training session, especially voluntarily or they've signed up to it, say, if it's a third-party one, and they know in advance that it's going to be shared and you said you're going to be recording it, so they can drop off if they want to at that point – it's kind of hard to see what legitimate interest they have. In it not going any further. Because yes, their legitimate interest may usually seem a bit more important, but they still need one. One like "I didn't get a proper haircut and my hair's not that good" is unlikely to cut it. "I was half asleep" is unlikely to cut it. "I picked my nose at minute 23" is unlikely to cut it. If they've got a real legitimate interest, then sure. But most of the time, it's kind of hard to think of what it is.

Anonymous
When is a subject access request considered excessive, and how do you respond when you think that one is excessive?

Jeremy Scott-Joynt
'Excessive' is a piece of string word, of course, isn't it? There's the obvious excessive, there's someone whose subjects access request, whether expressly or implicitly, is asking for 23 years' worth of back data, which amounts to 90,000 pages.

Daniel Barnett
I'm just going to put that in context, if I can, for anyone who's not sure. The relevance of it being 'excessive', is that the data controller can either refuse to comply with the request, or supply less information, or charge a fee for some information.

Jeremy Scott-Joynt
Volume is one issue; whether it is abusive or vexatious is, of course, also an issue; as is whether it's particularly complicated, or requires, on the face of it, a hugely expensive process of retrieving data. So for instance, if someone's subject access request was for stuff that was on paper from 1992 to 2003, then getting that stuff back, sorting it out and dealing with it is going to be an immense task - far harder than simply grabbing a bunch of files off a hard drive that you stuck in a cupboard last year.

Broadly speaking, 'excessive' means what it says. You can always say it's excessive. You're going to have to defend that, potentially, to the Information Commissioner, so it becomes a balancing act. What does the person want? Is the information that they're asking for related to what they're asking for? Now, obviously, a subject access request doesn't have to have a purpose. If it's your personal data, you have a right to your personal data.

The first thing you do, by the way, in such a case, is you can say, well, actually, I need the three months rather than the one month,

because built into the legislation is an ability to extend. But when you do that, make sure you do that for a good reason, not just because you're trying to push the person around or make trouble or your systems are rubbish.

Daniel Barnett
A question I'm asked a lot is do employment tribunal judges care about claimants' moans about subject access requests? Because you get so much information copied to a tribunal judge. I think the short answer to that is: usually not. Tribunal judges don't care at all. What's your view on that?

Jeremy Scott-Joynt
Frankly, we've both seen the faces of tribunal judges when they're in bundle six of 12 and they're digging through copies and copies and copies of emails - most of which, by the way, are the same email trail printed over and over again, just with a new three-line email at the top of it - And once they've done that a few times, you can see the judge just kind of going, I want to die. Unless you can make a case for why that failure has materially harmed your ability to make the case that you're making, on the whole, yes, a judge is going to say "And?..."

Elizabeth
If a settlement agreement has been signed, does this preclude the former employee ever submitting an SAR?

Daniel Barnett
I'm assuming, Elizabeth, a term of the settlement agreement is 'you will not submit a subject access request'.

I'll go with this one. I think you split it into two situations. Situation number one is where the subject access request has already been made at the time of the settlement agreement. And in that case, it's perfectly legitimate to say that the employee withdraws the subject access request and the employer is not obliged to do any further work in respect of it. I think that's fine. I think what's not fine is a clause in a settlement agreement that says the employee will never make a subject access request ever again. Because that's contracting out of legislation, which you're not allowed to contract out of, and I think that's where an employee would have run into problems. If I tried to rely on that.

Jeremy Scott-Joynt
That's roughly where I came down to. If you want to put a term like that in, by all means do, but I can't imagine it ever being enforceable. It'd be like contracting out of health and safety legislation. it's just not going to happen.

Sian Wilkinson
What extra precautions do you need to put in place when working from home, when you've got loved ones wandering around your workstation?

Jeremy Scott-Joynt
We are in a different situation, and working from home has taken on new meanings. Really simple, basic things like ensuring that if your computer has fingerprint control, you activate it. Personally, I like long complicated, difficult passwords because I'm paranoid and suspicious. Having to type a 23-character random password 82 times a day, every time I log back onto the computer means I'm almost certainly going to change the password to 'password1' or something like that. So if you do have biometrics on your computer, activate them and make the logoff really, really quick. Then if you do wander off to get a cup of coffee, actually, your computer is protected. So that's the easiest version straight off, if you can do it technologically.

Jeremy Scott-Joynt
Things like those screens that can go on top of a laptop or, or a desktop screen - polarisation screens - mean that if you're not looking at it straight on, you can barely see anything. It sounds silly, but it really works because it means that unless your kid or your spouse or their mate is standing immediately behind you, they're not going to see anything anyway. If

you still work on paper a lot of the time, I'd say don't if you can possibly avoid it. You're going to need lockable cabinets and you're going to have to be Mr Boring or Ms Boring clean desk policy even in your own house.

Someone has put in the chat to use Windows key and 'L'. Yes, if you're using a PC, Windows Key and 'L' instantly locks the machine. If you can get into 'Windows L' as a habit, so every time you get up you hit 'Windows L', basically, this problem pretty much goes away.

Daniel Barnett
Someone pointed out to me a few years ago that when I'm in the tribunal with my laptop, everyone sitting behind me can see my screen and can see the questions I've got planned to ask the witnesses. If a witness from the other side is sitting behind me, they can pass all of the information to their witnesses. And it just struck me that it was so obvious. I immediately bought one of those polarisation screens and they are life-changing, it means that you can only see what's on the screen if you're directly in front of it. No one else can see it. It makes such a difference.

Jeremy Scott-Joynt
The other point is, of course, it depends on the size of text you use. Frankly, if someone's sitting 12 feet behind me and can see my 10-point text on my 13-inch screen, then I'd like their eyes, please, because they're clearly far, far better than mine.

Mike Clyne
Should employees have any expectation of privacy if using work email or work phones?

Jeremy Scott-Joynt
Different jurisdictions do different things in this. If you're in the States, the answer is probably going to be: stuff that pal, no chance. As I said earlier, if you're in Germany, it's quite rigorously in the opposite direction. Here. again, make sure you've got the rules really clear to start with.

Jeremy Scott-Joynt

Just because someone's using a work device doesn't completely disrupt, for instance, their article eight rights. Everyone has a right to a certain degree of privacy. There's case law on this. Bărbulescu (*Bărbulescu v Romania [2017] ECHR 742)* shows that just because you happen to be using a work system, that doesn't mean your privacy rights evaporate. That said, as an employer, therefore, the important thing is to make it absolutely clear upfront. A sensible employer, on the whole, is going to recognise that a blanket prohibition is bluntly unworkable - maybe less so in a home environment where you know, people have their own devices knocking around - but certainly in the office. A blanket prohibition is always going to be problematic because people will break it. Human beings are human beings and if you're in the middle of something and your kid's school rings, etc. It's how it is. So get the rules straight upfront. Yes, you can use your work computer, but if it's anything on your work computer, we may have to look at, as long as we have a good reason to do so. But again, it comes back to good reason. Just because it's a work computer doesn't mean that you can read someone's love letters to their spouse because you feel like it. That is still an intrusion and bluntly, do you want to be that person? Do you want to have that relationship with your employees? On the whole? I'd suggest No.

Karen Bristow

On what grounds can you blanket redact grievance investigation meeting notes relating to other employees' interviews?

Jeremy Scott-Joynt

Let's take this from the point of view of a subject access request. I don't like the phrase 'blanket redact' because anytime you're dealing with an employee's personal data, as long as it actually is that employee's personal data, and if it's about them, it's their personal data. then your ability to 'blanket redact' anything - as in effectively refuse or stick

black lines across everything - is always going to be problematic. It's always a balancing exercise. And even though, as we said earlier - assuming we're talking about other employees' personal data as well - there's quite a wide margin of appreciation. You still have to consider the issues. You have to think through: have I sought consent? Is there a duty of confidentiality in here? A lot of the time, if you're dealing with quite sensitive stuff, then, yes, you may well be able to make the case for redacting large chunks of it. But simply blanket redacting everything without actually going through the process of considering whether it's genuinely something that shouldn't be shared or not, to be honest, I'd advise against that approach. It's boring, it's annoying and it's time-consuming to do a more case-by-case analysis, but it's a heck of a lot safer.

Daniel Barnett

A fundamental and important issue relating to data protection law is whether the correct acronym is SAR, meaning subject access request, or DSAR, for data subject access request.

Jeremy Scott-Joynt

For me, it's DSAR. And the reason is two-fold. Firstly, that's what actually appears in the legislation these days, and secondly, SAR also means 'suspicious activity report'. In my old world of banking, if you say 'SAR' to somebody, 90% of people are going to assume you're talking about money launderers rather than data protection. So I prefer DSAR.

Daniel Barnett

I prefer DSR but I always say SAR because I always think that people won't know what I'm talking about if I say DSAR or think I've got it wrong.

Tracey Munro

As an HR advisor, I was told by a solicitor to use the phrase 'advice given in view of potential litigation' on email correspondence that might become discoverable. Does that offer any protection?

Jeremy Scott-Joynt
It depends. Was it genuinely advice given in view of potential litigation? If yes, possibly, if no, then no. Investigators I used to work with - ex-cops mostly - would always put 'legally privileged and confidential' in their email signatures. And I'd look at it and think no, it just isn't. What matters is the substance, not the wording.

Daniel Barnett
Well, on that point, I've got to ask you about a bugbear of mine, which is people who put in their Twitter bios 'these are my views'. Who else's could they be? Does that have any legally enforceable power whatsoever?

Jeremy Scott-Joynt
I don't really understand what that means, legally or otherwise. I mean, it's your mouth. It's your fingers. It's your views. I mean, why are they saying it?

Daniel Barnett
A lot of employees have a policy that says if you tweet, you've got to say in the tweets or in your bio: 'These are my views. They're not the views of my organisation.'

Jeremy Scott-Joynt
That depends on whether you're doing it as part of your job or not. It's all a question of vicarious liability, isn't it? Ultimately, are you frolicking or are you doing your job?

Alison Clarke
Is there any way through a data subject access request that an employee could discover a situation where a senior manager has pressured an IT specialist to permanently delete questionable emails from that senior manager?

Jeremy Scott-Joynt
So hypothetically, if a manager tells an IT person to delete some emails, can the employee who is mentioned in those emails get hold of the instruction to the IT specialist under the powers of a subject access request?

Jeremy Scott-Joynt
In other words, is it personal data?

Daniel Barnett
It's a great question.

Jeremy Scott-Joynt
It's a really good question. I'm afraid it's going to come down to one of those twiddly points. There is a critical difference, I think between request one: "Daniel's asking us for information, so delete this bunch of emails", and request two: "Delete this bunch of emails". I would argue that request one may well be personal data because it's about Daniel. As for request two, that communication does not have in it any disclosable personal data, because it doesn't mention Daniel or it isn't connected to him in any jigsaw kind of way. Now, there are other ways in which one could get disclosure of that and different kinds of litigation, for instance, not least because - especially if there's litigation in prospect - deleting a whole bunch of stuff is likely to, under certain circumstances, result in someone getting banged up for contempt of court. But there's that narrow point there: is it personal data or not? Because if it is not personal data, a DSAR gives you no rights over at all. It's one of those 'head of pin' questions that we lawyers love.

AEO
What are your thoughts on Alexa while working from home and risks to personal data?

Jeremy Scott-Joynt
Now, I'm assuming that when we talk about Alexa, we're including HomePod, Cortana on Microsoft and Siri on Apple and all the rest of it. That is a little bit awkward, isn't it? Personally, I don't use those things. But I'm anal enough that I actually did read Apple's privacy policy and discover that the processing is going on at a device level rather than at a system level. It's not actually leaving the house,

so I'm not bothered. I would be quite nervous
if doing confidential work around a device
that was listening to me the whole time, unless
I'd taken steps to ensure that any processing
of speech was actually happening on device
rather than getting sent to a server somewhere.

Is it a big issue? Well, it's going to depend
partly on what you're doing. If I was doing
really confidential investigative stuff, or dealing
with someone's sensitive personal data, I'd
probably avoid having my Alexa speaker in
the room with me. But if not, these things are
always a matter of proportion. Take a sensible
view on what the risk is actually going to be.

Daniel Barnett
Jeremy Scott-Joynt, thank you very much.

EQUAL PAY AND GENDER PAY REPORTING

IJEOMA OMAMBALA QC, OLD SQUARE CHAMBERS

Daniel Barnett

I'm joined today by Ijeoma Omambala from Old Square Chambers, and she's going to be answering your questions on the subject of equal pay and gender pay reporting.

Ijeoma Omambala, good afternoon. I wanted to ask you this: what are the legal risks of voluntary reporting under the gender pay regulations?

Ijeoma Omambala

I think one of the potential problems about voluntary reporting is the risk of reputational damage. Generally, employers don't publish voluntarily unless they think they've got good news to publish. Perhaps the most significant risk is just placing information in the public domain, which individuals who may seek to bring equal pay claims within the employing organisation can use to support and develop their claims. It enables an employee to search the public registers and to look at company websites, to see what the pay gap is, and to see whether it's changed or got worse over recent years. It also enables an employee to say, well, look, clearly there is this gap, you knew about it, and you haven't taken steps to address it, and to use that to persuade an employment tribunal to perhaps draw some adverse inferences about the employer and the employer's policies. So, there's a risk of providing information to a potential claimant if you voluntarily publish information.

Anonymous

How does an employee find out what other employee salaries are without doing a subject access request?

Ijeoma Omambala

Well, of course, an employee has the right to request information about pay. There is a right to request disclosure of pay information from colleagues if they are interested in pay, and perhaps minded to bring any challenge in relation to pay. That right as set out in statute and it brings with it a degree of protection in that both the person who receives the request for information and the person making the request may be protected under the victimisation provisions in the Equality Act.

Victoria Duff

Is it ever acceptable to pay individuals with the same job role at different rates where common terms apply?

Ijeoma Omambala

That's one of those 'it depends' sort of questions, I'm afraid. It depends on whether there are any particular personal characteristics or circumstances that separate the two employees. For example, if an employee has been in a particular role, and has additional responsibilities that may warrant a difference in pay, or if the employee has recently arrived in the organisation from another organisation, that may, in the short term at least, justify the difference in pay. But it will certainly beg a number of questions. And what's important is that any employer has cogent evidence to support the responses to those questions.

Daniel Barnett
Would a very common reason for differential pay be something like different experience at the point of recruitment?

Ijeoma Omambala
Yes, that may well be. Also, if for example, there have been particular recruitment problems into a sector or into a particular part of an organisation, then that might justify a difference in salary.

Gillian Howard
In light of the report in the Financial Times today that the European Commission is planning to introduce tough gender pay reporting rules so that employees have transparency over their salaries, what do you think about the Equality and Human Rights Commission suspending gender pay gap reporting last month, and now allowing employers a six-month extension to report their gender pay gap figures?

Ijeoma Omambala
I think that the EHRC decision in consultation with the Government Equalities Office, is simply a pragmatic response to the Covid-19 pandemic and the difficulties, both real and imagined, that employers might face when collating their pay data. I think rather than having arguments down the line about whether there has been effective compliance, a pragmatic decision has been taken to extend the time for compliance until at least 5 October this year. The question talks about the EU Commission intending to introduce tough gender pay reporting rules, I'm not sure that they are significantly more rigorous than the rules that we currently have in place, and I'm not sure whether or not they will have the desired effect.

Daniel Barnett
Do proposals from the European Commission still bind the UK post-Brexit?

Ijeoma Omambala
Well, no. That's the other thing. We will look on with interest, but there is no obligation in the UK to take on any additional measures that the Commission ultimately develops. We are now on our own.

Anonymous
How does changing gender, transitioning gender, affect equal pay claims? Does a claimant always have to pursue any claim based on their biological sex at birth?

Ijeoma Omambala
I think the position as the law stands is that unless there has been a legally recognised transition supported by a recognition certificate, then a claimant will be pursuing a claim on the basis of their biological sex. If they have the relevant certification in terms of transition, then they would be in a position to bring their claim based on their certified sex at that time.

Daniel Barnett
And is there any overlap here with gender reassignment discrimination? If somebody was paid less than somebody else because they'd gone through gender reassignment, would they have a claim?

Ijeoma Omambala
They'd potentially have a claim. It would be a discrimination claim rather than an equal pay claim.

It's unlikely, I think, but if there was a situation where an employee who was a transgender employee had less favourable contractual terms than somebody of the opposite sex, then that might give rise to an equal pay claim. Otherwise, the claim would be under the sex discrimination provisions of the Equality Act.

Su Apps
What sort of evidence do you suggest to support a market forces argument as a material factor defence? Could you maybe start by explaining what a material factor defence is?

Ijeoma Omambala

Yes. So, in equal pay claims, there is a rebuttable presumption of discrimination in pay, and the employer can rebut that presumption by producing evidence that the difference in pay can be explained by a factor that is unrelated to sex and is untainted by sex discrimination more generally. And that is what we describe as a material factor defence. Market forces is an example of one such defence. What we generally mean by market forces are prevailing conditions in the labour market that have led to a scarcity of a particular type of employee or an oversupply of a particular set of skills.

Obviously, it depends on the scope and the size of the claim, but it is important for employers to produce evidence about the state of the market at the point of recruitment. That may be evidence that's gathered in relation to comparable employers, by way of a sort of benchmarking exercise. It may be by looking to organisations that provide that sort of information as part of an HR or data analysis service. But I think there needs to be some coherent information about the labour market in the area in which the employer operates. And, in particular, it's helpful to have evidence that relates to the particular type of jobs that the employee and her comparator are doing. Sometimes, organisations have the resource internally to collate that information. HR departments are often very able to do this work. But it may be that you go to your local Chamber of Commerce or a trade organisation to try and collate that sort of evidence.

Caroline Oliver

Caroline Oliver asks has the gender pay gap reporting deadline been delayed again this year, and what are your views on a further relaxation of these obligations?

Ijeoma Omambala

So, as we mentioned earlier, back in February, the decision was made to extend the time for reporting on the 2021 gender pay gap to 5 October this year. I wonder myself whether, in fact, that deadline may yet be moved again because I'm not entirely confident that matters will have settled sufficiently in relation to the pandemic for a comprehensive set of gender pay gap reporting exercises to be undertaken. As I said earlier, I think it's a pragmatic response. I hope that what it doesn't do is lead to a general sort of side-lining of gender pay gap reporting. I think it remains an important tool, both for employers to demonstrate what good employers they are and what desirable places they are to work because they can point to the steps that they're taking to close the gap, and also as part of a general effort to increase equality across organisations.

Mike Clyne

Do you think the government will reduce the 250-employee threshold over time?

Ijeoma Omambala

I think perhaps over time. But I think in the short to medium term, the 250-employee threshold is likely to remain in place, particularly at a time when we are still hearing lots of conversations around reducing the red tape burden on employers and industry and in allowing them to, to flourish and to innovate. So, I think it's unlikely that the numbers will be reduced anytime soon.

Daniel Barnett

My recollection is that when the white paper originally came out about gender pay reporting, it was always proposed that the number would drop from 250 down to 200, then 150 and settle at 100. But it's been pretty much knocked out by Covid because the government doesn't want to be introducing red tape at the moment.

Mike Clyne

If the threshold was reduced to say 50 employees, would small sample sizes for comparison cause issues?

Ijeoma Omambala

Well, I suppose it depends on how the information is presented. I think as long as it was possible to make comparisons between employers of similar sizes - so perhaps there is reporting in accordance with employee numbers - then one could still conduct relevant and intelligent comparison exercises.

Anonymous
If an employee moves to a new role and finds out their successor is paid more than they were paid in their previous role, when would limitation run from?

Ijeoma Omambala
First of all, I suppose we'd have to think about whether or not they could in fact bring a claim in relation to a successor. So, let's assume that, all things being equal, that claim is brought, I think the time would run in the first instance from the date at which the successor began their role. If there was any suggestion that there had been an attempt to obfuscate or hide the fact that the successor was being paid more, then it might run from the point at which the employee finds out.

In any event, there is a six-year period for bringing the claim. Assuming that nothing changes in the immediate term, then I would be hopeful that there wouldn't be arguments about limitation anyway.

Daniel Barnett
Just to clarify for anyone who's not sure, it's six years in the county court, but it's still a normal limitation period in the tribunal. So, if you wanted to go for the six years, you do have the risk of costs that you wouldn't have in a normal tribunal claim.

Sarah Matthews
What are your views on whether there should be race pay gap reporting?

Ijeoma Omambala
This is a nice short answer. I think there should be. I think there is, again, a reluctance to add administrative reporting burdens on employers - that reluctance existed before the pandemic, but it's heightened as a result of it. I think there

are also some logistical problems around how does one define race for the purposes of pay gap reporting, and we could no doubt spend hours talking about what the categorizations might be. That's something that has slowed some of the debates and the discussion around this, but my view is, none of that is insuperable and if there is a political will to address what we know is a pay gap that exists in relation to race, then it could be resolved. And I think there are some sensible arguments for mirroring the gender pay gap reporting regime.

Daniel Barnett
Do you know if any other countries have race pay gap reporting?

Ijeoma Omambala
In the form that the gender pay gap reporting is done here? I don't know. I think there are some parts of the states that do it, but I don't know about other European countries. I would be surprised if they did.

Christopher Temmink
Do you think that the gender pay gap means that unscrupulous employers have started to cheat the system and outsource lower-paid work, and if so, how can we address this?

Daniel Barnett
I'm not immediately seeing how one leads to the other.

Ijeoma Omambala
That was the point that I was going to make. I don't think that outsourcing lower paid work is a consequence of having gender pay gaps and reporting. I think employers who are unscrupulous would outsource that work in any event. Given that the enforcement provisions around gender pay gap reporting are so weak, there is no effective sanction in relation to a failure to report an inaccurate or even potentially fraudulent report that is going to discourage employers if they are so minded to cheat the system.

Anonymous
Which statutory provision gives an employee the right to request details of a colleague's pay?

Ijeoma Omambala
That's a really good question. I think I'm going to have to reach for my statutes. I think its s77 of the Equality Act.

Daniel Barnett
I think 77 is the one that outlaws discussions about pay. I don't know that section number off the top of my head, actually. Neither of us has the statute section number to hand.

Victoria Duff
Is it acceptable to top up furlough to 100% of salary for one employee and not for others?

Daniel Barnett
What I assume the question is getting at - and forgive me if I'm mistaken - is whether it is a breach of equal pay legislation to top one furloughed employee's up to 100% and not top someone of the other gender's up to 100%?

Ijeoma Omambala
Again, this is one of those where 'it depends'. If the others are both men and women doing the same job, then it's unlikely to be held unlawful because there are both men and women who are receiving the less favourable rate of pay. If there is sex segregation in the way that that topping up happens, then the topping up doesn't arise as a result of a contractual entitlement to pay, it arises as a result of the employer's exercise of the discretion in relation to pay. And so, whilst that is capable of being challenged, it will be challenged under the provisions of the sex discrimination provisions of the Equality Act, not as an equal pay claim.

Remziye
Do you anticipate there being gender pay gap issues if an employer appears to be putting more women on furlough?

Daniel Barnett
Or is that likely to be good old-fashioned sex discrimination?

Ijeoma Omambala
There will be issues in terms of reporting in the sense that the practice will impact on the gender pay gap or may impact on the gender pay gap. But it doesn't give rise to any cause of action in itself. There may be - if employees have access to that information, perhaps as a result of seeing the reports - they may then seek to run sex discrimination claims and those claims might be for direct or indirect sex discrimination. We know from the statistics that have been collated so far, that women are more likely to be placed on furlough and earn less money while they are on furlough also.

Ben Hunt
Can an employee raise an equal pay claim on behalf of lower-paid employees even if they're in the higher-paid category?

Daniel Barnett
I'm not sure I quite understand the question.

Ijeoma Omambala
I'm not sure I do either. So, if what the question is asking is whether a higher-paid employee can encourage lower-paid employees and assist them in bringing a claim, then, the answer is yes of course. They might, for example, volunteer to be a comparator for those lower-paid employees, and provide them with assistance in their claim in that way, and perhaps provide them with information as to their own pay and terms and conditions. So, in that way, they can assist. But I'm not sure if that's what the question was getting at.

Christopher Temmink
In your opinion, does gender pay gap reporting actually ask the right questions?

Ijeoma Omambala
I suppose it depends what one thinks the purpose of gender pay gap reporting is. At least a part of the reason that it was brought

in was to raise awareness of differences in pay between men and women, and to try and encourage employers to take steps to close the gap. As far as the way that the regime operates, I suppose there are always more questions that could be asked. It is a little bit complicated if one has employees with non-typical working hours, for example, but I'm not sure that there is a huge and obvious gap. There are areas where the complexities of pay in relation to deferred elements of pay and so on aren't most effectively dealt with. But it's better than nothing is probably where I sit on this.

Vanessa Hall
Gender pay gap is not the same as equal pay. I'm interested in claims made for equal pay for work of equal value. How many private sector claims for this succeed?

Daniel Barnett
I mean, there are statistics, of course, for equal pay claims, but I'm not sure they break them down into the different categories of equal pay claims. And of course, we've got on the one hand, the single equal pay claims, and then we've got the multi equal pay claims like Tesco, Lidl, Asda, etc. What's your gut feeling on that?

Ijeoma Omambala
In terms of succeeding by being litigated to judgment, I would say probably less than a third. But I think very many equal value claims involving private-sector employees settle. They resolve without a final determination on the question of equal value. Either that's because there is a hearing on any material factor defence, and that goes well or badly, or because there is a report from an independent expert or evidence at a tribunal that says there is equal value in any event. I think most equal pay cases tend to be resolved by settlement rather than by judgment in a court or tribunal.

Mike Clyne
As the sanctions are so weak, do you think the 'market will sort it out approach' will work?

Daniel Barnett
I assume he's talking about gender pay gap reporting.

Ijeoma Omambala
No, probably not. I think that those employers who have an interest in presenting themselves as progressive, modern, enlightened employers will take the steps that are needed to address pay inequality. And those employers who are not interested or who do not need to do anything, will not do anything. And I might say, it was ever thus.

Anonymous
Should you always claim sex discrimination in the alternative to an equal pay claim?

Daniel Barnett
It depends what the claim is about.

Ijeoma Omambala
Exactly so. And I think there are lots of judges who would say absolutely not. I think the important thing is to think through what your claim is about. And if you're defending a claim, to think through what the claim you're trying to defend is about. It's pointless claiming sex discrimination if there is no basis for a sex discrimination claim. Now, if your case is one where it's possible that it will be said, well, this is not a contractual provision, it's an exercise of discretion or it's a difference in treatment, then, of course, it makes sense to plead sex discrimination in the alternative. But I think the most important thing is to gather as much information as you can before you plead your case, and then try and understand what it's going to look like.

Helen
If a differential in pay has arisen historically, to what extent does an employer need to look into the exact circumstances that have resulted in the pay disparity when seeking to use a material factor defence?

Ijeoma Omambala
I think it's always helpful to understand how the current pay regime has come to pass.

How historic is the issue? Because if you're essentially relying on discrepancies that are a number of years old to justify your actions, then you're obviously going to be in a more difficult situation than if those historical factors are a little bit more recent. One can't just simply sit back and relax and say, well, 20 years ago, it was very, very difficult to get tech managers with this skill set, and that's why we've got this pay structure. One has to ongoingly review and consider that disparity and whether or not it remains justified by the market conditions.

Su Apps
When a material factor defence becomes outdated, does the employer have to increase other employees' pay to the enhanced level, or can the employer reduce the pay of the higher-paid employee down to that of the masses?

Ijeoma Omambala
Well, assuming that the pay provisions are contractual, there is a risk in reducing pay, which employees may be unhappy about, and may seek to take action in relation to. But it's, of course, possible to dismiss and offer re-engagement in appropriate cases, and some employers do that if they are in a particularly strong bargaining position. Other ways in which the disparity can be addressed might present themselves if there is discussion and consultation with the employees who are affected.

Anonymous
Can you claim injury to feelings for equal pay claims, or is it just the financial difference in salary?

Ijeoma Omambala
The answer is no, you cannot.

Daniel Barnett
No, you can't claim injury to feelings.

Anonymous
What tips would you give an employer to help them improve gender equality in the workplace?

Daniel Barnett
Let's limit it to pay equality.

Ijeoma Omambala
An obvious one is to think about the right pay for the role, as opposed to what a potential employee asks for or is currently getting. That immediately reduces the problems that arise from female prospective employees being on lower pay elsewhere and being reluctant to ask for higher pay when they start a new role. That's, I think, an obvious tip.

Florajane Lynch
If there was a claim to HR from an employee regarding the gender pay gap, what's the best first course of action to address the situation?

Ijeoma Omambala
I think the first thing that I would do would be to speak to the employee that has a concern and then obtain some information about the pay that she receives and the pay that those she is potentially comparing herself to, receive so that I could, first of all, understand what the factual landscape might be. It may be that there are elements in that pay that you need to find out about: how they've arisen, why they are being paid, and how long they have been paid for. I would make sure that I have as much information about the facts as I can before I undertake to do or say anything to try and resolve the situation.

James Fairchild
Can one do an age-based equal pay claim?

Ijeoma Omambala
One can. It wouldn't be an equal pay claim. It would be an age discrimination claim, arguing that you are being paid less because you are older or younger. And it may be a direct claim, or potentially may be an indirect claim.

Daniel Barnett
Presumably, the grounds for justifying an age discrimination claim would be wider than those for justifying an equal pay claim, which sounds wrong, but I think is what the law says.

Ijeoma Omambala

I think that's right. We say an equal pay claim. It wouldn't be called that, but essentially, you would either be saying, look, I'm doing exactly the same thing as somebody who's at a different age than I am, or I'm doing something that's worth the same as them, but I'm not being valued in the same way. So, I suppose that amounts to an equal pay type claim.

Anonymous

Asking about pay is a protected act for the purposes of victimisation, but does an employer actually have to give the pay information when asked?

Ijeoma Omambala

Well, the regime now means that an individual makes the request for pay information to other employees. So, the employer doesn't actually have any responsibility for providing that information if the request is made to a colleague. There is the ability for an employee who has concerns about pay to write to the employer and ask them for pay information, but again, there's no obligation on the part of the employer to provide that information. It may be something that there are good reasons for doing, and equally, it may be that there are very good reasons for not doing it. But there's no way that an employer can be compelled to provide information about pay.

Stuart Morely

Is it possible that the matters relied upon to defend a like-work claim on the basis there are differences of practical importance can also be used to defend the like-work claim on the basis of a material factor defence?

Daniel Barnett

Do you need to lead discrete evidence on each of the defences? Or do they overlap?

Ijeoma Omambala

There's a degree of overlap. But if you are running a claim, and you are having the evidence on like-work and the evidence on material factor defence being heard at the same time, all of the evidence will be led, and I think you would just pull out in submissions those things that you thought were particularly relevant either to the like-work issues or to the material factor defence. If those issues are being dealt with separately, of course, if you're an employer and you've lost the argument on like work, then a tribunal will have found that there are no differences of practical importance that distinguish the claimant and her comparator. And so, the evidence and arguments are unlikely to be more successful at the material factor defence stage.

Daniel Barnett

Ijeoma Omambala, thank you.

FAMILY-FRIENDLY RIGHTS
RACHEL CRASNOW QC, CLOISTERS

Daniel Barnett

Today's webinar is on family-friendly issues with Rachel Crasnow QC from Cloisters.

Rachel, good afternoon. A couple of questions from me. Over the last couple of years, we've seen a lot of debate about shared parental pay, and whether men, fathers, can ensure they're paid equitably with women and whether there can be some form of equality between shared parental pay and enhanced maternity pay. And can you update us on what the position currently is?

Rachel Crasnow

Of course. Let's first define our terms. contractual maternity pay is frequently enhanced to some extent so that it's worth more than statutory maternity pay, which is paid at just six weeks at 90% of your average pay, and then 33 weeks at a statutory rate of now around £151 a week. What's shared parental pay? To know about that we have to remember that shared parental leave is the leave which a woman can gift to her partner or spouse when she shortens or curtails her maternity leave for the purpose of being able to look after a new child at any point in their first year of life. And you can give up to 50 weeks to your partner to share, but only 37 of those weeks will be paid. Shared parental pay is paid at a flat rate throughout at just £151 a week from April 2021. And since it's so much more common for maternity pay to be enhanced than shared parental pay, a key question has arisen: is there a way for a father

or indeed a female partner, to challenge their employer's scheme whereby maternity pay is enhanced under a contract but shared parental pay remains at the statutory lower rate? The short answer to the question is no, according to recent Court of Appeal authority. But - there is a 'but' here - the longer answer is maybe, thanks to a European Court of Justice case in Luxembourg at the end of 2020.

One reason why this is such an important question is that it's the low rate of shared parental pay which is really seen as being the key reason why the take-up of shared parental leave has been so low since it was introduced in 2015. About 2% of eligible couples actually take it up. So this is the reason for the challenge in the case of Ali v Capita and Hextall v Leicestershire police force *(Ali v Capita and Hextall v The Chief Constable of Leicestershire Police [2020] ICR 87)* you may remember from the Court of Appeal decision in 2019. These claimants were two fathers whose workplace treated employees on these different kinds of leave differently. The two fathers in their separate workplaces brought sex discrimination claims, but they needed to be able to compare themselves to women on maternity leave. That was because the women who were taking shared parental leave were treated no more favourably than the fathers themselves; they simply got that flat rate. Mr Hextall and Mr Ali argued that after a certain point of maternity leave, the purpose of such leave was really to care for the child rather than to recover from childbirth or pregnancy.

They argued once you've got to a certain way along that leave, the reasons for both shared parental leave and maternity leave are similar enough to allow for comparison. They relied on legal and societal developments, such as the fact that shared parental leave could now be taken in the UK as early as two weeks after birth, which showed that maternity leave by some point must be, they said, for the purpose of caring for a baby. Well, the Court of Appeal disagreed in 2019 and said the purposes of maternity leave *throughout* remains linked to pregnancy and recovering from childbirth as well as looking after the baby generally. But the Court of Appeal wasn't really interested, in my view, about whether maternity leave and shared parental leave *continue* to serve different purposes, even much later on in the maternity leave period. And the point is surely, is the further away you get from birth, the more clear it is that the reason for the leave is not about recovery from childbirth, but about the care of the child. And that should make the comparison between shared parental leave and maternity leave easier.

Well, everyone thought that argument was dead in the water, and then at the very end of last year, just before the Brexit transition period ended, along came an European Court of Justice case called Syndicat CFTC *(Syndicat CFTC (C-463/19) [2021] IRLR 152)*. That focused on at what point, post-birth, does the period of leave cease being for the effects of pregnancy and motherhood and start just being for parenting? So that decision is part of EU retained law. Why is it important? Well, it somewhat changes the landscape from where we were after the Court of Appeal in *Hextall*. And I suggest it means that if a similar case were brought now, it will be easier to carry out that comparative exercise, which failed in *Hextall*, and it might mean that dads can get an enhanced rate of SPL.

In the Syndicat case, a French father was unable to take a certain kind of additional leave which was reserved just for mothers.

Not surprisingly, he was refused it on the grounds that he was a man and he brought a sex discrimination case before the National Court and then before the Court of Justice in Luxembourg. Before the judgment came out in November of last year, Advocate General Bobek produced an opinion where he looked at all the ways that society - and, indeed, the law - had developed in recent years where parental responsibilities of fathers had been enhanced. And parents now had a choice about who was going to care for the children in early years. And he said that when it came to additional periods of maternity leave going beyond the statutory period of maternity leave, which is just 14 weeks in EU law, the protection of the biological condition of women becomes less relevant. And therefore, families can choose how they're going to share the leave after that period, and so in every case, you need to look at the purpose of that additional leave where it's reserved for women to try and work out if it has aims additional to that are protecting the biological condition of women, and perhaps be for simple childcare. Also, he said, look at the length of the leave, because the longer that additional maternity leave is, the more difficult it will be to justify reserving it to women alone. And also, is there less pay at a later stage? Because that also may mean it should be regarded differently from the first 14 weeks.

Well, where does that leave us in this post-*Hextall* landscape? In my view, there are now better prospects, if the right case came along for comparing the two types of leave - maternity leave, and shared parental leave - and eventually getting these enhanced, shared parental pay rates. But should we be launching further lengthy litigation now after *Hextall* and *Ali* took so long to get to the Court of Appeal? It's probably preferable, instead, for the much-delayed reform of shared parental leave to come to pass. And when the long-heralded employment bill eventually comes in, it's really hoped that this will be used as an opportunity to replace shared parental leave with a fairer system of maternity and parental leave. What would that look like? Well, key items on the wish list include giving individuals non-transferable rights to better-paid leave for both parents - you might have heard that called 'use it or lose it' rights - and having those rights available to all working parents regardless of their employment status from day one. And lastly, of course, a new system would have to enhance the financial provision for fathers and other second parents, whilst also protecting existing rights of mothers.

Well, you might be thinking, this sounds expensive for employers. It would be more than it costs at the moment, but that's a short-sighted view in some terms because it would ultimately help retain those female employees that businesses have invested in over the years and narrowing the gender pay gap by keeping women in the workplace. So lots of food for thought there.

Daniel Barnett
Lots of food for thought. Let me just ask you one more question. How should an employer treat a pregnant employee if the pregnant employee is concerned about whether the workplace poses a risk to her pregnancy, especially during the current COVID-19 pandemic?

Rachel Crasnow
We know that the impact of the pandemic has had really significant effects on female workers. And they often stem from both employers' and workers' inability to understand the detail of existing rights and the complexity of all the options open to them, coupled with the fact that new guidance has come in very speedily. And we know that all employers have got a duty to assess workplace risks specific to pregnant women and new mothers, and that will include assessing the risks of COVID-19 infection and taking into account the fact that pregnant women are classed as particularly vulnerable after 28 weeks of pregnancy.

So, what action must an employer take? It should be straightforward. They must take reasonable action to remove health and safety risks following individual risk assessments. For example, by altering working conditions, providing suitable alternative work on the same terms and conditions - which could include working from home - or if working from home not possible and there simply is no other suitable alternative work, then they must suspend on full pay. Now, if suspension is the only safe option, and the employer fails to do that, a pregnant woman would have a right to bring a number of claims, including a tribunal claim for detriment on health and safety grounds under s44 Employment Rights Act 1996, and there might well be a discrimination claim for pregnancy discrimination there too under s18 of the Equality Act 2010. There are complicated questions for employers about whether it's preferable to furlough a pregnant woman or to suspend her on full pay - and we may come on to the details of that a bit later, because the different path you take can result in different financial outcomes for both employer and employee. But either course are surely better for a pregnant employee than being forced to take unpaid leave or being put on sick pay at the statutory rates, which are far lower than those alternatives.

There have of course, been calls for the government to reimburse employers for health and safety suspensions, and also furlough at 100% rather than an 80% rate. But there's been no guidance on whether that's going to come through as yet.

I really want to touch on the application of 'no job, no job' policies for pregnant women, which is really frightening a lot of people. If an employer says only employees with a vaccine can come back to work or even select for redundancy on the basis of who's agreed to take up an offer of a vaccine, to treat people who don't get vaccinated because of pregnancy will be pregnancy discrimination. But let's come back to that a bit later.

Su Apps

If you discover an employee on maternity leave has potentially committed misconduct or gross misconduct, should you wait until her return - or shortly before - to start disciplinary proceedings, or should you start disciplinary proceedings straight away?

Rachel Crasnow

The first thing for us to remember is that when you're on maternity leave, all your terms and conditions continue other than your remuneration rights. Therefore, you're only entitled to statutory maternity pay or contractual maternity pay rather than your usual earnings. But the fact that your other terms and conditions continue means that your employer is basically entitled to look into the details of your misconduct. But I think what a good employer would do in those circumstances is apply this question: why carry out an investigation which wouldn't require an employee to be working if it's not so urgent that it has to be dealt with prior to that employee coming back to work? You might think, well, in many investigations involving gross misconduct we might need to suspend the individual. But if that individual is already on maternity leave, and not in the workplace, then we don't need to do that. I think there is scope for being very careful before starting such a process if it's the case that there's no reason why it cannot wait. But an employer does retain a discretion to carry out such an investigation because the terms and conditions do continue in the maternity leave period.

Daniel Barnett

Could requiring an employee on maternity leave to come into work for an investigation, outside their ten keeping in touch days amount to a detriment?

Rachel Crasnow

Keeping in touch days are there to be agreed between employer and employee. If there's no agreement there, you couldn't even do it under keeping in touch days. But the question about whether it would amount to a detriment would depend on what the circumstances were. I've certainly seen cases where managers came to the individual's home to conduct interviews, dialogue, conversations about the misconduct in question. If you're going to get the employee to come in, you've got all the kinds of questions: what impact will that have on her with childcare? How will her pay be treated differently if she's required to come into work? Is the reason why she's being asked to come in linked to pregnancy and potentially risking a breach of s18 of the Equality Act? Care needs to be taken in each and every case.

Su Apps

If as a result of an employee going on maternity leave it becomes apparent that her role is redundant, when should you start the process and what risks are there?

Daniel Barnett

I think this is a very focused question based on not a general redundancy scenario, but suddenly realising you don't need that woman anymore now that she's no longer there.

Rachel Crasnow

The very fact that the pregnant woman is absent from the workplace may lead you to think actually, we can cope without her. Now, is that a redundancy situation? Sounds like it would be, but isn't it also the fact that she is being selected for redundancy because she is on maternity leave? It sounds strange, doesn't it, that you can have a lawful redundancy situation but the application of it is rendered unlawful when you select for redundancy because the reason is she's on maternity leave? In that situation, you would have to look very carefully at whether there were suitable alternative vacancies which you would consider offering to the individual. Because if you simply say, well, there's nothing; we're coping so well without you that we've realised we don't need you to come back and but for your absence, we'd never have realised it, I think that is a difficult situation for employers and they would be wary of running the risk of a s18 claim, and arguably, therefore, an automatically unfair dismissal claim.

Natalie White
How should employers handle redundancy consultations with employees who are on maternity leave?

Rachel Crasnow
That's a question where we can really draw a contrast to some extent with the onus upon an employer if a misconduct situation becomes known during the maternity leave period. If a redundancy situation arises and one of the people affected by it is likely to be on maternity leave, you absolutely do have to consult with the woman on maternity leave, in the same way that you would consult with everyone else in the workplace. That's really essential. How you do that will depend on each and every case. And in our age of Zoom, it may be far easier for those kinds of discussions and consultations to be carried out than we would have thought a few years ago. But what's important is that you give the individual on maternity leave exactly the same information as her colleagues have at work. We know it's very easy for people to feel left out, cut off and distanced from the workplace and what's going on there. There's no point having consultation unless it's meaningful, so make sure the individual in question has the information and that they can ask for more facts if they need it.

June Smith
A man who took five months shared parental leave, has had his annual bonus reduced to take account of this. Is this action a detriment as a result of asserting a statutory right and/or victimisation?

Rachel Crasnow
I am presuming that he had his bonus reduced by five twelfths based on the five months absence.

The first thing when looking at bonuses, whether they're being applied to somebody on maternity leave or shared parental leave, is that you have to consider what the purpose of the bonus is in the first place. Bonuses are usually either to reward you for your past work or to incentivise you for your future work. And in such a case, it's only if they're there to consider the specific period when the individual is absent, that it may be appropriate to reduce pro-rata. So where you say, you will get an extra £100 per month in 2021 simply for being here in the workplace and someone's not there, if it can be said that that's part of your general remuneration - you have to be there in order to get it and if you're off on leave, your remuneration isn't applicable in the way that your general salary isn't - then the employer is entitled to reduce it pro-rata, and I don't think it will be arguable that it amounts to either a detriment or victimisation.

Matilda Swanson
Where do employers most fall foul with family-friendly rights? What do people get wrong?

Rachel Crasnow
One thing that I find that people get wrong the most is making decisions too quickly about change. And this happens an awful lot with flexible working requests. And you can see why. If a system is working well, perhaps requiring employees to work in the office nine to five, Monday to Friday, and your clients like it, business is working well. As soon as there's a threatened change to that apple cart, managers can be nervous about it and react defensively. And therefore, when a request is put in for flexible working and someone suggests a change to the status quo: I want to work from home; I want to shift my work from ten till six, not nine till five; or I want to work avoiding school holidays and work longer days - there are many different kinds of flexible working patterns - people can react defensively and say no, this is bound to be bad for business. And I've seen that happen on so many occasions where there's been the

'our customers will all go elsewhere as soon as you're not there to pick up the phone every hour of the day' reaction. It's amazing how that kind of defensive reaction starts to erode trust and confidence between people because the individual applying for flexible working reacts badly as well and trust ebbs away.

Rachel Crasnow

Interestingly, I think the pandemic will make a real difference here because we've all been forced to work in different ways. Some of us have even had to work while doing schoolwork with a 10-year-old or making lunches for people we luckily don't usually have to make lunches for, and we've been able to cope despite that. What will be interesting to see as my when we return to the office is how flexible working requests are handled differently. Because you may be able to say to your employer, it's nonsense to suggest that our customers won't like it. I've been speaking to our customers from home for the last year and it's gone perfectly well! I think trying to avoid gut reactions and giving speedy answers rather than taking a request into proper consideration is a real lesson that will bear out well.

Daniel Barnett

I often find employers will say we can't possibly manage with Fred away from the office and away from the telephones today. And then you just ask them, well, how do you manage for the 5.6 weeks when Fred's on holiday? And their faces fall as they try to work out the conundrum. I'm not sure I agree that the pandemic is going to make a massive difference, though. I hope I'm wrong, but I suspect there's going to be a reversion to the mean within a couple of years, and we'll be back exactly where we were with middle managers saying, almost as a knee-jerk reaction, no, you can't work from home; It doesn't work. And they'll have no evidence to back it up.

Rachel Crasnow

We'll have the evidence base of the pandemic with which to test that.

Mike Clyne

What changes to family-friendly legislation do you predict will come next?

Rachel Crasnow

I think one of the likely developments we will see coming into force soon is a ban on making pregnant women redundant at all during the maternity leave period and for six months after they get back to work. A lot of commentators and legal workers in this field have been seeking that for years now. They say, well, regulation 10, The Maternity and Parental Leave etc. Regulations 1999 simply isn't working, those suitable alternative vacancies aren't being offered properly. Pregnant women are being made redundant and not being able to return from leave day in, day out. And one reason for that is it's too complicated to apply. It just isn't working.

I think a law reform which will go hand in hand with that is likely to be giving people in this position an extra few months to bring their claims for unfair dismissal or sex discrimination which arises from redundancy on maternity leave. And there's a suggestion that even following the pandemic, on a temporary basis, there should be an additional six months for women to bring their claims because it's really difficult to put in a claim when you're up all night with a screaming baby or far away from the workplace or not able to access the kind of rights you might be able to if you were, indeed, at work. I think those two factors we may well see come into work soon. Maria Miller MP has got her private members bill seeking those factors due for its second reading this Friday. Those points may also be part of the Employment Bill that has gone rather quiet at the moment.

James Fairchild

My client has a member of staff who doesn't have children. Whenever a colleague has time off for family-related reasons, he says can he have time off to deal with issues concerning his pet cats or his classic cars?

I think the second part of that is flippant. There isn't any danger that a court could, in the future, decide that pets or cars are part of the family. But I think James makes a serious point: are you treating men less favourably because you're not giving men the same family-friendly entitlements that you give women?

Rachel Crasnow
The first quick point I'd make on that is that the right to flexible working used to be related to people with caring responsibilities, but now it's open for everyone. So, I'm entitled to put in a request saying, "I want to go canoeing every Thursday afternoon, please. Can I leave at three?" It doesn't have to have anything to do with childcare whatsoever. So, remember, the right for flexible working would give someone the same right to ask to look after their cats, as to pick up a baby from nursery. And the reasons for denying it would have to be on the same prohibitive grounds as they are for any flexible working request.

When you're looking at whether you can treat women more favourably or not because of them being absent on maternity leave, you need to remember the specific provision of s13 Equality Act 2010 that came up in the case of De Belin v Eversheds *(Eversheds Legal Services Ltd v De Belin [2011] IRLR 448)* when the issue was whether it was appropriate to treat a woman who was on maternity leave more favourably in how you applied the selection criteria for redundancy than her male colleague who was simply sitting in the office. And what you have to do- in a nutshell -is be proportionate about it.

So, getting back to the question, if someone said, "it's really unfair that you're not letting me go and look after my cats at four o'clock on a Thursday, but you are letting Mrs Smith go and pick her baby up from nursery," well, the question would be, in a nutshell, is it proportionate to allow one and not the other? Whether it's enough to say, "Mrs Smith can sue me at least for indirect sex discrimination if

I don't let her, but you can't sue me for anti-cat treatment," may not be the end of the question. So proportionate responses are the way to go there.

Daniel Barnett
Ever since Eversheds v De Belin was decided, I've always thought what hope is there for us ordinary mortals of being able to handle maternity rights correctly if one of the best law firms on the planet gets it wrong?

Amelia Berriman
What legal rights are there, if any, for women wishing to go through IVF with regards to time off for treatment or sickness related to the IVF treatment?

Rachel Crasnow
Strictly speaking, although IVF treatment is specific to women {like pregnancy} there is no special protection give to a woman who seeks to undergo IVF, any more than for an employee of either sex who wishes to undergo medical treatment for a gender-specific medical condition. This always seems rather unfair to me and it would be a pretty harsh employer, I think, who simply didn't give an individual the right to time off for such treatment, at the very least allowing them to use their annual leave. But you don't have the same rights simply to have IVF treatment as you do, for example, to attend antenatal appointments when you do get paid time off. So there's a difference there. And protection from detrimental treatment for those on IVF starts from the point of egg removal: because either she is pregnant from them if the procedure is a success or since she is treated as being pregnant until she is informed otherwise: see further cases of *Sahota v The Home Office* [2010] ICR 772, [2010] 2 CMLR 77 and *Mayr v Bäckerei Und Konditorei Gerhard Flockner OHG: C-506/06*, [2008] IRLR 387.

Daniel Barnett
James Fairchild pointed out that he was being serious about whether cats might be seen as

extensions of the family, not flippant. Apologies if I was trivialising what you said. Rachel, would you care to comment on that?

Rachel Crasnow
Well, maybe there could be Article 8 rights supplied here; rights to privacy and family life. What's a family, Daniel? People are broad-minded in today's society. Maybe it depends on how long the individual's cats have been there as part of a unit...

Penelope Douglass
Is it possible for a single parent to use shared parental leave in order to have a break in maternity leave and then go back to work?

Rachel Crasnow
At the moment, you can't do that because in order for you to curtail your maternity leave, and thus change the status of what's left to 'shared parental leave,' you have to be doing sharing. But that point about how it really impacts unfairly on single parents has been talked about a lot in recent years specifically with the drive to have grandparents coming in and being able to do that sharing. About four years ago, this was really big on the agenda, but then, as Brexit took up more and more time, it simply got dropped and the whole idea of grandparents leave went very quiet indeed.

At the moment, single parents can't access shared parental leave and the most they can do is ask their employer if they are allowed, by virtue of an agreement, to take their maternity leave in separate blocks because if they did have a partner, they would be able to do that with shared parental leave. There's nothing to stop an employer consenting to such an agreement. That said, if I were that individual employee, I would be careful to get the agreement of my employer that I was still protected - for example, against redundancy selection - in my later periods of leave in the same way as I would be if my maternity leave continued in one single period.

Anonymous
Has furlough had an impact on women returning from maternity leave - so people who refuse to come back and ask to be furloughed to keep their baby and their family safe?

Rachel Crasnow
Furlough has thrown up all kinds of difficult issues for women on maternity leave. Firstly, there's this scenario where you might have a woman who's on the latter parts of her leave periods, the parts where she no longer gets any maternity pay at all, and she sees her colleagues are not at work but being furloughed on 80% of their pay. And she thinks well, hold on, this is crazy. I could be doing exactly the same as I'm doing every day at home with my baby but getting four-fifths of my salary. And she may say, "Please can I come back and you furlough me? It's no skin off your nose, Mr Employer because you'll get 80% back from the government in any event."

I would say to employees that they should be wary of doing that unless they get their employer's consent or agreement that they will still have redundancy protection even when a furlough period ends. This, of course, wouldn't apply to public sector employers, but I'm assuming the question applies to those who can. But as for individuals who are told, "at the end of your maternity leave period, we're going straight to furloughing you," a real question that arises is what will be looked at for the worth of your average wages to make up your furlough pay? And we know now that an employer mustn't take into account your maternity pay, which will be less than your normal salary. So in a nutshell, someone coming back from maternity leave won't lose out if they go straight onto furlough. They should get their normal wages, even if it's at the 80% rate.

Anonymous
Is it discriminatory to pay a less experienced male on maternity cover more than the employee who went on maternity leave?

Rachel Crasnow
The rules about comparators in equal pay are that a male comparator need not be employed at the same time as the claimant- that's from s64(2) of the Equality Act - but a claimant can't compare herself with her male successor, since that is too hypothetical (see *Walton Centre for Neurology & Neurosurgery Surgery NHS Trust v Bewley* [2008] IRLR 588. So if the cover had left by the time the women returned from maternity leave he could still be relied upon as a comparator.

A key issue would be the reason why the cover's pay was higher – did it amount to a material factor?

So some relevant questions would be did they advertise the locum post at her pay level? If so, what happened? Did they have to pay the cover that amount to get him to provide the cover? What had he been doing before? What would he be doing after? It may be that he is a contractor and so commands a higher rate of pay because it's a fixed term contract (with no benefits, pension, holiday pay etc). So each case has to be examined on its facts to see if a material factor defence in my view.

Another point is whilst it might immediately be thought that such a claim would not affect the rate of maternity pay itself, but rather the rate upon return, since of course maternity pay is based upon one's pre-leave pay, the lower leave rate itself might well be part of the loss arising from the breach of the equality clause

Christopher Temmink
How much proof does an employer need to give to the employee when turning down a request for flexible working on one or more of the eight set business grounds?

Daniel Barnett
As you know, they're things like burden of additional costs or detrimental effect on ability to meet customer demand.

Rachel Crasnow
Interestingly, if an employee wants to challenge any of those reasons by bringing a claim to a tribunal, saying their right to work flexibly was wrongly refused, you can challenge the business reasons put forward on the basis of the evidence rather than on the basis that the judgment call taken by the employer was wrong. It's a bit like a perversity appeal in that way. So suppose you, the employee, know very well that all your customers are absolutely happy to talk to you whether you're sitting in the park on your phone, whether you're at home in your study, or whether you're in the office, and you say, "You just don't have the evidence to back up that business reason," to that extent, you could challenge it. So I do think employers need to be very clear about what their evidence is that is going to their refusal for business reasons. And that comes back to what I was saying about not jumping to conclusions when deciding whether to accept or reject a request for flexible working.

Gillian Howard
Is it unlawful indirect sex discrimination, to refuse to allow a woman to have paid or unpaid time off to have fertility treatment, even if it needs to be once a month?

Rachel Crasnow
That's a really interesting question. I'm thinking of that Scottish EAT case called Wilson v Hacking *(Hacking & Paterson v Wilson EAT/0054/09)* a few years ago, where the EAT said don't assume it's indirect sex discrimination to not let women come back to work part-time. Couples rearrange their caring responsibilities in all kinds of ways now. That judge refused to assume that refusing a woman part-time working was any more discriminatory than refusing a man part-time working.

People reacted differently to that judgment. But in terms of how this kind of argument would work, you'd have to ask when looking at the merits of an indirect sex discrimination claim, whether women are more likely to be turned down for that kind of treatment than men would be. And the answer here would surely be yes, they are. And then you'd have to look at the basis of why the policy that the employer was applying didn't give the individual what they wanted. So, for example, what was the problem with taking sick pay? If you get a certain number of days sick pay a year, was there a discretionary basis which the employer could apply? If not, the question it would come down to - because I think you probably could establish disparate impact fairly easily - is what the justification is for not doing that. And I think one would really have to know what the employer was thinking of when they said their legitimate aim is to have all employer employees in the workplace at all the time, and it's proportionate for us to have some kind of bar, regardless of the need for it.

If I were doing a case like that, I would look at all of the other reasons for healthcare-related absence which were covered. There could be a whole range of things from physiotherapy to covering time off from recovering from operations. So you'd really want to get the evidence base and look at the employer's sickness absence policy and the occasions on which they were prepared to pay full pay for medically related absence. If you could show men undergoing medical treatment for a gender-specific medical condition had treated more favourably, you'd have the basis of a direct discrimination claim.

Daniel Barnett
Rachel Crasnow, thank you very much.

GIG ECONOMY WORKERS AND THE UBER CASE

JASON GALBRAITH-MARTEN QC, CLOISTERS

Daniel Barnett

I'm joined today by Jason Galbraith-Marten QC from Cloisters. Jason is going to be talking about the *Uber* case *(Uber BV and others v Aslam and others [2021] UKSC 5)*.

The *Uber* decision was handed down on Friday 19th March, and as you almost certainly know, it held that Uber drivers are workers. The Supreme Court said that tribunals are expected to look at the reality of the situation, the purpose of the statute, the minimum wage legislation, the whistleblowing legislation and the annual leave legislation. The purpose of all that legislation is to protect vulnerable workers and make sure they get minimum wage, and if workers are subordinate enough that they can't negotiate the terms and conditions under which they're engaged - such as Uber drivers who had to sign the standard Uber contract - that can very realistically be a pointer towards needing the very protection, such as the minimum wage, that the statute is there to give people in subordinate positions.

So the Supreme Court essentially said that you don't look at the contract as your starting point to see what the true relationship is between the parties. In fact, you don't look at the contract, really, at all to see what the relationship is. You look at the question from the other angle: are these people the sort of people who deserve the protection of the law and deserve the protection of worker status? Now Jason Galbraith-Marten is pretty much Mr Status at the moment. He's been in most of the leading

cases over the last year or so on employment status. He was in *B v Yodel (B v Yodel Delivery Network Ltd (C-692/19) [2020] IRLR 550)* in the CJEU, previously known as the ECJ, of course, he was in Uber in the Supreme Court, he was in *Varnish v British Cycling (Varnish v British Cycling Federation [2020] IRLR 822)* last summer. In fact, very shortly, he's back in the Supreme Court arguing the case of *Police Service of Northern Ireland v Agnew (Chief Constable of the Police Service of Northern Ireland v Agnew [2019] NICA 32)*, which covers the employment status of police officers.

Jason, do you want to just take a couple of minutes to summarise what the *Uber* case decided, and then we'll go to questions.

Jason Galbraith-Marten

In very simple terms, as most of you know, on Friday, the Supreme Court dismissed Uber's appeal, upholding the decision of the Employment Tribunal, which in turn had been upheld by the EAT and the Court of Appeal, confirming that the claimants in that case were workers for the purposes of the Working Time Regulations, National Minimum Wage legislation and also for the purposes of the Employment Rights Act and in particular, the right to bring a whistleblowing claim. The case will now go back to the Employment Tribunal to determine those claims on their merits. This was of course only a preliminary hearing, and there are lots of issues that will no doubt arise at the Employment Tribunal, for example, the

113

calculation of minimum wage for people such as my clients.

That short description, though, doesn't really do justice to the importance of the case. Because this wasn't just a case that upheld *Autoclenz (Autoclenz v Belcher & Ors [2011] UKSC 41)* and doesn't really say anything else. It goes quite a lot further than that. It was, in my view, a belt and braces win for the Claimants. In football parlance, it was a complete thumping for Uber. There were three main strands to the decision, and all of them are important in their own way, and they pretty much cover the full range of interest to lawyers. So for the black letter lawyers out there, there was the first strand on which Uber lost: the straightforward agency argument. We don't employ these drivers, said Uber, we're only their agent. They contract directly with passengers. No, said the Supreme Court in a unanimous decision. The lack of a written agreement appointing Uber as the agent is pretty much fatal. Yes, it's true, you can infer agency from conduct, but there was nothing here in the evidence that justifies such a finding, and more importantly, the regulatory regime - that which regulates minicab drivers in London, but also, in the rest of the UK - almost certainly requires that the operator, Uber in this case, which is the one that's authorised to accept bookings, does act as principal and not as agent. So for the black letter lawyers and agency lawyers out there, strand one found in favour of the workers.

Then the second strand, the *Autoclenz* strand that Daniel's just mentioned, is probably of more interest to us. Ever since I started as an employment lawyer, there's been a debate raging: is the employment contract the same as or different from other kinds of contracts? Do normal contract rules apply? Some cases say yes, some cases say no. Well, here we've got the Supreme Court unequivocally saying no, usual contract rules do not apply and an employment contract - an employment relationship - is not the

same as a normal contractual relationship. Daniel's already highlighted the buzz words that we're all going to take away from the Supreme Court judgment. The employment relationship is characterised by 'subordination' and 'dependency' on the one hand, and the correlative of that, said Lord Leggett, 'control' on the other - control by the putative employer over working conditions and pay. It's the nature of that hierarchical relationship, borrowing language from the Court of Justice of the EU, that means those in such a situation ought to be protected by employment legislation. The language of *Autoclenz* was slightly different. The language of *Autoclenz* asked us to look for 'the true agreement between the parties': if the true agreement of the parties is that this is a working relationship, then the tribunal's entitled to say fine, and to determine that the written agreement is a sham. We've moved away from that. This is a fuller explanation, said Lord Leggett, of the reasoning of the Supreme Court in *Autoclenz*. This is all about statutory interpretation and the need to protect individuals who are in that vulnerable situation. So that's the purposive strand of the judgment.

Then the novel strand, one I have to confess no one really argued that strongly. The idea that the contracting out provisions in various pieces of employment legislation - we all know you're not allowed to contract out of employment law rights - has effects so that any provision in a contract of employment, whether directly or indirectly preventing someone from bringing a claim before the employment tribunal, is void. In the past, we've thought that only applies to a straightforward term that says 'you're not allowed to bring a claim for unfair dismissal' (for example). No, says Lord Leggett - and I must admit he asked me a question about this during the course of the hearing, so we might have seen this one coming, though it wasn't at the forefront of our submissions - anything in a contract that either directly or indirectly has the effect of preventing someone getting to an employment tribunal is void and unenforceable.

So on those three strands, Uber lose.

Where do we go from here? Something really interesting to pick up is that on Friday, in The Guardian, Matthew Taylor, formerly the Government's 'Employment Rights Enforcement Tsar', but who is no longer in position, was bemoaning the fact that although the Government at the time of his Good Work Review said they were all in favour of his findings and recommendations, they had really been dragging their heels and done nothing to implement them. If you go back and look at that Taylor Review, on page 36 he talked about the essence of the employment relationship being about the degree of control exercised over individuals by putative employers. Parliament may well have been dragging its heels in relation to that; perhaps now the Supreme Court's done the job for them. That language of control is now central to the test for employment status and we don't need to wait for Parliament to do it.

One last thing: who does this affect? Strictly speaking, of course, just the claimants in the Uber case. I think it's much more important than that. It sets a precedent not just for Uber drivers, but for workers generally. Interestingly, Uber have come out and said that they think the decision only applies to those that were parties to the claim. I have to say, I think that's pretty outrageous. I think that given the thumping they got in the Supreme Court, it is disingenuous to suggest that that ruling only applies to those that were parties to the claim. I think if what they're relying on is tinkering with the written agreements to plug the gaps that they think Lord Leggett identified, then they are failing to grasp the spirit of this decision. They're really missing the central point of it, I'm very clear that this decision applies generally not just to the parties to this particular claim. So that's where we are. I'm happy to take some questions.

Patrick McNamee
If a person is an Uber driver, what can they now do to obtain the money they're owed?

Jason Galbraith-Marten
So assuming you are talking about an Uber driver that's not a party to the litigation, obviously - there was a small group that were - as I mentioned, it looks like Uber are going to say that the judgment does not apply generally, and can I just say, this is a feature I've noticed of these employment status cases. Let me tell you a little anecdote. I also represented the CitySprint courier in the *Dewhurst* case (*Dewhurst v Citysprint UK Ltd [2017] 1 WLUK 16*). We won that case for Mags Dewhurst. CitySprint appealed to the EAT, and a matter of days before the EAT hearing, they withdrew their appeal because they said they had rewritten their terms and conditions, and they no longer accepted that the decision of the employment tribunal had any relevance at all, and nor would the decision of the EAT because it wouldn't apply to the new terms as written.

We're seeing this pattern, with Uber now saying, well, the factual situation currently is different from the factual situation back in 2016, and therefore, the decision of the Supreme Court doesn't apply. It sounds like it's very unlikely Uber are going to automatically recognise that drivers have these rights, and individuals are going to have to certainly threaten to litigate or potentially even litigate. I've got no doubt that there will be any number of unions and solicitors ready, willing and able to bring class actions. I know that Leigh Day, who were acting with the GMB, will be keen to do that. I know that the ADCU, the union that my clients James Farrar and Yaseen Aslam have set up, are very keen to do so, and of course, the IWGB are also very keen to do so. So the short answer is: if Uber don't give you the money you're entitled to look up one of those trade unions and join it.

Allyn Walton
Was there any merit at all to the Underhill LJ minority view in the Court of Appeal,

saying that Uber is no different to how all taxi companies actually operate, as it's well established that most minicab drivers are not workers?

Daniel Barnett
Just pausing for a moment, Lord Justice Underhill gave the minority decision in the Court of Appeal, and he held that Uber drivers were not workers.

Jason Galbraith-Marten
Two points to that, really. First of all, the Supreme Court did not accept that it's well established that this is how all minicab firms operate. The two cases that were cited to them that dealt specifically with minicab drivers - the *Mingely v Pennock* case (*Mingely v Pennock (t/a Amber Cars) [2004] ICR 727*) and the *Khan v Checkers* case (*Khan v Checkers Cars Ltd [2005] UKEAT 0208/05/1612*) - neither of those were thought to be of any great assistance, and Lord Leggett came as close as you can to saying that they're probably wrong, that he disagreed effectively with some of the observations of the judges in those cases, and he expressly said he wasn't satisfied that evidence had been adduced to show what the usual practice was in relation to minicab firms. He also said, of course, that the regulatory regime on his reading of it, and he didn't finally decide the point, but on his reading of it, he thought the regulatory regime meant that you have to contract as an operator as principal. In other words, you can't have an agency relationship.

So that's really one answer to it. But more specifically, the important thing that Underhill LJ decided in the Court of Appeal in his dissenting judgment, was that the *Autoclenz* principle only applies where you can show there is a true inconsistency between what it says in the written agreement, and what the parties do in practice. So, if what the parties do practice is consistent with a written agreement, you cannot disregard the written agreement. It effectively determines the

situation. That was the real import of what Underhill LJ had to say in the Court of Appeal, and that Lord Leggett absolutely says is wrong. This is where he comes back to his 'statutory interpretation' rather than 'contractual interpretation' answer to this case. It's not about looking to see whether you can identify some inconsistency between what happens in practice and what it says in the contract. It's about, as Daniel said right at the beginning, looking to identify the type of relationship that's an issue, and whether that's the type of relationship that Parliament intended be covered by statutory employment protection. If it's the type of employment relationship that falls within the ambit of statutory employment protection, then you can effectively chuck the contract out the window. So absolutely, Leggett says Underhill LJ got it wrong.

Daniel Barnett
We've got a couple of questions that deal with that particular point.

Mike Clyne
Do you think this will affect the professional services gig economy, or do you think it will more affect those in the Uber-type roles such as app-based workers?

Anonymous
What are the implications for workers who aren't vulnerable, such as a consultant solicitor engaged by a law firm?

Jason Galbraith-Marten
I think those raise a similar point, which is: looking at the sort of people who are self-employed, but not necessarily those that we think of as being generally vulnerable. So whether it's a consultant with a solicitor's firm or anyone else involved in professional services. I think that's why the three buzzwords are so important. The domestic buzzwords are now 'subordination', 'dependency' and 'control', and the EU buzzwords were 'hierarchical relationship', but amounting to much the same sort of thing. And there is a

plain difference between those who are in that subordinate and dependent relationship - Matthew Taylor talked about those being the 'dependent contractors' - and those who are not in that dependent relationship, like the arbitrators in *Hashwani v Jivraj (Jivraj v Hashwani [2011] ICR 1004)*. Obviously, where that line is drawn in any particular case will be a matter of fact for an employment tribunal, but we understand at least, and are clear now about, the principled basis on which you would divide those two groups.

Julie Norris

Some contracts contain a clause stating that the individual will indemnify the company against all costs and any award if there's a claim. Are those sorts of clauses valid?

Jason Galbraith-Marten

I've been asked this so many times. I've seen so many contracts, and pretty much every one that I've dealt with in worker status cases has something similar: 'You're not an employee or worker, but if you sue us and it turns out you are, you'll pay us every single penny that you get when you establish that you are a worker or an employee'. In the past, we've thought of various ways in which that might not be enforceable - public policy grounds: does it infringe the restriction against contracting out? - and in the past, I must admit, I've taken a rather narrow view that the restrictions on contracting out would not invalidate those sorts of clauses. As soon as I saw the Supreme Court judgment, the first thought I had was, those sorts of clauses are now done. The third strand of Lord Leggett's argument that anything that either directly or indirectly prevents someone bringing a claim before an Employment Tribunal, where otherwise they'd be entitled to, is void and unenforceable, and absolutely, I think that captures those sorts of indemnity clauses now.

Sundeep Bhatia

Do you think the decision regarding when the drivers were workers in relation to when they were on call would be different in 2021, due to there being other similar companies that drivers can drive for?

Daniel Barnett

I think Sundeep is talking about the possibility of having multiple apps on at the same time.

Jason Galbraith-Marten

This was a point that really came to the fore in the EAT and the Court of Appeal. The idea that drivers can 'multi-app' was the phrase that we all landed on, the idea that a driver can have not only the Uber app open, but Addison Lee open, or Kapten, or any number of minicab companies now, driving around and take whichever trip request comes first. Does that influence the situation? And the reason we're being asked whether it's any different in 2021 from 2016, is at the time this case was determined in 2016, there weren't so many of those other platforms operating, and both of my clients did only work for Uber. It can't be right, said Uber in the appeal courts, because you've got the right to multi-app, that you can be working for us just because you've got the app on. That would mean in practice, you're working for us and all those other people, and we will all have to pay you minimum wage, and that can't possibly be right. Our primary response was this just wasn't argued before the Employment Tribunal, so we don't have the facts on which to base any argument or decision.

However my view has always been it's a bad argument anyway. I don't see any problem at all with the idea that you can work for a number of different employers at the same time. And yes, it might be a bit messy to work out who has to pay you and what, but I think that's an administrative problem rather than a problem of principle. As we all know, it's possible to have more than one boss - if you saw the James Corden play 'One Man, Two Guvnors', it can happen. How was it dealt with in the appeal courts? It came up and I have to say, none of them really gave a definitive answer. So none of the EAT, Court of Appeal or Supreme Court. In part because we didn't have sufficient factual material in front of us to enable them to give a principled decision as I have already mentioned. But if given the chance to argue it again on different facts, I'm pretty confident I could find a way through. You'll probably remember there is a decision of the CJEU that says it's not the responsibility of the employee to work out a solution to working time problems; it's the responsibility of the employer. And the short answer is Uber does so many incredibly sophisticated things with its software, it can't be beyond its reach to work out when drivers are genuinely willing and able to accept rides from Uber and therefore to be accountable in working time terms for that.

Caroline Lewis

In your argument, did you differentiate your Uber clients from Deliveroo drivers who've been found to be self-employed? Is it arguable that the Uber decision could now be applied to Deliveroo drivers?

Jason Galbraith-Marten

There is a really important distinction between the Deliveroo case and Uber. In Uber, personal service was not an issue: minicab drivers, because of the regulatory regime, have to be licensed. And anyone who's ever used an Uber will know, you're sent a message on your phone telling you the name of the driver that's coming to pick you up and the registration of their car, and only that person can drive that car on their licence. So there's no question at all of substituting in Uber. And everything that's said in Uber assumes personal service. Deliveroo lost, you'll remember, in the CAC, on the basis that there was a genuine right to substitute.

I am clear that both the domestic legislation and the case law requires that for someone to be a worker, there's got to be an obligation on them to undertake work personally. And in the words of McKenna, in the *Ready Mixed Concrete* case (*Ready Mixed Concrete Ltd*

v Minister of Pensions [1968] 2 QB 497), 'freedom to do work by one's own hand or by another's' is inconsistent with an employment relationship. I think that is still right. If you contract with someone to do work and that person has the right to either do the work themselves or send along someone else to do it in their place, they cannot be a worker. They fall on the wrong side of the line.

Now, that was the factual finding that was made in Deliveroo. As I understand it, and Alan Bogg was posting about this at the end of last week, it's gone up to the European Court of Human Rights in relation to the Article 11 point - the freedom of association point - I don't know yet, whether that's been heard or when we're due to get a decision from it. But we did have some argument in *B v Yodel* about whether this provision of domestic law - that essentially, if there's no obligation of personal service that's fatal to finding worker status - whether that was inconsistent with EU law. And the CJEU did not say that it was.

Jason Braier

Given the five key factors the Supreme Court found in the driver's favour, can we next expect a claim by the drivers to show they are employees?

Jason Galbraith-Marten

So, there's no doubt there were five key factual findings that were identified by Lord Leggett to suggest that this was an employment relationship. Again, two really interesting points to make about that.

The first point to note is that I understand that's why Uber is saying the decision doesn't apply now, because some of those facts have changed. Most notably, for example, the fact that back in 2016, at the point at which drivers accepted a trip request, they didn't know the destination. I understand that's now been changed, so drivers are told the destination and can choose whether they want to accept it or not. For reasons I've already given, I don't think that change is sufficient to mean that the judgment doesn't apply to Uber drivers now.

The second point is that I think there is still a valid distinction to be made between a worker - the self-employed individual who's nonetheless in a dependent relationship, sufficient to amount to an employment relationship - as opposed to an employee in the narrow sense, someone employed under a contract of employment (a contract 'of service' rather than 'for services').

Now, I know when Matthew Taylor produced his report, he thought we should stick with the tripartite categorisation of employee, worker and the truly self-employed. Daniel, you were telling me over the weekend that he's moved away from that position and he now thinks we should have a more binary categorisation just 'employed' and 'self-employed'. Certainly, as far as EU law is concerned, the wider definition of 'worker' is the one that applies, and EU law is still relevant for us. So I can still see a place for that intermediate category.

Interestingly, when the Uber Employment Tribunal decision came out, I remember a couple of Uber drivers being interviewed and saying, 'We don't like this decision. We like being self-employed; we don't want to be employees', and thinking, you don't understand: you can be self-employed and be a worker. It's a really important point to make. I suspect most drivers will say, "Well, we don't want to be employees; we want to be workers. We want to be self-employed, with the benefits that come with that - flexibility on working time, choosing when we work, not having to turn up at times dictated by Uber - and we're willing to give up, for example, the right to claim unfair dismissal, for that flexibility". So at the moment, I don't see drivers arguing specifically that they are employees rather than workers.

Gillian Howard
Given Uber, what can employers now do to try to establish someone as an independent contractor if the contract is irrelevant?

Jason Galbraith-Marten
I love the way that question has been phrased. And it reminds me of the number of times I've been instructed to redraft contracts to ensure that 'someone isn't a worker'. And my short answer is always: I can't do that; I can't just tinker around without knowing what really happens, the real nature of the relationship, just so as to avoid a finding of worker status. That would make me one of the 'armies of lawyers' that the then Mr. Justice Elias spoke about in the *Kalwak* case (*Consistent Group Ltd v Kalwak [2008] IRLR 505*). So what can employers do? Well, what employers can do is they can ensure that their written agreements properly reflect the relationship that they have with individuals who do work for them. Brian Langstaff said something about this in an industrial Law Journal article: you have to make a choice. Do you want to exercise a significant degree of control over those people that you have working for you, delivering services for you, and do you want them in a subordinate independent working relationship? Because if you do, they come within the ambit of the employment protection. If you want to avoid that state of affairs, then you can't have them in a subordinate relationship with you, you can't have them dependent on you, and you can't exercise a significant degree of control over them. Your choice as an employer is over what kind of relationship you want with the person delivering services on your behalf. And they're either within or without the statutory protection - that's your choice. It won't just be a matter of tinkering with the contract.

Shaun Duffy
Can claims be brought against Uber for the minimum wage in the County Court if the claims are out of time in the employment tribunal or limited by the two-year rule?

Daniel Barnett
There's some doubt, by the way, about whether the two-year rule is legal.

Jason Galbraith-Marten

I don't know the answer to that off top of my head, I haven't looked at whether National Minimum Wage claims can be brought in the county court, so I'm going to park that one I'm afraid.

Adam Turner
Does the decision apply to employees as much as workers?
Daniel Barnett

So, I think rather than asking whether people can be categorised as employees or why the Uber drivers aren't employees, he's asking in a more general sense.

Jason Galbraith-Marten

I think it does in broad terms. We know that prior to the Uber decision, the distinction between an 'employee' and a 'worker' was narrowing all the time anyway. Lord Justice Underhill, very famously said that the tests are essentially the same; there's just a slightly lower pass mark if you're seeking to establish that you're a worker rather than an employee. So you still have to show that there's an obligation of personal service, there's mutuality of obligation that's consistent with an employment relationship, other features of the relationship are not inconsistent with a contract of employment or worker contract. I must admit, I always struggled to know exactly what a 'lower pass mark' meant when you're applying it practically in an Employment Tribunal; what is a 'lower pass mark' in the context of personal service, for example? But that's the position we've got to. And if that's right, and a number of cases have said so, that the tests are essentially the same, then whatever's said in Uber, I think is just as applicable if you're seeking to establish that you are an employee working under a contract of employment,

Anonymous

What is your guess on the future of Uber? Will they revamp their business? Will this be the end of their business due to fines they might owe?

Jason Galbraith-Marten

It's a great question. It's not particularly a legal question and therefore I don't know that I'm necessarily the best person to answer it, although I've got a view about it. We know because of the press release that they've put out they're saying the judgment doesn't apply to current drivers; they're going to try and do a 'CitySprint' it seems, and say, well, we're not going to honour this decision in relation to any of our other drivers. But let's assume that either they recognise the spirit of the case and they decide to do so or enough people bring claims so that it makes a material difference to their business model.

Where do they go from here? There's no doubt that Uber is super cheap. We all use it and we all know that it's super cheap because the drivers are being paid so little. And if it means prices have to go up, and that's the cost to us the consumer of ensuring that workers are afforded the statutory rights that the Supreme Court said they're entitled to, then I personally think that's a price worth paying. What I'd hope, of course, is that Uber will absorb some of the cost themselves, rather than just passing on the cost directly to consumers. But I think they're so well embedded, not just in London now but elsewhere, that I can't see they're going to disappear. They might just become a little bit more expensive.

Henry Clinton-Davis

Does the Uber decision impact clients who engage contractors working through personal service companies, where under the new off-payroll working rules, clients need to assess whether those contractors are really employees? And if the answer is yes, do you have to put them on payroll from April?

Jason Galbraith-Marten

I think the answer to that is yes. The IR35 regime, effectively, all it does is it transfer the responsibility for assessing whether someone ought to be paying tax as an employee or they're truly self-employed, it transfers that responsibility from an intermediary such as a Personal Service Company to the employer. The regime is being extended to the private sector but even in relation to the public sector, the employment tests that we apply to decide whether someone was a worker or an employee, were those used. The extent to which the test has now changed as a result of the Uber decision will impact on the employer's assessment of whether someone falls within or without the definition of an employee. As a matter of practicality - and others will have more experience with this than me - but as a matter of practicality, it seems that employers, out of an abundance of caution, wherever they think someone might be an employee are treating them as an employee, because it's just easier for them to do it and not take the risk. So if what that means is they're going to be even more cautious going forward, I think that's probably the right effect of the Uber decision.

Jason Springer
Has Uber closed your account down yet?

Jason Galbraith-Marten
I happily take Ubers, because I know that I'm providing drivers with a source of income, but I feel obliged to tip them very generously now because I know how badly they get paid! I had to use a Pimlico Plumber very recently. A Pimlico Plumber came round to my house to fix some central heating. It was post the Supreme Court decision in that case (*Pimlico Plumbers Ltd v Smith [2018] UKSC 29*), and I said to the plumber, not wanting to give away that I was an employment lawyer; you must be very happy, I understand that you get paid holiday and all sorts of things like that. No, said the plumber. Well didn't that chap win the case in the Supreme Court? No. We were told he lost by Chris Mullins. If you remember the case was remitted to the employment tribunal and the individual lost his claim because it was presented out of time, notwithstanding the fact that he won on issue of principle. And that's what we fear Uber might now do: tell their drivers that it doesn't really apply to them, it

only applies to the half dozen or so people that brought claims. So no, they haven't closed the account yet, Jason, but thanks for asking.

Derian Kymes
Does the Uber decision leave the Pimlico Plumbers decision open for any sort of challenge?

Jason Galbraith-Marten
I don't see that it does because in the Supreme Court, they actually found in favour of Mr Smith, that he was in fact a worker for the purposes of the relevant statutory provisions. He only lost in the ET because his claim was presented out of time.

Pimlico Plumbers, though, was really about personal service, it was about whether the individual could substitute and you may remember that in the Court of Appeal, Terrence Etherton, the Master of the Rolls reviewed all of the cases on personal service. And I don't mean any disrespect to him, but he hadn't really said anything new about them, he had just summarised the case law to date. And what we were all hoping was that the Supreme Court would say something very interesting about the determinative nature of personal service. And rather disappointingly, they didn't. They decided the case purely on the basis of the written agreement and the facts of that case. So, if anything Uber goes further than Pimlico Plumbers did in terms of developing the law, in terms of the principled argument.

Val Stansfield
Does the Uber decision now mean that Uber drivers must have a statement of terms and conditions, in line with the revisions to s1 Employment Rights Act 1996, last year?

Jason Galbraith-Marten
Yes, I assume it does.

Daniel Barnett
It must do. Presumably, though, the incredibly detailed contracts they already have would pretty much tick every box.

Jason Galbraith-Marten

They would. I haven't looked at the detail of that, but those agreements would cover most of the statutory particulars that are required in a statement. I suppose the curious question is: the agreements relied on as evidencing an agency relationship - and it specifically and expressly provided individuals aren't workers - so whether you could rely on a document that says you're not a worker as providing the particulars that are required to show that you are a worker? It would be a nice black letter question, I think. But in principle, yes, absolutely, Uber are now required to issue that. And that's why I think they're saying we don't believe it still applies. So presumably, they're not intending to do so.

Daniel Barnett

Ruth Christie has helpfully added to the statement of terms conditions point that of course, only new workers are entitled to a new statement of particulars; existing workers aren't.

Dave Chaplin

Can we now ignore the fact that there's a limited company interposed between worker and end user, as seen in *James v Greenwich Borough Council (James v Greenwich London Borough Council [2008] EWCA Civ 35)*?

Jason Galbraith-Marten

For the most part, I think so. I mean, if it's a pure personal service company, it only exists in order to provide the services of the individual, then I think, then, yes. Obviously, if it's a genuine limited company, and that's going to be a factual inquiry, a genuine limited company that employs people - in some of the driving cases, for example, you've got a company that provides its own drivers and a number of them, albeit under a single contract with the putative employer - then, of course, that factual matrix is very different, and I suspect will lead to a finding that an individual is not an employee or a worker. But insofar as it's a pure personal service company, I know

there's been some authorities going both ways in relation to this - BBC personnel have been looked at in relation to it - but I think I'm pretty confident that if it's a pure personal service company, you can effectively ignore that.

Anonymous

Can you explain the rationale of the decision that drivers are entitled to minimum wage and other rights when the app is on, even if they haven't got a passenger in their cab?

Jason Galbraith-Marten

A number of the judges found this a difficult point. They all said so, HHJ Eadie, in the EAT said she found it a difficult point to resolve and all right up to and including the Supreme Court said the same sort of thing. There was a binary choice really, and I think that really gives you the rationale behind it. It was a binary choice between on the one hand Uber saying drivers only working when they're in fact, driving someone - they were prepared to be a little bit flexible and say it's from the point at which they've accepted a trip request, i.e., they've agreed that they will pick someone up - so their binary position was 'only when in fact working' as opposed to 'also when available to accept a trip request'. And you might remember the Employment Tribunal, in fabulously colourful and descriptive language, used the expression "they also serve who stand and wait", in support of it's finding that drivers are working whilst they are available to accept a trip request not just when they're actually driving a passenger to a destination.

So, essentially, the Supreme Court had to say it's one or the other, and they came down on the side of 'you're working not just when actually driving but also whilst you making yourself available to accept trip requests'. Lord Leggett, in fact, cited some of those cases on whether availability time counts as working time eg Firefighters who have to be on call or those in care homes who have to be on call. He didn't quite go as far as saying they are the same thing, being available to accept a trip request and being on call, but he said that if he had to go one way or the other, those cases push him towards 'if you're available to work, then that must count as your working time'.

This is where the multi-apping point raised its head, specifically. How can you be working for Uber when you're available to work for Uber if you're also available for Addison Lee, and you're also available for Kapten and the other apps. And that's where I say they didn't finally resolve the point, because they didn't have to on the facts that were in front of them. That's the one that I think is going to be tricky going forward - how you work that out. I think there is an answer to it. I'm not sure I can tell you exactly what it is at the moment, but I'm sure we'll find an answer to that problem. But I think that's the best I can do in terms of the rationale. It's either the narrow interpretation or the wide one, and we think it's more likely to be the wide than the narrow, so we're going to go that way. Ultimately, of course, they use the language of 'the employment tribunal was entitled to reach the findings that it did on this point'.

Anonymous
Other than with collective action, how does an Uber driver protect themselves if they've been threatened with dismissal?

Jason Galbraith-Marten
That's an interesting question. So how does one protect oneself if they've been threatened with dismissal? Clearly as workers they have certain protections, the right not to suffer a detriment for having made a protected disclosure for example. But how do they stop themselves being dismissed? I think that's a much tougher one. By collective action, I assume you mean other than by joining a trade union or associating yourself with others in some way? I have to say I've always been a collective lawyer. I did my pupillage under John Hendy and Jeremy McMullan, and I've always believed that's the best way of protecting yourself in the workplace. Don't try

and do it on your own, frankly. I can't think of anything off the top of my head over and above that, but if anyone's got any ideas, let me know.

Daniel Barnett
Of course, we know now that the impact of this decision is Uber drivers will have rights against discrimination or whistleblowing. Is it possible to take out an injunction to prevent a discrimination-based or whistleblowing-based dismissal?

Jason Galbraith-Marten
You'll remember *Edwards v Chesterfield (Edwards v Chesterfield Royal Hospital NHS Foundation Trust [2011] UKSC 58)*. Sir John Dyson at that time suggested that you can get an injunction to prevent disciplinary action being taken against you that's in breach of contract. So if disciplinary action is being threatened and a procedure is not being followed, then certainly an injunction is an available option to you. It's not a cheap or an easy one, obviously, and I'm not sure if it will assist most of the vulnerable individuals that we're talking about, but it's technically available. A bit more of a grey area as to whether you can get an injunction if what you're alleging is a breach of the trust and confidence term; so that you're not alleging a failure to constitute a panel in accordance with a written procedure for example, but that the way you're treating the individual is unfair. The view there appears to be no, your route's via the Employment Tribunal rather than the injunction route. But I think that's a bit of a grey area.

Daniel Barnett
Presumably, the remedy of interim relief wouldn't be available, because interim relief is associated with unfair dismissal - and that's only available to employees, not workers.

Jason Galbraith-Marten
It is. Although Chris Milsom did that very interesting case *(Steer v Stormsure Ltd*

UKEAT/0216/20/AT) recently about whether interim relief ought to be available in discrimination cases. Lost on the facts of the case, but the tribunal, I think, as you'll remember, held that UK law is out of sync with EU law in relation to that by not providing an interim relief remedy. So that's one to watch.

John Pascoe
If you're a contractor with multiple clients, and you invoice them for time worked, isn't that a key element indicating you're not an employee or worker, especially if you control when you're on or off an app with multiple apps? So can't Uber remodel their arrangement to insist their contractors use multiple apps?

Jason Galbraith-Marten
So again, fascinating. Lots of potential answers to that. First of all, it was recognised even at the Employment Tribunal that Uber could arrange their affairs in such a way so as to avoid a finding that their drivers are their workers. And just to hark back to one of the earlier questions, the one from Gillian Howard, I think: how can employers now draft contracts in a way that avoids a finding of employment status? Well, they need to decide what kind of relationship they want. And if Uber want less control over the product, and they genuinely want to contract with independent contractors, they can construct a model that looks like that.

Looking specifically at the multi-apping point, as to whether Uber can insist that someone multi-app, and the idea that a contractor can have multiple clients. It's really a factual point, isn't it? What we've always recognised is that the extent to which an individual is able to market their services to the world in general, is a factor that's taken into account by a tribunal in its factual assessment of whether that person is a worker i.e. are you genuinely in that subordinate and dependent position vis-a-vis any particular employer?

Lord Leggett did approve that Lord Justice Underhill said in the *Windle* case (*Secretary of State for Justice v Windle and Arada [2016] EWCA Civ 459*), that the gaps between assignments - i.e. the extent to which you work truly casually, or intermittently for any particular employer - is a relevant factor to be taken into account. So, how many clients have you got? Can you market yourself to the world in general? How intermittently do you work? These are factors that can be taken account in answering the factual question. And the more freedom you've got in that respect, the less likely it is you'll be found to be a worker. Subject to this caveat: Lord Leggett did recognise that the mere fact you've got flexibility about when you work or how much work you do, in and of itself isn't decisive in deciding whether you're a worker. And in fact, he said he disagreed with the *Khan v Checkers* case and the Mingeley case on that specific point.

Connie Cliff
Have you heard whether HMRC are going to take any investigation and enforcement action over the underpayment of the National Minimum Wage?

Jason Galbraith-Marten
Only what I read over the weekend, and there was lots of speculation in the financial pages of papers over the weekend that HMRC would, not only in relation to National Minimum Wage, but also in relation to VAT. Because if Uber is a principal in the supply of driving services, then it ought to have accounted for VAT rather than the drivers themselves. So there is lots of speculation that HMRC, with empty coffers to fill, might now look to Uber in various ways to see whether they can be recovered.

Daniel Barnett
I suspect - and I in no way speak for him - but if HMRC don't do anything about this, Jolyon Maugham, and the Good Law Project might want to look at judicially reviewing HMRC's failure to do so. I know that they're currently challenging the failure of Uber to charge and pass on VAT to the Revenue and Customs Service.

Anonymous

Can Uber now ask that their workers don't multi-app? I'm not sure why they'd want to ask that, but as a matter of law, can Uber say you work for us and us only when the app is on?

Jason Galbraith-Marten

That's interesting, isn't it? Presumably, the basis of that question is, if Uber is going to acknowledge that its drivers are workers, it will want to exercise more control over them, and it will want to stop them working for competitors: 'If we have to give you holiday pay, if we have to give you a National Minimum Wage, well you're only going to work for us then'. And they might use that, commercially, as a way of trying to put their rivals out of business. So in practice, can you require that your drivers do not work for others? Obviously, if you think of it as a zero-hours contract, any provision in the zero-hours contract that prevented you working for another provider of work would not be enforceable. But I think if Uber wanted to go the full employment route, if they wanted to say these individuals are employees and say they've got to work set times - your shift is a nine-to-five daytime shift - and they inserted a clause that during your working hours, you were to devote your time and attention to the work for Uber, I think that probably would be lawful. So not if it's a zero-hours contract. Yes, if they go all the way and say yes, you're our employees. Neither of those, I have to say, look likely at the moment, but yes, in principle.

David Price

Does the Uber decision in respect of working time provide any indication as to what to expect from the Supreme Court in the forthcoming decision in *Mencap v Tomlinson-Blake (Royal Mencap Society v Tomlinson-Blake* [2018] EWCA Civ 1641)?

Daniel Barnett

I think I see what David's getting at here, because of that part of the decision which covered on-call time. In essence Mencap is about whether people who are sleeping over at care homes or sleeping at their own home near a care home but on call, whether they're entitled to the National Minimum Wage for the periods when they're on call, but asleep. So does Uber give any indication as to which way the Supreme Court will jump in Mencap?

From memory, the Mencap case was heard in the Supreme Court before Uber, and I can't remember off top of my head how the court was constituted - as to whether it's the same or similar. But in theory, it's symbiotic, isn't it? Lord Leggett, in Uber, relies on what's said in the on-call working time cases in support of the conclusions that he reached in *Uber*. Does it work the other way? Does it reflect back? Certainly one would have thought, just speaking off top of my head, if a driver is working whilst he's got an app on and driving around, if working time extends to that individual in that circumstance, it's very likely to extend to someone who's in a care home and required to be there on call, whether sleeping or not. So I would have thought that it suggests that that case will go a certain way. I don't think I could say any more than that.

Anonymous

What are the time limit issues that new Uber Claimants would need to be aware of?

Jason Galbraith-Marten

So whilst they're continuing to work, obviously, time limits are not an issue. They can put in a claim at any time in respect of their current employment. As Daniel's already highlighted, there's controversy over how far you can go back, for example, in relation to claims for holiday pay. The interesting question that will be decided in *Agnew v PSNI*, the *Bear Scotland (Bear Scotland Ltd v David Fulton UKEATS/0047/13/BI)* question of whether a break of three months or more disentitles you from going back in relation to a series of deductions, so all of those issues that might flow in relation to someone that's currently in employment. Obviously, someone who's no longer working will be subject to the usual time limits. The interesting question that arises in relation to an Uber driver is given that there's no obligation on them to work, they can stop working, if you like, without necessarily ceasing to be one of Uber's workers, but do a day's work, you know, so I haven't done anything for Uber for a little while, but I'll do a day's work for them, and then say, time only begins to run from that day's work that I've done. So if still working, not a problem, if you've left, you might have to do a day's work in order to reinstate your right to bring a claim if you're outside the primary limitation period.

GRIEVANCES

DARREN NEWMAN,
DARREN NEWMAN EMPLOYMENT LAW

Daniel Barnett

I'm joined by Darren Newman, an employment law consultant, for this webinar on grievances.

Darren Newman, good morning. Let's start with a couple of questions from me. How do you deal with an employee who persistently raises grievances over the same or similar issues?

Darren Newman

Carefully and patiently but efficiently. I think the first thing to stress when dealing with grievances is that there's actually rather less law on this than lots of people think. It's not like a disciplinary process where you're potentially going to dismiss someone, you've got unfair dismissal rights and you've got to demonstrate that you've done something in a fair way to defend yourself against that sort of claim. There isn't that much law about what a grievance procedure has to contain.

We know that the written statement of terms and conditions has to give you a note that tells you who to speak to if you've got a grievance and tell you what the procedure is. There's an Acas Code of Practice that sets out a fair approach to grievances which is very light and really just tells you that you've got to have a meeting with the employee, and possibly adjourn for an investigation, but have a meeting, a determination and a right to appeal. And of course, there's a contractual right to have your grievances addressed. None of that necessarily means that you've got to

have a very detailed, very time-consuming grievance procedure.

Hopefully, if the grievance procedure that you have is relatively flexible, you can deal with serial grievances relatively quickly simply by going straight to the grievance meeting. If someone is raising a grievance that is incredibly similar to a grievance they've already raised and that has already been dealt with, then just arrange a meeting with them. Have a meeting, listen to what they have to say and decide what you're going to do. If they've raised something that makes you concerned, then by all means, have an investigation. But if what they saying is essentially something you think has already been dealt with, then say that. Tell them that that's the outcome and tell them that they've got the right to appeal. I don't see why that should be a particularly difficult or time-consuming thing to do.

It becomes more tricky if you've got a very cumbersome, inflexible grievance procedure that requires you to launch an investigation as soon as any grievance is raised. My advice is not to have one of those procedures. But if you do, by and large, you're going to have to follow the procedure you've got.

Daniel Barnett

You said it's quite difficult to actually recognise a grievance. You, me and the other ancient people amongst us will remember the statutory grievance procedures from 2002 to 2004, when you had to prove to a tribunal that you'd lodged a grievance before you were allowed to bring a tribunal claim. And as a result, the tribunals basically said anything was a grievance in order to allow people to bring their claims. So if you've got up and sneezed in the morning, the tribunals will say that was a grievance.

Darren Newman
I think a lot of the issues that people have with grievances have their roots in those dispute resolution procedures that were repealed by the Employment Act 2008, with effect from April 2009.

There are fossil remains of those statutory grievance procedures because a lot of people drafted quite complex grievance procedures to deal with the statute dispute resolution procedures. And they remember all that case law about having to deal with a grievance even if it's raised very informally, having to infer that something's a grievance even when that's not necessarily what was intended. Those are repealed now, so it shouldn't be something that we worry about too much. You really can be quite sensible and efficient about dealing with a grievance that someone has raised.

Daniel Barnett
Can you discipline an employee if you think that their grievance was malicious?

Darren Newman
The problem is with 'think', isn't it? I think most employers would regard raising a malicious grievance as misconduct, or potentially gross misconduct, and I think that's fair enough. The problem is demonstrating that it's a malicious grievance and identifying the difference between a grievance that is wholly mistaken, possibly irrational and wholly unreasonable in what it's asserting, and one that is actually malicious. That's to do with the motivation of the employee. You've got to get inside the head of the employee and figure out why they've raised this grievance. That's a very difficult thing to do.

The risk that you face is that a large number of grievances will be concerned with discrimination issues or they might be making an allegation about the employer that will amount to a public interest disclosure - whistleblowing. If they do, then any detriment that you subject somebody to as a result of raising that grievance is going to be either victimisation or an unlawful detriment under the whistleblowing provisions. So the risk that you're facing in disciplining someone who's making a malicious allegation is potentially quite a valuable claim. You've got to make sure that you're right. It's not going to be good enough to show that you reasonably think that this is a malicious allegation. You're going to have to persuade the tribunal that, in fact, it is a malicious allegation. And in the case of victimisation, you're also going to have to persuade the tribunal that it's a false allegation. Because it's perfectly possible that you can allege something that's true, but you allege it in bad faith. That in itself won't be enough to protect you against the victimization claim.

So by and large, my advice to employers is that unless it's a really stark claim, unless you've got it absolutely slam-dunked - there's an email somewhere that says, "I'm going to raise this malicious allegation! Ha ha ha! This is going to cause massive inconvenience for them!" Unless it's that clear, I wouldn't go down that route. I'd concentrate on dealing with the grievance as efficiently and quickly as I can and moving on. I think that's normally the best thing.

Daniel Barnett
What happens if an employee raises a grievance in the context of a disciplinary or performance management process? Have you got to put things on hold until the grievance is dealt with?

Darren Newman
Not generally. This is one of those issues that became a really tortured issue during

the currency of the statute dispute resolution procedures. The Acas Code of Practice agonised over exactly what you would do, and we all spend quite a lot of time trying to figure out how you could comply with both procedures that you have to comply with. Now that they've gone, I think the employer is free to deal with the issues in the way that best deals with the issues. So you have to look at the substance of the issues that you're dealing with and figure out the fairest way of dealing with them and the best way of limiting your risk in terms of employment law.

If you're going through a process of discipline or grievance, I think, generally speaking, it's better to get that process done. It's better to progress the disciplinary or performance issue and then deal with the grievance afterwards. And very often the thing that the grievance is concerned about, even if it's connected to the disciplinary, can best be dealt with in the disciplinary. So if, for example, you're saying that the reason you did that was because you were massively overworked and very stressed, and as a result, there was a lapse in your judgment. Well, that's a relevant factor for the disciplinary to take into account, so it seems to me that the most efficient way of dealing with that issue is to have the employee make that point in the disciplinary hearing, and the employer can then take it into account.

Where I'd be more careful is if there's something about the grievance that calls into question your ability to have a fair disciplinary process. So if for example, the grievance is that the person you've appointed to investigate this has been bullying the employee for the past two years and hates them, well, that's going to throw into doubt the reasonableness of the investigation. I would then want to look at whether there is substance to that grievance that makes me either want to change the investigator and get someone else to investigate it and then deal with the grievance later, or deal with the grievance first if that doesn't seem to be an option.

The priority should be on how you can best progress these things. You don't want to create a situation in which someone facing a gross misconduct charge, where they're going to get dismissed at the end of it, has a mechanism with which they can extend their suspension for another three months while you investigate their grievance. People are going to take that opportunity. So you don't want that to be an obvious option that people can take.

Daniel Barnett
Especially if they're on full pay, as they usually will be in that situation.

Darren Newman
Absolutely. And you really do need something contractual, if they're going to be suspended, not on full pay.

Daniel Barnett
Paragraph 46 of the ACAS Code of Practice touches on this. It says that where an employee raises a grievance during a disciplinary process, the disciplinary process MAY be - not MUST be - temporarily suspended to deal with the grievance. Where they're related, it may be appropriate to deal with both issues concurrently.

Darren Newman
I mean no offence to ACAS. It's a fine organisation. But you've got to say that in the Code of Practice on discipline and grievance, the bit on grievance is a little bit brief, isn't it? There's not a lot of detail to it. You do get the impression it was written a little bit as an afterthought. And that guidance on balancing disciplinary and grievance issues doesn't really say anything. It says you 'might' do this or you 'might' do that. Best of luck with it. It's not very prescriptive.

Daniel Barnett
In a shameless plug, I'm going to hold up a copy of this book on resolving grievances (https://amzn.to/3ltE2EM). There's a chapter on grievances lodged during a disciplinary or performance management process. The

other thing I find with grievances raised during disciplinaries or performance management is that the individual will often say, as you pointed, that they think the person hearing the disciplinary or hearing the performance management is racist, biased, hates them, slept with their mother, whatever it might be. And very often, the best way to deal with that, unless you are a very small company, is just to say that they're raising a really interesting point and that if they don't agree with it, as it's a relatively early stage in the proceedings, you can offer them two other names and ask them to pick one to deal with it.

Darren Newman
if you've got the resources to do that, absolutely.

Darren Newman
And then if the employee refuses either of those other names, no tribunal is going to criticise you for pressing ahead.

AJ Fraser
Where a grievance of bullying and harassment against a senior manager is not upheld, the complainant then refuses to work with the manager and also declines the offer of mediation or redeployment, what are the options? Can the employer move the complainant or would this be a constructive dismissal?

Darren Newman
It sounds to me that if you're in that situation, you're very likely to be staring down the barrel of an employment tribunal claim as it is. If you've investigated it and you are confident that bullying and harassment is not made out, you would then be confident that it is a reasonable instruction to tell this employee to continue to work with this manager. You'd have an employee who then refuses to do that. You want to then engage with them and see if you can find a way to deal with the problem. So there may be an offer of mediation, you may discuss redeployment with them and

explain that you understand the employee has had a falling out with this manager and perhaps they can work somewhere else. If you're prepared to consider that and you offer that, and the employee simply says no, then what is it the employee actually asking for in those circumstances? They insist on not moving but they also insist on not working with the manager. I don't think an employee can reasonably require you to move the manager when you've done your investigation and decided that there's no claim made out. So in those circumstances, you've got an employee refusing to work. I think that if you really have tried to engage with them and find an alternative solution, and they've refused to do that, then I think there is a natural consequence to somebody refusing to work, which is that you go down a disciplinary route and you end up dismissing them for it.

I'd probably say you'd end up giving notice, and you'd say that it's a breakdown in the relationship. You'd categorise it as some other substantial reason. You'd say it's about the breakdown in the relationship. The fact is, there's no workable relationship because the employee is refusing to work with this person and refusing to consider alternatives. So you have no choice but to go down the dismissal route. I think that's probably what you'd be stuck with. It's not risk free, but I genuinely can't think of anything else you can do.

Heidi Leybourne
Should we consider a grievance that's submitted after an employee has left?

Darren Newman
I'm going to really try not to say 'it depends on the circumstances'. I would want to look at the substance of the grievance. Generally speaking, I would say a grievance that's submitted literally AFTER someone's left, so not in the course of them leaving - and it might be slightly different if it's in the context of a resignation letter - I would say generally speaking, no. A grievance is about

an internal dispute between an employee and an employer, and it's about resolving the employment relationship. If there isn't an employment relationship, there's nothing to resolve.

It might be, however, that the substance of the grievance that they raise, makes you think it's something that you need to look at. They might tell you something that would genuinely be a useful thing for you to look at, and so it would be a good idea to talk to the employee about what happened and a good idea to investigate it. It might also give you a heads up that there's a potential dispute on the horizon, and that there's potentially going to be a claim. So you might want to look at that, and you might judge that the best way of forestalling that is to talk to the employee about it and take it seriously. You might say that you're very sorry that the employee unhappy about this, that you appreciate that they don't work for you anymore but you'd like to make sure that if you've done something wrong, you'd like to make sure that it doesn't happen in the future. So if they can tell you about it, that would be really helpful. I think that if you take that positive attitude with it, that might help the employee feel that they've resolved something following their resignation.

So, I wouldn't rule out investigating a grievance if it's raised after somebody left, but I don't think there's a legal obligation per se to. The query that people would have is that if you don't follow that as a grievance and the employee wins a tribunal claim, do they get the uplift with the Acas Code of Practice? And I think the answer is still that we don't know. The only case I've ever seen about it was a case called Childrenswear *(Base Childrenswear Ltd v Otshudi [2019] EWCA Civ 1648)* from 2019 that seems to accept an uplift for failure to follow a grievance procedure when the grievance was raised after the resignation. But if you pick that case apart, it's not quite that clear. It was both a grievance and an appeal against dismissal, so that's a slightly different

thing. And the appeal wasn't concerned with whether you could have the uplift. The other thing to remember is you only get the uplift if you've unreasonably failed to follow the grievance procedure. So you would have to show that it was actually unreasonable of the employer not to follow the grievance procedure. I think in many circumstances, it would be reasonable for the employer to wonder what the point would be if they've already left and there's nothing to resolve. But always look at the substance and address the substance rather than worry about whether you're strictly legally obliged to do it.

Melanie Bonas

An employee raises a grievance and the employer follows the correct procedure they have in place. The employee goes off sick and fails to engage despite all attempts by the employer. How should the employer deal with this?

Darren Newman

I'd probably just wait until they're better. I'm not saying the D word, but look at the substance of what they're alleging. What is the need for the employer to progress this quickly? If it's a disciplinary issue, if you've got someone facing disciplinary charges and they go off sick, there's no obvious reason why the employer wants to progress the disciplinary issue rather than pay someone sick pay all that time.

That might be less obvious in the case of a grievance. Although, of course, very often, a grievance doesn't just involve the employee and the employer. There are other people who are accused as well and that's hanging over them. So as an employer you may well think that you don't want to have this grievance ongoing while you've got other employees who feel that they're under investigation and under a cloud because a grievance has been raised that that concerns them.

In those circumstances, you might feel it's important to progress the grievance. And if you feel that that's the right thing to do, then try to conduct the grievance in a way that the employee can participate in it. So taking into account what their particular illness is, what can you do to adjust the process that would allow them to take part? Remember that the key thing you're looking at is how you can make sure you hear what the employee has to say and whether the employee is able to express themselves in a way that gives a fair account of what their grievance is so that you can give that proper consideration. I would look at whether you can ask the employee to give written submissions. I used to suggest remote hearings as some sort of great novelty, but of course, now it's almost the only kind of hearing you can do. So it may well be that someone can log in from work or you can give assurances about how quick the grievance will be. You can allow them to be accompanied by a member of their family to give them support. So, try to find a way to progress the grievance with them participating in it.

Other than that, I don't think there's much you can do. I'm not sure there's much to be gained from simply telling the employee that you've resolved the grievance and found against them, because when the employee comes back to work, they can raise the grievance again, and it'll be difficult to say that you've already dealt with it so you're not going to deal with it. So I think probably the options are to either find a way of progressing it or put it on hold and just accept that it might have to be picked up again when the employee comes back.

Paula Early
What should I do if a grievance is raised against me and I am the only person who can investigate the grievance?

Darren Newman
I'm assuming that that's because of resources and the size of the employer, rather than the skill set and it's not that other people could

do it, but you just don't think they'd be very good at it. I'm assuming it's simply that there is no one else who can really do it. In those circumstances, I think probably you just have to do the best you can. Remember, the Acas Code of Practice actually says that the first step the employer takes after someone has raised the grievance is that you go to the hearing stage and you talk to the employee about it. You may then need to investigate it. So you don't necessarily need to go through the process of investigating yourself. First of all, have the meeting with the employee, listen to what they have to say, reflect on what they have to say and see whether you're prepared to accept any of the points that they're making and make your decision accordingly.

I would think it's unlikely, if the employee is complaining specifically about your actions, that you're going to have to adjourn for an investigation stage while you investigate yourself. You're probably going to be in a position to respond to whatever is said, but you might want to adjourn while you check paperwork or check what was said in an email or something like that. So, by all means, do it. But I think that if that's the resource you've got, then all you can do is listen carefully to what the employee has to say, give them a fair hearing, and make the fairest decision you can. The tribunal. If it got to that, would take into account the fact that you're that size of employer. I wouldn't worry about it too much.

Daniel Barnett
Is there also the possibility of outsourcing to an external HR consultant?

Darren Newman
Well, there is. I hesitate to do that, partly because I make part of my living by doing independent grievances, so I don't want to plug, but yes, you can hire someone. But also, if you are a very small organisation and it's just you, it might be a little bit awkward if you have yourself investigated and you're found to have behaved appallingly. I'm not entirely sure

that would help you to move the issue forward. What you're going to do? Are you going to discipline yourself?

Really, you just need to reflect on what the employee is saying and decide what to do. In general, by all means, I think grievances sometimes do lend themselves well to external investigations because they often command the confidence of the employee rather better than an internal investigation would. I'd be less keen, for example, for external investigations into disciplinary issues. I think that by and large employers should manage those on their own rather than outsourcing decisions like that. But with grievances, it seems to me that it doesn't make sense to have some external help occasionally. But I wouldn't do it because my resources are too limited; I'd do it because it genuinely helps to have an independent voice.

Daniel Barnett
There's a large employment consultancy based in the north, that we all know the name of, that has a specialist division that runs disciplinaries for people. And the ones I've seen in tribunal hearings have been the most cack-handed, abjectly run and dishonest disciplinaries that I've come across. But it can work if you use a small independent HR professional or somebody like yourself, Darren. What are your contact details?

Darren Newman
I actually do that through another organisation. I'm on Twitter and you can find me on the web. Just search for @daznewman.

Daniel Barnett
I also maintain a list of recommended investigators by town or city (https://members.hrinnercircle.co.uk/list-of-recommended-investigators), and those are independent HR professionals who do independent investigations. So it's also quite a useful resource.

Darren Newman
I would definitely recommend doing it through a small, local HR person - I mean, not me - a small, local HR person - I mean, not me -

who knows local businesses and things like that. I think they're very often the ideal people to do this. I think I'd certainly query getting a large corporate to do it for you.

Julia Duncan
In what situations can management reject a grievance and not investigate it first?

Darren Newman
When it's clear that it doesn't have enough substance to warrant investigation. The Acas Code of Practice specifically says that the employee raises a grievance, the employee should then arrange a meeting with the employee to discuss the grievance, and consideration may then be given to an investigation. So if, on its face, a grievance is relatively trivial or obviously wrong, or there's some clear misunderstanding, there's no problem with going straight to the point at which you have the meeting, where you listen to what the employee has to say, and said, You know what, I've heard what you've had to say. That happens to everyone. That's not something you can complain about. Can you please go back to work? That's absolutely fine if that is genuinely a reflection of the substance of the grievance.

An important skill to have is to be able to look at a grievance when it comes in and basically do a triage where you consider whether it's something where someone is alleging something that's potentially very serious, or potentially very complicated and whether before you have a hearing with them, you should launch an investigation, or whether it's something where the employee is complaining that they don't like the view from their office window, and frankly, you just need to have a meeting where you explained to them that the view from the office window is not something you have much control over and they're stuck with it.

Obviously, there's a sliding scale between those two cases, but you need to be able to judge where you're going to put your resources. You shouldn't be in a position that every time any sort of grievance is raised, you have to launch an investigation process where two independent managers end up producing a written report that says that the view from the employee's office window is quite nice, really. That's just a waste of time. But you've got to exercise your judgment when you look at what the substance of the grievance is.

Daniel Barnett
Do you find there's a difference in approach between private sector employers and public sector employers?

Darren Newman
I think so. I spend quite a lot of my time explaining to public sector employers that private sector employers don't do it like this and that you can still be very fair and very thorough without necessarily being incredibly bureaucratic. You can still have a flexible grievance procedure that allows you to direct resources in a way that's efficient and doesn't take months and months of pointless paperwork but still give everyone a fair hearing and be responsive to the concerns that people have. So, yes, I think it has moved in recent years. I think public sector employers are quite a lot more flexible about things now. I think austerity had a big impact in terms of the capacity that public bodies have to absorb some of the bureaucracy that's created by this and they are a bit more nimble now. But it's a conversation I have a lot.

Nigel Forsyth
Should a grievance investigator disclose a copy of the grievance letter to the employee who's the subject of the complaint as part of the investigation process?

Darren Newman
I think that you have to disclose enough to be fair to the person who's being investigated so that when you're putting points to them, they know the point that they have to meet. It's not

quite right to say 'they are being investigated' because it's a grievance you're investigating rather than the individual. But it feels to them like they are being investigated, like they're the subject of investigation. If all you say to them, is that someone has raised a grievance against them and you have several questions, and you then take them back to a meeting they had six months ago and ask if they remember what they said, then they'll just have no idea what they're supposed to be responding to.

I would certainly give them enough information that they know what it is that's being said about them, what incidents I'm going to cover when I talk to them in the investigation. I'm not a fan of springing surprises on people to judge their reactions. I think you should fairly and openly tell people what it is you want to discuss, and give them an opportunity to think about what they have to say about it. So that can give you a considered response. Regarding whether that means you disclose the grievance letter, in my experience, the grievance letter is often 17 pages long and has lots of details about other people as well. I would disclose those parts of it that are relevant to the things I want to discuss with that person.

Su Apps
In practice, what proportion of grievances do you find actually resolve an issue for the better? There's always a concern when advising an employee that raising a grievance will mean the writing's on the wall and the relationship will ultimately end.

Darren Newman
I think it's a really powerful point to have made this late after I've been talking about grievances for so long! We haven't actually discussed whether they are a good thing or whether they are rubbish. I think grievances have their place. They are sometimes the only way you can formally close off an issue and make sure that you have dealt with it. I don't think that they are, in general, a good way of

resolving workplace conflict. I don't think that they genuinely result in everyone feeling happy that the situation has been resolved.

I would certainly advise an employer to have other tools at its disposal for resolving conflict rather than the grievance procedure. This is particularly the case where you have inter-employee grievances. It's one thing if you're raising a grievance about the fact that you didn't get a bonus last year, or the way in which the performance appraisal system works, or the resources that you've got because those are things the employer can control. It's also okay if you're raising a grievance about a manager because the manager is acting on behalf of the employer.

If you're raising a grievance about the person who sits next to you and how mean they are to you in the morning, I'm not sure it's helpful to have a grievance process as a sort of People's Court adjudicating between two people who don't get on. I don't think that I don't think it ever helps that situation. In those circumstances, whether it's mediation, some other form of conflict management, counselling, or a friendly chat with a manager who can help to smooth things over, there are better ways of dealing with the conflict. But I don't think there's any getting away from the fact that you have to have something that looks like a grievance procedure for some of the things that people will raise concerns about. It's a very valid point, and I'd have to say that the proportion that actually resolve issues is relatively small.

Daniel Barnett

I'm always a little sceptical about mediations between employees who don't get on, or some form of training for the manager. Although what inevitably comes out of a mediation or a clear the air meeting is that the two parties agree to draw a line in the sand and move on with life, the next time one of them blinks at the other the wrong way or fails to say good morning in a kind enough tone, the whole

thing kicks off again. And all it does is kick the problem six weeks down the line.

It can certainly be true. It is remarkable how many mediation outcomes have 'will say good morning to each other nicely' as one of the first things in the agreement. The research that's been done that I've seen - Paul Latreille in Sheffield has done a lot of good research on this - I think is very optimistic about the initial results of mediation as coming up with some sort of resolution. But I think there's a gap in the research about the long-term impact of it. So you have a mediation that resolves an issue. Is that issue still resolved a year later? I think there's less research as to whether that's true or not.

Mike Clyne

In your experience, how do tribunals distinguish between companies who try to handle a grievance but do it poorly and companies who go through the perfect procedures but are simply going through the motions and have no real intention of dealing with it?

Darren Newman

I'm not sure I know how tribunals do that. You've got much more litigation experience for me, Daniel, so you may have a view. My personal view of the best way of persuading the tribunal is to be open and honest about any failings that you identify and say that maybe you didn't handle that as well as you could have, but you were doing your best. There's nothing better than just coming across as really honest and open. I would hope that tribunals can tell the difference between the two, but you'll know better than me as to whether they, they can or not. It might depend on the skill of your advocate.

Daniel Barnett

I think that tribunals are made up of people, and they want to reward those who they like and punish those who they don't like. As a rule, a tribunal judge is going to like the well-meaning but slightly hapless employer far more than the malevolent, disingenuous and slightly dishonest, nasty, vicious employer who, like a certain large ride-hailing company we all know, has brilliant processes in place but doesn't actually mean any of what it says. I think the small, hapless employer who makes a mistake might get technical findings against them, but there'll generally be high levels of contributory fault if it turns to a constructive dismissal, or Polkey arguments *(Polkey v AE Dayton Services Ltd [1987] UKHL 8)*, whereas the slightly dishonest employer with fantastic procedures, who has no intention of actually finding for the employee under any circumstances and acts in bad faith is always going to be at the wrong end of a tribunal sharp stick.

Rachel Thompson

Should an employer treat a letter received via an employee's lawyer raising complaints and advising of an impending tribunal claim as a grievance?

Darren Newman

Well, this is the thing that we obsessed over during the statute dispute resolution procedures, isn't it? The question was whether that would be a grievance, and that had a legal consequence in terms of whether the claim could proceed or not. I think the way you deal now - and I'm assuming that the person is still your employee - is to say you've got a letter from their solicitors: would they like to raise a grievance, in which case you've got an internal grievance procedure to deal with it, or would they like it to be dealt with via your lawyers down the legal process? It's very much up to them.

I don't think there's a need to treat a solicitor's letter as a grievance. I would slightly discourage grievances being conducted by solicitors. I think everything I said about the fact that grievances don't necessarily resolve disputes gets multiplied by 10 once the letter has been written by a firm of solicitors - no

offence to the solicitors on the line. If an employee wants to use a grievance procedure, I would recommend that they write their own grievance and put it in the form that you want and deal with it then. But I don't see any harm in having the conversation with the employee, assuming they are still your employee, and asking them what they would like to do.

Julie Davis

A grievance by one employee against another employee isn't upheld. But that often leads to a counter grievance by the grieved-against employee against the original complainant, and that goes on and on and on. Can this retaliatory approach be avoided?

Darren Newman

I think, ultimately, it might just be that as the employer, you have to say that you understand that there's a disagreement between the two employees. You've heard one grievance, you've now got a further grievance that's been raised and you'll hear that but you're not going to hear any more. So you go quite quickly to the hearing of the second one and you don't do a separate investigation because as far as you're concerned, you have investigated or dealt with it. And you basically realise that you've now got a position of conflict between these two employees.

What is the best way of resolving that conflict? I'm not sure I know, but I'm confident the grievance procedure isn't it. The grievance procedure is not going to resolve this. You would then talk to the employees and say that you need to take this outside the grievance procedure and that you need to find some way that the two employees can work together - assuming they do have to work together - and come up with some sort of mediation, 'let's say good morning to each other' agreement or some other structured conflict resolution process that gets them to stop.

My concern is about inter-employee grievances is that to an extent, the employer is just facilitating disputes. It's just facilitating a method by which one employee can annoy another employee. And I think that as the employer you should be free to say that if the employee is not alleging that you've done anything wrong as the employer, you're not going to treat it as a grievance. You can say that this is just an accusation the employee is making against another employee, you'll consider it but if you think there's no misconduct, you'll just tell both of them to grow up and work together more carefully.

Victoria Clegg

What's the best way for a grievance handler who isn't legally qualified to deal with a grievance that's drawn up like a pleading, quoting the Equality Act and case law.

Daniel Barnett

I think that the best advice is to be a good witness in the employment tribunal when you're inevitably sued.

Darren Newman

In a grievance, I think it's not generally appropriate to get into arguments about case law, the Equality Act and provisions. The better thing to do is to say that you understand that there's a lot of law around these issues, but you're not adjudicating the law, you're trying to find a way of judging whether the employee has been treated badly and whether there's something you can do about that. So you can say that they shouldn't talk to you about what the case law says, they should tell you what happened so that you can make a decision as to whether what happened is something that you want to provide the employee with some redress for, or whether it's something you're prepared to stand by, or whether you think it didn't happen.

I don't see why a grievance would have to get into detailed legal arguments. And if you're presented with a grievance, that's got a whole paragraph about the Equality Act, or about what counts as being in the course of

employment and the case law around that, I think you could just say that that's legal stuff and you don't need to worry about that. Ask them to tell you what happened, and talk about the actual events and whether that's something that you're concerned about, and whether that's something you can do something about. Leave the law to the lawyers and just concentrate on dealing with the situation as fairly as you can.

Emma

In what circumstances would you say it's appropriate to have the same manager investigating and subsequently deciding a grievance?

Darren Newman

I think it is less of an issue than it is in a disciplinary case. So if you're investigating misconduct, I would say it's really very important to have a separate person investigate and then resolve the grievance. If it's a grievance and we're just talking about the employer deciding how to deal with a complaint the employees got, it is less of a thing. And the Acas Code of Practice doesn't specifically say that different people should conduct the investigation in the hearing. Whereas it does say that when it comes to disciplinary.

Daniel Barnett

I'm just going to interrupt for one second. You've used the word 'should' - that a different person 'should' do the investigation and the disciplinary - just to make it clear that the word 'should' in the Acas guide is used as a recommendation. It's not mandatory.

Darren Newman

There are cases where the same people have done the investigation and the disciplinary and that hasn't been a reason for it to be an unfair dismissal. It all depends on the circumstances of the case, to use our favourite phrase. But there is surely more of a requirement to do it in a disciplinary than there is in a grievance.

I think it's often perfectly appropriate for the person who's conducting the grievance to also do the investigation. I didn't see that's always necessarily a problem. Some employers will do it differently and that can be fine, too. That can be a helpful additional perspective. Maybe it's a question of what the procedure says and maybe it's a question of what resources the employer has and what's best. Are we going to fall out over that point?

Daniel Barnett
No, I don't think we are, I think we're fairly similar on that. I might take a slightly more robust view than you. I think that it should be the exception for more than one person to deal with it. The exception applying when you've either got a collective agreement that mandates two people look at it from a different perspective, or it's a public sector organisation where they've had that policy in place for years and years and they can't change it - although they should - because there's absolutely nothing wrong with one person, as long as they act in good faith, looking at the evidence and making a decision.

But if two people do it, you get all sorts of other problems, I think, and this applies and discipline was also. First of all, if you get two witnesses in front of a tribunal rather than one, there is double the opportunity for somebody to mess up. Second of all, when you get the investigator producing a written report and the disciplinary officer then making a decision based on it, I think you get the fundamental problem that the disciplinary officer hasn't seen the original witnesses, or often might not have done, feels hidebound by the report and the conclusions of the investigation officer who's never actually going to be tested or cross-examined on those conclusions, and also you often get a great deal of confusion in some organisations on the part of the disciplinary officer about whether they're bound by the findings of the investigation report or whether they can reopen it, listen to what the employer has to say and come to a completely different conclusion. When the disciplinary officer is then cross-examined, they can fall apart on that point. I find having two people investigating leads to much more likelihood of unfair dismissal.

Darren Newman
Interesting. I think that's partly a question of how you draft the disciplinary investigation report and what level of conclusion you reach, but that is possibly a separate webinar. I agree with you on the grievance point. The only point I'd make is that if you've got a relatively senior person hearing the grievance, it might be more efficient to have a less senior person doing the donkey work of trawling through the emails, doing the investigation report, talking to people and collating all the information. The more senior person doing the grievance might not have the time to do that. So it might be just efficient to have separate people doing it.

Daniel Barnett
Darren Newman, thank you very much.

DANIEL BARNETT'S HR POLICIES

INCLUDED IN THE LATEST COLLECTION ARE POLICIES ON...

STARTING EMPLOYMENT

1. Recruitment

BEING SUPPORTIVE

2. Holiday

3. Flexible Working

4. Equal Opportunities

5. Drugs & Alcohol

6. Wellbeing

7. Menopause

8. Maternity & Family Friendly

9. Homeworking

SETTING STANDARDS

10. Social Media

11. Harassment & Bullying

12. Performance Improvement

13. Absence management

14. Grievance Policy

BEING REGULATED

15. Whistleblowing

16. Bribery

17. Data Protection and GDPR

18. Modern Slavery

ENDING EMPLOYMENT

19.　Disciplinary

20.　Redundancy

WWW.POLICIES2020.COM

HARASSMENT

WILL YOUNG, OUTER TEMPLE CHAMBERS

Daniel Barnett

I'm joined today for this Q&A session by Will Young of Outer Temple Chambers and he is going to be answering all of your questions on harassment.

Will Young, good morning. I'm going to start by asking you a couple of questions. I just want to pull up s26 of the Equality Act, which is the legislation dealing with harassment and ask you a couple of questions about it. We're all very familiar with the definition in 26.1, which is:

26 Harassment

(1) A person (A) harasses another (B) if -
    (a) A engages in unwanted conduct related to a relevant protected characteristic, and
    (b) the conduct has the purpose or effect of -
        (i) violating B's dignity, or
        (ii) creating an intimidating, hostile, degrading, humiliating or offensive environment for B.

It's a phrase I see in almost every grievance letter in a tribunal bundle because people just tend to cut and paste it into their grievance letters. I'd like to ask first of all about the phrase 'related to' in 'someone harasses another if they engage in unwanted conduct related to a relevant protected characteristic'. What does that phrase mean?

Will Young

The first thing to note is that it's not the same as on grounds of a protected characteristic, unlike most of the old discrimination legislation. There doesn't have to be a direct causal link between the protected characteristic and the conduct. It's wider than that. There is some lack of clarity in the authorities about how close that connection must be. In the case of Warby v Wunda Group *(Warby v Wunda Group plc EAT/0434/11)*, from the EAT in 2011, it involved a manager accusing an employee of having lied about a miscarriage, and that was held not to be related to sex. But that case proceeded on the basis that 'related to' is not different to 'on the grounds of' so I think that must be questionable in the light of the change in the wording of the law.

The EHRC Employment Code adopts a broad interpretation. It gives the example of a female worker and a male manager having a relationship. He sees her with another male colleague and suspects she's having an affair and treats her badly as a result. The treatment is not because of sex, but it is because of sexual jealousy, which is related to sex and therefore could amount to harassment.

There are, however, a number of cases in which after consideration of the context, conduct has been found not to be related to a protected characteristic, essentially, because it was not the reason for the conduct. So to give two examples, there's the case of Kelly v Covance Laboratories *(Kelly v Covance*

Laboratories [2016] IRLR 338) in 2016, in which a Russian employee was instructed not to have telephone conversations in Russian at work. The reason for the request was found not to be the claimant's race or national origins but because the employer was worried about infiltration by animal rights activists, and so was suspicious of what they thought were the claimant's long and furtive conversations in a language managers couldn't understand.

To give a second example, in a case called Bakkali v Greater Manchester Buses (Bakkali v Greater Manchester Buses [2018] ICR 1481) in 2018, comments to a claimant who was a Muslim man of Moroccan origin to the effect of "are you still promoting ISIS?" were found to be because of an earlier conversation in which he had made comments which could have been interpreted as being positive about ISIS. It was held not to be related to religion or belief. Now, the problem with this is that logically, conduct can be not because of a protected characteristic, but can still be related to it.

I think the short version of that answer is that 'related to' is wider than 'because of' or 'on grounds of', but it's certainly a grey area, and it can be difficult for claims to prove. If the respondent can plausibly argue that there was some other reason for the conduct, one can readily imagine that in both of those examples it would not be perverse for an employment tribunal to have concluded that the conduct was not related to a protected characteristic. But of course, it's a question of fact, and therefore, it's very difficult to overturn on appeal.

Daniel Barnett
Thank you. Let's just go back to the statutory definition. There's this bit here, 'creating an intimidating, hostile, degrading, humiliating or offensive environment'. What does a claimant need to prove to establish that?

Will Young
Regarding the question of whether it has the statutory purpose or effect, most cases tend to be decided, in my experience on effects, so it's much harder to prove that somebody has the purpose of creating that sort of environment. And in terms of whether it has that effect, the employment tribunal must take into account the perception of the claimant, all other circumstances of the case and whether it's reasonable for the conduct to have had that particular effect on the claimant.

The leading case of Richmond Pharmacology v Dhaliwal (Richmond Pharmacology v Dhaliwal [2009] ICR 724) from 2009 confirmed that the claimant must have actually, i.e. subjectively, perceived him or herself to have suffered that effect. And then if they prove that, the tribunal must consider whether it was reasonable for the conduct to have had that effect.

The question of reasonableness of it having that effect is determinative; it's not merely one factor to be considered. That's confirmed in the case of Ahmed v Cardinal Hume Academies (Ahmed v Cardinal Hume Academies EAT/0196/18) in 2018. The other circumstances of the case, again, the EHRC says that these include the claimant's health, including mental health; mental capacity; cultural norms; and previous experiences of harassment, and it can include the environment in which the conduct takes place. Intent can be relevant to whether it's reasonable to have the statutory effects. And as an example, in the case of Exec Catering, v Kaczynska (Exec Catering Ltd v Kaczynska EAT/0182/13), a manager watched pornography on his computer at home, not intending it to be seen by the claimant. But it was seen and it had the required statutory effects despite the lack of intent.

Just to go back to Dhaliwal, there's an important statement in that case. It said that the reason that the statute has the objective element is to avoid a culture of hypersensitivity or the imposition of legal liability in respect of every unfortunate phrase. And so while it's important that tribunals are sensitive to the hurt that can be caused by racially offensive comments or conduct, not every racially slanted adverse comment or conduct constitutes a violation of a perfect person's dignity.

Finally, the employment tribunal does need to take into account the effect on a particular claimant of the conduct or comments. So if they're a vulnerable individual, for example, that might make it more reasonable for conduct to have had that effect. But again, it's a question of fact and so it will depend on all the circumstances.

Daniel Barnett
Jamie Anderson has just commented that one of the cases you mentioned was his and he has fame at last!

I've got an important question, in fact, I'm going to ask everybody this. So, ladies and gentlemen please vote on this: is it hArassment, or is it harASSment? Will, I'll ask you once everyone else has voted.

There is actually a clear winner here. Before I reveal the answer, Will Young, is it hArassment or harASSment?

Will Young
I think, slightly shamefully. I actually flit between the two of them, which is not very consistent. But I would say the correct one is probably hArassment.

Daniel Barnett
Most people seem to favour harASSment - 72% favour harASSment and 28% favour hArassment. So I'm going to make a conscious effort to call it harASSment during the rest of this talk.

AJ Fraser
How would you deal with an employee who frequently raises allegations of harassment by colleagues, but fails to provide you with

the specific details such as what, who, when, where, which?

Will Young
I think that you need to make it clear to them that it's very difficult, if not impossible, for an employer to investigate allegations of harassment without details of exactly what's going on. Obviously, there will be a range of the amount of information is provided, and if it's at the end of the scale, that is simply the employee is being harassed by someone but they're not going to tell you who or when or how, then, in reality, it's pretty much impossible for the employer to investigate that. I'd be surprised if a tribunal criticised an employer for not actually properly investigating, but I think they would expect an employer to perhaps meet with the employee and say that they need to provide more details so that it can be properly investigated. I think that's how you go about actually trying to deal with the situation.

The follow on from that, which isn't the direct focus of the question but I think is in the background, is what do you do if someone is making repeated allegations and there's a suspicion they're not being made in good faith? Do you need to do anything about that? I think maybe that will come up in another question. But I think, generally speaking, obviously, because of the victimisation provisions, you need to be very careful about taking any action against someone who makes allegations, even if they're not providing you with the material that you need in order to investigate it.

Daniel Barnett
You mentioned victimisation. If somebody is making allegations in bad faith and you subject them to some form of detriment, is that victimisation?

Will Young
In order to avoid liability victimisation, you need to be able to identify some part of their

conduct that is severable from the fact that they made allegations themselves, and that's the case of Martin v Devonshires *(Martin v Devonshires Solicitors [2011] ICR 352)*. So if the way someone goes about making allegations is something that can be properly treated as distinct from the fact that they've made the allegations, then you can take action about that. But it's very difficult to take any action solely because they've made repeated allegations.

Daniel Barnett

I think the Act also makes it clear - although it's some obviously very, very difficult for an employer to be confident that they can establish this - that if the allegation is made in bad faith, then it's not a protected act. But it's very high-risk for employers to take that approach.

Amir Gill

How can we investigate claims of potential office gossip and hearsay as a form of harassment?

Will Young

I think this gets to the question of whether it's reasonable for conduct to have had the statutory effect. I suppose the first thing to say is that I think it depends on whether the gossip and hearsay is being brought to the attention of the managers by someone who feels they are being harassed or whether it's just the managers becoming aware of the gossip and hearsay and thinking that they need to do something about this because it might be harassment.

I think in the first of those situations, in some ways, it's easier because you have someone who is saying they are feeling harassed by something. And therefore, you can do what you would normally do, i.e. meet with them, get some details and then interview the people who are named as also being involved. If it's a top-down decision from management who've become aware of the gossip and

hearsay and want to do something about it, I think that's a bit more difficult because unless you have someone who is saying that they feel that their dignity has been violated or they've been made to endure a humiliating, etc, etc, environment, then, potentially, you're wading into a situation that is very difficult to disentangle and there may not be any actual harassment. I think you'd obviously want to speak to the people involved, but I think it's hard to investigate that straight off the bat as harassment without anyone making a complaint.

That's not to say that employers shouldn't be concerned that employees are working in an environment where there is lots of gossip and things that might be categorised as good-natured, jocular behaviour between employees but might easily tip over into harassment and maybe it is good to get out ahead of that and try to avoid that happening.

Daniel Barnett

There are a couple of comments in the chat. Naomi has checked a copy of the Pronunciation Guide from the Cambridge Dictionary and says that hArassment is the correct version and harASSment is the US version. Anne Thompson says that the Oxford English Dictionary and the Cambridge English Dictionary both say the pronunciation is hArassment. So it looks like your gut feeling was right, Will.

In a 'he said, she said' unwitnessed harassment complaint, what evidence can an investigator rely on to tip the balance to help them decide which account is the more credible?

Will Young

I think it's always very difficult where there are no witnesses and it's literally one person's word against another. I suppose you could talk to other colleagues about the environment within the workplace. It depends on the nature of the allegation, but if you do further investigations and find that there is a culture of these kinds of comments being made, or of this particular employee doing or saying things that might not be appropriate, then that might, in theory, make it more likely that they did what they are accused of. But of course, we all know that sometimes people say things that are out of character, so that's not going to totally prove it either way.

I have to say that my experience from reading the notes of investigations by the time things get to tribunal is that employers almost always take the view that unless there is some pretty strong corroborative evidence that something actually happened, they tend to err on the side of not making a finding that it did happen. So lots of cases that I have that get to tribunal will be a 'he said, she said'-type situation where they can't prove it either way and the employer says that if it can't be proved, they're not going to uphold it. So I think that that tends to be the approach that most employers take. I think to be fair to them, it is difficult to find solid corroborative evidence where there aren't any other witnesses. But I think that the best you could do is probably just make further and wider inquiries about the culture within the workplace and about the particular employee about whom the allegation is made.

Daniel Barnett
I generally find a lot of employers will say in letters responding to grievances about harassment that there was nobody who could corroborate your account and since your account is uncorroborated, we cannot find in favour of you, which I always think is incredibly cowardly and ducking the question because it's the investigator's job to actually make up their mind. And if you're going to rely on the fact that the harasser didn't harass when there were 17 witnesses around as a reason for finding harassment didn't take place, you're a coward and you're not doing your job, to put it very, very bluntly. Your job is to make up your mind and if you refuse to make up your mind about who you believe simply because the harasser didn't harass in

public, you'll find an employment tribunal will pretty quickly make up its mind that you failed to discharge your responsibility under the statutory defence or indeed failed to provide a safe place of work for people of a particular protected characteristic. Do you agree with that, or am I being a little too harsh?

Will Young
I see your point, but I think it is pretty widespread for employers to say that. I think you're right that certainly, some tribunals will take a pretty dim view of that, but I think not necessarily all of them.

Gillian Howard
The tribunals have said individuals can't be over-sensitive to harassing words or conduct. How to tribunals approach the sensitivity issue of a claimant?

Will Young
There is a balance to be struck, obviously, between not encouraging the hypersensitivity that Underhill LJ as he then was in Dhaliwal was seeking to discourage. But on the other hand, you do have to take into account that some claimants might find something offensive that other claimants wouldn't and perhaps the tribunals themselves wouldn't. It's not a case of the tribunals substituting their own view as to whether they would have been offended by it, but I think both of those things do go into the mix when they're deciding the objective question. Perhaps the clearest example is that if you have an employee who is particularly vulnerable, let's say that they have some mental health difficulties or something like that, then that is obviously going to be something that the tribunal will take into account. It won't be a defence for an employer to say that most people wouldn't be offended by this. Because if you have a particularly vulnerable employee, then the tribunal is going to be sensitive to the argument that you've got to take into account the particular features of that employee. But there is obviously a line past which the tribunal just will not feel able to find that it meets the

objective test because they just find that it's not reasonable for it to have had that effect. So I think much depends on the particular circumstances or the employee. But that is always a balance, and both of those two impasses will be in tension when that arises.

Anonymous

I think that's 100% right because the definition of harassment is very clearly one that has a subjective and objective element to it. Just expanding on the question slightly, what about the position where the employee is subjected to some form of harassment, but overreacts and develops an unforeseeable psychiatric injury?

Will Young

That's a very interesting question and it's actually directly within the area of my special interest that you referred to earlier. Where a claimant has developed a psychiatric injury as a result of treatment at work, which could be harassment, they have a choice whether to bring a claim in the civil courts for personal injury alleging negligence on the part of the employer or to bring a discrimination claim. If you think, as a claimant, that you can prove discrimination, that you can meet the elements of the test, one of the key advantages to bringing a claim in the employment tribunal is that you don't have to prove foreseeability of the injury. So as long as you prove that the injury is directly related to the harassment, you can recover full damages for the personal injury, even if it's not foreseeable. In those kinds of stressful work cases in the civil courts, foreseeability is often the biggest hurdle for a claimant to get over. But you can entirely get round that in a discrimination claim because you simply don't have to prove foreseeability. The case is called Lang (Essa v Laing [2004] IRLR 313). So foreseeability is something you don't have to prove and that can be very important in those types of cases.

Anonymous

If an employee sends harassing text messages outside of work, to what extent are employers expected to investigate and take action?

Will Young

I think if it's possible to draw a clear line between the person's employment and the situation in which the alleged harassment has taken place, then it's arguable that the employer doesn't have an obligation to investigate the private lives of their employees outside of work. But I think in terms of being prudent and in terms of sort of good employee relations, it's probably not a good idea to completely turn a blind eye to things even if they happen in an area that is not clearly within the work environment. Those things are going to bleed into people's relationships at work, and if you have someone harassing someone outside of work, then it's pretty unlikely, I think, that then they would be completely unaffected by that when they are in work. So I think the employer does have a legitimate interest in allegations of harassment there are outside the work environment.

However, due to privacy concerns and things like that, I think the employer does need to tread quite carefully before wading into what might be characterised as someone's private life outside of work. So I think that the first thing that I'd want to do if I was an employer and I found out about it from the recipients of these messages, I would probably want to speak to them and see how they feel about it. And if they are of the view that they are being subjected to harassment, then I think that my instinct would be to do something about that and to try and investigate it. But I'd have to try it a little bit carefully, bearing in mind that it was not done in the work environment.

Matilda Swanson

What are the best tips you've got for an employer to show they did all they could to prevent any harassment in the workplace from occurring in general?

Daniel Barnett

If you could just introduce your answer by talking about the statutory defence and what that is, that would be helpful.

Will Young

Absolutely. I was going to go to that first. So under s109 of the Equality Act, an employer is not liable for the actions of its employees if it took all reasonable steps to prevent the employee from either doing the particular thing that is alleged to be harassment or from doing anything of that description. And there are various steps that employers can take. The EHRC Employment Code give the example of implementing an equality policy, ensuring workers are aware of that policy, providing equal opportunities training, reviewing the policy as appropriate and dealing effectively with complaints. It's important to note that the steps that the employer relies on have to be steps that are taken before the allegation. Remedying discrimination in a timely fashion after the complaint is not sufficient in order to rely on the statutory defence. Conversely, a lenient penalty for discrimination cannot in and of itself, defeat the defence, and that's a case called Al-Azzawi v Haringey Council (Al-Azzawi v Haringey Council EAT/0158/00), although, it can potentially shed light on the pre-allegation events, for example, by showing that an equality policy is really only for show.

The leading case, I think, is Canniffe v East Riding of Yorkshire Council (Canniffe v East Riding of Yorkshire Council [2000] IRLR 555), and it says that employment tribunals should ask (a) whether any preventative steps were taken in order to prevent this sort of thing happening, and (b) if so, whether there were any further preventative steps that could have been taken that were reasonably practicable.

In fact, there's a recent case called Allay v Gehlen (Allay v Gehlen EAT/0031/20), in which employees had been given training that covered harassment related to race but it had been delivered two years before the allegations of racial harassment. The tribunal found that it was clearly stale and went on to find that a reasonable step would have been to provide refresher training, and therefore the defence was not made out. The really interesting point

about that case is that the need for refresher training was illustrated by the fact that the remarks were made at all and that they were overheard by two managers who failed to respond appropriately. And that sort of reasoning, which is almost res ipsa loquitur, makes it more difficult for the respondent to rely on the defence and easier for the claimant to get around it. Because the very fact that the harassment occurred and, in particular, that it had been overheard by managers who didn't do anything about it is evidence that reasonable steps had not been taken. So I think that's a very interesting case and not a very helpful one for employers.

To get back to the direct question, I think, obviously, having a policy is important, having training that makes employees aware of the policy is important and having refresher training is also important. But on a slightly broader or more abstract level, I think that if you can show that this is something that is taken really seriously by the company, and that the culture of the organisation is to take discrimination seriously and to make people aware that it won't be tolerated, then I think that's really helpful. What you want to get away from is any suggestion that this is just a box-ticking exercise that you've handed out the policy and then that's the job done. So the more you can do to show a proactive and committed interest in preventing harassment and discrimination, the better off an employer will be and the easier it'll be to make out the defence.

Amaya Corcuera

What advice would you give employers when an employee claims they've been racially harassed by a third party? The third party is an employee of another company working on the same building site and if the employer does nothing, the employee could claim their failure to act and take the complaint seriously could also be motivated by discrimination.

Daniel Barnett

So what's the law on third-party harassment?

Will Young

It used to be possible to bring a claim against an employer for failing to prevent third-party harassment, but that's no longer possible under the Equality Act. I think that the employer's actual legal risk is probably relatively limited in these circumstances because it's very difficult for a claimant to prove that the failure to take a complaint seriously, or even higher than that, the failure to find in the claimants favour after an investigation or actively do something about this is itself motivated by discrimination. That is quite hard to prove. There are a number of authorities in which that argument has been run and failed. So in one sense, the employer is not necessarily at that great a legal risk, but on the other hand, and on a much more practical level, I think it's obviously going to be beneficial for the company to try and do something about it, even if only because it's the right thing to do and to keep your employees on site.

So I think my advice would be to do something about it if you can, for example, having a word with managers at the other company to report that this has happened and try and take steps to prevent it from happening. You'd want to explain to the employee what you've done and why you've done it and also what limitations there are to what you can actually do. Just try to do everything you can to show that the complaint is being taken seriously, even if there are limits to what can be done about it. And if you do that, then you ought to be fairly confident that you can be protected against any claim because the claimant would have to show that your actions or the company's actions were themselves motivated by discrimination which is quite a hard thing to show.

Yuri

In what circumstances can a culture of banter in a workplace help an employer's defence to a harassment claim?

Mike Clyne

Do barristers and solicitors have the same reaction as HR people when they hear a company mention banter?

Will Young

In answer to the second question, Yes.

Banter is not a defence to harassment if the conduct in question meets the statutory test. So there are cases - (English v Thomas Sanderson Blinds Ltd [2009] IRLR 206) - in which there is a culture within a workplace where there is what might be termed banter between people and there is a lot of teasing and things like that. Some of it related to a protected characteristic, and in this case, it was supposedly jocular homophobic insults, even though the claimant was himself not a homosexual man. But he decided that at one point it had crossed a line, he wasn't happy with it and he brought an allegation of discrimination. The employer tried to run the argument that because he'd engaged in this culture of banter beforehand, the conduct either wasn't unwanted, or it couldn't meet the statutory test. And looking at the test, those are the two arguments that are relevant to the question of banter because the employer might say that it's not unwanted because the claimant has engaged in this activity him or herself or that it's not reasonable for it to have had the statutory effect because, again, they've engaged in it themselves.

And I think what that case makes clear, is that it's perfectly possible for tribunals to accept that the claimant had engaged in this sort of back and forth him or herself, but that there is a line that once crossed, brings conduct over into harassment, even if there was a culture before so. So the short answer is that banter isn't a defence to a harassment claim, but it can provide context and it can potentially allow a respondent to argue that particular conduct was not unwanted, but it's not always that attractive an argument.

Matilda Swanson
With an employee on sick leave, if they claim the employer is harassing them by keeping in touch, what's your advice to handle that situation?

Will Young
My advice would be to go back to the sickness absence policy and see what it says about keeping in contact and to try and respect the employee's wishes as much as you can. If they say they don't want to be contacted or if they want a particular method of contact, try and respect that. But also make clear to them that you have an obligation to keep in contact with them to keep in touch and keep track of things, and try and do that in as light-touch a way as possible, consistent with the obligation to do that and to follow the policy.

Anonymous
Is there any way a company can investigate allegations of harassment if the victim doesn't want to proceed with an official statement?

Will Young
I think that the answer to that is a bit like the answer to one of the first questions, which is that it depends how much detail you have of the allegation. If you have a complainant who wants to remain anonymous and doesn't want to produce a statement to be given to the alleged harasser but provides you with details of what is alleged to have happened, then yes, you can investigate it. It will be more difficult to do so, particularly if there are no other witnesses, because without their evidence to rely on, it's very hard to come to any conclusion. But if you have enough details, you can investigate even if they didn't want to take part. If however, they just say that they feel they've been harassed and they're not going to give you any more details and they don't want to take part in the investigation, that makes it very difficult for an employer to do anything about it.

Su Apps
To what extent will the victim's own actions in participating actively in banter be relevant to a defence to a harassment claim and showing there was no effect?

Will Young
It is potentially relevant because it enables the respondent to argue firstly that the conduct can't be unwanted because the claimant was engaging in that sort of behaviour and also that it's not reasonable for it to have had that effect. But as I said a moment ago, (a) there's a line that can be crossed, even with banter - so that's not a complete defence - and (b) even if someone goes along with conduct on the part of their employer, even for a long time, that doesn't necessarily mean that it is unwanted.

There's a case called Munchkins *(Munchkins Restaurant Ltd v Karmazyn & Ors UKEAT/0359/09/LA)* where the waitresses were being harassed by the male owner of the restaurant and didn't say anything about it because of their precarious employment position - they didn't want to lose their jobs. The respondent tried to argue that that meant that the conduct wasn't unwanted and that they were effectively participating in it. The tribunal said that was not right. Just because you don't expressly object to something, it doesn't mean that it can't have the statutory effect or that it's wanted.

Robert
Would discussing the colour of the unborn child of a member of a close family business be regarded as harassment?

Will Young
I think it comes down to the objective question of when it's reasonable for someone to find that humiliating or oppressive and the various other statutory requirements for the environment. I suppose there's an argument that that is a factual question about which there may be a biological answer and therefore it's not necessarily inappropriate, but I think it's

certainly something that you will feel pretty uncomfortable about trying to defend in the employment tribunal if you're acting for the person who was alleged to have done that.

Anonymous
Can you please touch on the Protection From Harassment Act 1997 in respect of claims that aren't linked to a protected characteristic?

Will Young
That's a very good point. Earlier I made a point about the benefits of the employment tribunal if you have a claimant who has suffered psychiatric injury. Those benefits are only available if you can bring yourself within the discrimination rules of the Equality Act. And if you can't do that, mainly for the reason that I identified - if you don't have a protected characteristic on which to base the claim - then you're not going to be able to satisfy it that test. So the Protection From Harassment Act has the benefit of not having to pass the test for discrimination.

The definition, such as it is, of harassment within the 1997 Act is fairly broad. So that can be more easily met, perhaps, than the discrimination test. The significant difference is that it has to be a course of conduct on two or more occasions, which is not true of discrimination. So under the Equality Act, harassment can be one individual acts of harassment, whereas, under the 1997 Act, it has to be a course of conduct. So if you've only got one example, then the 1997 Act isn't going to help you. But if you've got a course of conduct or a campaign of harassment, then that might be a helpful option for you if you can't hang it onto a protected characteristic.

Daniel Barnett
Can a feisty employment judge be regarded as harassing the party or the representative?

Will Young
No, I don't think so. I think they would come within the ambit of litigation. I don't think that can be the subject of proceedings. I think if you got into that situation where a feisty employment judge was doing things that you might think are harassment, then your recourse is probably an appeal on grounds of bias rather than a separate harassment claim.

Anonymous
If an employee accidentally calls another employee by the name of another employee a few times, and both the employees are of a particular race, is that and that alone enough to amount to racial harassment?

Will Young
I think potentially, yes. I can think of a particular example of where a white football manager was alleged to have referred to his black players in his team by each other's names on a repeated basis. And the tenor of the reporting of that was that that was racist on his part. And I think that certainly, it's possible that that might amount to harassment, particularly bearing in mind that it wouldn't have to be the purpose - it could be completely accidental - but I think it's perfectly possible for that to have the statutory effect and therefore it could amount to harassment.

Anonymous
What's the best way for somebody to get in touch with you if they have any questions?

Will Young
Probably my chambers email, which is will.young@outertemple.com

Daniel Barnett
Will Young, thank you very much for joining us.

HEALTH AND SAFETY
GUS BAKER, OUTER TEMPLE CHAMBERS

Daniel Barnett
Today's webinar is on health and safety issues in employment, litigation and the workplace. I'm joined by Gus Baker from Outer Temple Chambers.

Gus Baker, good afternoon. There's a couple of questions I'd like to ask myself on health and safety. What duties do employers have to look after an employee's health and safety?

Gus Baker
So employers have a number of duties to look after employees' health and safety. Firstly, there's a criminal law-backed duty - s2 Health and Safety at Work Act 1974 - which is the duty to so far as reasonably practicable, take steps to ensure the health and safety of employees at work. Now employment lawyers don't deal with criminal law most of the time, but that's a section of criminal law all employers need to know. Because your client can very literally find themselves in the dock in a criminal court - and that includes the directors of the client - and they can face prison sentences if they don't abide by that. And one of the very difficult things about that duty is there is a reverse burden of proof. So the defendants have to prove that they did take reasonable steps to look after employees' health and safety. So aside from that, there's also an implied term in contracts employment, which amounts to much the same thing that you will take reasonable care to look after people's health and safety in the workplace. And then there may be duties to make

reasonable adjustments for employees who are disabled, and therefore particularly vulnerable too.

Daniel Barnett
We've all become hideously familiar with s44 of the Employment Rights Act since coronavirus broke last February/March. s44(1) provides a right for employees to stay at home and not go into work if they reasonably believe that they are in serious and imminent danger if they remain in the workplace. One of the raging questions which many lawyers disagree on is whether employees are entitled to be paid in those circumstances where they've decided to stay at home. Do they have a right to payment? Is not paying them considered a detriment and hence actionable under s44? What's your view on that?

Gus Baker
My view is that sometimes it will be a detriment. But the thing that you need to focus on is the grounds on which pay is being deprived from the employee. So I'll give you two opposite situations, and the task for lawyers advising is to work out which side of the line this falls.

So say your factory is burning down, well you can clearly leave work in those circumstances and refuse to return until the fire is over because that is clearly imminent danger to employees. On the other side, imagine you have someone who says they've recently had an operation, and they'll be in serious danger from any infectious diseases, like the flu if they come into work, and so they declined to go in the workplace on that basis.

Well, in the first circumstance, the reason why you're depriving the person of pay is the dangerous circumstances. So in my view, that fits squarely within s44, therefore, it is a detriment if you deny them pay if it's because of the workplace danger. But in the latter circumstance - when you properly think about it with a wet towel around your head - the reason you're denying someone pay is about them. So if someone says, look, the workplace is pretty safe for other people, but for me, it's really dangerous, the reason why they're not being paid if they refuse to attend work isn't within s44 if you think about it properly; it's effectively about sickness. And so in those circumstances, I'd say that people wouldn't be entitled to be paid.

Daniel Barnett
I take a slightly different view on it. Because although I agree with the ultimate conclusion you've put, which is that in a lot of these circumstances, people are not entitled to be paid. I look on it as part of the wage work bargain, which is that in order to be entitled to a wage, you've got to be ready, willing and able to work. Somebody who is staying at home because they're anxious about being infected with coronavirus might be ready to work, they might be able to work but they're just not willing to work. And so I take the view that because they're not upholding their their end of the work wage bargain, they're not entitled to a salary. But there's a lot of people out there who take a very, very different view. Michael Ford, in particular, I think, is quite clear on Twitter that he thinks that those of us who think employees don't have a claim for detriment under s44 - if they're not paid when they're off work due to Coronavirus anxiety - are wrong. How long do you think it's going to take for the courts to resolve this?

Gus Baker
It could take some time because no doubt there are arguments both ways. I mean, I'd be interested if you agree with me about the burning building analogy. Are employees entitled to be paid for the days of work where the building is burning down, so they run out of the fire? I'd say that's clearly over the line. And that is a detriment if they're deprived of pay. And so the questions for the courts, which will take them years to resolve is where is that line drawn? Where's the focus on the danger? And where's the focus on the employee's ability to work?

Daniel Barnett
What claims under the Equality Act can we expect to see brought in relation to people's safety?

Gus Baker
I expect these to be quite common. I'm already advising on a fair few of them. We know that coronavirus doesn't affect people equally. It affects older people more. It can affect ethnic minorities more, some statistics show. It affects men more. And so you have unequal burdens of danger. And what that will mean is where policies are put in place, which require someone to come into contact with other people who could give them an infection, you could well say that older people, men, ethnic minorities and disabled people are at a particular disadvantage in those circumstances. And that is effectively the beginning of a test for an indirect discrimination claim. And so I think it'd be quite easy for people to show that they're in those vulnerable groups, that they're at a particular disadvantage. The question will really come down to the justification the employer can give for putting them at that disadvantage. And the courts may not adopt a particularly high threshold of saying, well, obviously the business has to carry on. But if I wasn't devising an employer in that situation, I'd want the employer to have complied with all of the government guidance and done everything that they should have done. If they hadn't, I think I might be advising that an indirect discrimination claim - or a failure to make reasonable adjustments claim if the

employee was disabled - might have some prospects of success.

Alex

If a clinically vulnerable frontline key worker with a shielding letter wants to opt out of a COVID risk assessment - which says they should only work from home or shield at home - can they continue working?

Gus Baker

So if they are a key worker, can they opt out of a risk assessment? It might well be thought to be unreasonable to opt out of a risk assessment, is a starting point. The risk assessment is likely to take into account the person's vulnerabilities - or should take into account the vulnerabilities. It probably comes down to the test for reasonableness because what that person is going to be bringing - assuming that they may well be disabled - is a reasonable adjustments claim. And in that claim, the employer's duty is to take reasonable steps to avoid a substantial disadvantage. And so the focus of the tribunal and the reasonable adjustments claim is the ultimate result. But you've got to look at all of the situations for reasonableness there. What is it that the employer has done to keep them safe? How reasonable is working from home? It's not reasonable, perhaps, for a firefighter who's supposed to rescue people from burning buildings, but it might be reasonable for an accountant. All of those factors are going to get put into the mix, decided in a case like that.

Ed Jenneson

What happens if an employee has an exemption for face covering due to an underlying health condition? Can the employer still force that employee to wear a face covering?

Gus Baker

That is, again, a really interesting and difficult question. I suspect this might be litigated. Because what you have there is a conflict between the employee's rights under the Equality Act primarily, versus the interests of

the employers, customers and other members of staff. And so to address it from a reasonable adjustments point of view, let's assume that they'd be at a substantial disadvantage in complying with the policy of wearing face masks. Let's say that that's right. The question then becomes: is allowing them not to wear the face covering a reasonable step? Well, it meets one test of a reasonable step, because it will alleviate that disadvantage. But what an employer might say - backed up by government advice and medical evidence - is, well, it's a reasonable step for you, employee. It'll sort out the problem for you, but it doesn't help the rest of our employees and our customers, or service users. And so those are decisions that are going to be right on the threshold that employers are going to have to make. It will be really context dependent. And it may also be dependent on the stage we're at in the pandemic. Let's hope in a month or two's time, there are almost no cases, and so there's a little danger of someone like that not wearing a face covering. If we're back where we were in early January, I'd probably expect employers to insist that people wear face coverings if they're going to be in customer-facing roles.

Ken Morrison

If an employee wants to come into work and the employer also wants the employee to come into work, but the employee has been told to shield by the NHS, can they still come into work?

Daniel Barnett

I think that's a nice one-word answer, isn't it?

Gus Baker

You think the one-word answer is yes, don't you?

Daniel Barnett

I do.

Gus Baker

I think the answer is 'probably'. Because as I said, there's no employment law problem on its face there. You can come in, there's an agreement, but what about s2 Health and Safety at Work Act? Employers have a positive duty to take steps to ensure that people are reasonably safe. And so if the employer's judgment is it could be really dangerous for this person to come into work, there's a question about whether that positive duty is being fulfilled. Now, I think it would probably be fine, and again, it's really context dependent. But say you had someone who was a really high severity risk and COVID, who was working in a really high-risk area, I wonder - even if they volunteered to come in - whether the employer would be complying with their duty under the Health and Safety at Work Act if they allow them to put themselves at risk.

Daniel Barnett
Does their duty under s2 extend to where an employee gives their fully informed consent?

Gus Baker
It does. You can't consent to get rid of the employer's duty to look after your safety. So you can't say: no hardhats on this building site will be fine.

Andy Crisp
To what extent is an employer responsible for the health and safety of an employee who only works from home?

Gus Baker
Again, that is an absolutely great question. And there is no easy answer to it. It will come down to reasonableness. But we've all been working in very difficult and different ways. So people who are used to nice office chairs, like the one I've got, might find themselves with hard-back chairs in their kitchen. And so I think an employer needs to look like they're taking steps and have thought about it and investigated what steps they can take. But I think the courts will be quite generous to employers who aren't able to provide everything for employees when they're working in their own space, which they control.

Citizens Advice adviser
We're getting a lot of calls from people who are concerned they're not working in COVID-safe workplaces, but there seems to be guidance rather than law, and it's problematic for us to give much advice if the employer doesn't abide with guidance, particularly as many are low paid workers, any thoughts?

Daniel Barnett
I suppose what the adviser is asking is that if there's no black and white piece of law - other than perhaps s44 and s100 about the provision of safety equipment and safety policies, workplaces - what can people do if employers aren't complying with guidance?

Gus Baker
Well, I mean, if your workplace is unsafe, the employer may be in fundamental breach of your employment contract. And so in theory, an employee could resign and claim constructive dismissal. But that, of course, is the big red button for employment lawyers. It's an incredibly risky thing to do, and the only remedy for that step may be many years away after much cost and arguments in front of an employment tribunal. You could refer your employer to the HSE, the Health and Safety Executive, and make a complaint there. It might be sensible to write to the employer and express your concern. That will probably be a protected disclosure if you give information about the danger. And so depending on what the employer does next, you're quite likely to be protected from any action. But the adviser who asked that question is right, it's an invidious situation for employees who are working in dangerous environments, because it's hardly good advice for employment lawyers to say, well, pack up your stuff, resign and claim constructive dismissal. Because that doesn't engage with their needs to pay their bills the next month.

Jim Smith
Is it actually a legal requirement for an employer to carry out a risk assessment for

153

each and every person who announces they're pregnant?

Gus Baker
I'll say that I don't know that off the top of my head. It would be wise is to think about risk assessments for that, especially during COVID. I don't know of that legal obligation, but there may well be something like that.

Daniel Barnett
My understanding is that there is a duty to conduct a risk assessment for pregnant women if they work in environments with chemicals or hazardous materials as a discrete statutory obligation. But other than that, there's no specific requirement to conduct a risk assessment. But it is generally regarded as basic good practice for an employer to do so. But I'm not sure I'm right on that, and it sounds to me like you're not 100% sure, either.

Anonymous
How should you deal with employees who refuse to work with an individual who won't take the vaccine?

Gus Baker
It's a great question. I'm not sure that fellow employees are, at this stage, going to be able to insist that their co-workers take the vaccine. And I don't think that an employer faced with employees who said they won't work with someone who won't take the vaccine should have much sympathy with their employees there. Whether someone is able to and can take the vaccine may be affected by a multiplicity of different reasons. And we do know that there are certain groups with protective characteristics who are less likely to or less able to take the vaccine. So I think that employers are unlikely to be sympathetic to that. I think that an employee suing their employer for not taking action against a fellow employee for not taking the vaccine might not succeed.

Gillian Howard
What would an employment tribunal regard as a 'reasonable belief' pursuant to s44 Employment Rights Act?

Daniel Barnett
So just to expand on that for people who are listening, you have a right not to be subjected to detriments if you stay at home or leave work because of a reasonable belief that if you remain in work, you will face a serious and imminent danger to your health. What's a reasonable belief?

Gus Baker
It's a great question. A reasonable belief has to be a belief that you actually hold. So I've seen allegations of people saying that they are worried about COVID-19, so they won't go into their job, but then they were very happy to go down the pub with many people there at the same time back when pubs were open. And so the belief has to be one you actually hold about danger. And it has to be based on reasonable grounds. And so those can't be conspiratorial, they can't be overly worried or paranoid, but if you're able to say, around this time, there were X thousand people who were suffering from coronavirus in my local area and my job requires me to come into contact with them, the facts that you can assert need to be laid down like building blocks to make a reason for belief. Thinking about it like an office fire, just saying I believe there might be a fire won't be a reasonable belief. But saying, I smell smoke and all of the fire alarms are going off, those two facts would be enough to make a reasonable belief happen. So focus on those facts that the employee knows about to determine whether the belief is reasonable or not.

Daniel Barnett
it sounds a little bit like, in a whistleblowing context, the difference between making an allegation and disclosing facts that actually tend to disclose information.

We're getting some comments regarding the question about whether there's a requirement to have risk assessments for all pregnant women. And we don't seem to have very much common ground here. David Thomas has said there's a specific requirement for a risk assessment on being notified in writing of the pregnancy, usually on a MAT B1 form. Quentin Colborn says precisely the opposite, which reflects my understanding. Quentin is a lay member on employment tribunals. He says HSE on the website state that while it's a legal obligation for employers to regularly review general workplace risks, there's actually no legal requirement to conduct a specific separate risk assessment for new and expectant mothers. Adrian Barnes says your employers should ensure you adhere to national guidance and advice for pregnant women. I'm not sure that's bang on point.

Pardip Singhota
An employee has a number of medical conditions but hasn't been asked to shield. The workplace has had a COVID-19 risk assessment and it's safe for the employee to return but the employee doesn't want to come back. They're not giving any detail why they feel unsafe, other than referring back to a pre-existing medical condition for which they weren't invited to shield. Any suggestions on options available to the employer before dismissal?

Gus Baker
I think the key in any claims about danger in the workplace and dismissals for people not wanting to come back is a really clear exchange of information. So you as the employer need to explain what you are doing to make that workplace as safe as it possibly can be. And don't just say the workplace is COVID-secure, because that doesn't mean anything and it doesn't get you anywhere. List the facts that you rely on to say the workplace is as safe as you reasonably can make it, and then invite the employee to list the facts that they say mean that they feel unable to

come back to the workplace. They might point out something to you that you can address, and you might be able to persuade them to come back with no problems. Or their response might be so unreasonable that if an employment tribunal was ever to look at a dispute like that, they'd know the employer was in the right and the employee was in the wrong. But the key before any decisions are taken is to have a really clear list of facts on which you rely, explain to the employee and understand what they're saying as well. Because I think employers are going to get in most trouble where they take decisions thinking that what they've done is reasonable. But what they haven't done is explain that to the employee. Or on the contrary where they think that what they've done is reasonable, but they haven't heard about the employee's specific concerns and dealt with those. So that exchange of information is key and I would advise any employer to do it before anything else.

Daniel Barnett
I think we have an answer to the pregnancy question. It's found in regulation 16(1) Management of Health and Safety at Work Regulations 1999, which is that there's no general requirement to have a risk assessment specifically for any woman when she becomes pregnant unless the work is of a kind that involves risk because of a pregnancy to the health and safety of the baby because of physical, biological or chemical hazards.

Celine has reminded me of the decision of the Court of Appeal in Madarassy v Nomura (*Madarassy v Nomura International Plc [2006] EWHC 748 (QB)*) in which the Court of Appeal said there is no general duty to carry out risk assessments for pregnant women.

Diana Eguizabal
Does a carer with severe asthma, who because of her asthma can't wear a face mask, have a right to be paid if she can't work in a care home and no alternative work can be found?

Gus Baker

Well, you'll remember the difference I gave between where someone refuses to turn up to their work, because it's literally on fire, and the focus is on a problem with the workplace, versus someone who - forget COVID ever happened - had an operation, maybe in 2018, and said I had an operation and I'm really vulnerable to the flu. I'm not coming to work. So those are the two examples as far as I'm concerned. And I think the carer with asthma falls nearer to the latter example. What it really is is something about her that means she's unable to come and do her duties at work, not something about the workplace itself. And so in my view, it's unlikely that she'd be entitled to be paid under s44 if she refused to attend work. And so you might ask whether if her asthma was a disability, paying her would be a reasonable adjustment - I'm pretty sure the answer is no, paying her wouldn't be a reasonable adjustment. So my view there is I don't think it's likely she's entitled to pay when she's not able to attend the workplace.

Jim Jaffri

What case law is there around employers failing to protect an employee's mental health? And linked to that, is there a minimum standard employers should follow in order to protect mental health?

Gus Baker

So let's just take it from a point of general principle. The duty that I told you about earlier, under s2 of the Health and Safety at Work Act, just talks about the health, safety and welfare of employees. It doesn't explicitly say mental health, but mental health is included in that, as far as I understand. And that's the same for the Employment Rights Act and the Equality Act as far as claims under those acts would go. And so the employed contractual duty to take reasonable steps to look after employees' health will extend to their mental health. And as we know, mental health-related claims are very common in reasonable adjustment claims, discrimination arising from disability

claims and everything else. So there is that positive duty, again, for employers to think positively about employees' mental health, to take steps to make sure it's not being damaged workplace.

Jamie Anderson

Do the facts found by an employment tribunal on stress-related unfair dismissal claims bind a county court in a subsequent personal injury claim for breach of duty in respect of depression?

Gus Baker

I'm going to guess, but I don't think so. I don't see any statutory basis for employment tribunals to bind county courts. And as we know, employment tribunals are a statutory creation.

Daniel Barnett

I wonder if there's an issue relating to estoppel? Could that be a problem that might cause a county court judge to be bound?

Gus Baker

It might pose a problem. It would depend who is suing for what because an employee might well sue, for example, for unfair dismissal - that's something that the county court doesn't have jurisdiction to decide - and also sue for personal injury in a county court. There's no problem with an employee doing both because they can only make those claims in those respective jurisdictions. How employment tribunals and county courts would divvy up factual findings there is something I don't know off the top of my head.

Monica Beckles

Would a mandatory vaccine policy be discriminatory due to the disproportionate risk, perceived or otherwise, of the vaccine? For example, BAME individuals appear more worried about the vaccine. And the very low percentage of ethnic minorities involved in the trial appears to give grounds. Would such a policy requiring employees to have a vaccine be indirect discrimination?

Gus Baker

Here's the unhelpful lawyer's answer. I think maybe. A mandatory vaccine policy I'm sure would get over the first few steps of an indirect discrimination claim at the moment on two grounds. The questioner is quite right that BAME people are statistically less likely to have opted to take the vaccine, but I know another group who haven't been able to take the vaccine yet, which is young people - a protected characteristic under the Equality Act. So, a mandatory vaccination policy at the moment would certainly put people with certain protective characteristics at disadvantages compared to people with other protective characteristics. The question is whether that can be objectively justified. And that's a question on which there's going to be scientific evidence as well. If it turns out that in a few years' time, almost everyone has taken the vaccine, the vaccine is scientifically proven to be incredibly effective, but COVID is in such a form that it would be really dangerous for someone not to have taken the vaccine, that might move the needle for justification. And so when you're thinking about that justification test, all of the facts go into the pot, including the time at which the decisions were made. At the moment, I don't think the employer could justify a mandatory vaccination policy, but who knows where we'll be in two or three years' time?

Caroline Lewis

What are the health and safety protections for workers - as opposed to employees - given that many low-paid precarious positions are filled by workers, not employees?

Gus Baker

The good news for workers is that they're also protected under the Health and Safety at Work Act, as are members of the public, actually, who enter workplaces. There's no question there that employers have a duty to take positive steps to advance the health and safety of workers as well. Interestingly - and this emerged in the IWGD case - s44 and s100 of the Employment Rights Act are phrased with regards to employees rather than workers. But the UK failed to implement the European directives on which those provisions were based, which would have covered workers. But it's an incredibly difficult question of post-Brexit law whether anything can be done about that. There may be no remedy for workers there. But the other point is that in tort and in contracts, there will also be those implied terms and a duty of care to look after workers, and indeed members of the public as well, who come into workplaces. So in terms of personal injury claims people are protected.

Neil Coombes

Would it be a potentially fair dismissal to dismiss an employee who takes a risk at work in which only they were injured? For example, jumping over a wall to take a shortcut and breaking their ankle?

Gus Baker

My very short answer is yes, that would be a potentially fair dismissal. It could be a dismissal for conduct, doing something really dangerous, and it could constitute for some other substantial reason, I guess, as well. So yes, I think that could be a fair dismissal.

Anonymous

In the case of umbrella companies using agencies, who is ultimately legally responsible for health and safety?

Gus Baker

The employer will have positive duties under the Health and Safety at Work Act, the person who's controlling the workplace will have positive duties under that act as well, and to the extent to which Equality Act claims can be brought, that's quite a vexed question. And similarly, with regards to Employment Rights Act questions, because you'd have to untangle who was an employee of whom, looking at cases like London borough, Greenwich, which are really quite difficult too. But if you're thinking of personal injury claims, yes, there will be duties owed by those agencies, by the ultimate employer and by whoever's in control of the employees or agency workers and subjecting them to danger.

Melanie Bonas

If an employee works with farm animals, has received training on handling them, but has suddenly demonstrated they're no longer confident of working with the farm animals, what health and safety duties does an employer have to this employee, if any?

Gus Baker

Wow. There may be some specific handling of animals regulations that I've never come across in practice. Generally, the health and safety work activities, again, are going to be the ones that take place here, taking reasonable steps to ensure that as far as reasonably practicable, the health and safety of that employee is protected. And so that's the basic duty and I can't see why it wouldn't fly in those circumstances. It may be there's the People Handling Regulations 1998 that provide more detailed guidance, but if there is I haven't heard.

Anonymous

What are your thoughts about dismissing an employee for gross misconduct for failing to socially distance at work?

Daniel Barnett

It's similar to the mask question, but of course, people may not wear a mask for medical reasons. Social distancing wouldn't necessarily involve medical reasons.

Gus Baker

I think it's very simple. It's potentially fair to do that. If someone is repeatedly breaking workplace rules, that could count as insubordination, which would be a conduct dismissal, potentially fair, subject to everything. Now thinking about substantive things, and the test, would someone slapping someone else on the back to say well done very briefly, once, forgetting about COVID, constitute gross misconduct? I don't think it would. But if someone persistently refuses to follow workplace rules, I think that you've got a potentially and quite possibly substantively fair dismissal.

Mike Clyne

In your opinion, do you think there are going to be any changes to health and safety legislation as a result of the pandemic?

Gus Baker

I think s44 and s100 and the Employment Rights Act are inapt. They're not particularly helpful tools to think about infectious diseases under. Whether the government is going to take the bold step of changing those provisions would be a very difficult question and might raise problems with the Brexit agreement that they struck, because those provisions find their basis in EU law. But I do think that we'll end up with some sorts of regulations about dealing with infectious diseases at work. Because our current statutory framework isn't really set up to deal with this pandemic.

Daniel Barnett

Gus Baker from Outer Temple Chambers, thank you very much.

IR35

DAVID KIRK, DAVID KIRK AND CO

Daniel Barnett

Today I'm joined by David Kirk from David Kirk and Co, and he's here to talk about IR35. IR35 is coming into force for medium and large employers from 6 April and it's causing a lot of controversy and difficulty up and down the country.

David, good afternoon. Can I start by asking you a question off my own bat, if I may? Why is the government changing the rules?

David Kirk

Well, as with anything to do with tax, there's a history. Britain is, I think, probably unique, certainly almost unique in having a system whereby you can pay less tax by operating through a limited company than by having a direct relationship with your employer, or your engager. Limited companies have been around since 1854, and were set up for very different reasons. But in the world of tax, things appear and then stay when they should disappear. They were actually set up to encourage gun manufacturers to provide weapons for the Crimean War, which is not the sort of people who normally expect to get a tax break.

In 1999, to bring things forward, when it became easier and easier, and loads of people are operating through companies, Gordon Brown announced in the Budget, that he was going to introduce an anti-avoidance rule, and the press release with which this was announced was called IR35, hence the name, and that said, we're going to look through the company and what the

relationship would be if the person was directly engaged by his client or employer or whatever you like. There was uproar about this, and both contractors, people doing work and big business insisted that it should be the personal service companies, the little things, that were responsible for deciding whether IR35 should be there, whether it was actually an employment relationship.

But this left the Revenue with over 100,000 companies who they think ought to be applying it and haven't been. They can't possibly keep up. They went to the chancellor in 2015 and said, we can't manage this. We've got to put it back to where we originally intended, which is with the end clients, hirers, end users, whatever you'd like to call them, the businesses for which these people are actually working or might be the agencies that have hired them to be there. Now just to make one other point, the avoidance that's been going on, if it has, that's a matter of opinion, is about 82%, by my calculation, done by the employers that's big business and indeed big government up to 2017 because they have not been paying the Employers' National Insurance Contributions. The contractors, whilst they've been paying the wrong sort of tax, do actually pay quite a bit. So I hope that puts it in context.

Caroline Hitchen

Can you summarise the difference between the IR35 test and the employment law employment status test?

David Kirk

It depends where you start. There are several ways of looking at this, and the way I like to look at it, there is a fundamental employment status test, which is the same for employment law and tax law - and indeed other branches as well, as copyright law comes into this too. There are also statutory extensions, most of which are in tax. In employment law, if you've got a company in the middle, as I understand it, you aren't an employee. In tax law, there's a special provision to say that you are. The same applies if you're working through an agency, you can be an employee for tax and have to operate PAYE, otherwise you wouldn't get employment rights.

Amanda Coates

Are there are plans to extend IR35 to small firms - because at the moment, it only applies to large and medium firms - in the foreseeable future?

David Kirk

I think probably not. Small firms, where the small firm is the client, and it's the client we're talking about here, the end client, then it remains the case as under the present rules that the personal service company, the PSC, has to decide whether to operate it or not. And the same will be true for foreign clients as well. I don't think there are any plans to extend that because the financial secretary who was responsible for deciding this, the politician, actually, insisted that small firms should be kept out of this because of the compliance burden. But we shall see.

Julia MacDonald

If the CEST - the government website Check Employment Status for Tax - test comes back as unable to make a determination, what do we do next?

Daniel Barnett

Just before you answer that, David, let me just add some flesh to the bones there. The government has this tool, which is quite useful

for the obvious cases, which tells you whether you're going to fall within IR35 or not, whether you're an employee or not. I actually put myself into that tool and answered the questions, and I'm obviously - I could not be a better example of somebody who is self-employed. I have two limited companies, I'm a practicing barrister, I have a radio presenting career and I have a number of other things that I do as well, and the ridiculous CEST tool came back as 'cannot determine'. And I think I don't even get anywhere near the grey area - I'm obviously a self-employed individual contracting on my own behalf. But that's not the question. That's just me mocking the ridiculousness of the CEST tool. David, what happens if it comes back as 'employment status cannot be determined'?

David Kirk

Well, just to reassure you, I did the same and got the same result. So that's all. I'm afraid to say you have to take advice from somewhere else. The Revenue have made it quite clear they aren't going to help. They are only there to come after you afterwards and see whether you have been doing things correctly, and they will make their own decisions as to who they go for. The CEST tool, as it's called, is not producing a determination one way or the other in about 20% of cases. And these are just precisely the ones where you need to know because if it can't tell, you can't tell, there is a grey area. Round about 3% of the working population, according to academic studies, is difficult to determine.

Daniel Barnett

If the system spits out the assessed result saying somebody is subject to IR35 or is an employee etc., will HMRC consider itself bound by that result, or could it depart from it?

David Kirk

They say they will, provided that you filled in the questions correctly. Now you're dealing with a whole load of industries and different terminology here, and so there's quite a possibility that you may not have done. But

If you have filled them in correctly, then they should be bound.

Mandi
With the advent of the IR35 extension to the private sector, coupled with the Supreme Court's decision in the Uber case *(Uber BV and others v Aslam and others [2021] UKSC 5)*, is it possible or likely that ET judges may make the leap to finding off-payroll, personal service companies, employees, for the purposes of employment rights, or with the existence and benefits of the limited company intermediary, be fatal to giving personal service company individuals employee status?

Dvid Kirk
Well, I think there's quite a strong possibility that they will. This comes from a reading of the Uber judgments, which, to cut a long story short, they will decide to extend employment rights to people working through personal service companies. The Uber case, as I understand it, said that you start by looking at the relationship, not at the contract, which is not the way we've done things in the past, and certainly not tax. And with tax law already going in that direction, this is very much on the political agenda. A lot of people are saying 'if I'm paying taxes an employee, I ought to have employment rights. And with that approach, I think, well, it may well happen.

Beth Bearder
As employment lawyers, should we report to HMRC if we become aware that a client isn't complying with IR35?

Daniel Barnett
Now, Beth, David can't advise you on your ethical responsibilities as a lawyer, but is there an obligation in the tax legislation, David, that requires professional advisors to grass clients up to HMRC? Could it come within the money laundering regulations, for example?

David Kirk
It could come within the money laundering regulations, which I don't know quite how they apply to lawyers. I believe they don't all apply to barristers in the same way as to solicitors. I may be wrong there. There's also a corporate - it's got to be a company here - requirement to prevent tax evasion, which I don't really want to go into in this webinar, because it's pretty complicated, but you have to have to watch out.

Daniel Barnett
I'm going to just ask you a couple of supplemental questions on that. You said corporate requirement to prevent tax evasion, does that apply to LLPs, which is the form that many solicitors' firms take?

David Kirk
I'm not sure, to be honest, I'd have thought it quite likely does.

Daniel Barnett
And presumably, they all would have thought that legal professional privilege or legal advice privilege would be a defence to that. In other words, a lawyer is not normally obliged to grass up its clients.

David Kirk
I think that's correct, but I don't have expertise in this area. I have a limited company myself, so I have to have to watch out.

Gillian Buxton
If a contractor states that they incur expenses or financial risk, and they work for other clients as well, is there an obligation to look behind these statements if you're a hirer, or can those statements be taken on face value?

David Kirk
I don't think there's an obligation to look behind them, but you might be wise to do so. One of the problems with employment status is that there are things when it comes to determining whether you're in business on your own account, which are only known to the worker. And certainly, the advice I have been giving is that if you're a client needing to determine this, and somebody tries to say that,

you say, well, fine, I hear what you say, but you've got to prove it.

Kelly Millar
Where the fee payer and the end user are different entities, for example, where an agency is involved, who makes the IR35 decision, and who is potentially liable for the tax?

David Kirk
Well, generally speaking, the fee payer is liable for the tax, and so has to make the decision. The problem is the fee payer doesn't really know very much about the situation to be able to do that. And that's why there's a regime called status determination statements, which are done by the client, and the client has to pass them on to the fee payer. The fee payer is not bound by them, and in particular, there may be problems if the status says outside IR35 and Revenue come along and say, actually, inside. Generally speaking, the fee payer will still be liable then, so if you're working for an agency, who will be a fee payer, I would say make sure it's in your contract that you can get back to the client about that.

Lawrence Guyner
Does IR35 apply if somebody hires staff from an employment agency rather than through a personal service company?

David Kirk
If there's no personal service company in the chain, so you've got a chain: client, agency, worker, no, it doesn't. The test there is different. It's called the supervision, direction and control test and it's a lot narrower, and certainly, if you've got somebody wanting to be self-employed, I think it's going to be the safest thing to do to pay them in that way. That said, this isn't the law at the moment. But we are expecting, we've been promised an announcement in the budget on Monday week to change it so that is so.

Dave Chaplin
Why are some firms running so scared of off-payroll, and as a result blanket banning contractors?

David Kirk
Well, first of all, 'off-payroll' is the new generic term for IR35, which the Revenue are using for the new public sector rules, which you might hear referred to as Chapter 10, because of the chapter in the act, whereas the old ones are Chapter 8. Big business doesn't like risk. If you pay somebody you think is self-employed £1,000, and the Revenue come along afterwards and say, 'hey, you've got that wrong, you ought to have deducted PAYE', you have to pay £458 over to the Revenue, of which £320 ought to have been deducted and wasn't, and you're going to have to whistle to get it back. Now, when you're doing things on a large scale, people simply can't afford that, and so that's why they are running scared. It's not in anybody's budgets to take a risk on that sort of thing, and to be safe they're blanket banning contractors or finding other ways of making them fit into the system.

Daniel Barnett
Caroline Hitchen, you will recall, asked the very first question about whether there's going to be a divergence or convergence in the test for employment status between employment rights on the one hand, and tax assessment on the other. Caroline has a follow up question.

Caroline Hitchen
Could you comment on whether there's that divergence or convergence for individuals who don't operate through an intermediary, but nevertheless are possibly self-employed?

David Kirk
In other words, you're talking about people in the grey area who have just them and the people are working for. Basically, the state of determination for these people is, as far as I can see, and I've done a lot of research on this, exactly the same, but for one thing, which is that you can't enforce employment rights until - I think it's two years, isn't it, Daniel? - you've been an employee. In tax, it's used to determine which set of tax rules you go under, including PAYE deductions, and that starts

straight away, obviously. Other than that they should be the same.

Liz Burley
What are the particular factors which tend to put people into the grey area of 'can't determine status'?

Daniel Barnett
I assume, Liz, you're talking about CEST.

David Kirk
If it's CEST, I try to avoid looking at it. There are three basic tests for employment status, and a whole lot of subtests. Some of the tests are black and white, others are anything but. Then we'll get some value judgments, and there are really two areas where value judgments come into play. One is the level of control exercised over the putative employee, and the other is all the factors that make up being a business on your own account. Now, in CEST, in particular, if there's any sign of any control, they'll say you're nicked, if I could use a colloquial expression. So that's one example of people being pushed out of the grey area when they should be more likely in it actually, and they don't really look at all the tests of being in business on their own account.

Steven Eckett
What's the best way for contractors to protect themselves from the impact of IR35? Should they just accept they're likely to be workers or employees?

David Kirk
If you're a contractor, you've really got to assess your own bargaining power. For a great many people, I'm afraid to say they won't be able to get out of it now, because it's not their decision. Those who can, well, if you're in, you might like to ask for some more money to cover it. In particular, one big issue is going to be expenses, because you won't be able to claim expenses for getting to work now, whereas with your own personal service company, you could. Otherwise do make sure that you don't have a contract which allows the employer to

push down your gross pay if they decide that you're inside IR35. That's actually illegal.

Su Apps
Where there is a right to substitute - but this has never been exercised in practice - is it for the client or personal service company to prove it's genuine, or for HMRC to prove that it isn't?

Daniel Barnett
Maybe a third option there, it's for the hirer to make a decision. But what's your view, David?

David Kirk
In tax law, you have to prove that you're not liable for tax. So basically, you start off by looking at the contract here. But the tribunals do look at whether a right to substitute is realistic or not. And curiously, the higher up you go in the chain, the more niche your particular expertise, the less likely it is to be realistic. So you've got to look at that. But if you can substitute in any circumstances so that you don't actually have to turn up to work at all, then that should be all right.

Daniel Barnett
David, I'm wondering myself whether it's possible, if you're a contractor, to challenge a hirer's determination that you fall within IR35. So let's say the hirer has taken the cautious view and said IR35, because we don't want to be liable for lots of extra tax if we get this the wrong way round, but the end user, the individual worker, disagrees, what can the worker do to challenge it?

David Kirk
There is a provision in the law for making representations, which the client then has to consider; remember, it's the client who has issued the status determination statement, and they have to do that within 45 days and give reasons as well. Whether that's going to be any good remains to be seen, and I suspect it very often won't. You might have rights in contract to say that money shouldn't have been deducted, although where it has been you can sue for the price

of the contract, and you probably don't want to do that. You can go back to HMRC, who will probably hand you the money and ask questions afterwards, which means if they have to hand it back again, it's really not very easy. Bearing in mind, though, that if that hirer or fee payer is now paying Employers' National Insurance Contributions, there won't be so much money in it, as there has been up to now. So whether it would be worthwhile is really up to you.

Daniel Barnett
Presumably, the first thing to do is - if you're going against HMRC, or asking for a refund from HMRC - to make a request for the return of the National Insurance Contributions deducted in error.

David Kirk
That's right. That's the best thing to do, and you can do that as soon as they've been deducted. For income tax, you have to deal with that in your self-assessment tax return, by declaring a lot of PAYE paid, and the income as self-employed, not employment income, or some such thing, and you have to do that manually, which means by 31st of October, because the Revenue software will reject it.

Leonie Woodward
I know IR35 applies to some companies, is it the same rules for all?

Daniel Barnett
I'm not sure if she's asking whether IR35 is going to be extended to small businesses, or whether she's asking if there's a different approach between public sector employers and, now, large and medium private sector employees.

David Kirk
Well, put it this way, there are two sets of rules already. At the moment, there's one for the public sector and one for the private sector; the public sector rules are being extended to cases where the client is large or medium-sized, and British, in the private sector as from April the

sixth. So there will still be two sets of rules. Whether it applies or not depends on your employment status. That's the most important thing to remember about all this. I hope that answers the question.

Nicola Tager
Are sole traders unaffected by IR35? And if they're unaffected, please explain why companies aren't encouraging sole traders as contractors.

David Kirk
If you're genuinely a sole trader, you should be unaffected. The problem is that the client might not agree with that, and it's now the client's decision as to whether you're within the rules or not. If you've got a direct relationship, no company, it's just you and the person you're working for, it is already the position that your client or customer has to determine your employment status, and there have been cases at employment tribunals on that sort of thing. So it's not something you can just decide for yourself.

Daniel Barnett
And presumably as well, I'm just adding to that, David, the fact that there is an intermediary, limited company or personal service company in the middle of hirer and contractor to a very large extent, certainly up to now, has protected the hirer from many of the employment rights that would otherwise fall due.

David Kirk
I'm sure that's true. And up to now, from having to pay tax as well.

Nick Hine
If a company uses contractors and falls into the small business exemption, would you still recommend they conduct a status determination test just in case HMRC asks?

David Kirk
No, I wouldn't. I think it's an enormous bureaucracy, and small companies have been left out of this, because it's deemed by the

politicians to be too much for them. And I'd take what they say at face value and not do it. Why do you need to? You are not going to have to pay the tax yourself. If you know that somebody is not operating IR35 when they should, well that goes back to the corporate requirement to prevent tax evasion, which I was talking about earlier. But I think you pretty well have to be on notice on that.

Daniel Barnett
David, before I come to the next question, just give some idea from your own experience. How many organisations are you personally advising on IR35, and what does the general consensus of employers tend to be about it?

David Kirk
I'm a sole practitioner, so I don't have a huge number of clients, probably in double figures, and a number of personal service companies as well. I've shepherded some through the tax tribunal over the last few years, so I've seen this from both sides of the equation. Most of the people who have come to approach me have really done so because I think they're finding it very complicated and want to know what's going on. Certainly, solutions have to be tailored, and sometimes it's possible to have a mass testing regime, with quite a lot of it done by IT. But that can be very expensive if you've got a lot of people on one-day contracts, so for example, a training company might. You need to have something more generic for that.

Andy Crisp
If HMRC decide that a contractor should have been on payroll, and subsequently charges tax to the business, will HMRC take into account the tax the individual contracts has already paid under self-assessment?

David Kirk
This is a very contentious issue. If you've got a direct relationship, there's no personal service company, yes, they will if you make them. They hate it because it's an awful lot of work

and they like to do things on a big scale, but they will do it. Under IR35, it's more difficult because you've got an extra tax they can take into account, that's corporation tax, and also, they're not sure, it's not always obvious how much income that's been passed down the line, and so they're resisting doing that. Now on the IR35 forum, we've been making representations about this. I'm not afraid at liberty to tell you where they've got to, except to say that I'm not impressed with their response so far.

James Fairchild
If one is a small company, is IR35 a concern at all?

David Kirk
Yes, well, it's a question of whether you're a small company contractor or a small company client. If you're a small company client, as I say, make sure you still are a small company, but beyond that, I really wouldn't be bothered with it. If you're a contractor, you've got to know who you're looking for. If your client is a small company, a status determination statement shouldn't come down. But you'll find out whether you've had tax deducted or not when the money arrives anyway. If you don't get one, you can ask the company whether it's small, but I have to say I'm afraid you're very much on your own there.

Anonymous
Can you offer any guidance about drafting contracts for genuinely self-employed contractors?

Daniel Barnett
I think you've, in a way, answered this already in slightly different terms, David,

David Kirk
Well, not being a lawyer, I look at contracts and I suggest amendments to them, but I don't draft them because there are all sorts of things that have to go in there, which I don't know. I always say, first of all, make sure the contract reflects the reality on the ground. It will be

picked to pieces and trampled over mercilessly if you don't. Also, try and make sure that if you are looking at a right of substitution for somebody being self-employed, make sure that's realistic. Don't say too much about control because I think that just invites further questions. But beyond that, it's very much down to individual circumstances. I don't think I can say anything general.

Su Apps
Following up from Caroline Hitchen's questions, can we dig a little deeper into what the difference is in the definition of 'employee' for tax and employment purposes, because it's been established for a very long time - I mean you can be an employee for tax purposes, but not for employment purposes - when could that happen?

Daniel Barnett
I'm going to point out that for employment law purposes, you have three categories: employee, worker, self-employed, and for tax purposes you only have two: employ or not. So that very simple analysis immediately tells you that there's that middle category, workers, who could conceivably fall into either category.

David Kirk
In principle, there oughtn't to be, on the basic fundamental definition of who is an employee. Both employment and tax law derived from the case in 1968 concerning some Ready Mixed Concrete truck drivers (*Ready Mixed Concrete Ltd v Minister of Pensions [1968] 2 QB 497*), which is actually a National Insurance case. However, there are what I call statutory extensions, and there are quite a lot on the tax side. The main one, which affects a lot of people, is agency workers - people working through an agency. They don't get employment rights but they do have tax deducted under PAYE. The main other ones are managed service company workers, which, that's an avoidance provision; officers have tax deducted under PAYE, so company directors very often, for that reason, rather than any

other; and all sorts of local authority personnel as well, coroners and people like that. That's a statutory extension. But the basic fundamental thing is the same and has by and large been interpreted in the same way by the courts. There are some differences, but they're more differences of nuance than actual different criteria.

Su Apps
I'm sorry to keep harping on about this, but I think it's one that a lot of employment lawyers do struggle with, and we're always told there's a subtle difference between this test, and it was just to understand where that difference lies, whether we are still talking about control. All the things we put into the CEST test seem to me the same things when we're looking at employment status for employment law purposes. So I've always struggled to find when someone might be an employee for tax purposes, but not for employment status.

David Kirk
I think it is what I've said, it's where you've got a statutory extension. But otherwise, the tests are the same. The three basic tests, mutuality of obligation, control and the third one, which I shan't name, are the same for both, and they've been interpreted the same way. Except there are some minor differences on mutuality of obligation, which it would I would be very happy to correspond with you about. It's a very arcane subject, but they oughtn't to be there. As I was saying earlier, employment status in copyright law, negligence law, all derive from the same test as well.

Su Apps
Can I ask one more follow-up on that? I think you touched on it earlier. For IR35 purposes, there's more of a risk than I think has necessarily been out there in the guidance that someone if they are assessed as falling within IR35 could then acquire employment rights.

David Kirk

There is a risk, but that's for a slightly different reason. IR35 is a statutory extension. It comes from a statute and is explicitly designed to work for tax only. But I think the Uber case does actually give judges the green light to interpret it, and to interpret the law as giving people employment rights, who are in personal service companies as well. So the fact that the two are coming at the same time is probably coincidental. But there's no doubt the risk is there.

Daniel Barnett

I'm going to have a stab at answering as well. I think that a lot of the cases - and I'm certainly aware they exist, though I don't know the names off the top of my head - say that somebody can be an employee for tax purposes, but not for employment status, employment rights, or vice versa. I think those are all fairly old cases and they are used to justify a court struggling to distinguish precedence handed down from different tribunals. So on a particular set of facts, the EAT might want to find one thing, but it considers itself bound or embarrassed by something a tax tribunal's found. The only way to get around that without saying the tax tribunal got it wrong and doesn't know what it's talking about because they're a bunch of ignoramuses, is by saying although the tests look the same on the statute, book, in practice, they can have different results. I think it's nothing more than sophistry, and most of the cases that you're talking about - unless you know of any I don't - are all at least 20 years old. Am I right about that point?

David Kirk

I'd put it slightly differently, because some of the cases that look odd are tax cases and we haven't really time to get into that. I'd say one other thing, we've got around about 40 cases coming from the Court of Appeal and higher up now on this subject. I tend to look at what's coming out of there because at a low level it's actually relatively settled now to my mind.

Anonymous

If an end user has assessed a contractor as being outside IR35, but HMRC disagrees - so HMRC says they're inside IR35 - will a contractual indemnity for tax and Employers' National Insurance in the contract be effective? So is there any restriction in tax law that stops such recovery of Employers' National Insurance from the intermediary?

David Kirk

If we talk about Employers' National Insurance, yes, there is. From recollection, it's the Social Security Contribution and Benefits Act 1992, schedule one, paragraph 3a: "*You cannot try and recover Employers' National Insurance from anybody who's working for you, either in the contract or in practice, either directly or indirectly*". It's against the law.

Tracy Seymour

Are there clearly outlined criteria from the government as to what constitutes a small versus a medium employer?

David Kirk

Yes. They're not all that complex. I was looking at this only last week for somebody who's got a particularly unusual problem, and it's probably going to have to be within the regime for one year before they've got a way of getting out of it, because they're going to split the group up into two. And the solution that the government's come up with, I think is absolutely bonkers. You have to look at the small print here. Most of it is in guidance, which you'll find in the HMRC's employment status manual. It's actually one of the better ones and it is largely accurate - I do have one or two quibbles with it - but it gives a good guide to employment status. The trouble is, it's about 400 pages long.

Daniel Barnett

David, I think the question was just what's the test for a small company versus a medium company?

David Kirk

Small company versus medium company? I can't answer that briefly because there are several things that come into it. Basically, you're a medium company if you fit in two of the following three criteria. One is turnover of £10.2 million or more, a balance sheet of £5.1 million or more - and that's gross assets, not net assets - and 50 or more employees. But there are rules for groups, there are rules for people coming in and out of being small - all sorts of things you have to cope with - there are rules for non-companies - individuals, unincorporated associations. Anything to do with tax, I'm afraid to say you have to look at the small print.

Daniel Barnett

And for a final question - it's a nice easy one with a yes or no answer, I think.

Helen Shuttleworth

Does IR35 apply to contractors who work from the Republic of Ireland?

Daniel Barnett

Work FROM the Republic of Ireland? It shouldn't do, and I would make sure that you don't have a UK company. That can complicate things.

Daniel Barnett

David, thank you very much. That was David Kirk from David Kirk and Co. chartered accountants.

MENTAL HEALTH IN THE WORKPLACE

JODIE HILL, THRIVE LAW

Daniel Barnett

This afternoon's Q&A session is with Jodie Hill of Thrive Law on mental health in the workplace.

Jodie Hill, good afternoon. A couple of questions for me to start with. As a manager or somebody in HR, if you're told by someone that an employee is struggling with their mental health, what should you do?

Jodie Hill

If you are within the workplace and you actually suspect that someone is struggling, you should approach that individual, especially if you know them personally. If you are their manager, it would be sensible to arrange a one to one. Ultimately, what you're trying to do is create a safe place in which you want that individual to open up about their condition. Now, if you haven't got any information other than 'you just know', then, obviously, it's for that individual to share that information with you. You can ask some probing questions and you can ask them about their behaviours or ask them about any information that you've been given from other people, provided they've said that you can pass that information on.

Essentially, in order to create that safe environment, you do need to already have, in my view, quite an open culture. So, it really does depend on the culture of each workplace. But ultimately, I would be advocating for you to create a psychologically safe place for that individual to open up first, then explore if there are any reasonable adjustments for them if it's affecting their workplace. So, it really depends what comes out of that conversation as to where it goes next.

Daniel Barnett

I'm going to ask you for some top tips. What are the three things that every company, whether big or small, should have in place to support an employee's mental health?

Jodie Hill

I think the first thing is actually the culture. I think that's a really difficult thing to say, as a top tip, but essentially, it's a key element in creating a positive place where people can be open about their mental health. If you don't have a positive work culture where there's a genuine open-door policy and where people genuinely know that, if they're struggling, they can go to their manager or there's a designated person in the workplace to go to, then it's going to be really difficult to implement any effective or meaningful initiatives throughout the organisation because people don't feel engaged. So that's the first thing.

The second thing is that I would actually advocate Mental Health First Aiders. I think they are really, really helpful in an employment context for a few reasons. The first reason would be more from a proactive perspective. You can have those Mental Health First Aiders who generally have a deeper understanding of conditions on some of your committees, they can help with HR, but they can also help with any initiatives that you're running because they're generally people who've volunteered at all levels, and can actually give you a bit of insight into what individuals might be wanting. They also have a better understanding of mental health conditions. So Mental Health First Aiders from a proactive sense, but also in a reactive sense, where there's a crisis. We are seeing so many more people, unfortunately, taking their lives at work. Just as a physical first aider would help with a physical emergency, a Mental Health First Aider would help out in that situation. They would get the individual to a safe place, they would be able to support them in that immediate crisis moment, and they would signpost them and get emergency services there to help them.

The third top tip would have to be the mental health risk assessment, the One Mind Campaign (https://www.change.org/p/onemind-we-all-have-one-mind-and-we-need-to-protect-this-starting-in-the-workplace). It's something I'm personally very passionate about, mainly because I've seen it work so well in organisations. Essentially, it's asking individuals what their problems are at the moment, but not in an invasive way, using technology so that it's anonymous and actually trying to understand what people need in terms of support and training. It's also about identifying risks, so where someone might be already suffering with either depression or anxiety or another condition and they might be either a risk to themselves or to others. So it helps proactive analysis, but also, you've got the whole preventative piece. But actually, if there is a risk, can you put anything in place to support those individuals? That might be training, it might be an individual risk assessment on that person as well as the organisation.

Essentially, what we're doing is moving away from the tick-box approach that a lot of organisations have by just putting people on training, and actually looking at it more proactively and more preventatively when it comes to the wider initiative within the workplace.

Daniel Barnett
Presumably, something like that either cannot be anonymous or it has to rely on people being willing to volunteer information about their mental health and personal circumstances.

Jodie Hill
There are organisations that offer these assessments now. And you can do it anonymously, where the individual actually, in my experience, opens up more. It's a data-driven project and that data drives the organisation in terms of their investment in initiatives and training. The individual gets a self-care report, and that report then identifies to them if they're at risk and who to go to, but the manager doesn't see it. The other way you can do it is an individual risk assessment where you would obviously have to have that conversation directly with the individual to understand and they would obviously have to volunteer that information to their manager.

Daniel Barnett
There's often a tension in the workplace between managing performance and managing somebody's mental health. How do you reconcile that tension?

Jodie Hill
It's a difficult one. In my view, I would deal with a mental health problem first - make sure that that person is safe, make sure that they have the right support in place in the workplace, and also making sure that they know exactly what they need to be doing within their role. Then separately I'd deal with the performance issues because the adjustments are already in place. Now, as part of your process - it might be a long-term sickness absence process or a capability process - you may need to adjust those processes for the disability, depending on whether that's reasonable or not. But ultimately, balancing the needs of the organisation with

the mental health of the individual is a really difficult one. And it's taken very much on a by case-by-case basis, in my view.

Anonymous
We acknowledge how so many experience poor mental health and the effect this has. However, it does feel some employees play the system and claim mental health issues when informed of conduct or performance issues. Do you have any tips to handle this?

Jodie Hill
I think, as an employment lawyer myself, it comes up quite a lot in terms of a challenge that organisations tend to have. I would certainly say that if that does come up, first of all, explore whether it's a genuine concern or whether it's reactive to a situation that's stressful. If you're being managed for performance-related issues or misconduct, it is a stressful process, so it's natural to feel stressed. And I think that in those circumstances, it's differentiating between the stress of the circumstance and a genuine condition that may have caused the poor performance or may be contributing to the current situation.

So I think trying to do a bit of investigative work is really helpful at that stage because if you just dive straight into the misconduct or issues and don't deal with it, especially if they've brought it up - I know there was that case, not that long ago, where they didn't do any investigation around whether it could be contributing towards their poor mental health or whether the conduct could be in any way linked to their mental health - you do need to make sure that you're balancing the two.

Nicki Jones
Should this situation be managed any differently if an employee has less than two years' service?

Jodie Hill
No. From my perspective, I'm not talking about managing something in a fair or unfair

way. It's really looking at it from a disability discrimination way. You will have already had the webinar on disability discrimination, and ultimately, a mental health condition could amount to a disability. So regardless of length of service, you do need to be mindful of that throughout the entire process because it could end up being that the dismissal itself is discriminatory.

Anonymous
A senior manager has bipolar disorder, which often causes them to behave in a confrontational or aggressive way to the point where the well being of other staff is being impacted. Where would we stand when disciplining this employee for unacceptable behaviours? Are we expected to just accept that the behaviour is related to mental illness? Staff don't know about the person's condition because they've declined for it to be shared.

Jodie Hill
That's a really, really difficult one to manage because ultimately, you're managing the impact of the condition (which could be a disability) on other people. I've had to advise on these issues many, many times. And ultimately, I would actually go back a step further and understand what that individual is doing to manage their own mental health condition, try to understand what they've got in place, what they've got in their toolbox to help them deal with the way that it manifests in the workplace and whether they understand the impact that it's having on the team. Now, it may be that there's nothing they can do about that, and that's then a decision for the organisation to take in terms of the impact moving forward on the rest of the team. Is everyone going to leave because of it? It's balancing the impact on the rest of the team with the individual. But let's not forget that the individual has a protected characteristic. So that's where you need to be really careful.

Now, if it's causing a lot of problems and the individual is not willing to do anything in terms of supporting themselves - what we often find is that people don't want to disclose it, they don't want any help, they don't want to go to the doctors and they don't want medication - then I think it could be reasonable to then take further action if their conduct is having a negative impact on everyone else. But if they are trying to manage it and they are in a process and they are going through therapy, then again, it's just balancing where that individual is and what they're actively doing to support themselves with the wider impact on the rest of the team.

Su Apps

Should Occupational Health referrals for mental health conditions be treated any differently from referrals for physical conditions? We find all Occupational Health experts really do is repeat what the employer is telling them, so it doesn't take our client much further.

Jodie Hill

I find that's so common with mental health. The best solution that I've found is actually finding Occupational Health therapists that deal with mental health conditions. What they can do is have a really deeper understanding of how that condition might be manifesting for the individual and make some sensible suggestions in terms of adapting their workplace. Now there are lots of organisations online that you can find. I found an organisation recently called Simply People (www.simply-people. co.uk) where you can find someone who's a specialist. And I found that that was really, really helpful rather than just a generalist, because of the nature of the condition. Try to go a bit deeper into the background of the therapist that you're referring to them to.

Daniel Barnett

In fact, Jim Harrington has said that that's not always the case. He's worked with Occupational Health practitioners who've uncovered rare and serious diseases that have gone undiagnosed up to that point.

Amaya Corcuera

What are the legal obligations of employers regarding the negative impact of remote working on employees' mental health?

Daniel Barnett

Perhaps you could talk a little bit, if you feel qualified - I know you're not a medic - about the impact of remote working on mental health and then what you would tell your employees.

Jodie Hill

Of course. I think this is something that's been incredibly worrying for the past few months, especially as we've gone into the third lockdown. Essentially, the impact on mental health has been caused by the social isolation, the lack of communication, the fact that we can't see the physical signs of decline in people's mental health from home working has been a real concern for employers. But one way in which we found to tackle that is actually around really improving your communication, making sure you have conversations that aren't just work-related social events - albeit on Zoom - still trying to engage with people socially so that we can be socially connected even though we're physically distanced. That communication piece and the culture piece around all of that is really, really helpful for people as they come out of lockdown.

We can't hide behind the fact that there has been a huge impact. So it's really about looking at how you can support that team when they come back into the workplace. What does the new normal look like? Really clearly communicate how often you expect them to be in the office and for how long, and whether they can still work from home once lockdown is lifted. So whatever your plans are, as an organisation, it's really important that you communicate that effectively to your entire team. Some people really hate working from home; get them to come back first. And if you're thinking about staggering your working hours or having some people work from home, find out who wants to work from home. Again, the risk assessments I talked about before can help you identify that and understand who's really at risk and needs to be in a more social setting, and who wants to actually be working from home still.

Karen
Should performance management processes be paused if an employee is off sick due to a stress-, anxiety- or depression-related condition?

Daniel Barnett
So do you put performance management on hold if someone's got mental health issues?

Jodie Hill
Well, to be honest, I think the answer is it depends. It depends on how long they're off sick for what the performance issues are and whether putting the process on pause is because that is a reasonable adjustment that you want to make to allow them to get better to engage with the process, or simply because they've been off on long-term sick for a year, they had poor performance prior to that, and they don't look like they're coming back. So in my view, it does depend on where that person is in the sickness process, what the poor performance was - whether it was linked to the mental health condition or not - and actually whether or not you could use that as a reasonable adjustment in itself by pausing it to allow them to engage in the process.

Anonymous
An employee's been off work with stress and anxiety for three months. We've tried to engage with the employee multiple times, but they're ignoring calls and emails. A friend at work has been in touch with them, so we know they're 'okay', but they won't engage with HR or management. What steps should we take?

Jodie Hill
Again, it's a difficult one when you can't force someone to actually engage with you. This is where your policies, in my view, are really helpful. If you've got a clear long-term sickness

absence policy in terms of touchpoints, when you will have things like welfare meetings or keeping in touch days whilst they're off, that can be really, really helpful. It manages the expectations from both the employer side and the employee side. Now, if the employee is already off and you don't have this process set out, it's still helpful to try and reach out to the individual on a welfare basis to ask how they're getting on and generally just touching base with them in a non-work-related way. So make sure it's not about work or a particular job or anything other than their welfare.

I do think it's a really difficult one because ultimately, you can't force them to contact you, especially if part of their recovery process is actually them not speaking to people. They just need that time. So those policies can be helpful, but if you don't already have the policies, do try and reach out to them in a very conciliatory manner in a welfare setting.

Anonymous
When would you use Occupational Health versus a GP report?

Jodie Hill
Again, it does depend. I think Occupational Health are really helpful if they're a specialist. I do find, in my experience, that GPs tend to just say what the employee has told them. If you are going to use a GP or an occupational therapist, I think it's more about the letter that you write to them as the employer, so actually asking the right questions. What is it that you want from them? If you want to understand whether they meet the definition of disability, are you asking the right types of questions? Are you asking about reasonable adjustments? If so, I think probably an occupational therapist is the better person. So it does depend on what information you're trying to elicit, the condition the individual has and who's treating them. Again, if their GP isn't treating them but psychiatry is, the GP might not know very much. So pick your expert depending on who the employee is engaging with.

Daniel Barnett
How far is an employer expected to go when an employee suddenly claims they have a mental health issue, yet refuses to agree to a medical report from either their GP or Occupational Health?

Jodie Hill
It will seem sudden regardless of whether it is actually sudden for that individual. If they're unwilling to engage, in my view, you can tell them that you can only deal with the information you've got in front of you. So as an employer, you can only deal with the information you've been given, and if they're unwilling to engage in that process, then just make it clear to them that whatever the process is - whether it's disciplinary or a capability issue - what the consequences are and encourage them to engage in seeing a medical practitioner so that you can either support them or understand, at the very least, what the impact of their condition is on their ability to do their job.

Paula Early
Does offering a staff counselling service guarantee a stress-related claim is more likely to fail?

Daniel Barnett
I think the answer has ebbed and flowed a little bit over the years on this one.

Jodie Hill
It's a difficult one. In my view, just offering that doesn't necessarily reduce the likelihood of the actual stress claim. It's more the workplace environment. I'm not sure that it actually reduces the likelihood of the claim happening.

Daniel Barnett
I'm thinking of Sutherland v Hatton (*Sutherland v Hatton [2002] IRLR 263*), which is about a 20-year-old case where the House of Lords said that in order to win a stress claim for a personal injury claim in the civil courts, it has to be foreseeable that the employer is going to suffer a breakdown or some form of stress and

the employer has to be a breach of their duty. The House of Lords said that if the employer provides access to a staff counselling service, that's normally going to be enough to show they haven't breached their duty of care. Not always, but normally. Is that something you find that courts follow in practice or not?

Jodie Hill
No, I don't think that's enough. It's more than simply offering counselling. I think you've got to do more in terms of the day-to-day, not just what happens when they actually need that support. It's about the preventative side as well. So what preventative measures are you putting in place to support individuals, as well as putting reasonable adjustments in place? So it's not just the counseling. I think you'd have to do more.

Gillian Howard
If an employee fails or refuses to be medication compliant and continues to behave in an unacceptable manner or fails to perform their role to the standard you require, what can an employer do?

Daniel Barnett
The question is essentially asking whether it's misconduct, or a factor you can take into account, if an employee doesn't take their medication.

Jodie Hill
I suppose it depends on why they're not taking the medication. If they're actively not taking it and they've been prescribed and told that they should be taking it, then potentially, it could be a misconduct issue. But for me, it's more of a capability issue, but I suppose it depends why, doesn't it? I think, ultimately, balancing whether it's misconduct or performance can be a real challenge. I've actually come across this in practice a few times, and the way that we've dealt with it is that the individual has basically been given an ultimatum as to whether or not they want to continue to be in that particular role. For example, if they're not taking the

medication, finding out why aren't they taking it and understanding the reasons behind it rather than simply going straight to dismissal. It's understanding the reasons behind it and giving them an ultimatum.

Anonymous

My board doesn't want to use the HSE management standards as they fear it will expose us to litigation risks if any failings are found. I think a judge would look favourably on us for using the HSE management standards and taking measures to address the problems where practicable, accepting that no organisation is perfect. Who is right?

Daniel Barnett

Could the answer be they're both right?

Jodie Hill

Potentially. Is the question just about the stress risk assessments and that side of it? I'm unclear what they mean by the question.

Daniel Barnett

HSE management standards are a series of standards set out prescribing what employers should do in terms of risk assessments and steps employers should take. Because the person's asked a question anonymously, I can't actually call them up to ask for clarification.

Jodie Hill

That's how I understood it - the risk assessments. I think it's a bit of both. I think I personally would go more down the risk assessment route. So I actually think it's really helpful to identify the risks and proactively deal with them rather than reactively dealing with things. Actually, the HSE do have their own guidelines on stress risk assessments on their website. It can be helpful - and it can't be as well. I think what often happens is employers are concerned that it will open a can of worms, and that's the issue that many organisations face. But the reality is that it doesn't. What actually happens is that it identifies risks early on and puts in support so that you actually

end up saving a role or saving someone from going down a performance management route that could potentially have been avoided.

Myra Tourick

An employee might not recognise they have a mental health issue, but their manager might suspect they do. How do you address that if when they're spoken to about the issue, they deny anything untoward?

Jodie Hill

In my view, it's a difficult one to approach because you can't, as an employer, diagnose someone. That's not your job. Your job is not to say you believe they have a condition or make any assumptions about what the condition might be. All you can do is address the issues that you have. If they're saying that they don't have a condition, then, in my view, they're not necessarily covered by the Equality Act. You have no knowledge of the condition or the impact. I would explore that with them first. It's a difficult conversation to have, and nobody likes having those difficult conversations, but you do need to explore it in a safe environment where they feel that they can open up. If they're still refusing to engage in that and saying that there isn't anything wrong, then I would deal with it in a way that you would ordinarily deal with a performance or misconduct issue.

Nigel Forsyth

How would you, as an employer, handle a redundancy process where the employee's mental issues have already caused them to self-harm because of the stress? Assume it's all a genuine condition.

Jodie Hill

We've had this quite a few times where the employee's quite high risk. I would actually try to approach them on a without prejudice basis and see whether they want to engage in a settlement rather than putting them through the process. Often, what you find is that attending the process and the uncertainty around all of that exacerbates their condition. So if you can come to an amicable resolution with them, and they have a bit of certainty around what's happening, in my view, that's the best way to proceed. Obviously, you can't force them to engage in that process. But ultimately, it's either that or obviously go through the redundancy process with everyone else. So that seems like the kind of thing to do in those circumstances.

Julie Davis
If an employee has no predisposition to stress or depression but goes off work with stress or depression during a performance management process, can an employer safely assume that the Equality Act won't apply?

Jodie Hill
Never assume the Equality Act doesn't apply is the first thing. The Equality Act could apply because it's not necessarily that it hasn't lasted for 12 months, it's that it is likely to last more than 12 months. So the fact that they've only just had an onset of a condition doesn't preclude them from meeting that definition. So I certainly wouldn't assume anything at that stage. It's more about the impact. Has that got a substantial and adverse effect on their ability to do their day-to-day or is this a reaction to a performance process? Again, I definitely don't think you should assume, but it certainly does have some red flags.

Mark Irlam
Because of coronavirus and the impact on mental health, how much should an employer engage with its staff regarding issues they may have regarding working from home or in the office or both?

Daniel Barnett
This is similar to a question we had just before, but this question is really asking whether we, as an employer, should keep our mouth shut or take active steps.

Jodie Hill
I think we should take active steps. That honest communication is really important, especially

as we're working from home. If you, as the employer, procrastinate on an issue or you don't deal with it, or if the individual, likewise, doesn't raise an issue that they've got, all that will happen is that the situation will get worse. And actually, if it's a performance issue or, potentially, misconduct, you do need to deal with issues promptly. The fact that we're working from home doesn't preclude that. I think just crack on with it and make sure that you're really clear in your communication and if you are doing an online disciplinary or grievance process, make sure that everyone's got a safe environment in which to do that. I know a lot of people have been house-sharing and not had a room on their own, for example, to deal with those kinds of issues. So if you are dealing with any issues, just make sure that they have a separate room to deal with them privately.

Daniel Barnett
Is it fair to say that if companies follow your recommendations, and what indeed is best practice for dealing with mental health, it would involve investing an enormous amount of time and money resource?

Jodie Hill
Absolutely, it would. At Thrive, all of our staff have always worked from home and so we deal with issues as and when they arise. I think you would be dealing with it whether in person or not. So it's six and two threes to me. Yes, it does cost to engage in that process, but essentially, if they were in the office, you'd have to do that anyway. So I think you should still carry on and investigate.

Joseph
Must an employee tell an employer that they're taking medication for a mental health problem?

Jodie Hill
There's no obligation to disclose that information. What I would say is that as an individual, I've suffered with anxiety and

PTSD in my career as a lawyer, and one of the things that I found really helpful was that when I was open about my own condition and the medication I was taking, when I had bad days, it was actually really helpful because I was able to talk about that. And I still do that now with my team. Obviously, I don't go into loads of detail, but I do think it's helpful for people to be really open if they actually want the support. Sometimes you can get side effects from medication, and it is helpful if your employer knows about that because they can manage that and support you at work.

Robert

Is it discriminatory to question a job applicant about their mental health, to question a previous employer about the job applicant's mental health or to decline to employ them if it appears likely they'll be off sick with mental health problems once they're taken on?

Jodie Hill

I do think that would be discriminatory in itself to ask the question. I think, ultimately, the only reason why you should be asking for details about people's mental health is if they need support as a reasonable adjustment in that interview process. If you're choosing not to take them on and that mental health condition amounts to a disability, that could potentially give rise to a claim for disability discrimination. So yes, I do think it would be discriminatory to act in that way.

Mark Irlam

What are a director's responsibilities to a fellow director where that fellow director is suffering with depression?

Jodie Hill

I take the same view as an employee. One of the first questions you asked me was about how you approach someone if you think that they have a mental health condition. I think that applies to everyone. It doesn't matter the level of seniority. If you think someone is struggling, approach them and try to establish, in a safe

and private conversation, how you might be able to help them - whether there is anything from a business perspective but also from a personal perspective, director to director, peer to peer. I think it can be even harder to open up when you're in that more senior role because you've got fewer people to open up to. So I'd certainly approach that conversation sensitively, but equally in a supportive manner, and just see what you can do to support them.

Ebi

What are the legal requirements of the employer to an employee if they've told a member of staff to stay at home on sick leave? The staff member has a disability, and they didn't make the required reasonable adjustments for the employee to stay at work.

It was just regarding the reasonable adjustments the employer hasn't made the reasonable adjustments for the employee to stay at work, so in terms of them being off sick at home, what are the legal requirements that they have to that employee whilst they are off sick at home?

Jodie Hill

So are you meaning in terms of pay?

Ebi

No. The employee is on full pay but doesn't get the bonus or the commission that they would at work. The disability is anxiety and depression, which they have a medical diagnosis for. So, what are the legal requirements that the employer would have with regard to that employee's mental health?

Jodie Hill

It depends whether the adjustments that were requested were reasonable and whether they've been unreasonably refused. So I'd just explore that with them and basically understand what it is that they need to get back into the workplace. And if those adjustments would have enabled the employee to come back in, exploring why they were refused. Obviously, the employee has to meet the definition of disability - just having a diagnosis doesn't automatically mean that they do.

Then, secondly, it's looking at whether there has been a failure to make what are reasonable adjustments, or whether they're just adjustments that aren't reasonable. So again, it's about into a bit more detail as to why these decisions have been made. In terms of legal obligations, they're still employed, so the duty to make adjustments will continue. Are there any other adjustments that the employer could explore as well? It may be that one adjustment didn't work, but there could be something else that they could do to bring them back into the workplace. Does that help?

Ebi
I was thinking more in terms of the mental health aspect. So are they required to check in on the employee as they're not actually sick? It was the company that said they should stay at home.

Jodie Hill
So, they're physically saying you have to be off sick because we can't make adjustments. They haven't called in sick. That's a really difficult one because actually, like you say, they're being paid in full. Ultimately, it's for the employer and the employee to come to an agreement and understand how the employer can bring the employee back to work. I can't understand why an employer would keep someone on sick indefinitely on full pay. So there's got to be a point where they can't pay the employee in full anymore. There's going to be a crunch point. In terms of keeping in touch, it's very much dependent on the employer. So I would always say check the policies and procedures in relation to welfare, and the frequency and method of contact. So have they said that they'd contact the employee every three weeks and they're not doing that? If so, there might be a breach of an internal policy. But they remain an employee by the sounds of it, so those duties to make adjustments will continue.

Kay Moody
Are there any specific mental health conditions which you've seen on the rise during the past year?

Jodie Hill
Yes. Anxiety. I think the lack of certainty in our current lives has definitely increased the amount of anxiety people are experiencing. Whether that's just because of the pandemic or because people are talking about it more because they are able to self-reflect and be at home and have so much more time with their own thoughts. So, yes, anxiety, I'd say.

Pam Dosanjh
How do you become a Mental Health First Aider?

Daniel Barnett
Mental Health First Aid England have absolutely loads of instructors. All you need to do is go onto their website (mhfaengland. org). You can find someone either near you or you can do it virtually now, so you don't have to physically do it in person. It's especially helpful if you've got an organisation split across several offices, so you don't have to bring everybody into the same office. It's a two-day course. We actually deliver the training at Thrive, but there are absolutely loads of providers across the whole of the UK. They do have to be MHFA accredited, so just double-check that they are actually accredited. Organisations can actually engage from other countries into the MHFA England scheme as well. The person becomes a qualified first aider and then, three years later, they have to do a refresher. If you go on their website, there's loads of information.

We also offer this training at Thrive with peer to peer support community.

Mike Clyne
Given the chance, I imagine we would like all managers or companies to undergo good mental health at work training. Assuming that situation isn't prevalent, what simple messages

would you recommend companies and managers think about relating to mental health in the workplace?

Jodie Hill
I think it has to go back to the culture piece. Are you the kind of manager that someone could open up to? If you say there's an open-door policy, do you genuinely have your door - obviously, your virtual door – is it open? How do people communicate with you? What we're finding is that people say and do things and don't follow through with them. So leading by example and actually following through with what you say you're going to do is half of the battle when it comes to being a manager. I've certainly found that leading by example really opens up the door. People are so much more open with me because I'm open about my own struggles with my mental health. So I think it starts with us as people. You don't need mental health training to actually follow through with what you say you're going to do. If you say you're going to support someone with reasonable adjustments, follow that up.

Daniel Barnett
Jodie Hill, what's the best way for somebody to contact you if they have any further issues?

Jodie Hill
Yes, it's Jodie.hill@thrivelaw.co.uk and you can get me on Twitter as well. It's @iamjodiehill and @thrive_law on Twitter and Instagram.

Daniel Barnett
Thanks for your time, Jodie Hill. Thank you very much.

PARTNERSHIPS AND LLPs
CLARE MURRAY, CM MURRAY LLP

Daniel Barnett

I'm joined by Clare Murray of CM Murray LLP. She's here to talk about partnership and LLP matters. In March 2018, she was appointed as the specialist advisor to the House of Commons Women's and Equalities Committee, in respect of its year-long sexual harassment in the workplace inquiry, something that I think sounds like absolutely fascinating work. In fact, Clare, before I ask you my own questions, I might just ask you about that. What was it like being the advisor to the House of Commons Women's and Equalities Committee?

Clare Murray

It was possibly the most extraordinary thing that I've ever done in my career. It gave me such insight not just to the law, but to the real application of it and how sexual harassment is perceived by victims and the experience of victims. It gave me an insight that I just didn't feel I had before. So to have a role in that was hugely rewarding. We're all looking for purpose in our lives, and it really gave me a sense of purpose.

Daniel Barnett

You've very kindly agreed to answer a couple of specific questions I have first and because partnership and limited liability partnership law is perhaps a little niche for a few of the people who might be on this webinar, you've actually agreed to give slightly fuller answers than normal. It's acting very much as an introduction to the topic.

Can partners and LLP members accept a repudiatory breach of their partnership agreement so as to release them for partnership obligations? I suppose, in the vernacular, can a partner be constructively dismissed?

Clare Murray

Before I get into the meat of that, I should say that we're saying that we're covering partnerships and LLPs, and it's like we're wrapping them all up as one. But in fact, they are two very distinct species. When I'm talking about partners, I'm primarily talking about partners who are in a traditional 1890 partnership with unlimited liability, etc., and when I'm talking about LLP members, I'm talking about those members of an LLP whose work is governed by the Limited Liability Partnerships Act 2000, and the regulations of 2001. I'll try not to use them too interchangeably because they do differ in some respects.

So, the short answer is that we do get a lot of partners and LLP members who come to us and say that they've been excluded from management, they've actually been excluded from the office, they've been demoted, or they've been subjected to discrimination. They might say they've got a mate who's an employment lawyer, and they told them that this must be constructive dismissal. And, unfortunately, the position for partners and LLP members is that there's not an equivalent constructive dismissal scenario. The reason for that is that the doctrine of acceptance of repudiatory breach has been excluded from what's called multi-party partnership agreements and LLP agreements, although there is some uncertainty if you've got a two-partner LLP agreement - it's not clear yet through case law whether you could still claim constructive dismissal equivalent in that kind of 2 partner/LLP member context.

Where does this all come from? The origin of it is a case called Hurst v Bryk (Hurst v Bryk [2000] UKHL 19), which is an 1890 partnership case that basically ruled out the possibility for a partner to claim repudiatory breach to release him from his obligations. And there were two main reasons for this. One is that the relationship between partners is regarded as not being just a contractual thing. It's a living, breathing personal relationship; it's a commercial relationship. So it was felt that it was not something that was an equivalent to a contractual employment-type relationship. Also, under s35 of the Partnership Act, there are specific grounds on which the court has the discretion to dissolve a partnership. They include, under s35d, for example, if a partner persistently commits breaches of the partnership agreement. So they're saying that if you allowed this principle to come into partnership law, you'd effectively be undermining the Partnership Act and the discretionary powers of the court to order a winding up in appropriate circumstances. So that's the partnership position.

You then come to the LLP position and whether or not it's possible to claim constructive dismissal as an LLP member. For a number of years, actually, it was a little bit like the Wild West because this was new law that we were all kind of professionally growing up with. There were no answers so there were amazing opportunities there, so people were arguing left, right and centre that constructive dismissal did apply to LLPs. Some of the leading textbooks were saying that it was a

possibility because you've got a separate body, a separate entity with an LLP.

Eventually, we had the case of Flanagan v Liontrust (Flanagan v Liontrust Investment Partners LLP [2017] EWCA Civ 985), which decided the position and took away, frankly, all of our fun in these matters. But that was a case where there was a member of an LLP who was a fixed share member and he had certain arrangements and certain contractual entitlements, including on exit. He said that he was treated unlawfully in the way that the firm tried to expel him. As a result of that, he said he was going to accept that breach and that it was going to do two things. Firstly, it was going to remove entirely all of his partnership obligations so that he was no longer bound by the LLP agreement that bound the rest of the LLP members. Secondly, somehow, magically, the default rules under the LLP regulations would spring into place to fill this void left by the absence of the LLP agreement, and what that meant was that his little old £125,000 fixed share was suddenly magically converted under the default rules into a fully living and breathing equal equity partner status, so that he would have an equal right to participate in management, in profits and in capital profit sharing as well. So it would have completely elevated him and his legal entitlements.

He took this to the High Court and he was seeking a declaration of his rights and a buyout of what he considered to be the value of his share now that these magic default rules were in place, that would turn, in his view, his £125,000 fixed share into a claim with a value of £8 million. In that particular case, the court said, actually, he was absolutely right, it was unlawful conduct by the LLP. But the court said it didn't have the consequences that he thought. It said the notice against him was invalid. It wasn't done properly; it wasn't served at the right time, in the right way and by the right decision-making bodies. So therefore his exclusion was a repudiatory breach. So in an employment world, this would have been a constructive dismissal situation, but because it was an LLP world, it didn't have that effect.

There were two main reasons that the court took that decision. One was that it was just unconscionable and legally incoherent that you would have an organisation where you have not one constitution, but, basically, two. You've got the constitution that's existing that applies to everybody else who wasn't involved in these breaches, and then you've got a separate constitution that applies to the victim of the breach. That just couldn't work because you don't then know how to make management decisions and how to share profits, etc. The court also said it was just unconscionable to expect that you could take a £125,000 fixed profit share and convert it in the way suggested into a full £8 million equity.

So he was told, basically, that he was right in terms of unlawful conduct, but the consequences, instead, lay with a declaration that he still continued to be a member of the LLP and also damages for breach of contract for any losses that he could show from being excluded.

What that means in practice is that if you are advising individuals, and constructive dismissal is off the table, you're naturally going to be looking to see whether there might be any discrimination aspects to the unlawful treatment, or whether there might be a whistleblowing detriment, for example. If there is unlawful whistleblowing detriment and the individual lawfully and properly resigns in response and then has post-termination losses that are directly caused by the original detriment then on a Wilsons Solicitors v Roberts *(Wilsons Solicitors LLP & Ors v Roberts [2018] EWCA Civ 52)* basis, you may be able to found a claim for compensation.

Although it's not particularly attractive, you're also potentially going to be looking at an unfair prejudice claim here under s994

Companies Act 2006. Most professional partnership agreements will automatically exclude that right, but some investment management firm agreements will still leave it open. Also, if someone's a fully functioning equity member and a contributory on a winding up, then, in theory again, you could also seek or at least consider a winding-up petition. For most individual LLP members, these are however not necessarily real-world options.

I should, again, just make the point that if it's two members in the LLP, it may well be that constructive dismissal might be an option that should still at least be explored. I hope that answers your question.

Daniel Barnett
It answers my question very thoroughly. I'm just going to ask you one other question. Can an individual have both partner status and employee status, or LLP member status and employee status at the same time?

Clare Murray
I'd say the short answer to that is no in respect of a pure employment status, so contract of service status. That applies both in partnership law and in respect of LLPs too. Essentially, that's because, under partnership law, there is what's called the rule against dual status that says you can't be a partner and have pure employment status, say, for redundancy, unfair dismissal or maternity rights. That also controls the position in relation to LLP members, which I'll explain a bit further in a minute.

Of course, we all know that LLP members are workers under s230(3)(b), following the Supreme Court decision in Clyde & Co v Bates van Winklehof *(Clyde & Co LLP v Bates van Winklehof [2014] IRLR 641)*, and that means that if you're an individual worker providing personal services - because, obviously, you can also have LLP members that are corporates for example - and you satisfy the requirements of s230(3))(b), then you are a worker and you benefit from the whole range of worker rights, including whistleblowing detriment, etc., and the right to be accompanied, which is often forgotten for LLP members who might be going through disciplinary and grievance processes. You've got a right to be accompanied as an LLP member during that process.

Gillian Howard
What are the most frequent partnership disputes and how have you resolved them?

Clare Murray
The most frequent partnership disputes are typically around exits, around the lawfulness of exits and around the discrimination and whistleblowing aspects to them. We have lots and lots of partnership-related disputes about that. We also do a lot of litigation around team moves and restrictive covenants. So they are very common areas where we would have experience of advising on all sides, though not on the same matter obviously Was there a second part to the question?

Daniel Barnett
How have you resolved them?

Clare Murray
Diplomatically but diligently.

Su Apps
Is there any way to remove a partner against whom valid grievances have been raised if the partnership deed doesn't expressly allow for their removal?

Clare Murray
No.

Daniel Barnett
Can you dissolve the partnership?

Clare Murray
You'd normally have to seek a dissolution by the court. If it's a general partnership and there's no right to remove (and it's not a partnership at will), then you're going to have to seek a dissolution or negotiate an agreement

around it – otherwise you need to make a reasonable offer that's going to be hard for them to refuse.

Mike Clyne
How do partnerships or LLPs handle allegations of discrimination or harassment raised by a partner?

Daniel Barnett
So how do partnerships handle allegations of discrimination or harassment raised by one partner against another?

Clare Murray
Certainly, in the way that we would advise, they treat them as you would advise in an employment context. In the ideal partnership, even for partners, there would be partner policies regarding grievances and disciplinary processes and how they're handled. The reality is that a lot of firms don't have those. You would be looking at those policies to see how the particular firm determines them. They will typically look like the Acas guidance, but they will be tailored to the individual circumstances and the partnership terms in the particular firm. You would be treating them as a grievance. You would take them through the process, there would be an investigation, then if there were findings which supported that, then there would be a disciplinary process involving the partner in respect to the factual findings and then sanctions.

From our experience, LLP agreements and partnership agreements are often unequipped for these sorts of issues. You do also need a pretty solid body of policies that apply to the partners that just allow for consistency, allow for natural justice and give you the grounding for good-faith decision making and good old rational decision-making as well.

Tracey Munro
If an LLP ceases to trade, do the employees of that LLP have the same protection as employees of a limited company so that they can claim redundancy payments?

Clare Murray

I can't see any reason from the employee's perspective why they would be treated any differently than if they were employed by another normal employer.

Daniel Barnett

It's just the closure of a place of work that triggers the right to a redundancy payment, whether the employer is a limited company or an LLP.

Clare Murray

Exactly, the entity itself won't make a difference.

Su Apps

Is there a TUPE transfer every time a partner joins or an old partner leaves a partnership given the identity of the employer and the ownership of the business changes?

Daniel Barnett

I'm going to ask a follow up to that after you've answered, depending on what your answer is.

Clare Murray

it's a great question. I personally don't think there's a very clear answer to this. I would say that there are lots of professional services firms in the country who are general partnerships and they have partners come and go, and they certainly don't treat it as a TUPE transfer each time. These partnership agreements usually provide that there's no cessation, there's no dissolution when people come in and go out – the partnership simply continues. In that case, there's not going to be any triggering event for TUPE purposes. My instinct is that no, it would not be a TUPE event. A new partner will come in and sign up to a deed of adherence, there won't be a dissolution, other than maybe just a technical dissolution, and I don't consider that would trigger a TUPE transfer.

Daniel Barnett

If before there was a change of partners, the partners and the employer were individuals A,

B and C, and after a partnership change it's A, B and D, even if that was enough to amount to a TUPE transfer, would it actually make any difference to anybody?

Clare Murray

No, because there is a specific protection in any event. For example, even if there's a change in the partnership continuity of employment is preserved and your terms and conditions are going to stay the same. I don't think it would make a difference in reality.

Daniel Barnett

Actually, it might do because it would trigger the consultation obligations, of course, on the TUPE.

Clare Murray

I mean, information, surely, but not necessarily consultation.

Daniel Barnett

Yes. It just makes me wonder why no one has run this argument before. I'm unaware anyone's ever run this argument before.

Clare Murray

We've looked at it in the past and we've come to the conclusion that there's no obvious answer and we couldn't find any obvious case law on the point. Su Apps has commented that there could be a technical protective award if there's a TUPE transfer.

Mike Clyne

What are the main problems you see in the drafting of partnership agreements?

Clare Murray

Where do you start? Particular bugbears are around the right to take advice in respect of your own LLP or partnership matters. Unless litigation is contemplated, there's the real risk that if you're instructed by a partnership or LLP using firm monies etc., to take that advice, that advice might actually not be protected by legal privilege: the partner or the member who is the subject of it might be entitled to say that you're using partnership money, LLP money, and therefore as a partner or member of the firm they should be entitled to see a copy of that advice which shouldn't be privileged.

Say, for example, you're advising someone on a partner performance management situation so there's no dispute, no litigation, but there is a risk that the advice that the firm takes could be compromised, and the partner could say show me the advice that you're getting on this. It's not ideal, but firms would deal with that by actually having an instructing body that instructs you personally as senior management but in their personal capacity. There are lots of arguments and there's no clear answer. It's not helpful to have that used against you if people are looking for leverage, and so preferable to have an express power in the partnership or LLP agreement to take legal advice at the cost of the firm, and for that advice to remain confidential unless the management committee decides to disclose it and to whom it should be disclosed.

James Fairchild

Is it feasible for, say, six friends who do similar consulting work, which would now fall under IR35, to form an LLP? And could the LLP then send any of the six to undertake client work?

Daniel Barnett

I was wondering if there's an inherent flaw in the question, which is that if they're going to fall under IR35, there's probably some element of a requirement for them to do the work personally - personal provision of worker labour - and, as a result, if they're under some sort of obligation to provide the work personally, then, by definition, the LLP couldn't be free to send any of the six of them because they'd be in breach of their obligation to personally perform the work. Instinctively, I think what you're suggesting wouldn't be possible, but I'd need to give it some thought, I'm afraid. I don't know the answer off the top of my head.

Steven Eckett

Why should a firm become an LLP? What are the benefits?

Clare Murray

That's a really interesting question. The driving force originally for it all was to retain the collegiality and the internal flexibility of a partnership in its old sense, so you can control your own constitution, but having that shell of limited liability around it, and also the benefit that it's tax transparent. It has the benefits of a partnership from a tax perspective, but with the LLP protections that go with it.

Just to play devil's advocate, the reasons why you might not want to do it would be things like the financial disclosure that's required, the Companies House regulatory requirements that go with it as if you were a company. I'm obviously not an accountant, but things like having to bring things like annuities onto the balance sheet can really change how the finances of the firm look post-conversion.

It's immensely flexible and I much prefer the LLP to a limited company. Although, I do know that lots of smaller professional services businesses prefer a limited company as well.

Robert

When filing a claim against a partnership at will, who may or should be named as respondent?

Daniel Barnett

Could you explain what a partnership at will is, please?

Clare Murray

A partnership at will is a partnership under the 1890 Act that has been set up with an indefinite duration. It's something that can be dissolved at any time, by any partner and without notice. It's a really vulnerable position to be in. You become a partnership but you've not really agreed much and you've certainly not agreed a duration. It's a really vulnerable type of arrangement to be in. How do you sue a partnership like that? I think as you would sue any other partnership, you would do it in the name of the firm. That would be my view.

Robert
What happens if a partnership has arisen since the employment started, but the employee doesn't know about it?

Daniel Barnett
I'm struggling to understand the circumstances that could give rise to that. Presumably, a one-person employer has somehow formed a partnership but not told the employee? I suspect it's just as simple as you continue your claim against the one person because they'll remain liable for the debts of the partnership.

Nigel Forsyth
Given that repudiatory breach isn't an option for LLP members, what advice would you give to an LLP member who's trying to challenge their post-termination restrictive covenants?

Clare Murray
Firstly, I'd be looking at status. What's my actual status as the LLP member? Am I really a genuine living and breathing LLP member or am I, perhaps, in reality, a genuine employee. You've got to look at cases like Reinhard v Ondra (Reinhard v Ondra LLP & Ors (Rev 1) | [2015] EWHC 26), where it basically says you've got to get into the meat of the document and the relationship to work out whether someone is genuinely an employee or genuinely an LLP member. It's perfectly acceptable to look at the old partnership law on partner status in that context. So the first thing I'd look at is status. What is the person's status? Is there any angle there?

Secondly, I would be looking at the drafting and the parameters of the restrictions, in terms of enforceability. Is there anything I can do to work around those restrictions?

Thirdly, I would be considering whether there are any overseas aspects. So people have argued in the past, from a UK perspective,

unsuccessfully, that lawyers' professional conduct obligations prevent them from complying with restrictive covenants like non-dealing with clients, etc. But actually, the main case on restrictive covenants in this area for partners, Bridge v Deacons (Bridge v Deacons [1984] AC 705), said that under English law, those regulatory rules won't have an impact. But if there's any kind of connection with overseas jurisdictions, for example, a New York State Bar, they have very clear ethical rules which prevent any kind of restriction that puts a distance between you and your client. For example, it can prevent garden leave provisions, it can prevent non-dealing clauses, etc.

The reality with partner and LLP member restrictive covenants is that if you're a genuine partner, or a genuine member, firstly your restrictive covenants are far more likely to be enforceable that if you are an employee and secondly the firm that you're leaving behind is going to be holding your capital balances, your current account and they've probably got your tax reserve too. That is a really big lever that they've got against you. The first thing that these firms do is say that you've caused us this much loss as a result of your breaches of your restrictive covenants, and you're going to have to sue us to recover your balances. So that's the first thing some firms think about and it puts the partner or LLP member in a vulnerable position.

If you've got enough time, on a very narrow basis, you could consider or threaten seeking a declaration. You could look at the arbitration provisions, which there usually are in a partnership agreement and trigger those, threatening to seek a declaration in relation to the enforceability of the restrictive covenant. Certainly, they're the sort of things that we've looked at. Although, again, it comes down to the appetite of individuals to pursue those types of proceedings. Ultimately, these things are negotiated. That's the reality of them. There's almost always a negotiation. And just from a practical perspective, I would say that certainly for professional services, firms recognise that clients are often loyal to individuals, and they will recognise that in negotiations. So you'll have a carved out list of clients commercially negotiated. But the worst thing I think you can do is to try and speak to those clients in advance, or try and take associates. Again, it just ups the ante, puts you in breach of all your obligations and makes it really hard to negotiate those carve-outs.

Anonymous
Have there been any changes affecting partnerships and LLPs stemming from the pandemic and the introduction of emergency regulations?

Clare Murray
The only thing that springs to mind is in relation to the wrongful trading provisions. There was a qualification up to 30 September last year, where there was a potential insolvency risk as a result of the COVID pandemic and it gave a slightly lighter-touch approach. (Under s12 Corporate Insolvency and Governance Act 2020 the wrongful trading regime was modified so that some breathing space was allowed for LLPs and their members in terms of wrongful trading – broadly, the members are regarded as not responsible for any worsening of the financial position of the LLP between 1 March and 30 September 2020 as a result of the pandemic). I can't think of anything else, specifically, off the top of my head. LLPs and partnerships have though been affected like every other business and practice.

Gary
Are members of an LLP personally liable?

Daniel Barnett
There are two aspects to this. Are they personally liable for the debts of the LLP? To which the answer is a very clear no. Or is it more complicated?

Clare Murray
The whole reason for going into an LLP is that you should get the benefit of limited liability protection, but there are some caveats to that. For example, if I'm acting for someone, the engagement is with the firm and all of your letters of engagement will make it clear that I'm an agent acting for and on behalf of CM Murray LLP. But there is always a risk that a client could argue that if I'm providing that advice, I have assumed a personal responsibility and the nature of the relationship and the fiduciary relationship means that I personally can be sued.

Daniel Barnett
More so than any normal provider of any professional service?

Clare Murray
Well, I think the courts look at each type of relationship, but there is a risk. Law firms in particular spend a lot of time looking at that their engagement letters, making it clear the status the individuals who are advising - that they are doing so on behalf of the firm rather than in their own capacity, and they also include a contractual cap on the firm's liability too, etc. But the risk does remain. There's also a risk on an insolvency situation if there's a winding up. If the firm goes into insolvency then there is a personal risk for LLP members in that regard in terms of either fraudulent or wrongful trading or also if a member has withdrawn money that (along with other member's withdrawals) has had the consequence of making the LLP unable to pay its debts, then there's potential there for a liquidator to claw back up to two years' worth of drawings from the LLP member, basically any monies that you might have taken out during that period. And it's all about the extent to which you knew or may have known that taking money out like that would have put the firm into an insolvent position. So the principle is yes, there's limited liability protection. But there are one or two points of risk that you do need to be aware of.

Ben Payne
What evidence is needed to prove that a quasi-partnership exists?

Daniel Barnett
What is a quasi-partnership?

Clare Murray
That's not a type of partnership with which I have particular experience. You're going to start though with s1 Partnership Act, which is "is there a relationship between two or more people carrying on a business in common with a view to profit?" The 1890 Partnership Act also sets out circumstances when a partnership isn't a partnership. But then, also, the court is going to look at the facts in the particular case and what the intention of the parties was as to whether a partnership has been created.

Ben Payne
It's been argued there is a quasi-partnership between two directors or shareholders of a limited company, as it was agreed they could both make payments of funds without the authorisation of the other.

Simon Tovey
A quasi-partnership is the term used to reference a corporate entity that operates akin to a partnership, i.e. one which has two director shareholders, both holding 50% of the shares.

Daniel Barnett
Clare, does that help?

Clare Murray
It informs me. I have to say I personally haven't advised on that but that my partner Zulon Begum will almost certainly advise on that as this is her space, that corporate/partnership overlap. I would not have anything useful to add to that. But I'd be happy to take the question back to Zulon and get an answer if that would be helpful.

Daniel Barnett
What's the best way for somebody to get in touch with you?

Clare Murray
Clare.murray@cm-murray.com. I'm always happy to chat.

Daniel Barnett
Clare Murray, thank you very much for your time.

RECRUITMENT
ELEENA MISRA, OLD SQUARE CHAMBERS

Daniel Barnett

I'm joined today by Eleena Misra from Old Square Chambers. She's going to be talking and answering your questions about recruitment.

Eleena Misra, good afternoon. A couple of questions from me if I could. First of all, if a male interviewee is asked in a job interview whether he is planning to start a family, is that discrimination?

Eleena Misra

Quite possibly. And the reason why it might be discrimination - direct sex discrimination in particular - is if the person asking that question wouldn't have asked a female who was attending an interview that question because it was thought to be too sensitive a question. Now if you would not ask a female that question, why would you ask a male? So there's quite a clear path to potential direct discrimination. It also could be a proxy for other protected characteristics, such as age or marital status, for example. So quite possibly, yes.

Daniel Barnett

If you've got someone who's applying for jobs internally, can their sickness absence records be taken into account when considering them for the job?

Eleena Misra

With an internal job application, yes, you're likely to have lawful access to things such as sickness absence records, and there's

nothing to prevent you from doing that. So the straightforward answer is yes, you can have regard to them. But what are the risks of doing that? Well, the risks are that someone who has a sickness absence record that is significant might be disabled. And if you take that into account, you may well fall foul of the discrimination provisions relating to disability including, for example, s15, disability-related discrimination. And also, if you only look at sickness absence records for some individuals, but not others, so you cherry-pick which records you look at, you may be creating a situation of unlawful discrimination there as well. So just to be very clear, I think with an internal application, when it comes to sickness absence records, you're probably not in s60 Equality Act territory because you're not asking health questions, for example, but I think you could be running the risk. So yes, you can, but be careful.

Gillian Howard

If an offer of employment is subject to receipt of satisfactory references, how is the word 'satisfactory' viewed by an employment tribunal? Is that the employer's subjective view? Is that the view of a reasonable employer? Or is it what the employment tribunal, a year down the line, thinks is reasonable?

Eleena Misra

Well, actually, this question came up in a case that was determined back in 1990, called Wishart *(Wishart v National Association of Citizens Advice Bureaux Ltd [1990] ICR*

794), although, that was in the context of an application for interim relief, so an injunction, so it didn't actually go to trial. What the Court of Appeal said in the Wishart case is that, actually, the determinative thing is likely to be the employer's subjective view because at the end of the day, it is what is satisfactory to the employer. However, two words of caution there: the law has obviously moved on quite a bit since 1990, although, the Court of Appeal normally gets these things right. So we've now seen a lot more of this kind of discretionary approach that we saw in the case of Braganza (*Braganza v BP Shipping Limited and another [2015] IRLR 487*), and I think an issue that would be important in assessing whether the employer acted reasonably in saying that references were not satisfactory would be the good faith test and the Braganza approach, potentially.

Gillian Howard

If the employer dismisses a new recruit because of an unsatisfactory reference, should dismissal be with or without notice, or pay in lieu, and how much should the employer tell the employee about what that reference actually said?

Eleena Misra

If I split this question down, the first really important question is whether the offer that has been made was a conditional or unconditional offer. Now, if it was a conditional offer - which many of them are - in other words, the offer was conditional on the receipt of satisfactory references, then there should be no contract of employment arising because the offer is not capable of being accepted. It was effectively a condition precedent. In those circumstances, there's not an issue in terms of having to dismiss with notice or pay in lieu of notice.

Of course, if it is an unconditional offer, then the position will be that you have to dismiss with either notice or pay in lieu because a contract of employment has arisen. Now, there may be some cases in which you can

argue that it has basically become a condition subsequent, but that's in slightly murkier territory. So the take-home point is to make sure that if you're looking to check references, as you ordinarily would, make sure that it's a conditional offer that you make. So that's to deal with the notice point, and it'll depend on the contract as to whether you can pay in lieu of notice. Alternatively, you could actually pay damages in advance.

What should the employer tell the employee about the bad reference? Well, good practice would dictate that you say that you've had some adverse feedback, and this is why you considered the person not suitable for the position. That's essentially good practice, in my view. But there's no concrete legal provision or rule that requires you to say something in particular. Giving feedback is a very important way of staving off claims, though.

Su Apps

If a non-conditional contract of employment has been entered into - so not dependent on references - but the employee hasn't yet started work and the employer withdraws the offer for whatever reason before the employee starts work, does the employee have to give any notice, the probationary period notice or full contractual notice?

Eleena Misra

In this situation, the likely analysis, in my view, is that it's an unconditional offer, it's been accepted, so there is a contract of employment, but the parties have effectively agreed to delay performance of the contract. That's why work hasn't started. And that's certainly the analysis that has been favoured by, I think, for example, Mr Justice Elias, in various cases, including that we've seen in the EAT. So if that's the correct analysis - and I think it probably is - then in that situation, first of all, you can't withdraw the offer because a contract has been entered into. So you're going to have to terminate the contract in accordance with the contractual provisions, which will mean giving the notice set out within the contract. And it seems to me there are mixed authorities, I think, in relation to whether you can rely on the probationary period clause. But if you are effectively ending the contract, you're entitled as an employer to do so in the most favourable way you could as a matter of contract. So, probably, you could refer to the minimum period by reference to the probation period clause.

Rebecca
What are we legally allowed to do to attract a more diverse candidate pool?

Eleena Misra
Great question. There are loads of things that you can legally do. Information dissemination is a really important thing, so making sure you connect with local groups and making sure that people are aware of vacancies. One of the things that increase diversity is not just restricting a pool to internal candidates. You might want to look at how diverse your existing workforce is and then look at whether you need to go to external candidates, for example. There are plenty of things you can do, but cutting to the heart of this, positive action, s158 and 159 provide, first of all, the ability to take steps to attract diverse candidates. If you've got someone who falls within s158 of the Equality Act and you're trying to, in fact, meet the needs of a particularly disadvantaged group, for example, then you can have particular forms of advertisement, you can make broader arrangements to increase the attractiveness of an offer or the attractiveness of the job. So s158 of the Equality Act is a good one to remember in relation to attracting a more diverse candidate pool.

Quentin Colborn
Employers receive many applications for vacancies nowadays. How much information should they provide to unsuccessful applicants given the need to be able to demonstrate they've not discriminated, yet be practical in how information can be provided?

Eleena Misra
It seems to me that a lot will depend on how the arrangements are actually set up by the employer. So if they've done an initial sift, which many will - if you're dealing with a volume of applications, you're probably going to have an initial sift - then you may just be able to refer to the fact that someone simply didn't meet the essential criteria. It may be that you want to say something more if it's an applicant who's got further down the line. It seems to me that the further down the line you get in terms of the journey of the applicant, the more information you might want to give. But for someone who simply hasn't made the first cut, I would have thought a very modest amount of information is entirely permissible, and indeed desirable, perhaps, given the time you might have to deal with it.

AJ Fraser
Where an external job applicant has accepted an offer of employment but has since informed the employer she's pregnant and wants to delay her start date by 12 months, can the employer retract the offer of employment?

Eleena Misra
No, you can't. So first of all, in this scenario, the external job applicant has accepted an offer of employment. So I'm reading from this question that it's not a conditional offer of employment. Even if it was a conditional offer, the condition precedent wouldn't be that you're not pregnant. It causes massive difficulties. So we've got s18 of the Equality Act 2010, which creates a particular form of discrimination protection for pregnant women during the protected period, which begins with a pregnancy. They do not need to have a comparator in relation to s18. So no, you can't do that. But one thing I will flag up because I think it's pretty clear is that in the Equality and Human Rights Commission's Code of Practice, it's very well worth looking at chapter 16: avoiding discrimination in recruitment. In paragraph 16.70 of the code, the example given is an initial vacancy to cover another

woman on maternity leave. The code of practice says that it's irrelevant that the woman has failed to disclose that she is pregnant and, basically, it's tough luck for the employer. There's a very special protection for pregnant women.

Paula Early

Can an employer use social media to vet potential new employees?

Eleena Misra

That is an excellent question, especially given current recruitment practices. So the short answer is yes. The slightly longer answer is to be careful in how you go about doing it. Why is it important to be careful? The first reason is GDPR. So we're obviously required to have regard to data protection, the 2018 Act and the six core principles of data protection. Something that people forget is that processing information includes obtaining information as it doesn't sit very comfortably with that language. But obtaining information about someone from social media is processing their personal data, certainly within the meaning of the legislation. So if you're going to be processing someone's personal data, then you need to have regard to those principles. Why are you doing it? Is it proportionate and necessary with regard to what you're looking for?

There's probably generally a distinction to be drawn between going to professional sites such as LinkedIn, where you're looking at someone's professional outward face, particularly, for example, if you're recruiting someone senior, you need to know what sort of reputation they bring with them. That's quite different to trawling someone's Facebook if they've been foolish enough not to sort out their privacy settings, and having a look at pictures. Let's give you the classic example, which I think is given in some of the guidance, you stumble across a picture that shows that someone's got young children. You've used that information so you need to keep a record and it leaves you

wide open to potential discrimination claims. So it's a good idea to have a social media policy in terms of what you do in recruitment terms. And also it's very good to make clear to candidates that you may, within reason, be carrying out those sorts of searches.

David Price

Where does an employer stand if they need to recruit for a male-only role - specialist adult social care with a male-only service - and the employer receives an application from a trans candidate who identifies as male, but is at a stage of their transition where they objectively appear female?

Daniel Barnett

I'll just say that when Eleena answers this question, she's arguing it from a legal perspective, not from a political perspective or revealing her own views.

Eleena Misra

One of the first things to ask in relation to this potential application, or indeed any application, is whether you can legitimately require a man or a woman at all. The answer to that is to be found in the provisions that govern occupational requirements. So the first thing you need to determine is whether there's an occupational requirement for a man or woman. So if it's specialist adult social care, and there is indeed an occupational requirement, say, if it involves intimate care or something that means you do just need someone of a particular sex, then that's the first question. And of course, the legislation deals with this in terms of sex.

The next layer is whether someone's legal sex has been affected by obtaining a gender recognition certificate. That would then need to be analysed in terms of their legal sex. There would have to be a very careful record as to why you acted as you did. And you'd have to be very careful that you were not discriminating against someone on the grounds of gender reassignment as well. So if they're in the process of transitioning, you must bear in mind the provisions which protect persons in that group from discrimination as well.

I'm not going to pretend that it's anything but a very knotty issue. But you've got to take a very sequential approach to these things. The language in our statutes on gender and sex can be quite confusing, and we have very different strands of discrimination that come together. I hope that doesn't sound like I'm ducking the answer, but it is quite a nuanced one.

Anonymous

What can an employer do when no disability is mentioned in the recruitment process, either in an optional questionnaire or in an interview, and then shortly after recruitment, the candidate discloses that they have a disability but the adjustments that are required impact the needs of the role?

Daniel Barnett

I'm not quite sure what 'impacts the needs of the role' means, but we can probably have a guess.

Eleena Misra

In circumstances in which the employer didn't know that the employee that they just recruited was disabled, but they then become aware, they're then affixed with actual knowledge, and they're then affixed with the duty to make reasonable adjustments contained in s20 of the Equality Act. So it doesn't really matter, in a sense, that this person has not disclosed that disability at an early stage. Once you know that they're disabled, you're under that duty to take such steps as are reasonable in all circumstances. The legal analysis is exactly the same. I should say, I think there are some authorities where employers effectively decided to dismiss on the basis that it had been dishonest not to reveal the extent of sick leave that they'd had in a previous job or something that was a consequence of disability. And they got pretty short shrift on that one. So not helpful, I appreciate, in those circumstances, but the

minute you know that someone is disabled and you've already employed them, and let's assume that in this scenario you haven't required them to go through medical checks or health checks, you then need to just analyse your duty in terms of reasonable adjustments.

Beth Bearder

What's the most common mistake employers make in a recruitment process?

Daniel Barnett

We'll both have a go at this one. Do you want to go first?

Eleena Misra

Oh, my goodness! I'm trying to summarise the last 15 plus years of cases I've been doing. What's been the worst mistake? Probably the most basic mistake is just not keeping a proper paper trail of what's been done and why. It's utterly basic. I've often dealt with a company that has actually got a human resources department, it's got a lot of resources, but when it comes down to it, there's been a very poor paper trail kept about the interviews or the sift or something else. And when you face a claim, you then just don't have the tools to deal with it and it's very difficult for everyone. So that's not the most legal answer to the question, but from years of experience, to my mind, that's the most common mistake.

Daniel Barnett

I agree with you. I think another very common mistake is not having clear criteria for the skills required and the details of the role you're recruiting for, and recruiting based on who you like best or have the best rapport with rather than the person who's going to be the best fit for the job.

AJ Fraser

When a job applicant has failed to disclose spent convictions, as required for roles that are exempt from the rehabilitation of offenders act, do we have reasonable grounds to withdraw the offer due to lack of honesty, trust and integrity?

Eleena Misra

If I understand this question rightly, we've got a situation in which someone would ordinarily not have to disclose the spent convictions, but because of the Exceptions Order 2013, or a combination of that and another act, they're within an exception of the exception, for example, professionals who work with vulnerable people. So assuming, therefore, that they are required to disclose spent convictions because of the legal framework, and they don't do so, well, that would quite likely go to the heart of trust and confidence. So it seems to me that there would be reasonable grounds to either withdraw the offer if it has not been accepted, or if the offer has been accepted and there is a contract of employment that has come into being, then it may be that's actually grounds for summary dismissal, and that may be conduct, it may be something that it amounts to a breach of trust and confidence or it may be some other substantial reason. But, of course, while it's plainly going to be something most people would consider egregious, you have to take a step back and just wonder whether, in light of that particular role, going down the route of requiring those spent convictions to be disclosed was actually necessary. I would imagine that in this scenario because it's an exemption for an exemption, it probably is. So I think you're probably on good ground there.

Daniel Barnett

I think there's also the practical point that 95% of the time when you discover their convictions, the person is going to have less than two years' employment. And I don't think any discrimination issues will arise here. So you can just get rid of them without worrying that much about the consequences other than possibly notice pay. Would notice pay be due in this situation? I think the job has been obtained and the contract's been entered into through misrepresentation.

Loads of people have put their views about the biggest mistake made in recruitment into the chat.

Eleena Misra

There are some great ones on diversity which I think are really good.

Daniel Barnett

Pick a couple and read them out if you would.

Eleena Misra

I quite like the one about unconscious bias. I think it was Liz who mentioned unconscious bias and recruiting people like you, which I think it's a really good point.

Karen

If you advertise a role asking for specific memberships or qualifications and you have a strong candidate who doesn't meet those criteria, are there any reasons why you shouldn't select them over other applicants who do meet the criteria but weren't as strong in other areas?

Eleena Misra

It's one of those where maybe, in hindsight, when you look at it, you think that possibly something should have been desirable, rather than in the essential criteria. There's nothing to stop you from picking the best candidate for the job, which is essentially what you're trying to do, to recruit on merit. The risk of deviating from your essential criteria is that someone who is unsuccessful will, if they know about it, seize upon that and say that they don't understand why you've preferred this person when they don't meet one of the essential criteria. So as long as you have a good reason and you've looked at the applications holistically in the round, and you record it and keep a good paper trail, ultimately, none of these laws are there to stop you from picking the best person for the job as long as you do so in a way that's on merit.

Paula Early

What can you do as an employer if a job applicant doesn't disclose a pregnancy during interview?

Eleena Misra

The answer is nothing. Nothing.

AJ Fraser

Where an individual has accepted an offer of employment but has since told the employer they can't start on the agreed date, can the employer retract the offer?

Daniel Barnett

Of course, it's not an offer at that stage, it's a contract.

Eleena Misra

Assuming that the start date had been agreed - it is an agreed start date and they say that they can't do it, well, you could just have a simple issue of unless the employee agrees, it's an unauthorised absence. That was the start date and that was when they were required to attend for work. Now, you'd have to look and see what the reasons were. You certainly wouldn't want to prevent someone starting a bit later if there was a family emergency or something that you knew was a good reason. But otherwise, you've got a contract to implement, you have an agreed start date, and unless there's a good reason not to, you can effectively act on their failure to start when they're meant to.

St Cox

I've had a few fights over the giving of references and the potential for negligent misstatement by omission. Have you any advice on leaving out matters in a reference, bearing in mind the risk that that might be deemed failing to give a full, accurate and fair reference as required by Spring v Guardian Assurance (*Spring v Guardian Assurance [1994] UKHL 7*)?

Eleena Misra

If you're just giving a straightforward factual statement that says 'Bloggins worked here from X to Y dates in such and such a position', one of those references that doesn't do anything other than state the very, very basic facts of the employment, then I think, in those circumstances, you're on pretty safe ground. You might want to make sure that you set out if it's the policy of the company to give nothing other than a factual reference. Otherwise, someone reading it may wonder what's gone on here and why you won't say any more. Although, of course, they might be savvy enough to know that there's a compromise agreement, for example.

When you go on to say something more, the acid test is to look at everything that you're proposing to say in that reference, then stand back from it and think, reading this, does it give a fair and accurate summary to the person who's receiving it? One thing that you might want to do if you have got a very sensible prospective employer who has actually contacted you with, for example, a job description or person specification and you're aware of that, is just make sure you try and link your answers to that, and that everything you're going to be saying can be backed up somewhere. It's not just piecemeal opinion-making.

Liz Hayward

What advice do you have for employers about when to consider status to work in the UK as part of a recruitment process?

Eleena Misra

One of the things that the Home Office tells us is that when you're going to carry out checks in terms of the right to work, you don't want to do that too early because, obviously, that could change. You want to carry out those checks reasonably close in time to when the employment is meant to be starting. That's really to do with checks. But in terms of status, yes, you're going to have to keep that under review throughout, really, and comply with the regime in terms of the information that you have.

What is the purpose of carrying out these checks as to status of work? It's to prevent you, as an employer, either going down on civil liability with a fine of up to £20,000 for hiring someone who's working illegally in your business or worst-case scenario, proceeding in a way that exposes you to a criminal sanction of up to five years in prison where you reasonably believe that someone is illegally working. So the purpose of why you're doing this is really important. And that's down to your appetite for risk, I suppose. But yes, I'd say do it close to the start of employment and keep it under review.

Steven Eckett

Are there any problems in recruiting for an employee and stating in the job specification that it's a requirement that they speak another language fluently, for example, Punjabi, Polish or Welsh?

Eleena Misra

I'm sure there won't be a job that necessarily requires all three languages, but you never know! The first point is if it's a genuine requirement of the job that you need someone who speaks any of those languages fluently, then no problem at all. Let's just bear in mind that people speak different languages; it's not linked necessarily to their own ethnic or national origins. You get people who are conversant in lots of different languages. So if it's an essential part of the role, then it will probably help you if you end up in an indirect discrimination scenario because you can objectively justify why you have got a requirement for someone to speak fluently in those languages.

Anonymous

If a candidate is invited for an interview and they refuse to be seen on a remote video meeting, and they'll only attend the interview by audio because they suffer with anxiety and don't want to be seen, do you have to proceed with the interview on that basis? And is the answer the same if there's a requirement in the job for the person in that role to attend meetings remotely on camera?

Eleena Misra

That's a really good question. First of all, I think we can all recognise that there is something about interacting with a person, detecting their visual cues and their body language; there's more than just hearing someone and speaking to them. So my starting point would be that it's quite a normal thing to want to see someone during a job interview and not just to hear them speak. But if the person said that they suffer from anxiety, then as a reasonable adjustment, would you allow them to attend the interview without video? You might want to ask, first of all, if there's anything else you could do to make them feel comfortable in engaging by video. For example, rather than having a panel, you might want to have a one-to-one discussion first of all. So just think about other reasonable adjustments you couldn't make. But if the person in question says that they just absolutely can't do it other than by not having their video switched on, then probably it would be a reasonable adjustment, depending on the nature of the role.

That's where the second part of this question comes in. I think if this person does need to engage with people face to face on a regular basis, whether that's remotely or otherwise, I think that's a perfectly good reason to say you think openly and honestly that you have to have the interview face to face and it's not a reasonable adjustment in view of the nature of the role we're advertising for.

It's a really interesting one and I'm sure that must come up. I've done an investigation in recent times where someone was too anxious to actually have their video on the whole time. We agreed that the interviewee would speak to me with video on briefly at the beginning and at the end, but would feel more comfortable having it switched off in between. So you sometimes have to think on your feet with these things. That was a different context to interviewing someone for a job though, I appreciate.

Daniel Barnett
I'm not sure I'd be happy with that because I would be worried at the back of my mind that somebody was sitting there next to them whispering the answers or passing them notes.

Eleena Misra
That's the other risk. You don't know.

Natalie White
What advice would you give to an employer who's heard on the grapevine that a candidate had conduct or capability in a previous role if their nominated references from those other roles don't disclose the conduct or capability issues?

Daniel Barnett
I may have misread that question, actually. I made up that last bit.

Eleena Misra
So my understanding is that there's something on the grapevine that the referees are not going to speak to, for whatever reason.

Daniel Barnett
That's relevant to the question. But if you read it literally, the question is actually saying the referees are from a different role, not the one that gave rise to the problems. Can you answer both?

Eleena Misra
If there's anything that's effectively entered your mind that is going to be playing on your mind when you make a decision, then the thing to do is keep a note of what it is you've been told, and by whom. And I think the starting point might be to actually explore those issues with the candidate themselves. So you might actually want to explore those issues and see what answers they give you, and then based on those answers, you might say that it would really help you to have referees who can speak to the person's performance, their abilities in X

role rather than this role so I can gain a better understanding. It seems to me that's the better way forward, to try and elicit the information from the candidate first of all in a fairly open way. I'm not sure you'd go into that saying you've heard something pretty bad about them. But you might want to just explore those areas a bit more and see if you can do it in a more transparent way rather than just dealing with information you've heard on the grapevine that will play on your mind and taint your decision without giving a candidate an opportunity to answer those points or find a way of talking to the right referee.

Daniel Barnett
What happens if a former employer says in a reference 'this person is absolutely awful. They have appalling body odour and nobody likes them, but please keep this strictly confidential and don't let on that I've told you. Is a potential new employer entitled to discuss those points with the candidate in interview, or are they prohibited from doing so because the old employer's asked for it to be kept confidential?

Eleena Misra
I guess it depends on the context in which that information is being given. But as you say, if you've just asked for a reference and it's been provided confidentially, without going into the details, you could say that you have received a reference that has matters of concern without going into the absolute ins and outs of it and that you'd like to explore those issues. The first thing that I would do is probably go back to the person who had given the reference to say, that in those circumstances, surely you must appreciate that it isn't fair for me not to explore this further and I'm going to need to so. I really would be grateful if you could agree that I can explore this with the individual concerned.

Anonymous
Can an employer seek to recover the recruitment fee from the employee if the employee leaves

within a specified period of time and there's an express clause in the employment contract permitting the employer to recover the recruitment fee on a sliding scale?

Eleena Misra
So can they enforce the provision of the contract agreed with the employee that lets them do that? Well, unless it amounts to a penalty clause, it seems that would be permissible as a matter of contract.

Daniel Barnett
Is there anything in the Agency Workers Regulations that renders unlawful any clause in the contract that charges an employee a fee for the recruitment process, which might include contracts of employment as well?

Eleena Misra
I don't know the precise details. There might be something for that specific agency worker provision, but otherwise, in a situation where there's no agency involved (in recovering the fee).

Daniel Barnett
I think I'd need to check the wording of the Agency Workers Regulations.

Eleena Misra
I think I would too. I'm afraid I don't know off the top of my head, either. But I think the basic principle would be that unless it amounts to a penalty clause and unless there's a specific prohibition, by virtue of being an agency worker arrangement, then that would be alright. Harsh but permissible.

Gillian Howard
What legal recourse does an employer have if the job candidate accepts the role and on the day they should have started they call to say they're not starting the job with you because their current employer has persuaded them to stay?

We all know you can't injunct an employee to work for you, but what measure of damages would the new employer have in that situation?

Eleena Misra
We know that employers very rarely go to court over these sorts of issues because it ends up being more costly trying to pursue it than actually recovering it, but in principle, the losses that flow from that breach of contract. So if you had to hire some agency cover or an interim member of staff while you recruit someone else, in principle, that would be a recoverable loss. Certainly not too remote, in my view.

Daniel Barnett
I agree. It never happens in practice, but in theory, I suppose that the measure of damages or whatever the notice period would be - so if the notice period was a month - for a month, it would be the additional costs that you might incur having a temporary worker in over and above the salary you would have paid. I suppose theoretically, you could bring a claim for loss of profit that flowed from that employee not being in post, even though that would be difficult to prove.

Eleena Misra
It would be a nightmare to prove, but I don't see why, as a matter of analysis, you couldn't do that.

There's an interesting comment from Claire Palmer (regarding the recruitment fee issue). She says: it seems to me that you might not be able to do so if it meant that the employee had not received the minimum wage for the time they had worked. Yes, I hadn't actually thought about whether that that would result in less than minimum wage being paid. But I think that's a very valid point if the recoupment resulted in the hourly rate dropping below the statutory minimum for the reference period?

Vish Dhall
Would it be reasonable for an employer to ask their employees to refrain from publishing who they work for on LinkedIn to prevent recruiters trying to poach their employees?

Eleena Misra

So, to prevent an employee from stating who their employer is on LinkedIn? That's a very difficult one. I think that probably trespasses on their human rights to be honest with you. So, in other words, not identifying who you currently work for on your LinkedIn profile so that you can't be poached? I think that's a very difficult one. And I think that's a step too far. You're entitled to have your identity outside of work, which includes your career profile. So I think that would probably amount to a breach of that employee's human rights. I can't see a court enforcing that if I'm honest. But if anyone knows of an authority where they've done that, I'd be very interested to know.

What you can do, of course, in your contracts of employment, is to have provisions which try to deal with the situation of employees being poached. But at the end of the day, if someone comes along with a very generous job offer, and your employee thinks that's a better bet, so they resign and give you the correct notice, I'm afraid it's one of those things.

Amelia Berriman

What do you think of Ban the Box?

Daniel Barnett

Ban the Box, I'm sure people know, is a campaign to increase opportunities for people with convictions to find employment and compete for jobs.

Eleena Misra

I think that they are a particularly disadvantaged sector of the job market because notwithstanding the legislative framework that provides for convictions having to be disclosed in some situations but not in others, if you're in one of those categories where your conviction is not going to be spent - there are certain convictions which are never spent - you're going to find it really difficult to find a job. I suppose it's the idea of whether people can ever change. Well, I'd like to think that people would be open-minded as to the prospect of people

changing over time, particularly for things done in youth or done in different circumstances. So yes, I think, overall, anything that's going to assist a disadvantaged sector of the job market has got to be a good thing, in my view, and I can see why that would be helpful.

Ed B

Should you give more feedback to a disabled candidate, such as a candidate with Asperger's, if they are unsuccessful in their role?

Daniel Barnett

Can you watch that from a legal perspective rather than a moral perspective?

Eleena Misra

There's actually no obligation to give feedback or to give a particular type, nature or quantity of feedback to anybody. In giving feedback, you're either minimising the risks or enhancing your position in the event of a challenge as to your decisions. I'm not going to stray into whether you should do that morally or not - that's a question for each employer. But in terms of why other than for moral reasons you would do that, it's really to do with managing the risk of challenge. To give you another example, you might think that that candidate would be well-suited to a different role in the future, so you might want to give feedback that gives them encouragement to apply again. That could be something that's good for increasing the diversity of your business. So risk and diversity are two things that would come to mind for me.

Daniel Barnett

Eleena Misra from Old Square, what's the best way for somebody to get in touch with me if somebody wants to ask any further questions or instruct you?

Eleena Misra

So if you go to our chambers website, which is www.oldsquare.co.uk or my email is misra@oldsquare.co.uk

Daniel Barnett

Eleena Misra, thank you very much.

REDUNDANCY

PAMAN SINGH, LAW AT WORK

Daniel Barnett

For today's Q&A webinar session on individual redundancy consultation, I'm joined by Paman Singh from Law At Work.

Paman Singh, good morning. I'm going to ask you a couple of questions first. Where you have a number of individuals volunteering for redundancy, and there are more volunteers than there are redundancy spaces, how should an employer choose which volunteers to accept?

Paman Singh

Voluntary redundancy actually seems to be coming up a lot more these days. And it's something that I advise on quite regularly. I don't think it's a bad thing. In fact, it shows that employers and employees are willing to sort of think beyond just a blinkered approach to a redundancy scenario. But if we're talking about how to select volunteers, if you've had more than one come forward, I suppose there are a few wee tips I can give you to take into account.

Firstly, set the rules of the game. So as an employer, you should always set the parameters for VR. And what I mean is that you want to build yourself in an escape hatch of discretion. Make it clear to the employees that when you're seeking volunteers, there's no obligation upon you, as an employer, to accept any. You might want to do that for a number of reasons. It could be for cost - you don't want to lose particular employees or the skills that the employees have. There's nothing wrong with that. It's just good business practice

and it really wouldn't - or at least it shouldn't - affect the fairness of compulsory redundancies further down the line. But I would say to just watch out for the spectre of discrimination. There's a 2016 case, Donkor v RBS *(Donkor v The Royal Bank of Scotland [2016] IRLR 268)*. I won't go into the great detail of the case, but it was found that offering voluntary redundancy to a group of people and then not offering it to someone who is over 50 was, on the face of it, age discrimination, and the EAT remitted the case back to the employment tribunal to consider whether that discrimination could be objectively justified.

The other practical point to make is that it is a good opportunity to consider who the poorer performing employees are and offer them voluntary redundancy and keep your better-performing individuals.

Keep your comms sharp when you're going out to the employees. It's very much a case of 'we accept your request to be selected for voluntary redundancy'. Again, you're keeping a paper trail from an early point to show the intention of the parties. I think Karen Jackson might have mentioned it a few days ago when she was presenting on discrimination law: paperwork and paper trail are your friends! Whenever you're in a tribunal, there's nothing quite like holding up a piece of paper showing what the intention of the parties was at the time.

Daniel Barnett

Can you have a trial period? As you know, when you're offering alternative work, you have to allow the employee to have a statutory trial period of four weeks. Can you offer a longer trial period, say, of 12 weeks?

Paman Singh
That's something I've been asked a couple of times by clients, and it is understandable. You've got an employee being placed into a new role and it can often take more than four weeks to get up to speed with a new way of working. I won't embarrass myself and tell you how long it took me to get up to the speed of working here.

Trial periods are set out in statute in s138 of the Employment Rights Act. That allows a four week trial period. Of course, we know that that can't be extended for anything other than retraining purposes. And even then, that's an extra two weeks, so it is fairly strict. And then if the statutory trial period is unsuccessful, then you're deemed to be dismissed, for the purposes of redundancy payment, on the date that the original contract ended.

Susan Sidell
If an employee is on a fixed-term contract with a specified end date and the contract naturally comes to an end, does the employer have a liability to make a redundancy payment if the individual has over two years' service?

Daniel Barnett
So I suppose what Susan's asking is whether that is a redundancy dismissal or some other substantial reason dismissal.

Paman Singh
Did you say two years' service?

Daniel Barnett
More than two years' service.

Paman Singh
If the fixed term is due to expire fairly soon, then you could be creative and argue that it is, in reality, for some other substantial reason. It could be that if it's mat leave cover or something or someone is imminently about

to return, then you could deem the fixed-term employee to be a replacement employee under s106 of the Employment Rights Act. But you still obviously have to carry out a fair procedure. If they have sufficient service and the fixed-term contract's not due to end anytime soon...

Daniel Barnett
The question says the fixed-term contract is coming to an end. So if the fixed-term contract is coming to an end and they've got more than two years' service, is that a redundancy dismissal if they're not renewed, or at some other substantial reason?

Paman Singh
You can argue some other substantial reason, I think, and there's some case law that suggests that that's perfectly fine.

Natalie White
How much discretion does an employer have in choosing its criteria for redundancy situations if the employee disagrees with those criteria?

Paman Singh
In short, you have a wide range, you have quite a lot of discretion there. An employment tribunal will tend not to look too much into pools. As long as you can show that it wasn't completely unreasonable, then there's a range of reasonable responses that would apply.

Daniel Barnett
But do employees have any grounds to challenge criteria?

Paman Singh
Did you say 'employees'? Yes? That is one of the fundamental hallmarks of the consultation process. Yes, we would say, and actually, you should welcome the opportunity to have some challenge because it shows that the process is a fluid and evolving process. The tribunal has been on record on this many times to say you don't want to blinkered approach - "blind faith in process" I think, is one of the terms from

the Biluan case *(Mental Health Care (UK) Ltd v Biluan UKEAT/0248/12/SM)*. That is not advisable. So, yes, in short, you would want to have the challenge, consider the challenge and provide a response.

Daniel Barnett
My experience is that tribunals will apply the range of reasonable responses test, as they do with all matters relating to unfair dismissal, but they'll expect there to have been consultation over the criteria under Compair Maxam *(Williams v Compair Maxam Limited [1982] IRLR 83)* which sets out consultation on criteria as one of the key matters for selecting the criteria. But as long as the employers jump through the hoops of consulting over criteria and listen fairly to what the employees say, it's almost impossible to challenge the criteria the employer selects unless they are tainted by some form of discrimination, such as people having to work five days a week, which would be discriminated against women, or people having to have worked for a certain number of years, which would be discriminatory against younger people. Is that your understanding also?

Paman Singh
Absolutely. And I think that there was a Rolls-Royce case *(Rolls-Royce Plc v Unite the Union [2009] IRLR 576)* in 2009 that dealt with potentially discriminatory selection criteria. I think length of service was something that was considered and eventually justified in that case. But certainly, you've got to watch for any sort of selection criteria tainted by discrimination. Especially now that we're looking at furlough then you'll perhaps be looking at things like attendance and performance. If you can't measure performance when someone has been off on furlough, then you'd need to make sure that there's an equal application.

Adriana Pantaleon
Can employers avoid redundancy if the employee is on a zero-hour contract, knowing you can run someone's contract forever with

their hours dialled down to zero without the need of offering them work?

Daniel Barnett
Does this turn on the rules about lay-off and short-time?

Paman Singh
Yes. I think that you're looking at things like lay-off and short-time where there is a period of time when you can, if you have a contractual right to do so, dial someone's hours done. I think, off the top of my head, the specified period is either for four or five weeks out of twelve, I think it might be, after which there are certain statutory processes that need to be followed so that an employee can notify an employer of their intent that they want to apply for a redundancy payment.

Daniel Barnett
If the employee is genuinely on a zero-hours contract, so the employer isn't purporting to exercise a lay-off or short-time clause, what's the position? Are they entitled to redundancy payments? Or can the employer just say you don't get a redundancy payment because we're reducing your hours to zero and that's all we have to do? I think that's one of the big holes with zero-hour contracts, isn't it? It's one of the big problems that the government's looking at legislating to fill.

Paman Singh
I don't know of any case law on this topic. I don't know. I've not come across that so far.

Daniel Barnett
My view, for what it's worth, and I don't profess to be any great expert in this area, is that an employer is entitled just to dial the hours down to zero, and there's absolutely nothing an employee can do about it. They won't have an entitlement to a redundancy payment unless they can somehow argue that the dialling down to zero - which is, of course, a contractual right - has been exercised in bad faith so as to give rise to a constructive dismissal. If it's a constructive dismissal, then

the reason for the dismissal is redundancy and you get a redundancy payment. But unless you can fit yourself within that pigeonhole, I think zero-hour contract employees are pretty much shafted by that technique. Is there something about the government looking at changing the law on this to give more rights to employees?

Paman Singh
I think there was a consultation that the Government recently concluded.

AJ Fraser
How would you deal with individual consultation for a woman on maternity leave who fails or refuses to engage with the process?

Daniel Barnett
Let's just take that back a step. Can you make a woman on maternity leave redundant?

Paman Singh
In short, yes.

Daniel Barnett
If she refuses or fails to engage in the consultation process, what should an employer do?

Paman Singh
We need to be careful here and we need to unpack the reasons. It's not just a case that if the employee is not engaging, then that's it; off she goes. We need to try and at least show an employment tribunal what steps we've taken and how we have tried to encourage her to communicate. It could be that she's not comfortable with dealing with these issues while she's obviously looking after her newborn child. It could all be very overwhelming for her if she's not been in the workplace for some time. So you want to show a little bit of empathy. It's quite easy to get dragged down into process-driven thought. But I think things like potentially offering telephone conversations or even consultations in writing setting out the reasons that we want to speak to her clearly and advising her that if we can't

eventually get hold of her, then we will have to make a decision.

Daniel Barnett
Is there a legal obligation on an employer to put a redundancy process on hold for a woman on maternity leave? I don't think there is.

Paman Singh
No, The only thing that I would point out is if you have a suitable alternative vacancy, then there is obviously an automatic right to that suitable alternative under the MPL regs.

Daniel Barnett
If the woman doesn't engage, notwithstanding the employer's attempts to engage her, ultimately, it's just the usual range of reasonable responses test for the employer, isn't it? Has the employer made reasonable attempts to consultant and help and do what it can do to avoid redundancy?

Paman Singh
Yes, absolutely.

Daniel Barnett
Karen Teago has sent a message, commenting that the position is different depending on what stage of maternity leave the woman is at. I've asked Karen to pop into the webinar. Karen is one of the principal solicitors at Yess Law.

Karen Teago
We're working on a three-year project with Maternity Action, whereby we're doing casework for women, many of whom are in it in this exact situation. One of the women I helped recently was contacted when her baby was eight or 10 weeks old to say that she needed to go through a competitive selection process for a new role. Now, at that stage of maternity leave, that's a huge ask, particularly if it's your first baby. So the way in which she was dealt with was inappropriate. There was too much communication, bearing in mind the stage that she was at. And I think the 'too focused on the process approach' was what was happening there. I don't think it was

necessarily deliberate, but it was having a big impact on her.

If you contrast that with a woman who's in the latter stages of maternity leave, she's potentially thinking about childcare and how she's going to manage going back to work. And then towards the end of maternity leave, if an employer says they'll just wait until she gets back and then start the process. Actually, that doesn't necessarily do the woman any favours because she may have secured a place with a childminder or nursery and paid a deposit for that. There are all sorts of reasons why, towards the end of maternity leave, actually, it's better to engage as soon as you know you've got that situation, but always taking account of the woman's circumstances anyway. It can make a difference where the woman is on her maternity journey.

Natalie White

What advice would you give an employer who makes a position redundant but then has unexpected changes in their financial situation, meaning they need to rehire for the same role. Morally, should they offer the redundant employee their job back, and is there a legal obligation to do so?

Daniel Barnett

I'm assuming this is after the individual has gone.

Paman Singh

This is assuming that they've been paid their statutory redundancy payment and the contract has come to an end.

Daniel Barnett

I'm assuming Natalie meant they've gone because if they were still there, then obviously you have to offer them the job.

Daniel Barnett

Natalie says yes. Assume they've gone.

Paman Singh

There's no obligation per se. What would you do morally? That's interesting. I would

probably see that it's a good idea to offer them the role back. We're thinking about this practically, and we're thinking about how this affects business. Well, it engenders trust, I think, and it engenders a sense of loyalty from your staff if they can see that actually, you are fairly applying your mind to things and you genuinely care about them. So if there is an upturn or a sudden need for them, then absolutely, yes.

Daniel Barnett

That covers the moral aspect. Can I have a stab at the legal one? I think from a legal perspective there's no obligation whatsoever to offer the job back. Once they're dismissed, they're dismissed and when you're determining the fairness of the dismissal, you can only look at what happened up to the point that the notice period ended. Anything that happens after that is totally irrelevant. The fact that a position reopens cannot make a dismissal for redundancy unfair if it was otherwise fair.

But there are two caveats. Point one is that our failure to offer the job back could be evidence from which a tribunal might infer discrimination - if the employee was alleging discrimination in the selection process. Point two is that the fact that the job reopens at a later date - and I'm now hypothesising that it's weeks or months later, not a few days later - would be a valid reason for extending time for an unfair dismissal claim. There's EAT case law on that, the name of which I can't remember for the life of me, but it's been held that it wouldn't be reasonably practicable for an employee to bring a claim about the unfairness of a redundancy situation if they only discovered crucial information that the job might not have been genuinely redundant months later.

Mike Clyne

Where you're starting or in the process of individual consultation and the employee says, "I know what's happening here; I know I'm going to get sacked. Just give me the numbers," what steps should the employer take to protect themselves whilst not forcing the employee to go through the whole probably pyrrhic and futile process?

Paman Singh
A paper trail again. So let's make sure that it is absolutely clear that the employee is saying this. There is case law on this as well. If an employee has previously said, for example, "You know what? That's fine. We don't want to be consulted with; we just want the redundancy," then the tribunal is very, very keen to at least have some form of consultation. So that is very much a last resort. I would slightly say still protect yourself. A useful case Thomas v BNP Paribas *(Thomas v BNP Paribas Real Estate Advisory & Property Management UK Ltd UKEAT/0134/16/JOJ)* around 2006. In that case, actually, the tribunal went on the record and said things like getting the name wrong or immediately putting someone on garden leave at short notice are all contributory factors towards a finding of unfair dismissal - a highly insensitive and depersonalised process. So I would just protect yourself and make sure that you have a paper trail to show and that you're still trying to follow as full a process as you can.

Karen Teago
We're seeing an increasing number of employers using 'bumping' - a classic example of something incredibly unfair being potentially lawful. Have there been any developments in the law around this in recent years?

Daniel Barnett
Bumping is also known as transferred redundancy. Could you explain what bumping is before you go on to answer whether there have been any recent cases on it?

Paman Singh
Bumping seems to be this mythical kind of thing that every HR professional has heard of, is worried about and is fascinated by! The clue in the title. So generally speaking, you have one employee, usually senior, who is at risk of redundancy and there is a junior role open. The employee sets out the fact that they're willing or able to do that role and the employer agrees and 'bumps' the junior person out of the role so that there's a knock-on effect.

Daniel Barnett
Have there been any recent cases on it?

Paman Singh
There's a 2012 case. There was maybe a case in 2014. But there was a case of Fulcrum Pharma v Bonassera *(Fulcrum Pharma (Europe) Ltd v Bonassera & Anor UKEAT/0198/10/DM)*, and I think that in that case, it went up to the EAT and the EAT did find that the employer could have asked further questions about the issue of bumping. And what I'd say, again, in terms of practical solutions, keep a note of whether you have considered bumping and if you don't think it's appropriate, why you don't think it's appropriate. It's always good to be able to refer to that further down the line.

Daniel Barnett
I have the slightly unfair advantage of being able to do some research while you're talking. So I've just I just typed the word 'bumping' into the archive of my Employment Law Bulletins and came up with this case, which I had no recollection of. It's in 2018 and it's authority from the Employment Appeal Tribunal, Mirab v Mentor Graphics *(Mirab v Mentor Graphics (UK) Ltd UKEAT/0172/17/DA)* that an employee doesn't need to specifically raise bumping before an employer needs to consider it. But a decision not to consider bumping must be viewed through the range of reasonable responses tests.

That, of course, is the opposite to what the question is asking. The question is asking whether there's a way of stopping bumping because it's a tremendously unfair process. I agree that it is tremendously unfair. But I don't think there's any way of stopping it. The decision to bump is now well established in law and, of course, it stems from very, very old, well-established union-approved principles. Not so much anymore, but this was an older position of unions that used to encourage bumping. It's so firmly ingrained in the law now that I just don't think it's ever going to disappear. So yes, it can be an excuse to get rid of the employees you want to get rid of, and yes, I agree that it's tremendously unfair.

Paman Singh

Just one other thing. I think that the Bonassera principles still would apply. So again, if we're thinking about bumping on a practical point, what would you look at? You'd look at whether or not there's a vacancy; how different the two jobs are; the difference in remuneration will probably be a relevant factor, the EAT said; the difference in the length of service is another factor; and then, I suppose, the qualifications of the employee who's in danger of the redundancy and whether or not they specified in the consultation that they'd accept a reduced salary. So those are factors for someone who's dealing with that situation.

Daniel Barnett

Karen Teago has very generously offered to write a blog or an article on some of the scenarios she sees and how comms should be adapted with women on maternity leave. Lots of people are commenting that that would be really useful. Karen, that would be amazing. If you do it, I'll send out a link to everybody who's on these webinars.

Allyn Walton

How best can an employer avoid the appearance of individually targeting somebody if considering a pool of one?

Paman Singh

I suppose what we've got to look at first of all is identifying the pool. So what is the particular type of work that is either ceasing or diminishing? That's the first thing. Remember, it is not the person, it's the role that you're making redundant. You need to be able to

establish that first of all. Once you've done that and you can genuinely show that there is a pool of one, again, you've generally got a wide discretion over how you select your pool.

What I would say - certainly from my experience - is that if you have a pool of one, the tribunal will certainly give it more scrutiny. So you have to be able to justify your reason there. Make sure you can show that there is there's a genuine pool of one, there's not a lot of interchangeability or that the skills for that person or that role cannot then be easily transposed or other people can't do that role.

Daniel Barnett

I generally find that tribunals are reasonably accepting of a pool of one provided that the employee hasn't challenged the pool of one. But if the employee has said this shouldn't be a pool of one, you should be drawing people with similar skills or similar roles in during the consultation process, then a tribunal expects to see damn good contemporaneous evidence of why the employee is wrong. Because although the range of reasonable responses test is quite wide, tribunals will be very, very willing to find that an employer hasn't addressed its mind properly to the pool, so as to allow itself to come within the range of reasonable responses unless there is contemporaneous evidence of the employer saying that they don't accept that the roles are similar and they don't accept the skills are comparable, because of X, Y or Z. There needs to be some sort of contemporaneous file note showing that it's been actively considered. And as long as you can show that it's been considered, generally, you'll get away with it if you're an employer.

Paman Singh

I think that's absolutely right. But like you said, contemporaneous notes and file records - show your working. If you remember the heady days of school and being in maths class, you get one point for the right answer, but you get a multitude of points for showing you're working all the way through.

AJ Fraser

How would you deal with individual consultation for an employee who's going off sick with stress because of the redundancy process?

Daniel Barnett

Is the answer to just get on with it?

Paman Singh

Get on with it to an extent. Again, show that you are trying to reach out to them and show that you're trying alternative methods to communicate with them. But, ultimately, if it's just stress, then I'm afraid that it is a stressful time. Make sure there are no underlying health conditions and cover yourself in terms of discrimination, etc. But certainly, try and consult with them if you can. Resort to a written exercise, try phone calls, but ultimately, yes, if there is a redundancy process, then it's not going to be halted just for stress. It's a bit cynical, unfortunately,

Daniel Barnett

It sounds callous, but it's true. What you really need to be remembering is that the stress is never going to go away, while the cause of the stress is still there. And if the cause of the stress is an elongated redundancy consultation, well the stress is going to continue as long as the elongated redundancy consultation. So you just have to get on with it and try alternative means like written representations and getting a friend to speak on the phone, that sort of thing.

Su Apps

To what extent will it be fatal to the redundancy consultation process if the selection takes place before employees are put at risk?

Daniel Barnett

In other words, there's no consultation around the proposed pool and no consultation around the proposed scoring until employees are already provisionally selected.

Paman Singh

Generally fatal. There is a 1994 case - I can't remember it off the top of my head - about

a pre-determined decision in terms of going ahead with the redundancy and making people redundant. The whole point of the consultation is to engage your employees in the process. If you're not really showing and you can't show that you've engaged with them, then nine times out of 10 it's going to be unfair.

AJ Fraser

What are the best questions to ask during individual consultation meetings?

Daniel Barnett

I've got very clear ideas on this, but let's hear yours first.

Paman Singh

That's a good question. It is very much a case of setting out your stall - the who, what, when, where, why and how of the redundancy process - almost like you're going through all these questions, you're explaining it to them, and then you're trying to extract information from them. You want to be able to show that the redundancy is generally a last alternative that you've thought about. So have they got any input? Have they got any ideas about how redundancies can be avoided? Have they got any solutions that they can give? Give them the opportunity to contribute towards that. But in terms of if you're what you're asking them, specifically, you'd be asking them if they have any contribution that they'd like to make or whether they can provide you with any guidance because it is employer-led, but it's not solely down to what the employer says.

Daniel Barnett

One of the questions that I find particularly helpful is just to say over and over again to the employee, as you're going through each stage - the need for the redundancy, the criteria, etc, etc. - what would you do if you were me? Because sometimes, not always, but sometimes, you can get an employee to say "I accept that you've got to do this and I accept the financial situation is such that you have to make redundancies. I accept these criteria result in me being selected." And if they say that, you've slammed any unfair dismissal claim on the head.

Another useful couple of questions to finish off, I would always just use the stock question, "do you have anything you want to add?" Of course, you have to make sure that this is all minuted carefully or recorded because that closes down an argument at a later date that you didn't give them the chance to say something they wanted to say. And you always finish by saying "Do you think you've had a fair hearing?" And 99% of employees will say, "Yes, I've had a fair hearing because they're still keen to stay on your good side and keep their job. And that makes it much harder for them to argue at a later stage that the hearing was unfair. And if they say no, I think the hearing has been unfair because of X, Y and Z, that's actually great because it gives you the chance to think about it and fix a problem if there is one, rather than having it thrust at you for the first time in the ET1. So "Do you think you've had a fair hearing?" is a win-win question every time. Do you have any questions that you always like to ask?

Paman Singh
It's important to be able to analyse issues before they had the ET1. Although there isn't a built-in right of appeal, actually, in relation to the redundancy process, always make sure that you do allow for an appeal. I think that's stock. I know that most people do, but generally, some small employers that we sometimes deal with tend not to. But, absolutely, it's an internal mechanism to allow an assessor to assess the process if you will.

Daniel Barnett
And what's your reasoning for saying always allow an appeal?

Paman Singh
It's like a canary down the mineshaft. It gives you the early warning signal that there could

be issues here. The employee might say they've not had an opportunity to challenge the selection criteria, or they don't agree with the scoring. It lets you iron out any issues ahead of time. You're heading off trouble at the pass.

Daniel Barnett
I'm slightly more ambivalent on whether to allow an appeal or not. I think we might take different views on this and I recognise that there's lots of room for different views. You said there's normally no legal obligation to offer an appeal, which is absolutely right. There's a case called Robinson v Ulster Carpet Mills (Robinson v Ulster Carpet Mills [1991] IRLR 348) that makes it clear there's no obligation. There's also a more recent case called Gwynedd Council and Shirley Barratt (Gwynedd Council v Barratt UKEAT/0206/18/VP) that says there is no obligation to offer an appeal.

There's a very good argument, I think, against having an appeal process in redundancy dismissals. Tell me I'm wrong by all means, but unlike performance and conduct dismissals, where no one else is affected by dismissal being reversed on appeal, in redundancy situations, other people are affected by a decision being reversed on appeal. There might be someone who's been put through the redundancy scoring process and come above the break-point but now finds themselves being told they are redundant because someone who originally scored lower than them has been allowed back on appeal. I think there's a powerful argument for finality in redundancy selection processes, and allowing an appeal undermines finality. There's also the second point that allowing a right of appeal allows a second manager the chance to mess things up. Persuade me I'm wrong.

Paman Singh
The only thing I would say is, like you said, if you've got one manager who's possibly got it wrong, or you are concerned, then an appeal allows you to bring in a panel, perhaps, that

alleviates any concerns and goes against any issues of subjectivity in the scoring process. There's not really any law that obliges you to. I prefer to tie it in. Again, like you said, it's personal preference.

Daniel Barnett

Jamie Anderson from Trinity Chambers has said that he agrees with you and not me regarding appeals because it's a chance to rectify something that's gone wrong. I think there's legitimate room for disagreement here.

Anonymous

Can the cost of keeping the employee on the payroll be a fair criterion?

Paman Singh

Cost on its own?

Daniel Barnett

The question isn't specific, but I think you've just highlighted the precise issue that will make the difference.

Paman Singh

Cost on its own is a slippery slope. Again, I mentioned the Rolls-Royce case - it can be linked to all sorts of other issues, so you'd need to know more. I don't want to just be giving you generic answers, but that's fact-specific. Sorry. I know that you're asking for more specific details, but that is a bit vague.

Leszek Werenowski

Is Polkey (Polkey v AE Dayton Services Ltd [1987] IRLR 503) a 'get out of jail free' card for employers in a redundancy scenario?

Paman Singh

No. Any dismissal is still unfair. You may be able to show that it was an inevitability and that there still would be a 100% chance, for example, of the redundancy occurring, but no, it still would be an unfair dismissal. And Polkey and Compair Maxim set out very clear guidelines, and the House of Lords were very, very clear. And another case was De Grasse v Stockwell Tools (De Grasse v Stockwell Tools Ltd [1992] IRLR 269) that was about a very small employer who was still required to consult. So, no, it isn't a get out per se. It is something that you would then argue further down the line, but no, it's not a get out in itself in terms of mitigation.

Daniel Barnett

I think that Polkey is by no means a get out of jail free because, as you say, it's still going to be an unfair dismissal. Hence a basic award, which is equivalent to the redundancy payment. But more significantly, tribunals don't like making Polkey findings because when the employer comes along and says, "Yeah, okay, we fluffed this up; we ignored procedure, but we would have dismissed anyway." It's an entirely self-serving statement, and unless there's pretty credible evidence that the employer would have dismissed anyway or selected that particular employee, tribunals are just quite sceptical about Polkey arguments. I find it's often harder to win the Polkey argument than it is to win the unfair dismissal claim in the first place.

Daniel Barnett

Paman Singh, thank you very much.

GETTING REDUNDANCY RIGHT

MODULE 1: Introduction

MODULE 2: Definition of Redundancy and Challenging

MODULE 3: Avoiding Redundancies

MODULE 4: Choosing your selection pool

MODULE 5: Choosing your selection criteria

MODULE 6: Scoring and individual consultation

MODULE 7: Collective consultation

MODULE 8: Alternative employment

MODULE 9: Dismissal

MODULE 10: Miscellaneous issues

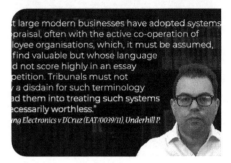

THESE BONUS RESOURCES ARE AVAILABLE IN THE VAULT TO ALL PURCHASERS OF GETTING REDUNDANCY RIGHT:

Daniel Barnett's template redundancy selection matrix, which you can use to score employees during a selection process
Value: £75

Daniel Barnett's redundancy policy, which he uses with his regular corporate clients
Value: £100

Private online forum, where you can discuss issues arising from redundancies and ask questions
Value: £125

Access to videos of 31 webinars chaired by Daniel Barnett in early 2020, with 31 employment barristers on 31 aspects of employment law
Value: £60

WWW.GETTINGREDUNDANCYRIGHT.COM

RELIGION AND BELIEF DISCRIMINATION

NAOMI LING, OUTER TEMPLE CHAMBERS

Daniel Barnett

I'm joined by Naomi Ling from Outer Temple Chambers for this webinar on religion and belief discrimination. Naomi recently acted successfully for the respondents in Page v the Lord Chancellor and the Lord Chief Justice (*Page v Lord Chancellor & Anor [2021] EWCA Civ 254*), which was a religion and belief claim brought by a former magistrate and in which the judgment was handed down by the Court of Appeal about 10 days ago. She's also the person who worked with me to produce a video recently on the five hot issues for employment law in 2021. And you can see that if you go to www.YouTubelegal.co.uk.

Daniel Barnett

Naomi Ling, good afternoon. I want to ask you a couple of questions, if I may. Let's start with the basics. You're talking about religion and belief. We all know what a religion is. Tell us what belief means in this context. What beliefs are protected by the Equality Act?

Naomi Ling

Well, the Equality Act itself is very broad. It says that a belief means any religious or philosophical belief. So the courts have interpreted that broadly and in line with the interpretation given to freedom of religion and belief in the European Convention on Human Rights. The test that was developed effectively by the ECHR is that to be a protected belief it must be genuinely held, it must be a belief as to a weighty or substantial aspect of human life and behaviour, it must have a certain

level of cogency, seriousness, coherence and importance, and it must be worthy of respect in a democratic society.

So for it to be a belief, it can't be an opinion based on some real or perceived logic or based on the evidence available. An example of that was a case some time ago called McClintock v the Secretary of State for Constitutional Affairs (*McClintock v Department of Constitutional Affairs [2008] IRLR 29*). He said, well, I don't believe that there's currently enough evidence to show that we should be allowing children to be adopted by same sex couples. That was found to be not a belief because it was essentially a judgement on the basis of the current state of the evidence. And in the recent Page case the belief that children should be adopted by same sex couples was said to be something founded on a conviction based on religion. That was a protected belief because it was based on that conviction as opposed to the state of the evidence.

So in a secular society, we're in a slightly uncomfortable position because where the belief relies upon something there's evidence for, you're less likely to be protected. But I would say that where beliefs tend to relate to factual matters that are provable or disprovable one way, I think it's unlikely that in that case the courts would find that it was a protected belief. We've had an ET case, for example, where Holocaust denial was found not to be a protected belief because that is something that could actually be proved or disproved, according to the historical record. And similarly, I suspect that conspiracy theories, including vaccination conspiracy theories, might also, on that basis, not be a protected belief.

Daniel Barnett
We've got some questions about anti-vax views, so we'll come to that in a bit more detail in a moment, if we can.

Naomi Ling
I would also say that even if a belief seems to be founded in reason or founded in evidence, it can amount to a belief if it amounts to a sufficient conviction. So for example, there was a case called Grainger v Nicholson (*Grainger Plc v Nicholson [2010] IRLR 4*), where the claimant had a belief that mankind was heading towards catastrophic climate change and that we were all under a moral duty to seek to avert that. That was a qualifying belief. And similarly, we have other examples such as people having a profound belief in the proper efficient use of money in the public sector and that kind of thing, which would seem to be based on evidence and other matters, but do attain that status of a protected belief because the person has sufficient conviction.

In relation to the requirement of cogency, seriousness or importance, there's quite a low threshold for that. Cogent means intelligible and capable of being understood. But there is an additional requirement that not only must the belief that you rely on be capable of being understood, you must also give it cogency in the way that you manifest it. So for example, there's a recent case called Gray v Mulberry Company (*Gray v Mulberry Company (Design) Ltd [2020] ICR 715*), the well-known handbag designer and maker. And in that case, the claimant relied on her moral right to own the copyright of her own creative works and output. The Court of Appeal in that case upheld the employment tribunal's finding that that didn't have sufficient cogency because it

didn't amount of philosophical touchstone in her own life. So the way that she manifested that belief didn't have sufficient cogency in order to give it protected status.

The final qualification is that it must not be worthy of respect in a democratic society. So for example, Marxist and Trotskyist views that involved a belief in the right of the individual to break the law to achieve political aims and deprive individuals of their property was found not to be worthy of respect in a democratic society. And in another example from 2005, Williamson v Secretary of State for Education (*R (on the application of Williamson) v Secretary of State for Education and Employment [2005] UKHL 15*), a belief in corporal punishment as a means of discipline necessary for the proper upbringing of children was capable of protection as long as it was a mild nature such as a smack. So the courts are saying this far and no further. There's obviously a subjective element from the court to say something's not worthy of respect in a democratic society.

Daniel Barnett
Linked to that, there's a difference between a belief in a philosophical view or a religion and manifestation of that belief. So, for example, I might believe that I need to go around proselytising about my beliefs to others, but my employer might have a problem with me doing that. Is there any protection offered to the manifestation of beliefs?

Naomi Ling
Yes. I would say that the protected characteristic of religion belief parts company from the other protected characteristics that we have under the Equality Act because there is this additional element of manifestation that is protected. I think this really stems from article nine in the Human Rights Act, which also treats the manifestation of religion as something that is requiring protection. And you can see why that is because if you never told anyone about your religion or belief, then they'd never

know about it. So, it is necessary to have this additional element. But also, if you treat someone differently or less favourably because of the way they manifest their religion or belief, it is possible to justify that.

So this does raise questions for the tribunals as to how they give effect to article nine within the structures of the Equality Act. And so the way they've found to do that is to say, well, if you are claiming direct discrimination and you're saying you've been directly discriminated against because of the way you've manifested your belief and that manifestation is really just simply an extension of the belief itself, the courts draw a distinction between the belief and its manifestation - which are offered equal protection - or the manifestation of the belief in a particular way to which objection could be taken. What they say is, if you've treated someone for that second reason, you are essentially not treating someone less favourably by reason of their belief or its manifestation. So for example, if you have someone who, as you say, is proselytising inappropriately to clients or to junior employees, the defence the respondent would run is well, we weren't treating this person less favourably because of their belief or the way they manifested it - we recognise that there is an entitlement to proselytise if the faith requires it - but we take objection to the way it was done or to whom it was done. And that applies the standard 'direct discrimination because of' test to say what is lawful and what isn't. And that is the way in which you incorporate the justification that is permissible under the European Convention on Human Rights.

It's also possible, of course, to bring a claim for indirect discrimination. And you would want to do that if your manifestation of your belief plus a provision criterion or practice applied to everyone puts you at a disadvantage. So, a classic example would be believing that you shouldn't work on the Sabbath because of what the Bible says about that and your employer having a requirement

that all of its employees work on the Sabbath. In those cases, you would need to bring a claim for indirect discrimination, which has the additional hurdle that you need to show that there is group disadvantage. And in those cases, you would need to show that some people who practice the same faith or who hold the same belief as you are disadvantaged by this particular manifestation, which is that you believe you shouldn't work on the Sabbath or whatever it is that applies to you. And so this additional element of manifestation does add an additional layer of complexity to the way in which we have to analyse the protected characteristic of religion and belief in the context of the Equality Act.

Mark Mason
The most popular question is from Mark Mason, which I think looks like a really interesting one, but I don't quite understand it. So I've asked Mark to join us. I'll read it out, Mark, and then then maybe you can explain a little more.

Daniel Barnett
What would be your advice, Naomi Ling, to an employer who believes there's an occupational requirement that a role must be undertaken by someone of a certain religious belief to help the employer establish if they're right, and demonstrate this requirement to potential candidates?

Mark, can you put a little flesh on the bones to explain what the occupational requirement and the religion is?

Mark Mason
I'm thinking about a potential scenario where a Christian church wants to appoint a church administrator, and they think that because of the nature of the role and the context in which it's carried out that they need a Christian to be in that role. So it's just a question around how they actually analyse that to make sure that they're right and it's proper to have that requirement, and then what they could

maybe do to demonstrate that through the job description, so that anybody coming along to query that or say they don't agree that you need to be a Christian to do that role, could perhaps see through the documentation that actually the Church has about this and they think that they're right.

Naomi Ling

I have a little bit of a feeling that there's been a case a bit like this recently. I think there is an exception in the Equality Act to scenarios where you actually need to appoint someone of a particular belief to a particular role. I think that, as with so many things in equality law, it really is a question of looking - and the courts will probably say with intense focus - at the facts. Is it actually necessary for someone in an administrative role to share the faith of the religious establishment itself? And I think the case that I may have in the back of my mind, was actually one in which the courts found that the employer hadn't demonstrated that the employee needed to share their religious faith.

It will really be a question of looking at what the role is and working out to one's own satisfaction the reasons why one felt that role needed to be occupied by someone sharing the faith. For example, did that person need to, in any way, encourage young people to become involved? Was there a public facing element to the role in which that person needed to be able to speak about their own faith in order to do that role properly? Or was it purely a kind of backroom role, purely administrative, where there simply wasn't anything of that nature that needed to be fulfilled by that person? So I think that it really would be a question of looking honestly and dispassionately at what that person was going to need to do. Because if it's a question of just feeling more comfortable or feeling that they should include people who share or give opportunities to people who share their faith, I don't think that's going to cut it.

Daniel Barnett

Mark, does that answer the question?

Mark Mason

Yes, it does. I think it's just about, as Naomi says, looking at the actual requirements of the roles.

Adrienne Rosen

How is it best to manage an employee in a care home who doesn't want a COVID vaccine because of their religious belief? She is Rastafarian.

Naomi Ling

So I think that the first question would be, why does the individual not want to have the vaccine? Is the reason very closely related to the religion, or is it only incidentally related? It needs to be intimately linked with a close and direct nexus. And if there isn't an intimate connection, or close and direct nexus, then we're not really in the territory of this being related to religion and belief at all.

I think that then feeds into the next question, which is that even if it's not related to religion and belief, is the desire to have members of staff vaccinated objectively justifiable? Because even if the reluctance isn't related to religion and belief, you're still dealing with people's article eight rights to their bodily integrity when you require them or ask them to have this kind of vaccine. At the moment, I think it's still the situation that there is very little evidence that the vaccine will prevent transmission of disease. I think scientists are confident that we will acquire scientific evidence that it does prevent transmission. When that happens, I think it is likely to be open to care homes to say that they have a duty to protect their residents and other staff. They could say that due to the nature of their work as a care home, they do think it's justified that they require staff to be vaccinated. And so I think that's likely to be where care homes end up. Where there is no such duty to residents or clients of a business, I think the picture is likely to be different, but I think that that's likely to be the case for care homes.

Su Apps

Where an existing employee has already brought tribunal proceedings, could the offer of a settlement of the existing claim, which includes the termination of employment, be an act of victimisation in itself?

Daniel Barnett

The question is talking about religion and belief descrimination. I think it's probably a one word answer, isn't it?

Naomi Ling

I don't think so. I think that this would fall within some protected privileged communications as with any other employment tribunal proceedings,

Amelia Berriman

What level would an employer need to become involved in with two or more colleagues arguing over political, religious or other beliefs on social media outside of work if complaints are raised?

Daniel Barnett

So is there an obligation on employers to intervene if employees are having arguments about religion on social media outside of work?

Naomi Ling

Good question. I don't think there's an obligation on employers to intervene, except insofar as it becomes relevant to relationships at work. If there are problems arising and there is a suggestion that it's becoming sufficiently out of hand that it could start to breach the obligations the employer owes employees, then obviously, the employer is going to need to step in. And I'd suspect that's particularly likely to be the case if you have someone who is junior to the other person or if particularly derogatory comments are being made if these people are have a work relationship that needs to be managed and preserved. Obviously, if it's people who never really work together at all, then that's almost as if two strangers are arguing. But if you have

to manage a relationship where two people have to work alongside each other, that's quite different. So I would say that that's probably the moment at which an employer needs to start getting involved.

If a debate on social media is bringing the employer into disrepute, or is in any way affecting the employer's commercial interests, then I would say that that is also a point at which the employer is entitled to become involved and to take action against one or both of the two individuals. That said, the way in which the employer gets involved obviously has to be proportionate. And it would need to see, first of all, whether it could induce the individuals to stop doing what they're doing, or to have a debate in more moderate terms. And it's only really if they aren't able to manage this debate in that way that they can then move to more disciplinary type action.

Amaya Corcuera

How would you deal with conflicting sets of beliefs and protected characteristics? A Christian employee who believes the Bible does not condone homosexuality expresses his preference not to be assigned on tasks with a homosexual colleague, and the homosexual colleague claims this is harassment.

Naomi Ling

I have to say that that scenario is one that has actually arisen in cases like Ladele (Ladele v London Borough of Islington [2009] EWCA Civ 1357) where there was a registrar who didn't want to officiate over same sex marriages. I don't think that preference is likely to be acceptable.

Daniel Barnett

Is the Ashers Bakery case (Lee v Ashers Baking Company Ltd and others [2018] UKSC 49) going to be relevant here?

Naomi Ling

I would say not because that was all about whether it's fair to require someone with a particular belief to make a statement that is inconsistent with that belief. In the example, this is about whether you'd be prepared to work with someone rather than whether you'd be prepared to make a statement in support of their status.

Steven Eckett
Can having anti-vaxxer views legally be classed as a philosophical belief? You touched on this at the beginning. Maybe you could give a little more detail.

Naomi Ling
I suspect that were a belief is capable of being disproved factually, it may well not be a protected belief. So, for example, Holocaust denial has been found by the employment tribunal not to be a protected belief. Not only because it was not worthy of respect in a democratic society, but also because it was contrary to the historic record. If you have a belief that is contrary to what is provable as a matter of fact, then I doubt that that is going to be a protected belief.

Su Apps
Can it be discrimination to end the employment of an employee with less than two years' service, because they've been active in an extreme right wing organisation.

Naomi Ling
That would depend on whether their activity was a manifestation of a protected belief. And that would depend on whether the political beliefs or the right-wing organisation otherwise met the tests of a protected belief, and that would depend very much on the specific facts of what was espoused by that organisation.

Daniel Barnett
There was a first instance case of this last week involving an English nationalist. A tribunal held that English nationalism could be a protected belief, but when it tips over into racism as part of those beliefs then it can't be because it's not worthy of protection in a democratic society.

Naomi Ling
And that goes back to what I was saying earlier about how you have to look at the manifestation of the belief by the individual. It's not just a question of looking globally at whether English nationalism could be a protected belief, it's whether the specific beliefs manifested by the individual qualify.

Anonymous
An employee is claiming a first come, first served holiday request policy is indirectly discriminatory against their religion because their significant festival is an ever-moving date depending on the lunar cycle, like Eid. The legitimate aim of the employer seems straightforward - having a fair system of allocating holidays - But is the PCP (the provision, criterion or practice) proportionate?

Naomi Ling
Well, obviously, that will depend on the ease the employer had in allocating holiday, I think. If it's an employer that could be entirely flexible on when it required people to take holiday, then it would probably not be proportionate. But if it was an employer that had a lot of different employees to juggle and a lot of difficulty in scheduling its workforce, and I suspect it would be.

Daniel Barnett
Mike Clyne and Penny Douglass have commented that lots of religions have moving dates, such as Easter, and lunar cycles can be looked up. So, in fact, an employee who followed a religion that was based on a lunar calendar could be booking their holidays years in advance anyway.

Naomi Ling
Again, one thing that we've emphasised in the course of this is that it really does depend very much on the facts of each case. It's difficult to give a global principled answer to many of these questions because it really is a question of looking at what the specific circumstances of the individual and the employer are.

Jamie Anderson

A philosophical belief must be worthy of respect in a democratic society, not be incompatible with human dignity and not conflict with the fundamental rights of others. Do you think that this creates too great a risk of a judge being required to deal with matters of politics and social policy, unlike any other area of employment law?

Naomi Ling

I do think that that is a real issue with this particular protected characteristic and I suspect that is why this is an area that is actually quite dynamic and interesting at the moment. I slightly hinted at this when I was talking about the 2005 case of Williamson against the Secretary of State for Education, where there was a belief relied upon, which was that it was necessary to use physical punishment to chastise and discipline children. And the House of Lords said, yes, as long as it's quite a light smack. And that was a very good example of how the House of Lords was relying very much on what was acceptable in society at that time to define what was a religion and belief.

I think that if one is sitting in judgment on this kind of case, a good rule of thumb is what rights are actually protected by the law in terms of either rights under the Equality Act or rights under the Human Rights Act? But, of course, in particular with the Human Rights Act, when you decide what is a right that's protected, that is quite a moveable feast and quite a subjective matter. So I do agree that judges are likely to get drawn into quite political decisions when they give judgment on this kind of case.

Karen Bristow

Do you think that someone who is a staunch royalist, who believes that any attack on the integrity of the monarchy is treachery, is enough to amount to a philosophical belief?

Daniel Barnett

As well as answering that, which is quite a general question, I'd like you specifically to answer that if I think Harry and Megan were right and I'm passionate about it, does that qualify as a philosophical belief?

Naomi Ling

To answer your question first, Daniel, I think that your issue would possibly founder on the question of whether or not it was a cohesive philosophy and a touchstone according to which you lived your life. I think it's far too narrow and discrete a topic for you to treat as a belief. And there's also the required criterion that it must be a belief as to a weighty or substantial aspect of human life or behaviour.

Coming on to Karen's question about the staunch royalism, I think that I would probably need to unpack that a little by asking what you mean by 'treachery' and whether that that carries any implications. Because if what you're saying is that any attack on the integrity of the monarchy is treachery in the sense that we ought to have heads on pikes and that kind of thing, I suspect that that would not be worthy of respect in a democratic society. If it is someone who's a staunch royalist who has lived their life by a belief in the monarchy, I don't see why that actually couldn't be a reasonable belief that is capable of protection.

Daniel Barnett

Hina has pointed out that the date of Eid is not known in advance in the way that Easter is. If you passionately believe that people should not be allowed to demand equality and should not be allowed to emote on matters relating to mental health, is that enough to amount to a religious or philosophical belief?

Naomi Ling

Well, I think there's two questions there. The first is about equality. I suspect that that would founder on must be worthy of respect in a democratic society. If it's a question of believing that someone should never emote, I think we're slightly getting into territory of it not being possible, actually, to answer questions on the basis of these very high-level philosophical precepts. Because, actually, what an employment tribunal always has to do is to look at the way it's manifested by the individual and look at the way in which it informs their lives or is used as a fundamental precept for their life.

Robert
A Jewish employer gives his Jewish employees significant Jewish holidays off in addition to their regular holidays. Is that employer discriminating against their non-Jewish staff?

Naomi Ling
My instinct would be yes. Why can't they have other holidays to be taken when they wish?

Daniel Barnett
Yes, that has to be right.

Mike Clyne
Do you think the diminishing influence of European law will affect religion and belief discrimination?

Daniel Barnett
Of course, religion and belief discrimination was one of those areas we introduced because we were compelled to under European law.

Naomi Ling
What's quite interesting is the way in which we've had a massive resurgence of reliance on the Human Rights Act, which started, actually, before we left Europe. The Human Rights Act, particularly with article 14 and the ability to pray in aid protected characteristics has actually become far more significant and dynamic than even claims based on European law. And I think I've already touched on the fact that the European directive has actually had to be interpreted in order to give effect to article nine of the European Convention on Human Rights. And additionally, article 10, which the freedom of expression, is an article that is relevant to the freedom to manifest your religion and belief. So I would say that these issues are only going to become more

pressing, and not less, despite the fact that we've left the EU.

Nicola
Is chivalry capable of being a philosophical belief?

Daniel Barnett
I'm not sure I could define chivalry.

Naomi Ling
I suppose it conjures up ideas according to what your cultural consciousness tells you chivalry means, but I suspect I'm going to start repeating myself by saying that is a question of how it's manifested. Let's say, for example, that a person lives his life on the basis that it's his duty to behave in a chivalrous manner to every woman he meets, he must hold the door open for her, he must offer her his seat on the tube and if he doesn't, he's going to have failed himself on everything he believes in. I don't see why that couldn't be a protected belief, but it would have to meet the tests of cogency, seriousness, cohesion and importance, and it would also have to not in any way attack the rights of women to be treated equally.

Daniel Barnett
I'm not sure whether I'm asking this mischievously or seriously. But the point that strikes me is: is it worthy of belief in a democratic society because not offering men seats on trains and not holding the door open for men is discriminatory against men.

Naomi Ling
I think the question is whether you owe men a duty to treat them equally. As an employer you do. I don't think that behaving in that way to the whole world could be said to be discriminating against men. I think, perhaps if there was a difficulty at work with treating men less favourably because you weren't holding doors open for them? Could that be said realistically to be less favourable treatment? I don't know. Would it meet the Shamoon test? The question would then be, yes, it's fine for you to hold this belief, but is the way in

which you're manifesting it problematic for us? Would we need to take action against you? That might be the way in which the question would be answered rather than asking if it's a belief in the first place.

Daniel Barnett
GGM has pointed out that a belief in chivalry includes dragon slaying, which might take it outside normal philosophical belief, but I won't ask you to comment on that.

Anonymous
Where a staff member refuses to undertake certain duties on the basis of being vegan, what steps would be deemed to be reasonable in terms of expecting them to provide evidence that they believe or practice ethical veganism as opposed to it being a dietary preference only, which in itself wouldn't constitute a belief?

Naomi Ling
Well, that's very interesting. I mean, I expect that certainly a tribunal would ask the person to demonstrate the way in which it's been a touchstone of their lives. If the belief is that you must never slaughter an animal and you must treat animals well, is that belief carried over into other aspects of the individual's life? Do they wear leather clothing? Do they take other steps in order to ensure that animals are treated well? I can see that it's a slightly more tricky conversation to have as an employer.

I suppose that if the question is being asked in the context of the individual saying that they don't want to perform particular tasks, then it would be fair enough to sit down with the individual and have a discussion with them about what veganism actually means to them. Ultimately, it's going to come down to objective justification as well, isn't it? And I suppose as

part of that discussion, you might also talk about how feasible it is to exempt an individual from these tasks and that's why you need to really drill down to find out how important it is to the individual.

Anonymous
Can a requirement not to discuss religious and philosophical beliefs in the workplace itself be discriminatory?

Naomi Ling
I think if it's applied across the board, then it would seem to be unlikely to be directly discriminatory. I mean, plainly, if you have a religious belief that it's your duty to proselytise, you could argue that you are being discriminated against indirectly by such a policy. And so I think that really comes down to why have you got this policy? Have you had problems in the past? Is it really necessary to actually say to everyone, right, no more politics and no more religion in order to keep the peace at work or to ensure an effective working relationship.

Daniel Barnett
What's the best way for somebody to get in touch with you?

Naomi Ling
I think probably by email would be the best way.

Daniel Barnett
What's your email address?

Naomi Ling
It's naomi.ling@outertemple.com.

Daniel Barnett
Naomi Ling, thank you very much.

RESTRICTIVE COVENANTS

ADAM SOLOMON QC, LITTLETON CHAMBERS

Daniel Barnett

I'm joined by Adam Solomon QC from Littleton Chambers for this Q&A session on restrictive covenants. You might have noticed that Adam and I are dressed slightly differently this morning. About four weeks ago, when I was encouraging people to register for these webinars, I tweeted that if any organisation booked 10 spaces on the webinars on that day, Adam Solomon and I would do our webinar dressed up in full barrister's wigs and gowns. Well, three firms booked 10 places on that day and true to our word, Adam and I have dressed up in our wigs and gowns. Thank you to everyone for registering and helping to raise £30,000 for the Free Representation Unit.

Adam Solomon

Mike Clyne has thanked us for dressing up in fancy dress. It's a great pleasure to do this. It's a great cause we're doing it for and it's a real honour for me to be helping on these webinars and helping the FRU.

Daniel Barnett

Adam Solomon, good morning. I have a few questions to throw at you. First of all, is a former employee in breach of a non-solicitation covenant if their new employer but not the employee themselves, solicits one of the clients affected by that covenant?

Adam Solomon

Well, the answer is that they might or might not be. Now, of course, an employee has a contract with the employer and that's what contains the post-termination restrictions. And normally speaking, the ex-employer will be relying on their contractual rights to enforce any restraints. And so it's only if the ex-employee is in breach themselves of the post-termination restraints that the ex-employer is able to get any form of relief, whether that's in the form of an injunction or damages. However, if the new employer is suddenly dealing with clients of the ex-employer, then there's a real suspicion that the only reason they're doing that is because the ex-employee is giving them the details of the client contact information or other confidential information about the clients to enable them to do so.

Faced with evidence that their clients are suddenly being taken by a new employer, even if they've got no direct evidence that the ex-employee is doing it themselves, the ex-employer might well think that something's up and might rely on that to seek to obtain interim relief. But the short answer to the question is that if the ex-employee has done nothing themselves at all, then strictly speaking, they're not in breach of a non-solicitation covenant. And this question throws up the difficulty of policing and enforcing non-solicitation covenants, which is why they're often in a suite of covenants along with, classically, the non-compete covenant.

Daniel Barnett

Should a six-month non-compete restrictive covenant take the probationary period into account?

Adam Solomon

The question is, when you give someone a new contract of employment, can you immediately restrain them if they're going to leave or do you have to wait six months for a probationary period to have started? The answer is you don't have to wait at all. And if someone contracts with you on day one, and they have post-termination restrictions in their contract of employment, then those restrictions are enforceable immediately. It comes as quite a shock to some employees, especially junior ones, if they sign up to a new job and then want to get another job that's slightly better immediately afterwards. Suddenly, the ex-employer comes along and tries to enforce restrictive covenants. And that happened in the case I was doing recently. So long as the ex-employer can show that the covenant is reasonable and protects the legitimate business interest, then even if the ex-employee has only been there for a day, from the second they sign the contract and then terminate, it's potentially enforceable. So that's really something to for employees to watch out for. They can be caught by restrictive covenants even if they're very junior or only been there for a short period of time. They don't need to have been there for the entirety of the probationary period in order for it to be enforceable.

Daniel Barnett

One more question from me. If an employee resigns in response to a repudiatory breach of contract, so there's a constructive dismissal, are they discharged from their restrictive covenants or can the employer still enforce them?

Adam Solomon

That's a very interesting question. There's a lot of case law on this. The historic answer has been that the General Billposting rule applies (General Billposting Co v Atkinson [1908] UKHL 701), and that's that if an employer has acted in repudiatory breach of contract, the employee accepts that repudiatory breach and there's a constructive dismissal, thereafter, both parties are released from all of their obligations to the other. That includes post-termination restrictions but potentially doesn't include obligations of confidentiality, but that's a separate point.

Now, there are lots of dicta in various cases that say that rule is wrong and needs to be relooked at. I'm sorry to say that in a case I was in, this was argued definitively, contrary to the arguments I made, and the General Billpasting rule was upheld. So if an employer is in repudiatory breach, the employees are released from their covenants. It will have to take a case going to the Supreme Court, I think, for that rule to be changed.

However, that's not the total answer to the question because practically speaking, the vast majority of restrictive covenant cases never get to trial. The case I was in, Brown and Neon (Brown v Neon Management Services Ltd [2019] IRLR 30), was a case at trial. The vast majority are resolved at the interim stage. At the interim stage, first, a judge will look with great suspicion at an employee running an argument that the post-termination restrictions aren't enforceable because of some repudiatory breach - because that's the sort of thing employers always say and there's case law to say the judges should raise a judicial eyebrow about that - and secondly, if there's a conflict of fact about whether there's a constructive dismissal, that's a classic example of something the court can't resolve at the interim stage. There's a serious issue to be tried, and so it won't be resolved and the covenant will be upheld. And because the vast majority of cases never get to trial and are resolved after interim relief, in fact, this argument never really gets determined and an employee will often not be successful in running that point.

Matilda Swanson

If an employee breaches a restrictive covenant, so works for a competitor soon after leaving, what can the former employer actually do about it?

Adam Solomon

Well, this is exactly the sort of thing I do on a daily basis. What the employer can do is get interim relief. The first thing the employer will normally need to do is write a letter before claim saying to the ex employee and the new employer, "Here are your covenants. There's a non-competition covenant that's enforceable and you've got to stop acting in breach. You've got to stop working for the new employer."

If they don't, or if it's very urgent, then normally speaking, on three clear days notice, you go to court and seek interim relief. That's the classic sort of relief that restrictive covenants call for. And so the vast majority of cases are resolved at the interim relief stage. That's exactly what an ex-employer should do. They shouldn't say that all covenants are unenforceable, so they're just going to let their ex-employees go. They should get advice very quickly and then potentially go to court very quickly as well. Speed is of the essence.

Matilda Swanson

Is it enforceable if you name precise competitors that an employee can't go and work for?

Adam Solomon

Yes, you can do that. If your client works in a restricted area, say, there are five competitors that if your ex-employee went to work for, they would definitely have damaging confidential information that would undermine your business and undermine your legitimate business interests, then you can name them. Sometimes that's useful. Sometimes, when you have such a list, you can go to court and say that it's is definitely within the non-compete covenant because they're on the list of names that you've set out in advance.

However, sometimes things change. So if you have a list of five competitors when you sign up to the covenants and by the time the employee has left two years later the number of competitors has changed to six or seven, and they're not named, then that can undermine you. So you've got to think very carefully about whether or not you have a list at all, whether you want it to be an inclusive or exclusive list, or whether you just want a general non-compete covenant that you think will be more or less enforceable.

Daniel Barnett

I often tell employers or suggest to employers that it's a good idea to actually not bother with a general restrictive covenant just to avoid or to limit problems of enforceability. Just have an annex to the employment contract which is reviewed every three months just naming the most popular or most important six clients. I generally think, not always, that that's likely to have more chance of being enforced at an interim stage than a general covenant.

Adam Solomon

Maybe. I mean, I'm sure that's right; I'm sure that if you review it every three months then you're going to be on top of it. But the vast majority of employees don't do that. We all know they don't. In my experience, the vast majority of covenants that I've seen, certainly at the interim stage, have not had named competitors. Courts are willing to enforce general non-competes as long as they're reasonably drafted. So my tendency, I think, is to be slightly more aggressive than your approach and just to go for a general non-compete, unless you can be certain that the named competitors are all you're concerned about. Sometimes, for example, in an industry that has lots of different competitors, you just don't know. It's your confidential information that you're concerned with, and if the employee goes and starts up their own business, for example, and you have five named competitors, that won't protect you. So to cover every eventuality, I still prefer a general covenant, I think.

Mark Irlam

What's the one top tip you can give an employer to make sure a restrictive covenant is enforceable?

Adam Solomon

I'd get Daniel to draft it. That would be my number one tip. But ignore his advice about having a list of named competitors. I think that the top tip about enforcing is to act quickly. What clients often do is see someone has done something wrong and just sit on it for ages. The longer you sit on it, the more the court is likely to think that you've sat on your rights, therefore, the court doesn't need to exercise its discretion to act in your favour. But if you act quickly, if you write a very speedily but not a hastily put together, well-structured letter for claim and then, thereafter, within a few days, issue proceedings and go to court, then you're much more likely to be able to enforce those rights. This is at the enforceability stage. Obviously, if you're talking about drafting, that's a different matter. Doing it slowly and carefully would be my advice. Tailor the covenants to the individual employer and even to the individual employee. And, as Daniel says, update them regularly. So two top tips for the price of one.

Mike Clyne

Do you foresee any legislation from Parliament that will make restrictive covenants less likely to be enforced and is there any trend on changing case law on restrictive covenants?

Daniel Barnett

There has, of course, been a recent consultation.

Adam Solomon

There has been a consultation. And my chambers, Littleton Chambers, has put in a lengthy consultation response as part of the team that responded on that front (https://www.danielbarnett.co.uk/site/blog/employment-blog/restrictive-covenants-government-consultation-041220). If the government legislates, and it's not clear how they will legislate or whether or whether they will - you might think the government at the moment has more important things on its plate than tinkering with the law on restrictive

covenants - but if it legislates, then everything's going to change. For example, they're thinking about whether there should be non-competes at all, or whether there should be a maximum time limit for non-competes. And obviously, if those things are brought in, then that changes the whole basis of what we understand and how things work.

Adam Solomon

At the moment, generally speaking, you see non-competes of six months, sometimes, at the outside, 12 months. But I've been in cases where non-competes have been upheld for longer, 13 months, for example, in an insurance situation where there's a 12 month renewal cycle, and that's justified in those terms. But if government legislates to say you can't have longer than, say six or nine months for a non-compete, one might imagine that everyone suddenly starts putting the maximum six or nine months as the standard non-compete, just like university admission fees have all gone to the maximum. And so how will the courts interpret those in that context? It is very different. It might change completely.

My hope is that the government doesn't legislate and leaves it to the courts. At the moment, I think the courts have struck the right balance between fairness to ex-employees and competitors and protection of ex-employers and their rights to confidential information, trade relations and stability in the workforce. I think the balance is right, but who knows what will happen if they do legislate?

You asked about trends as well. Broadly speaking, I think the trend over the last 15 years has been narrowing the enforceability of covenants. So 15 or 20 years ago, you saw covenants of, say, two years that were being enforced, or even longer in non-competes. Now, it's very rare to have anything longer than six months or a year at the outside. So I think the courts are becoming stricter and more protective of employee rights. But there is a willingness if the covenant is reasonable to enforce. I think Egon Zehnder (*Tillman v Egon Zehnder Ltd [2019] IRLR 838*) in the Supreme Court is an example of that. The ex-employee and the new employer took a point that was sort of fanciful about the meaning of a clause and the Supreme Court cut through it by simply removing the offending wording in order to make the covenant enforceable. So there you see the courts striving to enforce. But so long as it's reasonable, and there's been a reduction of what the courts think is reasonable over the last 15 or 20 years, then the courts will enforce.

James Fairchild

An employee who's left has given confidential information to their new employer. We know this because they've told us gleefully. No specific contract point deals with this. Can we do anything?

Adam Solomon

That is the classic question that I'm often asked. The answer is maybe. It turns on what type of confidential information it is that the employee has given to their new employer. And the law is that during employment, an employee may not misuse their employer's confidential information. But if it is mere confidential information - and I don't know why the courts use the phrase 'mere confidential information' - then the employee is free to use it after they leave employment to the extent they're not subject to any restrictive covenant that impinges on that right. However, if the confidential information amounts to a trade secret, then the employee may not use that post termination, irrespective of what the contract says. That's a right in equity or an implied term.

So the question is really about what type of confidential information it is. And there's lots of arguments about where on that spectrum between confidential information and trade secrets matters sit. I'm doing a case at the moment where there's a dispute about whether client contact information - an ex-employers client contact details - can amount

to confidential information. I think the better argument is, yes, it can. That's my argument, as a matter of fact, in the case. I think it is right that client contact details - the type of goods they buy and the prices they pay - are considered information that would amount to a trade secret. So if that is the sort of information you're talking about, if it's that sort of quality, then you can protect it as a matter of equity, and you can get injunctive relief to prevent the ex-employer and the new employer from using and or disclosing that information.

Helen Hancock

When introducing new restrictive covenants into existing contracts, how much consideration should be offered?

Adam Solomon

It's a classic contract question. How much consideration do you need to provide in order to make the contract enforceable? There must be some form of consideration. It doesn't need to be equal to the promise. It must be sufficient but need not be adequate. So you can give £100 or £50 or some nominal amount. However, some courts and some dicta have also looked at the consideration for the covenant in order to determine its enforceability. Sometimes, courts will say that if a chap was paid £1 million a year, you could have more restrictive covenants in the contract. So, arguably, if you want it to be more enforceable, give more consideration. Although, as a strict matter of law, you're not obliged to as long as there is some consideration. Peppercorn, classically, is given for consideration in leasehold agreements. Some consideration that's sufficient is all you need.

Julie Davis

Should maternity leave that's taken immediately before termination reduce the duration of the covenants as garden leave reduces the duration of covenants and might the same apply to furlough?

Adam Solomon

That's an excellent question. I've never seen a case on that point, and, obviously, no cases on furlough have come up yet. But there is no case on garden leave in which it has been stated that because an employee took garden leave then the post-termination restriction which didn't set off the amount of garden leave is unenforceable. On the contrary, the courts have consistently upheld the covenants or struck them down, irrespective of the garden leave. So I think the answer could be that it doesn't make any difference.

The classic explanation for upholding covenants is that you've got to show it's reasonable and protecting a legitimate business aim at the date of entering into the agreement. So, actually, what you've done immediately before you terminate shouldn't make any difference. And I think that's part of the reasons why the garden leave argument has failed so far. If the employer wants to protect, for example, it's confidential information with the non-compete covenant, then it shouldn't really matter - if the employee has that confidential information - if they've taken maternity leave immediately before leaving, unless you can show that the confidential information will necessarily have decayed in that six-month period that they've been off. But that's going to be very difficult to show. My view is that it won't make any difference and they should be upheld.

Mark Mason

Does the role an employee proposes to move to affect the enforceability of a non-compete clause? So for example, if a salesperson moves to work for a competitor in a non-customer-facing admin role, will it make the covenant less enforceable than if they're moving to a sales role with that competitor?

Adam Solomon

That's a great question. It goes to the heart of what non-compete clauses are trying to protect. There are two lines of cases that go

in different directions on this very point. Some cases, like the Tradition v Gamberoni case (Tradition Financial Services Ltd v Gamberoni [2017] IRLR 698) or the case I was in, Egon Zehnder, have general non-compete clauses in which it doesn't matter what role the person's going into the clause bites in any event. The basis for that is that the non-compete is there to protect the confidential information. And it doesn't matter, for example, if the employee is sitting in the backroom because they could feed the confidential information, even unconsciously, to their employer even they're not doing the sales-facing role themselves.

There are other cases that go in the opposite direction and in the Tradition v Gamborini case, these were discussed. And in those cases, the court said that the covenant is there to protect trade relations. And so if the employee is going from a sales role to a back office role, then the trade relation is unaffected and therefore the covenant is too broad if it says you can't compete in any role and you should have a more specific role. Both lines of authority are arguable. The answer is, what's the covenant there to protect? And what's the evidence on which the ex-employer is relying in order to enforce that covenant?

Nigel Targett

In the event of an employer wishing to tie an employee into post-termination restrictions and a new contract, does there have to be some further consideration, such as promotion or cash, or is it sufficient for the contract to be entered into as a deed?

Adam Solomon

It's similar to the question we were asked before about consideration. You have to have consideration for an amendment to a contract, if it's done as a contract. The consideration is a question of fact. It just has to be sufficient; it doesn't have to be equal. Can you do it as a deed? Yes, and deeds don't need consideration. I very rarely see employment contracts done as deeds but it's possible to.

However, if you enter into a whole new contract of employment, a whole new suite of obligations, then that's a novation and that doesn't need specific allocated consideration because both parties are entering to a new agreement. It's the wage labor bargain that will be consideration for all of the contract. So there are various ways of skinning that particular cat, but the suggestions you've put in your question would work: deed, novation or just sufficient consideration.

Daniel Barnett
Just explain what the word 'novation' means. Maybe some people don't know what it means.

Adam Solomon
It means entering into an entirely new contract. 'Novation' means new. An employer and an employee can end the old contract and have a new contract to start their relations again. It almost certainly won't affect continuity of employment, but that's a statutory concept, not a contractual concept. You can have a new contract of employment called a novation.

Anonymous
Can an employer ever reasonably claim ownership of an ex-employee's LinkedIn connections?

Daniel Barnett
I'm going to split that question into two. Can an employer claim ownership? And does it have to be subject to the test of reasonableness?

Adam Solomon
I'm not sure I know what ownership is. Ownership is a difficult question when you're dealing with confidential information because, classically, you can protect it, but it's not a property right. But can an ex-employer say that the LinkedIn contacts that you make are protectable, that when you leave, you have to, for example, delete of all your LinkedIn contacts and you may not use your LinkedIn contacts for business purposes after you leave? Yes, that's a possible type of information

that can be protected. I've done a couple of cases recently where we've argued precisely that. They happen to be expressed in the contract. Now, if they're not expressed in the contract, it might be more difficult, but you just apply standard arguments about confidential information to the questions and you get the answer. But I think that if you want to protect them, the safest bet is to make sure that's expressed in the contract.

Ruth Christy
David Reade QC suggested he would add consideration for a restriction about keeping the terms of a settlement agreement confidential. We've always used reciprocal terms by the employer as consideration. Do you agree with David Reade that there should be an offer of some cash for a confidentiality clause, and if so, how much?

Adam Solomon
David and I have agreed that I would pay him cash if I agreed with him on this one. He's a brilliant barrister and an ingenious lawyer, and it would take a very brave person to disagree what he says. What he said is eminently sensible, as well. If you can show specific consideration for a point, it's very difficult for the ex-employee at that point to argue that it is void for want of consideration. Do you need to? Well, that's a different question. Maybe not. If there is a suite of agreements, a suite of different clauses in a settlement agreement, and you're paying a lump sum for that settlement, then generally speaking, all the clauses are enforceable because of the consideration of the lump sum.

Daniel Barnett
I think David was actually talking about keeping a separate sum attributable to confidentiality for tax purposes within a compromise agreement, which I think may be more sensible and probably is right.

Adam Solomon
Yes, I see. For tax reasons, I'm sure that's sensible.

Sat Gill

Can you share an example of the most bizarre or hilarious restrictive covenants you've seen in place?

Daniel Barnett

I'm not sure restrictive covenants normally qualify as bizarre and certainly not hilarious. By the time you've read the 75-word verbiage, you want to kill yourself.

Adam Solomon

I very rarely find covenants funny. Can I come back to that one and maybe answer it at the end if something comes to me? There's nothing immediately that leaps out as bizarre or hilarious. In Egon Zehnder, we were arguing in the Supreme Court that if the covenant is subject to restraint of trade, then you have to apply reasonableness to it. But if an obligation isn't subject to this restraint of trade, you don't need to apply reasonableness and it's just a matter of contract. If you contracted for something, then that's that, that's what it is. We gave the example of wearing ruby slippers. That has nothing to do with somebody's trade, it's just a restraint. "You may not wear ruby slippers for six months after you've left our employment" has nothing to do with restraint of trade, and therefore, is enforceable. And that was a bizarre covenant but, obviously, it doesn't exist. It was just our example in the argument. But I've never come across anything as bizarre as that in real life.

Daniel Barnett

Catrina Smith has put in the chat that apparently James Bonds have to agree not to wear a black tie in other films. I didn't know about that restrictive covenant.

Misbah Sadiq

What advice would you give to help draft restrictive covenants so that they are enforceable and they don't amount to restraint of trade?

Daniel Barnett

So, your top tip for drafting a covenant..

Adam Solomon

You've got to tailor it. Ask the employer precisely what they need to protect. Think about the heads of legitimate business interests, for example, trade relations, confidential information, workforce stability and protecting your supplier rights. Tailor your covenants so that they protect precisely those elements for the ex-employer and do no more than is reasonable. If the employer thinks that the confidential information will subsist in that valuable form for six months, or eight months then don't have any more than that, and maybe tailor those restrictions for specific employees as well. So my biggest single bit of advice about drafting is speak to the client, get their precise instructions on why it is they need it and what it is they want to protect. And have a different one for each employee. And then, as Daniel says, review every few months.

Julie Davis

If a new employee brings a following it to their new employer, should those clients be excluded from any future restrictions, and if so, how long could it be before the employer argues those clients and now theirs, the employer's, to protect?

Adam Solomon

That is a classic example of something that is up for negotiation. But if you don't specifically agree it, and if the employee goes to a new employer brings a following of clients, they are not his or her clients at that point. They are the clients of the employer. And they are protectable by restrictive covenants. So if I start at Daniel Barnett's business tomorrow with my 100 client followers and I have restrictive covenants in place, six months later, I can't leave with those clients because my restrictive covenants would prevent me from doing so. They would be Daniel's clients because he'd be the person investing in the business by paying me, for example. However, as you rightly say, you can negotiate. A regular carve out on covenants that I've seen is that if the employee has themselves introduced the client or if the client came with the employee before a certain date, then they are unprotectable by the employer, and they can remain unprotected forever as long as they fall within that carve out. But unless there's a specific carve out, if there's a restrictive covenant preventing, say, dealing with clients, then the employee is prevented.

Steven Eckett
In 2021, is it better to have a six-month restricted period for restrictive covenants or a 12 month period?

Adam Solomon
What are you wanting to protect? I gave the example earlier of an insurance business with annual renewal periods. A six month covenant doesn't protect them in that situation because the employee goes away, the employee knows, for example, the names of the clients and the dates that their contracts will renew, and if that would fall in the period between six months and 12 months, then a six month restriction won't be enough. There isn't a simple answer in 2021 regarding the maximum period you can have. You've got to tailor it to the business. However, there is always the sort of gut feeling that anything over a year looks very long indeed and courts have to be persuaded with convincing evidence to enforce something every year.

At the interim stage - which is where the vast majority of cases are resolved, if they even get that far - the length of time of a covenant is a classic example of something the courts won't determine, because it depends on matters of fact. As long as there's a serious issue to be tried, that the length is enforceable, then a court will grant an interim injunction based on that. That might be the end of the argument, and 99% of the time, it is.

Pritti Bajaria
In your view, should an employee entering into a contract accept badly drafted restrictions in the hope they'll be unenforceable or should the employee seek to negotiate them at the outset to make them more acceptable?

Adam Solomon
That's a brilliant question. It depends on the risk appetite of the employee. So I did a case very recently where the employees were legally advised and there were separate payments made to independent lawyers at the time of entering into the agreement to advise the employees on the enforceability of the covenants. The ex-employer said you had independent legal advice and so you knew that these covenants were enforceable when you signed them up. You knew about the risks. And the ex-employees said that they knew they weren't enforceable, which is why they signed up to them. It's a classic example.

Do you try and negotiate, say something's reasonable for you, or do you take a punt on something being held to be unenforceable at trial or at interim relief? I think it depends on the risk appetite of the individual employee and what their intentions are as well. If they know they want to compete in breach of covenant then their risk appetite might change. But if what they're saying to you, as their legal advisor, when they're signing up to the covenant is that broadly, they want to comply with their obligations, they want to comply with what they think is reasonable, then you might think it's better to negotiate at that stage for a reasonable covenant.

Robert
What's the leading case on enforceability and covenants from the Supreme Court or the Court of Appeal?

Adam Solomon
There's only been one case in the Supreme Court in the last 100 years and that's Egon Zehnder. That is to some extent about enforceability because it upheld a covenant. It's about what words you can delete or blue pencil in a covenant. But the touchstone for covenants, the case that has been relied upon

in every case that I've ever been in is TFS Derivatives (*TFS Derivatives Ltd v Morgan [2005] IRLR 246*), a judgment of Mrs Justice Cox that sets out the three-stage-plus-one approach to covenants: What does it mean? What is the legitimate business interests that it's protecting? Does it go no further than is reasonable? And the fourth stage is judicial discretion. And that's the classic approach.

John Halson
Does the inclusion of a restrictive covenant in a settlement agreement make it any more likely it's going to be enforceable than if it had just been in a normal employment contract?

Adam Solomon
Yes, the answer is a bit more likely. There are some cases that say a contract's a contract, and it doesn't matter whether it's an employment contract or a settlement agreement, and other cases that go much further and say a settlement agreement has a public policy behind it of trying to prevent litigation, and therefore courts should uphold it without looking at the reasonableness of the covenant. Also, at the time of entering into a settlement agreement, there's no longer a disparate, hierarchical employer-employee relationship. There are just two parties trying to agree a commercial transaction.

I think the answer is - and there's a case called Capgemini (*Capgemini India Private Ltd & Anor v Krishnan [2014] EWHC 1092 (QB)*) that deals with the different strands of judicial authority - that it's a bit more likely to be enforced at the settlement stage. So the courts will look with slightly less anxious scrutiny at the terms of the covenant to enforce it if it's in a settlement agreement. But if it's unreasonable and doesn't protect a legitimate business interest, it doesn't matter that it's in a settlement agreement, it won't be enforced.

Su Apps
We all know that injunction proceedings need to be taken without delay. So how long can or should an employer spend writing to the employee warning them off and asking for undertakings before actually initiating court proceedings?

Adam Solomon
The answer is: not too long. There was a case about a year ago where an ex-employer was trying to be very reasonable and spent a few months writing and seeking undertakings and the ex-employee was just saying no, and not playing ball. Eventually, they went to court and the court held that the employer had waited too long. So my view is in general, write a letter before claim seeking undertakings. But if you don't get them, or if they say no, I think the next stage is to apply for injunctive relief. That's the classic approach.

Sometimes, you need to apply for injunctive relief without a letter before claim. You just put them on notice that you're going to court. Sometimes, you can even go to court without notice at all or only informal notice, depending on the urgency of the situation and whether or not tipping off the other side would somehow negate the injunction that you're seeking. But certainly don't wait too long. There's a risk if you do that you're undermining the relief that you're seeking.

Daniel Barnett
Adam Solomon, what's the best way for somebody to get in touch with you if they have any cases involving restrictive covenants?

Adam Solomon
Email me at asolomon@littletonchambers.com or call Littleton Chambers on 0207 797 8600 and ask to be put through to me.

Daniel Barnett
Adam Solomon QC, thank you.

SEX AND MATERNITY DISCRIMINATION

GARETH BRAHAMS, BDBF

Daniel Barnett

Today I'm joined by Gareth Brahams from BDBF and he's going to be answering your questions on sex and maternity discrimination.

Gareth Brahams, good morning. A couple of questions from me first of all. Let's think about the position of a woman returning from maternity leave. If there's a reorganisation of a team and the woman who returns from maternity leave ends up having a less senior role, is that a contravention of their right to return?

Gareth Brahams

The short answer is that it may or may not be. The employer is trying to navigate two rights. So obviously, the employee has got the right to return to the same job on the same terms and the same conditions as would have applied if she'd not been absent. It's slightly different when they return from additional maternity leave, but not actually that much different in reality. And the second rule, of course, is that if the employee is redundant, but is in the protected period, so, in other words, the change is so radical that it actually is a different job and she's been made redundant in the old job, then she's got the right to jump to the top of the queue when it comes to being offered suitable alternative employment.

Really, what the employer needs to do is try to get the situation into one of those two boxes. The first question is can you get it into the box that says this is the same job and the same terms conditions as would have applied had

she not taken leave? And the question is what makes it the same job and what makes it a different job? And, of course, something like "less senior" can cover a multitude of sins. The role might be downgraded, an additional layer of management might be inserted between the employee and their former line manager, someone might be appointed to work alongside her when she previously had sole responsibility, she might lose management responsibility or it may just be as simple as the day-to-day job that she's doing just being less responsible than it was before she commenced maternity leave. So, if any of this happens, the question is still: Is this the same job?

The good news is that the regulations actually define what a job is. And they say that the job is the nature of the work that she is employed to do in accordance with her contract and the capacity and place in which she's employed. So there are three aspects: the nature of the work, the capacity in which she does it and the place. I think we all know what place is.

What do we mean by the nature of the work? In particular, it has to relate to what under the contract she's required to do. There's one example, it's donkey's years old, about loss of responsibility involving someone no longer reporting for the person who had the responsibility to sign the cheques. It was a case from the 1970s. It was held that that didn't mean that she didn't have the same job. Ultimately, she was doing the same role.

In terms of capacity, what do we mean by that? Well, I think that definitely conveys something about status. And when it comes to status, lawyers at least will know that there are few people who care more about their status than secretaries in law firms. And there have been a number of cases involving secretaries in law firms. There's been one that's gone either way, in relation to that. So there was a secretary who was employed in the financial services department and she was offered, on her return, the position as a float. And there was a secretary who'd been employed as a 'grade one' secretary and as a personal secretary to a partner in a law firm, and on return from maternity leave, she was also offered the role of a float.

In the first case, which was a case called Banks (Banks v Carter Hodge and anor ET/28362/94), it was held that the employee still had the same job because her contractual role was to be a secretary. There was nothing beyond that and she was still going back to the same job, even if it was a float role rather than a specific role working for one person, which might seem quite harsh. But in the other case, because she was employed as a partner's secretary, it was held that she was not being brought back to the same job. So that's the fundamental position.

I think, in short, there are certain kinds of things that are unlikely to mean it's a different job: the normal variations of a role, administrative changes, immaterial changes to capacity and status and changes to reporting lines that don't really undermine authority. But it's a spectrum. There are things at the other end of the spectrum where you're losing a skilled part of the role, losing key client contact etc. So I'm afraid it is all a matter of degree. Probably just one irony of it all, though, is that if it's minor, the employer is going to get away with it. If it's more material, the employer won't. But if it's really material, they might get away with it again because at that point, the employee might be redundant. And if the employee is redundant, the employee does not actually benefit from the right to return. What they benefit from is the right to be first in the queue for suitable alternative employment.

Daniel Barnett

Can an employer withdraw a job offer that's made to a maternity cover applicant on the basis that she, the cover, is herself pregnant?

Gareth Brahams

So we're looking at a situation where an employee is going to be off for perhaps a year and the employer has hired someone else to cover her for that year only to find out that the cover herself is pregnant and going to be off for either some or perhaps all of that year. Can you just say that it's not going to work? The short answer to that is that yes, you can say it's not going to work - but it'd be unlawful and you'd get sued for lots of money.

Daniel Barnett

I did start to panic when you were saying that.

Gareth Brahams

I saw your eyebrow raise. I thought I would put it that way just to amuse you. I've got to say I've actually both defended and fought a couple of these claims in my time. I think employers find it particularly galling to shell out such large sums of money to people who've never done a day's work for them. It's a sort of new level of irritation with employment law when you get these kinds of cases.

I just want to add a couple of things on this subject more broadly before we move on. Never ask a candidate about their plans to have a family in an interview. If the candidate volunteers such information, you obviously shouldn't take it into account when you're considering suitability. Perhaps most importantly, you could understand that an employer might feel duped if they were hiring someone specifically to do a maternity cover, that person knew they were pregnant, didn't disclose that they're pregnant in the interview and then turns up and says that they're pregnant and they're going to be off in a month themselves. Can you say that's bad faith? The answer is that you just cannot. There's very clear case law on it. I'm afraid the answer is that you just have to suck that one up, say you're very pleased for them and go and find another replacement.

Daniel Barnett

I was actually in a job interview where I was recruiting with a partner. He asked a woman we were interviewing whether she was planning to start a family. I kicked him under the table, but he didn't even know what he was doing wrong. We ended up offering her the job. I insisted that we had to offer her the job because had we not offered her the job, she would have sued us. She wasn't the best person for the role. It was immensely frustrating. It's often just a level of ignorance on the part of the people interviewing, even today, that they don't know that's a wholly improper question to ask.

Does a requirement to repay company maternity pay raise the same penalty clause issues and the same restraint of trade and discrimination issues as requiring someone to repay training costs?

Gareth Brahams

That's an interesting legal question, actually. We're talking about a situation here where some companies offer enhanced maternity pay, but they say that if the employee doesn't come back for six months or a year or something like that, then they're going to have to pay the money back. Is it lawful? Is it a penalty clause? Or is it restraint of trade? While the short answer is that there's no case law exactly on the point, in relation to penalty clauses and restraint of trade, at least, when it comes to repaying enhanced maternity pay, there is.

Can you draw any conclusions from equivalent rules about people having to repay training costs? There've been a few employers over the years who've said that they've spent an awful lot

of money training an employee, they've paid for the employee to go on courses and they don't want to pay for the employee to go on another course just for the employee to leave. So if the employee leaves within a certain period of time, the money has to be repaid.

Employees have sought to challenge that and not repay the money on the basis that these are penalty clauses, or that they're in restraint of trade. I think the answer on penalty clauses you can deal with pretty shortly, actually. If you draft the policies properly, they won't be penalty clauses. You need to draft the clause to say that you will loan them the money and then the loan will be forgiven at the point at which they've achieved a certain level of service. And further, in any event, even if policies are drafted in a way that they are penalty clauses, particularly if you reduce the amount that has to be repaid each month, I think it's very unlikely, actually, to be a penalty clause. So I'm reasonably relaxed about that.

In terms of restraint of trade, the equivalent law on training costs is actually that there are cases going either way. So it may simply not be a restraint of trade at all. But I think probably the better view on the authorities is to say it can potentially be a restraint of trade. But I think the kind of sums we're talking about and the lengths of periods that normally apply on repayment of maternity pay, I think, make it pretty unlikely. So I'm pretty relaxed about it as I am, by the way, about discrimination because I think essentially, this is a benefit to employees that they wouldn't otherwise get. You can get very clever and try and draw some very fine distinctions. For example, if this was something that didn't apply to people returning from adoption leave or parental leave or that kind of thing, then you might be able to say it's discriminatory. But I think, in essence, it's generally fine.

I would just say this, though - and this is not an employment law point - I just question whether it's good as a matter of policy to make women repay their maternity pay if they don't serve, for example, an extra six months. I think what you're doing is incentivising women to return from maternity leave who don't want to return. I'm not sure how much a business benefits from someone who's been off for a year coming back for six months only because they would otherwise have to repay money they can't afford to repay.

I'm all in favour of enhancing maternity pay, and we enhance maternity pay at BDBF because we want to retain good female talent. But what we don't want to do is encourage people to come back for the wrong reasons. That's definitely more a matter for the HR people out there than me, but I just wanted to add my two pennies' worth on that.

Anonymous

If the boss's wife is the first woman to go on maternity leave in a small company and is given full pay for a year even though the written policy is statutory pay only, does this set a precedent that has to be followed for future women?

Gareth Brahams

It's a matter of contract law. For something to become a legal right, a contractual right, it has to be reasonable, notorious and certain. So I'm not sure that one person, particularly if they're the boss's wife, I'm not sure that action can be taken to generate a contractual entitlement. That's my instinctive reaction to it.

Daniel Barnett

I would have thought it's a fairly hopeless argument.

Matilda Swanson

A pregnant woman is subject to disciplinary or performance proceedings. She thinks it's a sham because she's pregnant and she's getting stressed. What's your advice?

Gareth Brahams

It raises a number of things because, obviously, you have duties to care for her health and

well-being you've got to do risk assessments, typically for pregnant employees, and that will quite often include avoiding stress and so on. But all of that said, if it's genuinely unrelated to her condition, then you're not treating her less favourably by continuing with the disciplinary process. She may well allege that you are, but if it's genuinely unconnected, that is ultimately something that you ought to be able to do. You're bound to tread a bit carefully in terms of taking care of their wellbeing and your applications in that regard.

The reality is that all disciplinary processes are stressful for the employees on the wrong end of them. They're even quite stressful for the employers, but it's best not to be indulgent about that. You'd rather be on the employer's side of the table than the other. And of course, it's something one frequently faces, whether someone's pregnant or not. Usually, the best way to deal with stress is just to get it over and done with.

Keith H

A pregnant employee has been advised by their midwife that they shouldn't come into the workplace because of COVID. The role can't be done from home. The employee's role does not involve dealing with members of the public face to face. We, as the employer, think the workplace is safe following a risk assessment and we think the midwife has got it wrong. We therefore require them to come into the office. Do we need to suspend them? If we do, can they claim they're being discriminated against?

Gareth Brahams

Well, that's a good question. You only have to suspend them if that's the only sensible thing that you can do. The first question is whether there's a genuine health risk to the employee as a pregnant woman. I think the science on that is fairly undeveloped. I think generally, the government's taken a very cautious line about pregnant women and COVID. But I don't think there's actually much science to support that view, other than just generally being precautionary about it. You could, of course, get into a debate about whether it's medically required or not. If it is medically required for health and safety, then, if there's no other role for her, you do need to suspend her as a last resort. That's correct. But one questions whether there are alternatives, in particular, noting that she doesn't deal with the public face to face. Why is there a COVID risk? I'm not sure a midwife who's not actually been to the workplace is necessarily best placed to assess that.

Daniel Barnett
Agreed. If the employer presumably is fairly confident that it's right that there's no particular COVID risk there, it's entitled to just say that the employee is not turning up to work; they're not ready, willing and able to work; and they don't have any right to statutory sick pay under the COVID rules, so stay at home on no pay.

Gareth Brahams
Yes. You could take, I suppose, a hard view that they're absent without leave. But the reality is that people rightly tread carefully around pregnant women when it comes to these situations.

Anonymous
At what point is an employer required to conduct the risk assessment for a pregnant woman under the Management of Health and Safety at Work Regulations 1999?

Daniel Barnett
I was advising on this wrongly for years. I discovered a few years ago that, in fact, there is no obligation to conduct a risk assessment under the 1999 regs for a pregnant woman. There's a general obligation under s16.1(b) to conduct a risk assessment to see what the workplace is like in general for pregnant women, but you don't have to conduct a separate risk assessment every time a woman says she's pregnant, unless she works in a job that involves particular hazardous biological and chemical agents.

So to come back to the question, at what point is an employer required to conduct the risk assessment for a pregnant woman under the regulation?

Gareth Brahams
You've given the answer. They should have a generic assessment in place. I've got to say, I think in ordinary circumstances, one does conduct a risk assessment. I think that's what women expect to happen, and appreciate it happening. So I think you're right that it's not required, probably, at all, because you've done a more generic assessment - and we're presuming we're not working with hazardous biological agents for this purpose – but once she's told you that she's pregnant, I think it's not a bad idea to sit down with her and discuss any adjustments to the workplace she might want to think of in terms of looking after her health and safety and that of the baby.

Anonymous
Does the right to jump to the top of the queue in a redundancy mean that maternity cover should be sacked in favour of the returning mother?

Gareth Brahams
If you've got two people available for one role then the short answer is yes, assuming that the maternity cover is not themselves in a protected period. The maternity cover could already have told you that she's pregnant, in which case, they could both jump to the top of the queue and then you're going to have an even fight.

Daniel Barnett
I'm just struggling with the concept behind the question very slightly because, of course, if there's a redundancy situation, the maternity cover would be sacked anyway because there's no longer any role.

Gareth Brahams
Yes. I think the question is that if there are two people going for one role - the maternity cover and the person returning from maternity

leave - is the person returning from maternity leave automatically going to get that role? And I think the answer is yes. Unless, as I said, the employee doing the maternity cover is themselves pregnant and in a protective period.

Tracey Munro
When an employer gives performance-related pay increases, how should they deal with a woman on maternity leave at review time if she's not been at work long enough to assess her performance?

Gareth Brahams
That's a good question. I think the normal practice is that you try and make an assessment of their performance prior to them going on maternity leave. Obviously, if you're early in the year, you might look to prior years for performance. I'm not sure there is a right answer to this. You'd probably just try and treat them fairly and probably give them an average pay increase. You'd make the best judgment that you can on the information available.

Mark Irlam
What's your top tip for dealing with a male director who's constantly belittling and berating a pregnant director?

Daniel Barnett
Don't do it. That's the top tip.

Gareth Brahams
Yes. That would be a very good start. You might want to warn them that they themselves could become liable for damages for discrimination in their personal capacity if they were to carry on doing that. That might scare them rather more than risking the company's money. It should, of course, be a disciplinary offence as well, and something for which they could ultimately be fired.

Anonymous
What do you advise when an employee on maternity leave refuses keeping in touch days?

Gareth Brahams
It's entirely up to them. Keeping in touch days are an entirely voluntary matter.

Paula Early
It's been discovered that an employee has committed gross misconduct, but she's on maternity leave. Does the employer have to wait until she returns to deal with this?

Daniel Barnett
It's a very common problem.

Gareth Brahams
Obviously, the reason why you might want to dismiss someone for gross misconduct is primarily because you're continuing to pay them. And if they qualify for maternity pay, that pay still has to be paid after the termination of employment if they were employed in a qualifying week, no matter what the reason for them leaving employment is. So, just pragmatically, there may be no particular saving in not waiting until that employee returns.

I'm trying to think. I'm not sure I can give you a better answer than that, actually. I think you would speak to the employee, saying that an issue has arisen and you'd like to deal with it. But if they say they don't want to deal with it now and they'll deal with it when they're back from maternity leave, I don't think there's anything you can do. Going back to the previous point, keeping in touch days are optional. There may be exceptions if there's a regulatory breach or something like that.

Daniel Barnett
Is there anything in the point that leaving aside the two weeks surrounding childbirth, which have special rules, during maternity leave the contract of employment remains in place, save terms relating to remuneration, which means that normal practices such as disciplinary processes don't vanish? And if you insist on somebody facing a disciplinary allegation, they don't have to join in, but dealing with it from an unfair dismissal point

of view, if you've given them a chance to respond, you're probably okay from an unfair dismissal perspective. And dealing with it from a discrimination point of view, you're not dismissing them or subjecting them to a detriment because they're on maternity leave, you're dismissing them or subjecting them to a detriment because they've committed an act of gross misconduct.

Gareth Brahams

I hear that, and that makes some good sense. I'm just wondering about whether you're requiring them to work, though. I mean, there's a question about whether attending a disciplinary hearing is work. And of course, one view is to say that it's not work, it's just attending a meeting. But in the ordinary course, you would attend a disciplinary meeting during your working day and be paid for it. I'm just wondering whether that's a keeping in touch day or not.

I am inclined, on balance, to take the view that you're right, Daniel. But I also would add that there's a whole real-world danger of dealing with people on maternity leave in this way. For example, there'll be issues about organising childcare and they wouldn't be getting paid. So I think there are some circumstances where you would have to try and force it through, like if there's been a regulatory breach and you're a regulated employer. I think in most cases, you'd be better off just biding your time, I'm afraid, but I think legally, you might well be right.

Daniel Barnett

Noeleen Farnan makes a practical point here: leaving the issue might allow the employee to say they can no longer remember the incident and therefore it's an unfair process. I think that's very much six of one and half a dozen of the other.

Gareth Brahams

I certainly don't think there's anything wrong with giving the employee the opportunity to

deal with it straight away. That's generally the way to deal with these things more generally when something pops up at work. You'd tell the employee you can deal with it now or you can deal with it later. And you would have thought that most employees wouldn't want that hanging over their head for the remaining six months of their maternity leave whatever they were planning. There'll be some who would prefer to just get it done.

Paula Early

An employee wants to return from maternity leave earlier than she thought. She's given more than eight weeks' notice, but it's not convenient to have her back. Is there anything the employer can do?

Gareth Brahams

Correct me if I'm wrong, but I don't think there is. I think she's got the right to return as long as she gives at least eight weeks' notice.

Daniel Barnett

Gillian Howard has sent the ACAS guidance on disciplining someone pregnant on maternity leave. The ACAS guidance, although it's not supported by authority, seems to say an employee can be disciplined while pregnant or on maternity leave as long as the reason for the disciplinary action is genuine and fair and not related to pregnancy or maternity in any way. Although, exhibit caution if there are any pregnancy-related illnesses going on and make sure that you've followed a fair process that's not affected in any way by the pregnancy. I'm summarising.

Mike Clyne

Is the title of the campaigning organisation 'Pregnant then Screwed' an accurate reflection on maternity in the workplace?

Gareth Brahams

I'm afraid that I think it is. Of all of the forms of discrimination that exist, I actually think it's the one that is most commonly practised. You can actually understand the reason why. A rational human being, I think, would accept that people on the grounds of sex, race, disability, sexual orientation, religion, belief, age, and all rest of it are no different. And, of course, the same is true when someone's had a child. But it's also true that some of the people who've had children will come back with different calls on their time. In fact, most people will come back with different calls on their time. The reality is that it does change some people's perceptions about how they want to work. Some people actually want to work harder, some want to work less hard, some want to work different hours and all sorts of different things. Very dangerous presumptions can be made. But of course, the law is not interested in any of those presumptions and the law requires you to disregard pregnancy and maternity leave altogether as reasons, and rightly so. I'm not saying otherwise.

But you can see how, in the real world, people struggle with what they may describe as a legal fiction. I only have to think about the women who were in my NCT class some years ago. They came in with quite high-powered jobs and then when they were returning I suddenly had a whole bunch of new clients. And I notice with my team that whenever someone comes back from having their first baby, they come back with a new caseload of claims from people they knew from their NCT classes who don't have the jobs they thought they had. I think it's very real, unfortunately. I think there's an awful lot of it around - much more, as I said, than probably most other forms of discrimination.

Patrick McNamee
is there an identifiable discrimination issue if a male single parent is disciplined for failing to attend work if his disabled three-year-old child's childcare isn't available?

Gareth Brahams
Employees have a right to urgent time off for family reasons. It's unpaid, but one would have thought that that's actually the applicable right. And if they are being disciplined for exercising

that right then they're being disciplined for asserting a statutory right and they aren't being protected. And actually, if it's related to disability, you might have an associative disability claim. So if you treat someone worse for a reason related to disability, then they have a claim. That disability doesn't have to be the employee's own disability. It can be a disability of someone close to them, as per the example you gave me. So there are two reasons why you shouldn't treat that employee that way.

Daniel Barnett
There might be a third as well, actually, if you don't mind me butting in. I notice the question says it's a male single parent. So maybe, the question is implying that a female single parent in the same situation would be treated differently.

Gareth Brahams
It's a very fair point. Yes. I'm so inured. I can't imagine there being sexism in the world. But it didn't occur to me that that was the point. But yes, it was a completely sound one, of course.

Emma
If an employee is going through IVF in an attempt to get pregnant, has been open and honest about it and is then treated less favourably, does that count as discrimination and are there any cases discussing it in any detail?

Gareth Brahams
I'm sure there are. But off the top of my head, I'm struggling. They may come to me, so bear with me. But I have no doubt that if you treated someone worse because they were undergoing IVF, you'd be treating them worse because they're a woman. And on that basis, it would be unlawful.

Daniel Barnett
There's a case on IVF which says that IVF is treated the same as sex and maternity discrimination and it's called Sahota v Home office and Pipkin (Sahota v Home Office and Pipkin [2010] ICR 772).

June Smith

After returning from maternity leave, an annual bonus payment was reduced to take account of the five months a woman was off on maternity leave. Should she have been paid that five-month bonus?

Gareth Brahams

I can answer that one. The law says that whilst you're on maternity leave, you should obviously be awarded the bonus for the period of time that you worked, you should also be awarded a bonus for the compulsory maternity leave period - that's the two weeks after childbirth - and the rest can be prorated. The only exception to that might be if the bonus is sort of the equivalent of a Christmas hamper that everyone gets. I don't think an employer can give them a Christmas hamper of half the size. You get some employers, for example, who give an additional month's pay in December. I'm not sure you can take that away because the employee hadn't been working over the previous period. But where it's performance-related, the employer is entitled to prorate the bonus other than in relation to the two-week compulsory potential leave period.

Anonymous

Can a company lawfully state that to be able to get six months' fully paid shared parental leave, the employee - the father - has to be the primary carer of the child? What if the mother loses her job part way through the shared parental leave? How would you decide who's the primary carer of the child?

Daniel Barnett

I wouldn't. I'd ask someone else. But do you know the answer?

Gareth Brahams

I think I would likewise ask someone else.

Daniel Barnett

To be fair, that's exactly what the anonymous attendee has done. They've just asked two of

the wrong people. I'm sorry we can answer that one.

Rachel Hughes

Does bank holiday entitlement, which is separated out from annual leave entitlement in the contract and the holiday policy, maintain during maternity leave?

Gareth Brahams

That's a good question. So obviously, the bank holiday cannot be taken because you can't take holiday when you're on maternity leave. Therefore, I think, to the extent that it forms part of the working time regulation irreducible minimum of 28 days inclusive of bank holidays, then then the entitlement goes over.

Mark Irlam

How would you deal with a male employee who thinks that what women wear at work is designed to entice men?

Gareth Brahams

If he privately thinks that and doesn't act on it at all, you don't need to worry about it. But I suspect that's not the problem. I suspect that the concern is that this person is acting on it and thinks he is being enticed by women wearing short skirts or whatever the issue is. And clearly, that is going to expose the employer and this individual to a claim of sexual harassment because there's going to be unwanted conduct of a sexual nature arising from this person's rather curious beliefs.

Leszek Werenowski

Can the protected period ever be extended by a tribunal?

Gareth Brahams

No. Although, the protected period is looking like it's going to be extended by statute for everyone. But that's all in the pipeline.

Anonymous

What data protection or GDPR consequences are there if an employee's pregnancy is blabbed by someone senior in the office or blabbed by HR?

Gareth Brahams
There might be a data protection consequence, but I don't think that's the real concern. I think where the exposure is likely to lie is in that person's motivations for blabbing that. Is that going to be a case of people making assumptions about their career and so on, like the example of a miscarriage I gave earlier, and is that going to be prejudiced against them? I mean, yes, I suppose it's right to say that the fact that someone is pregnant is sensitive personal data and may be a confidential matter - special category data is the proper term - but I think the more real issues will turn on actually why they flagged it and what consequences flow from them blabbing it. The chances of any claims arising out of that are, in reality, non-existent probably.

Anonymous
Do you now use or not use non-disclosure clauses in settlement agreements?

Gareth Brahams
That's a good question. The answer is yes, we still use non-disclosure clauses in settlement agreements. The evidence I gave to the select committee was that I think non-disclosure agreements are to the benefit of people who bring claims. And the reason for that is it that makes those claims a lot easier to settle. And the reality is that for the vast majority of people bringing those claims, what they would prefer is to have a settlement rather than to have a public determination of their rights.

However, these days, the non-disclosure provisions have a large number of carve-outs in them. The kind of things that we saw in the Harvey Weinstein case where she was being told that she couldn't speak to her doctor and she couldn't speak to the police, all of that has long gone. And of course, there are exceptions for making protected disclosures, but there are a number of further exceptions which are set out in the Solicitors Regulation Authority's warning notice that gives us very extensive carve-outs. So the answer is that NDAs are still there. They're actually quite important. They protect the employee who often wants the benefit of the NDA because they don't want the whole world knowing or talking about the situation, and there's also a whole category of people that people don't like to talk about when you talk about sexual harassment, but that's the wrongly accused - typically men - and they are also entitled to protection. NDAs, of course, enable those people to be protected as well.

Daniel Barnett
Gareth Brahams what's the best way for someone to get in contact with you if they have any litigation or need advice regarding discrimination?

Gareth Brahams
You know, I'm the only Gareth Brahams on the internet. If you type 'Gareth Brahams' into Google, out will pop my name and you can get in touch with me by email.

Daniel Barnett
Gareth Brahams, thank you very much.

TAXATION
DAVID READE QC, LITTLETON CHAMBERS

Daniel Barnett

I'm joined today by David Reade QC from Littleton Chambers who's going to be answering all of your questions on taxation.

David Reade, thank you for joining us. I'd like to start by asking a couple of questions of my own. First of all, we all live in fear of post-employment notice pay, which has been around for a couple of years, and many of us are still very much getting to grips with it. Can you reduce post-employment notice pay liability by diverting some of the termination payment to legal fees?

David Reade

Yes. Post-employment termination notice came in in 2018. And there have been various modifications and changes that have come in. And the essential purpose of it was, of course, to resolve the ambiguity that existed about whether or not payments in lieu of notice - if they were contractual or non-contractual - were subject to tax and National Insurance. And they did that by amending part of the termination code, that part of ITEPA that deals with termination payments and their taxation. And if you look at that section, that's where you also find the exemption in relation to the payment of legal costs. And the payment of legal costs exempts the entirety of that subsection. So in principle, if you have a legitimate payment of legal costs in connection with the termination of employment that fits within the concession in that - which is going to involve paying those legal costs directly to

the legal advisor who's incurred those costs only in connection with advising in relation to the termination - that payment falls outside the taxation regime, and therefore could reduce the amount that would fall to be taxable under the post-employment notice period payment. So the answer is yes. Of course. We've got to be careful always in any tax context about abuse, and we're obviously looking to ensure that that's a genuine legal expense. And I'm sure of course it's going to involve the external lawyers that you're paying legitimately confirming that those are expenses incurred in connection with the termination of employment.

Anonymous

Can the parties agree that settlement compensation is for termination of employment rather than unpaid notice pay - for example, in a redundancy situation where there's no notice pay paid - and could the reclassification of what would otherwise be noticed pay as a termination payment attract any issues?

David Reade

Yes, is the answer to that. So reclassification - it doesn't matter what you call it, what matters is what it is. The problem is that if you're making a payment in connection with termination, however we classify it, if it's not caught by any other taxation element - in which case, it will be subject to tax and National Insurance anyway - it gets caught by the termination provisions I've mentioned. And the minute it's caught by the termination provisions I've mentioned, one has to look at whether or not there has been a payment of notice pay, as would be required under the contract of employment. And so if there hasn't been that payment of notice pay, then the deemed provisions that require an element of pay attributable to that last notice pay - to be subject to tax and National Insurance - would apply, and they would eat out of the redundancy, payment that you've made. The only thing they don't eat out of is statutory redundancy entitlement. So if, for example, I classified it as being immediate termination, no notice pay, but £15,000 worth of redundancy payment, the statute redundancy payment would come out. But in relation to the remaining £15,000, you'd have to calculate the actual notice entitlement. And the post-employment notice payment would be taxable, with normal tax, normal employers' and employees' National Insurance.

But of course, what we have to remember is that it's the employer who's primarily always going to be at risk in relation to this. When it comes to enforcement, that's always a direction of travel that the Revenue have got. If an employer has chosen to chance their arm in relation to this, the prospect is that they're going to find themselves with that liability. And absent an express indemnity from the employee - and even that may be very difficult to enforce in these circumstances - they're going to end up with that liability. So clever sidestepping around that is unlikely to achieve the desired result.

Daniel Barnett

I'm occasionally asked about confidentiality obligations or post-termination restrictive covenants in settlement agreements. And you often see a clause in a settlement agreement that says we are going to pay£100 for you to continue to be bound by confidentiality or post-termination restrictive covenants. What's the reason for that? Does it affect the taxation of the rest of the settlement amount?

David Reade

I think, just to step back a bit, as employment lawyers were quite used to people being

aware of the 30k tax-free limit, and people often approach these questions by focusing on the 30k, and then looking at the world through that particular perspective. That isn't the way that the Revenue looks at the world. There's no surprise there. They look at the world from the point of view that at the end of any set of payments in relation to an employee or former employee, there's a prospect of termination payments being taxable, and in that taxation, there's an exemption of 30k. But, and the point is this, before you ever get there, they look at a whole succession of other provisions that may apply to any particular payment that's made to an individual by their employer or their former employer and ask whether or not they're taxable in relation to those particular provisions.

Now, obviously, one bit of those provisions is straightforward - your salary is quite clearly taxable. But buried in ITEPA are two sections. s225 and 226 are provisions that deal with restrictive covenants. Now, we as employment lawyers think restrictive covenants must mean post-termination restrictions about not competing, but from the Revenue's perspective under the Act, they mean restrictions that are imposed upon an employee and if you make a payment in relation to an employee or a former employee that restricts their future behaviour, that payment can be completely taxable under s225 or s226.

A few years ago, there was a case that caused quite a lot of consternation about this, and the Revenue issued a practice statement, that still operates, that if you merely restate existing restrictions and don't have any new changed restrictions, they don't regard any settlement agreement as being taxable. So if I do a settlement agreement and in that settlement agreement I merely articulate the restrictions on confidentiality that are contained in your contract of employment, or indeed, the normal post-termination restrictions and I have a settlement provision, there's no issue. But the minute that I start tinkering with those, and I introduce something which is modified or changed - and of course, potentially, that might be a restriction about keeping the confidentiality of the entire settlement agreement - suddenly there's a risk that the Revenue may say that's a restrictive covenant that falls within this tax provision.

So my approach has been, and I see it in a lot of other people's settlement agreements, is to attribute a discrete element of consideration in relation to any modified or restricted restrictions, including confidentiality about the agreement itself and identifying that separate consideration so that it can be treated separately for tax purposes. That always begs a separate question, which is what figure do you put in relation to that? And there's no easy answer to that, other than that it looks rather unsustainable if you have a completely nominal figure, like £5, or £50 or £100. So I normally put something which is not a huge amount of money, less than £1000, but certainly something that looks like a significant element of consideration for that particular obligation.

Daniel Barnett
You've mentioned 'ITEPA' a couple of times. That's the Income Tax (Earnings and Pensions) Act 2003.

Caroline
Can you please update us on umbrella companies and what evidence a hirer or end user can request to show that tax and National Insurance have been deducted through an umbrella company?

David Reade
Obviously, we've got IR35 and the changes coming into force later on this year, and the most significant change in relation to this, of course, is the off-payroll earnings position. The real risk in relation to the off-payroll provisions is in relation to the putative employer because they are contracting with the intermediary for services, but they have to make a determination as to the status of the provided worker. Th at requires them to look closely at the status of the intermediary to determine whether or not it meets any of the criteria that mean that you move to the second question of whether or not the relationship will be one that will be treated as being one as if there was employment of the provided worker. And those criteria are factors typically related to the degree of control that the end worker has or interests that they have, and in an umbrella company, they wouldn't have sufficient interest for that to be brought and engaged.

I think the difficulty is that there's limited capacity to compel the provision of information. From the point of view of the end user, they are always subject to an obligation that they have to take reasonable steps in order to ascertain the true position of the intermediary, which is clearly going to involve asking the questions. I suppose the unclear question is if you don't get answers to those questions, are you simply going to default to the view that we should treat it as being a deemed employment and deduct tax and National Insurance? Or does one take the view that absent the provision of that information in a satisfactory way that persuades you that the intermediary is a true organisation that can exist as an intermediary without the off-payroll regulations applying, that you just wouldn't touch the intermediary? But I don't think there's a direct power that compels the provision of that information. You're left to make your own assessment on that and take a view. It may be that the view you have to take absent the information is the cautious one of either saying we're going to operate the deduction of tax and National Insurance at source in relation to this individual, or we just simply won't engage with them through that body.

Julie Norris
Within PENP rules - post-employment notice pay rules - can you argue that there's no tax if there's been a dismissal for gross misconduct,

on the basis that no notice pay would have been payable?

David Reade

It's a slightly vexing question in the sense that if you dismiss someone for gross misconduct, why are you paying them anything anyway? Because obviously, the only issue you'd ever have with the PENP rules or the payment would be in circumstances where you're paying them something despite gross misconduct. The answer to that is, you've dismissed them for gross misconduct, they haven't accepted that they've been guilty of gross misconduct, they've purported to bring a claim in the employment tribunal and you're settling that claim.

The minute that you're settling that claim and you're making a payment in relation to the individual, I think your problem is that the PENP rules engage. So you can, in principle, say it's gross misconduct, I didn't have to pay anything and there is no liability in relation to non-paid notice tax. But PENP only engages once you're paying, and the minute you're paying in terms of settlement, then you've got the problem that that tax position will be there. And that's absolutely true if you have an engagement, for example, where there's a tribunal settlement that you're engaged in. Even if you dispute it, the entitlement to bring a dismissal claim, because you said it was gross misconduct, is still engaging with these principles if you pay a settlement in relation to matters, because that's a payment in connection with the termination of employment.

Andy Crisp

Can an employer and an employee agree to defer payment of salary until the next tax year, if it's tax-efficient to do so?

David Reade

I was doing some research in anticipation of this talk, and my approach has always been that you couldn't on the basis that the minute that you crystallise the deal in relation to the

entitlement, it's treated as being payable at the point of the original agreement. And if you look at the payments in relation to termination, it does talk about the entitlement being an entitlement the individual can enforce or be paid at the point of payment.

Having looked at a few pieces of information, there does seem to be an argument to the effect that you could have deferred payment, particularly if they're genuine staged payments for tax-efficient purposes. And you can imagine an employer having a particular interest in that. So you do sometimes see people, particularly with long notice periods, that have encouraged individuals to mitigate their loss and have provided staged payments as part of the settlement agreement with a proviso, for example, that a payment isn't made if someone has sought and succeeded in obtaining full employment elsewhere, or, for example, with conditions that they comply with post-termination restrictions. And having looked at that, in those circumstances, the employee wouldn't be able to enforce the payment in the earlier tax year. They would only be able to enforce to payment in the later tax year, and that would then be taxable as a point of receipt. But obviously, the important thing here is that if you've got someone who is taxable at a higher rate, it will be helpful to be able to have a break in the payments. And also if you've got someone who potentially may not recoup or recover their earnings in that second tax year, they'd obviously be taxed at with the advantage of their personal allowance in relation to the year's taxation.

Gillian Howard

How can damages for injury to feelings be paid tax free?

Daniel Barnett

I think what she's asking is if the only amount being paid to the employee is in respect of injury to feelings, whether you'd still have to make the deductions you would for PENP?

David Reade

Yes. One of the changes as a result of the changes that were made when we talked about post-employment notice pay was tightening up the position about compensation for injury to feelings. There had been a debate in the law, about whether or not injury to feelings could fit within an exemption from the termination of taxation regime. If you pause to think about it, if I have an accident at work and I bring a claim for damages for my accident at work, and that accident at work caused me to lose my job, that's a payment in connection with the termination of my employment. It's not treated as being taxable in itself because of a specific exemption under the ITEPA rules. The debate had been as to whether that exemption extended to cover payments in connection with injury to feelings.

David Reade

People tried to argue that injury to feelings could fit within that provision. And it's absolutely clear now that if it's treated as a termination payment - for example, if they've got a claim where they say that they were the subject of discrimination leading to their constructive dismissal, or discrimination, or their termination, and they've got an injury to feelings element to it - unless they can say that the injury to feelings is actually such that there is identifiable medical harm - so a psychological injury of a medically definable nature, not simply an injury to feelings, but something that amounts to an injury - it's treated as being taxable as a termination payment.

The only caveat to add to that is the position before termination. The Revenue may take a slightly different view about this, and so one certainly has to be cautious about it, but when one's looking at positions before termination, there's a line of authority to say that if you're looking at compensation for injury to feelings in the course of employment, that's statutory compensation. It's not paid as an emolument of your employment and it's not paid in connection with termination. That is an area where one can look at injury to feelings being payable without taxation. I should say that that's the point where there are some first instance tax tribunal decisions in support of that view. The Revenue itself may be more quizzical about whether or not that's the position. But certainly, most of the commentators say that in employment injury to feelings compensation for acts in the course of employment, rather than in connection with termination, could be paid without deduction of tax.

Anonymous

For the purpose of post-employment notice pay, can notice be deemed to be served and worked from the date the employee and employer reach agreement on settlement terms, even if the settlement agreement isn't signed until the following week? Is it the date of signature that matters or the effective date of termination?

David Reade

The critical date is the date of termination. One of the earlier questions was slightly similar, which was whether or not you could effectively deem notice as running from an earlier point in time. So let's say you're entitled to six months' notice, we reach a settlement agreement, and then we say actually, we gave you your notice six months ago, and the termination date is now, so there's no question of a post-employment notice period because of your last six months of working. And that sounds to me like a simple fraud on the Revenue to be honest. You're actually then falsely stating your position. I don't think it's true if all you're doing is in the exercise of signing off the agreement on the basis of statutory notice, and it's not the signature that matters, it's the termination date. Because the first thing you have to do for the purposes of post-employment notice pay is identify the termination date, that's the effective date of the employment, that is a pivot point.

The significance of the date of the settlement agreement and the termination date. are perhaps more important from the point of view of how you treat the tax payment. Because if you make the payment before the end of the employment after the settlement agreement is reached, so we've got a date in the future, you deal with it under the normal PAYE regime. If you make the payment after the end of the employment, you have to use the special tax code for post-termination terminations. That has the practical effect for the employee that you start off by deducting more tax to begin with, and then it's necessary, typically, for them to reclaim some tax at the end of the year.

Jamie Anderson
When drafting a schedule of loss, how do you properly present the correct position under ITEPA in high-value cases? Is it good enough to just put at the bottom 'ITEPA will apply' and let someone else have the headache of working out?

David Reade
Well, it depends on what your schedule of loss is aspiring to do. If your schedule of loss is merely creating a ballpark structure for a negotiation, I can see that doing that is going to be a convenient shortcut. But if your schedule of loss is actually going to be trying to assist a tribunal, to calculate those particular payments out, I'm afraid you've got to do the legwork.

It's absolutely true that when you're bringing any form of claim - in an employment tribunal, or indeed in the County Court or High Court in relation to notice pay - that the basic assessment is always done on a net basis, because you compensate people for their net loss. But the difficulty is that because of the regime of ITEPA, if you're looking at a claim that's based on the termination of employment, the damages themselves will be taxable. And it means that if you've got a high-value claim, and we're talking about, for example whistleblowing claims or discrimination

claims, in order to assess the true net loss, you have to gross that award up so that after the application of the termination provisions - the first £30,000 tax free and the remainder subject to the highest incidental rate of tax for the individual in the applicable period - the gross-up can be very, very significant. I do think that it's very important to get how big that figure is out there, because the worst thing in the world in negotiation terms, if you're acting for a claimant, is to start off with a claim that looks X, with a notional provision about tax in there, and when it comes down to the reality of arguing out the position, you've actually got to get X plus Y, and Y is a much bigger figure. Suddenly you're engaging with an employer who's seeing the claim as looking much bigger than they might have immediately anticipated. And it's always harder to talk people up from what they originally contemplated your claim was at its highest than the talk them down.

David Reade
When I work as a mediator, the first thing I always say in a mediation process in any employment dispute is let's get our language clear. Are we talking net of tax or gross of tax? And if we're talking gross of tax, we need to work out how tax will apply. You can get people who fail to be on even the same plane in terms of those levels.

I will just add my bugbear which is that it's always seemed to be a complete inequity that no one in an unfair dismissal claim that is subject to the cap can ever have their true net loss. If you get the maximum unfair dismissal award, and it's calculated on a net basis, the tribunal can't gross up above the cap. You will be subject to tax as a termination payment and the net amount that you got will always be significantly lower than the employment tribunal cap. It will be very significantly lower if, for example, you had an unfair dismissal claim, but have already received redundancy payments that used up part of your entitlement.

And it's always seems to be completely wrong that that is the case, but that remains the law.

Julie Norris

If an employee claims monies that the employee says are due, or holiday pay that is paid without admission of liability via a settlement agreement, can you argue that this is compensation because there's no admission of liability, or would it be taxable as income?

David Reade

I think that even so far as compensation for failure pay holiday pay properly, the Revenue have taken the position that it's taxable as an emolument of employment. The basic position is going to be that the Revenue will look at the underlying payment claim. So if I'm claiming unpaid holiday pay, that's treated as being arrears of salary. It's an unlawful deduction from wages claim. If I'm seeking claims for contractual back pay, it's a wages claim. So when they're paid, they're fully taxable and fully subject to employers' and employees' National Insurance. Just because I settle the claim for a particular sum doesn't change that status, and the Revenue will look at it and say it's taxable.

Andy Crisp

If an employer and an employee agree to evade tax on a termination payment, and the solicitor advises it's unlawful, but signs the advisor certificate anyway, has the solicitor done anything wrong?

David Reade

Well, aren't you facilitating a fraud on the Revenue you sign off as a party? I would have thought your professional obligations would require you not to be complicit in something which is a conscious evasion of tax.

Daniel Barnett

Would you regard this as being complicit in a conscious evasion of tax? Or would you simply take a more restricted view that all the advisor

is doing is signing that he's given advice and he has insurance?

David Reade

The agreement can't be affected unless you've signed it off, can it? Aren't you an operative party in achieving something which is an unlawful purpose?

Anonymous

Should employment solicitors carry out PENP calculations?

Daniel Barnett

I'm not quite sure of the context of that. Presumably, it's when advising on settlement sums.

David Reade

I personally would regard that as being a sensible thing to do for an employment Lawyer. I know that they typically might be considered as part of a payroll exercise, but if you need to give practical advice, whether you are for the employer or the employee, you need to be able to advise people what the true effect of that provision will be. Obviously from an employer's point of view, quite a significant change in settlement agreements is the existence of the PENP, which has got normal tax and National Insurance. But also, of course, these days, you've got to be quite careful to advise people that the minute they're an employer paying more than 30k, they're going to be subject to employers' National Insurance on those termination payments that never used to be the case. I suspect that that's led to a lot of employers being rather less generous in relation to termination arrangements than they have been historically.

St. Cox

How would the Revenue hear about a settlement agreement?

David Reade

You're required to report termination settlement payments as part of your reporting obligations. The other side of the coin, as an individual, is that if I receive a payment in relation to a settlement agreement in respect of my earnings, and I do a tax return, I should also be declaring it there. But termination payments are a reportable obligation on an employer.

Ian Jones

In a summary termination case, if a settlement agreement is agreed, is notice always deemed to have been included in the settlement for tax purposes?

David Reade

I assume that we're talking about a situation where there's a settlement agreement that simply provides that someone's employment will terminate. In those circumstances, the PENP obligation kicks in. So it is assumed that you've agreed to make a payment without notice, and the whole of the notice provision under the contract would be engaged in the calculation of that PENP settlement.

Somebody did ask a question anonymously, which was whether or not you could agree to vary your contract to reduce your notice entitlement. You couldn't reduce your notice entitlement below the statutory minimum, because even you as an individual can't contract out of that effectively. So you can agree to immediate termination, but you still would have your statutory notice; you can never lose that. I think it'll be a moot question whether I could, for example, if I had six months' notice, agree a contractual variation before my settlement agreement took effect, to reduce my contractual notice pay down to a period of, say, three months. Instinctively, I feel that that will be something that the Revenue would look very closely at as being some form of device.

Anonymous

If an employee is on long-term sick and leaves without working notice because of constructive unfair dismissal and their entitlement to pay during the notice period would have been nil

- because they had a notice period, at least one week greater than statutory notice - and they've exhausted their SSP and occupational sick pay, what's the tax position on any settlement?

David Reade

My understanding of the tax position from the point of view of payment is that obviously, we've got to have a payment to them. So if they simply leave and you're not making a payment to them, then there is no taxable payment that's due. Let's say they left and they brought a claim, and you end up settling that claim, then my understanding of tax position is that when you calculate the PENP, their earnings in the last month, their basic earnings, would be zero and therefore there is no PENP notice. Now, that may not be the end of the story, because if there was a contractual payment in lieu clause in relation to the contract and you end up doing some form of settlement claim, the Revenue might say that an element of that sum is taxable because it is preferable to a contractual payment in lieu clause. The PENP doesn't create a basic pay liability. It looks at the last month before termination and says What is the pay there? I checked up a few of the provisions before I came on, and I think for those purposes it's also true that statutory maternity pay doesn't count for that particular purpose either.

Anonymous

If there's a senior employee with no written contract and the employer pays pay in lieu of notice on the basis of the statutory notice period, what's the risk of Her Majesty's Revenue and Customs saying notice should be greater on the basis that statutory notice is not reasonable notice?

David Reade

There's no explicit notice provision, but we, as lawyers, would say there's an implied reasonable notice provision. I've not seen or heard of that happening. We've had a culture in the last few years where there's been a much more robust approach to looking at taxation questions, and I could well see that being argued. For example, the Revenue for years have run an argument about automatic PILON , where they've looked at habitual payments and said that they would regard regular payment of payment in lieu, even without a contractual payment, as giving rise to an obligation. So they are prepared to look at what they regard as being the deemed or implicit contractual obligations. So I could well see an argument that reasonable notice could be read in.

Mike Clyne
Other than payment of legal costs and payment towards outplacement fees, are there any other payments that a company can make without attracting tax?

David Reade
Well, we identified genuine payments in relation to an injury occasioned o the employee. So if you've got a situation where someone was genuinely incapacitated and although work had occasioned them injury in respect of matters, you could make a payment in reference to that. One always has to be slightly careful about this because there is lurking in ITEPA something that you occasionally see, which is that the Revenue can sometimes look at a payment and say that it's a payment referable to a non-approved retirement income scheme. Basically, what that means is if you've got someone who might be retiring from employment, or ending their employment, then the Revenue can look at a payment and say, it's not really a termination payment, it's a payment of a retirement benefit under a non-approved pension scheme, and tax it. Scheme can include a one off payment. So if you had someone who was effectively ending their employment career in circumstances where there might have been an injury, for example, and you wanted to make a payment in relation to that, but it wasn't fully commensurate with their injury claim, you might be in danger of walking into another tax liability. So I think, to be frank, the safest things are legal expenses, outplacement costs and consultation.

Daniel Barnett
David Reade from Littleton Chambers, thank you very much.

THE MENCAP CASE

SEAN JONES QC, 11KBW

Daniel Barnett

I am joined by Sean Jones QC, who was one of the counsel in Tomlinson-Blake against Mencap *(Royal Mencap Society v Tomlinson-Blake [2021] UKSC 8)*, which was a decision handed down by the Supreme Court this morning. Sean is the barrister who represented Ms Tomlinson-Blake, and he's going to be talking very briefly on the impact of that decision and on how the decision was reached.

Sean, could you start off just by explaining what the decision was about?

Sean Jones

It concerned sleep-in workers and time work. So we're dealing with a question of the National Minimum Wage. And there are various different ways in which the National Minimum Wage is calculated, but essentially what it does is ask how many hours you have worked and then it wants to know whether you have received a level of pay which produces at least the National Minimum Wage for each hour of work that counts. But not every hour necessarily counts. So the question is which count and which don't.

This arises in the particular context of what we call 'sleep-in workers'. And let me start immediately with a problem, which is that 'sleep-in workers' is not a narrow category. So various different people who call themselves sleep-in workers might be doing very different sorts of work. And that, I think, is a problem

with the reasoning in the decision. I'll come back to that in a moment to explain exactly why.

When they were considering introducing the National Minimum Wage Regulations, they went first to a body called the Low Pay Commission. The principal purpose of the Low Pay Commission is to set the rate of the National Minimum Wage, and they do that periodically. In order to do that, they take a lot of evidence, and they produce a big report. The report contains certain recommendations. Their first report was produced before the original set of National Minimum Wage Regulations came into effect and provided something of a framework for what the Low Pay Commission had intended the law should be. The National Minimum Wage Act said that the government had to consider these recommendations and if they were not going to implement them, they had to say that they weren't going to implement them and explain why. The reason why that is significant is that when the National Minimum Wage Regulations first came into effect, the government did not suggest that it was doing anything other than accepting the Low Pay Commission's recommendations - it said it was. So nothing was identified as being wrong, nothing was identified as being problematic, they just issued the regulation.

So we're dealing with time work, which is where you're effectively paid a rate per hour. Let's say you're a care worker and you go along during the day and do eight hours of work, caring for someone in their own home. That's eight hours of work and you need the National Minimum Wage for each of those eight hours.

But let's say that instead of going along during the day, you go along at night. Your job is effectively to put the person you're caring for to bed and tidy up. You're then allowed to sleep in a bed with which you are provided. Your job is effectively to keep what was described in the authorities as 'a listening ear'. So it's your job to work out whether there is something that requires your intervention and requires you to exercise your judgment as to whether you do or not, and if you do intervene, to make sure that you do it well and that the person that you care for is properly looked after.

You're generally there because of a local authority, and the local authority has you there because it has a duty to ensure the welfare of the people who are being looked after. So the local authority has a statutory duty to discharge, it needs people to discharge that duty on their behalf, it employs you, it sends you along, you put people to bed, you sleep, you wait to deal with an emergency, you go back to sleep and you wake up in the morning.

Let's say you're there for eight hours. Do you get eight hours worth of pay? Well, I said on behalf of Ms Tomlinson-Blake that yes, you do. And the reason why you get that is because you're really working all the time. You're working because you're helping the local authority discharge its duties and you're working because it is your job effectively - whether awake or asleep - to be in a position to respond immediately to anything that should arise. So the nature of your job is not endlessly assembling things on an assembly line as they come back past you one after another. The whole purpose of your job is to be there in case something happens and to exercise your judgment as to whether to intervene or not. In other words, the nature of your job is to wait to see if something happens.

Does that justify the National Minimum Wage? Effectively, yes, had said a long series of EAT decisions, including the one in the Tomlinson-Blake case itself. It said that is a kind of work. "They also serve who only stand and wait", quoted Brian Langstaff in one of the early EAT decisions. So this is the kind of work for which you hire people. You require their attendance for a period of hours, they're disciplined if they leave, they should get the money. So why isn't that obviously the answer? The reason why it isn't obviously the answer is that when you look at the regulations, it pays you for time work which it doesn't really define, but it then says what also counts as time work is availability for work. So you're not working, but you're making yourself available for work, and it says that, too, counts, except it doesn't count in certain narrowly defined circumstances. And, massively, massively oversimplifying, what was a series of provisions that evolved over time, one of the circumstances in which you're not treated as being available for work is if you are permitted to sleep using facilities which have been provided by your employer.

So, the approach taken by the other side was to say that you reason back from the , to the extension, to the definition of time work and you say that if being allowed to sleep means you aren't treated as being available for work, that must mean that in circumstances where you're allowed to sleep it would otherwise be a subset of availability for work, which wouldn't count as work unless the extension applied, and the extension doesn't apply. Sorry, if that's blown a few minds. Essentially, what you're doing is working from the exception to the extension backwards to the definition of time work.

What we argued was that you should do what the EAT had done, which was to argue forwards from the definition of time work. So you start by asking: Is this work? And if the answer is yes, it is, then you don't have to ask whether it would fall into the category of availability for work and would it then fall into the exception from the extension to availability for work because it just is work. That is the approach that the EAT had taken pretty consistently. It worked substantial justice, but there were two problems with it. One problem was that no one had ever cited the Low Pay Commission report to them, or taken the point that was taken in this case, so it hadn't really been looked at head-on by any of the big, most important authorities. The second problem was that once you'd taken that Low Pay Commission report into acount, because they had recommended in relation to sleep-in workers that they shouldn't get the National Minimum Wage for time where they were not awake for the purposes of working but should instead, as they put it, get an agreed allowance, as is now the practice, it began to look like the EAT was effectively working around that issue, that it had created a way of frustrating the Low Pay Commission's plans.

It all got a lot more complicated because what happened was that we were dealing with the 2015 regulations and by then the government had surrendered. It was issuing guidance which said the EAT was right. So the argument that David Reade was running was, to our mind, the rather unattractive one that although the government was actually saying in terms, in guidance, that the EAT was right, that this can constitute work and if it does constitute work, you're entitled to time work, you should nevertheless read the regulations which were also issued in the spring of 2015 as having the exact opposite effect. We said that was obviously absurd. They wouldn't be issuing guidance and regulations which are materially identical to their predecessors in circumstances where it would utterly undercut all the guidance they had given.

What Lady Arden said is yes, they might be, and the reason why we take this approach is that we are statutorily entitled, statutorily obliged in fact, to take into account the Low Pay Commission recommendation from back in 1998. But we aren't obliged to take into account the guidance which had been issued by government departments in 2015. So in other words, we wipe away all of the EAT reasoning, we wipe away the government's apparent acceptance of the EAT reasoning in its guidance, and we just go right back to square one, to where the Low Pay Commission was 30 years ago, and we apply that. So that's how we get where we are.

Obviously, my eyes are boiling out of my head with disappointment. But I can see how they got there. What would have been lovely is for the Low Pay Commission to have stepped in and said that things have moved on and they no longer consider that what they had to say 30 years ago is of any real relevance, but they didn't.

Daniel Barnett
I suppose that one of the things that people need to remember is that the Supreme Court wasn't ruling on whether sleep-in workers are working. They were ruling on whether the work they were doing attracted minimum wage under the Minimum Wage Regulations, and it didn't.

Sean Jones
Yeah, so they ruled on whether they're working for the purposes of the regs. It's not a working time issue. One of the issues which really does befuddle me is that they had to say what amounts to being awake for the purposes of working. Bear in mind that the way the Supreme Court looked at it was that you were dealing with a subset of availability for work and not actual work. They said that the only point at which you're awake for the purposes of working is when you're up and doing something, which seemed to me to go way too far because, on any basis, when you're up and doing something, you're doing time work. It's not a subset of availability for work. So I think their reasoning goes too far.

There's some disturbing stuff in it. Without wanting to give bad employers ideas, we were relying on a case called BNA *(British Nursing*

Association v Inland Revenue [2003] ICR 19), which was about home workers. Working at home is another exception to the extension to cover availability for work, so people who are sat at home waiting for a phone to ring. As a matter of fact, they were also entitled to sleep. We kept saying that's completely indistinguishable from our case. So if BNA is right - and the other side was saying that it was - we're also right. So we were able to say in the Supreme Court that you can't adopt the position they've adopted. If you agree with them and with us that BNA is entirely correct, then you must find for us. But unfortunately, the Supreme Court said they agree that it's indistinguishable, and they overruled BNA. Although that's a matter in which there's a difference between the majority and some of the additional decisions, and that really does require some fine-tooth combing as to what position they took in relation to that.

But certainly, giving the lead judgment, Lady Arden thinks BNA goes too; so that means people who are performing irregular tasks at home now may find themselves in a position where they're no longer entitled to the National Minimum Wage throughout that period.

Daniel Barnett
Sean Jones, thank you so much. I'm so sorry about the result in the Tomlinson-Blake case.

Sean Jones
Well, that's my fault! Thanks very much, everyone. It's been a pleasure to participate. Thank you, Daniel, for this incredibly generous thing you've done for FRU. Speaking on behalf of FRU, we just couldn't be more delighted or more grateful. Thanks to everyone who bought tickets for this. You've made a huge difference to a really important legal charity.

TIME LIMITS

REBECCA TUCK QC, OLD SQUARE CHAMBERS

Daniel Barnett

Today I'm joined by Rebecca Tuck. Rebecca is a silk at Old Square Chambers who specialises in employment and discrimination law. She's head of their employment group. She sits as a fee-paid judge and is a qualified mediator.

So, on the subject of time limits in employment tribunals, I've got a couple of questions. In employment law, time limits are usually three months, leaving aside ACAS early conciliation extensions. What are the tests for extending time if that three-month time limit is missed?

Rebecca Tuck

So, there are two principal tests, and whenever you're looking at a cause of action, you need to know which of the two tests you're concerned with. The test which is found in the Employment Rights Act - and is the relevant test for unfair dismissal, whistleblowing and a lot of the Wages Act type claims - is you've got to have presented the claim within three months, unless it was not reasonably practicable to do so. And if it wasn't reasonably practicable, then have you presented the claim within such further period as is reasonable? Now, the reasonable practicability test traditionally has been seen as the stricter of the two tests, and you've got to have jolly good reasons as to why you didn't present the claim within three months. I think it will be interesting in terms of the pandemic as to whether we see more of these out-of-time claims with people being unwell or having even more limited availability of advice, but we'll see what transpires with

that. The second test, which is the one found in s123 of the Equality Act and applies to all discrimination claims, is that you must present the claim within three months. But if you haven't, is it just and equitable to extend the time limit? So reasonable practicability or just and equitable.

Daniel Barnett

There was a case in January this year called Adedeji v University Hospitals Birmingham NHS Trust *(Adedeji v University Hospitals Birmingham NHS Foundation Trust [2021] EWCA Civ 23)*, from the Court of Appeal, which regard to time limits. Can you explain what that case was about?

Rebecca Tuck

You might come across this case when Andrew Short QC is talking to you as well because confusion as to the time limit on behalf of the claimant arose because he wanted to start the ACAS early conciliation process and named his BMA rep without their permission. The BMA rep said, No, we're not on record. And so he sought to withdraw his ACAS early conciliation process, and they issued a certificate. That certificate was valid, so time started to run. When a paralegal explained this to Mr Adedeji, he thought that she was a bit confused and must have got it wrong and didn't accept her advice. So he ended up presenting his complaint out of time. The employment judge found that the claim was out of time and refused to extend the limitation period for both the unfair dismissal and discrimination claims. The appeal concerned just the discrimination claim.

The Court of Appeal judgment is of particular interest because of the approach of Underhill LJ to what are known as the *Keeble* factors. Keeble v British Coal *(British Coal Corporation v Keeble [1997] IRLR 336)* years ago said when you're looking at extending the time limit on the basis of just and equitable, look at the factors in s33 of the Limitation Act - the reasons for the delay, what steps are taken to get legal advice, and so forth - and Underhill LJ, in this case, warns us to be careful not to treat that as any kind of checklist.

What you should really do is go back to the wording of s123 Equality Act 2010, which is: take into account the circumstances which might render it to be just and equitable to extend time, and look at all the factors in the particular case, including the length of and reasons for the delay, but there is a broad general discretion. So you don't have to go through the checklist of s33 factors. The key things that tribunals will be looking at are the length of delay, the reasons for the delay, and whether there's been any prejudice to the respondent.

Daniel Barnett
Under detriment rules, discrimination rules and unlawful deduction rules, there's a concept of acts extending over a period, which means that if there've been a number of consecutive detriments, which are acts that extend over a period or acts of discrimination extending over a period or unlawful deductions extending over a period, you can take the trigger date for time limit purposes within which a claim has to be lodged as being the last of those dates. How do you actually know, though, if an act extends over a period?

Rebecca Tuck
I think that this is one of the areas which creates litigation risk whenever you've got a set of facts in front of you. The leading

case is still the Court of Appeal judgment in Hendricks v the Metropolitan Police *(Hendricks v Metropolitan Police Commissioner [2002] EWCA Civ 1686)* from years ago. And it says that you look at all the circumstances. In Hendricks they said it was a discriminatory environment. So even though you had a very long time period involving different places and different people, they were looking at the overarching environment within the respondent. And I think that there is a whole array of ways people can look at this issue. And then to some extent, it depends on the underlying merits of the claims as to whether tribunals are willing to say, well, yes, that's an act extending over a time. So on some specific issues, like suspension, there is authority. We know that suspension acts over a period, we know that sometimes there are decisions that are made that have got lasting effects. Say you haven't got a promotion, the decision is made on the date that you're told you haven't got the promotion and while that is an act with lasting consequences, time will run from the date of the decision.

In any set of circumstances you must consider factors such as whether the same people are involved? Are the acts of a similar nature? But there's a great deal of discretion there.

Ed Jenneson
Does a grievance extend time? For example, if harassment has taken place in January, and a grievance is raised in February, will time run from the harassment in January? Or can it be extended by the grievance in February?

Rebecca Tuck
The short answer is for a claimant it is always safer to the time limit as running from the act that you have complained about. The grievance is not going to extend the time period. If a claimant has missed that primary limitation period, the fact of having raised a grievance is a relevant factor in a just and equitable extension, not least because you can say well, the respondent hasn't suffered the

prejudice of having to investigate a stale claim, because they were investigating it at the time. They know all about it. But the short answer is no, it's not going to operate to extend time.

Jamie Anderson

Aside from the prejudice on the specific facts of a case, what's the best argument against a just and equitable extension that actually works for respondents?

Rebecca Tuck

That is the $64,000 question, isn't it? I'd love to know what Jamie thinks the answer to that is! I mean, I always think that if the claimants have got knowledge of the fact that they can go to a tribunal, and that there are time limits to operate, I think that that is very relevant. And when you're looking at the prejudice to the parties, I think that whether or not it is expressed out loud - because frequently it isn't - I think a claimant will suffer less prejudice from losing a weak claim, and more prejudice from losing a strong claim. But tribunals can be very wary about weighing that up before they've had a full exploration of the facts. For a respondent, you'd always want to say, well, they're not losing a great deal anyway! Trade union membership is very relevant because then they're taken to have had access to legal advice that will include advice on time limits. I think really you're juggling a lot of balls or platting in a lot of threads here and bringing them all together to create this entire picture. They know that they've got a cause of action. They know all the facts that make up the cause of action. They could have put it in earlier, and they should have put it in earlier.

Daniel Barnett

I sometimes find when I'm arguing about prejudice or lack of prejudice, that tribunals take a very inconsistent approach. So for example, if a respondent says we're prejudiced because the delay means that one of our key witnesses has left employment, some employment judges will say that's a pretty knockout point and they won't extend time. And some judges will say,

well, you can always witness summons them, can't you? What's the problem? Is that your experience as well? Is it really licking your finger holding it up in the air and not knowing what's going to happen?

Rebecca Tuck

It's another one, which is very much an art rather than a science. And it's why you've got such litigation risk around any area where there is an exercise of discretion. Yes, I agree with you.

Mark Irlam

What's the biggest mistake you see with time limits committed by claimants?

Rebecca Tuck

Well, one has just been raised in the first question we had. I think that claimants can often think that a grievance is going to operate to extend the time limit. And then you end up with people saying, well, the way in which the grievance was dealt with was discriminatory. And that's often a much weaker argument, because you end up alleging that the employer would have dealt with a grievance from a man in a more favourable way than the grievance from a woman (or a grievance from somebody who's got a different protected characteristic). So I think that the operation of appeals and grievances can lead to mistakes. Listen carefully to Andy Short, because as the *Adedeji* case itself shows, the complexity that is introduced by the ACAS early conciliation process has created a lot of mistakes for claimants. This is especially the case if the name on the certificate is wrong, so somebody has obtained a second certificate. What does that do with the time limit for the first claim? So that has created a great deal of confusion, I think.

Daniel Barnett

I find as well that something claimants often get wrong is linked to grievances - it's the appeal against dismissal. Claimants often think that putting in an appeal against dismissal means that the time limit won't start running until after the appeal is dealt with, which of course, is totally wrong in most cases. It might be a good reason for just and equitable extension in discrimination claims, but it's very, very rarely enough to get an extension in an unfair dismissal claim.

Rebecca Tuck

Yes. And then do you have the concept of vanishing dismissals? We know that we don't have that in discrimination law, it will still be a detriment, but in terms of unfair dismissal, if the appeal is successful, and they're reinstated, you have got this vanishing dismissal. So yes, it can be difficult for claimants. But if in doubt, put the claim in. And if your appeal is successful, you can always withdraw the claim.

Leszek Werenowski

In an unfair dismissal claim, where the three-month limit is passed, how strong would a depression-based reason need to be?

Rebecca Tuck

The test here, of course, is was it reasonably practicable to put the claim in earlier? If you're relying on depression, you'd certainly want to see some medical evidence. You'd want to see statements about how people are dealing with their day-to-day affairs and what impact the depression has had on that, in order to try and show that it wasn't reasonably practicable to have done it earlier. A short answer is it would really have to be very significant depression.

Daniel Barnett

I think it also helps if the claimant can show that they've suffered from depression over the entire three-month period, not just in the last couple of weeks.

Rebecca Tuck

Yes, because otherwise, you get judges just saying you shouldn't have left until the end of the period. I always think that the difficulty with this is what changed to enable them then to put the claim in when they did? Because if they're still suffering from that serious depression in months four and five but they put the claim in,

then that suggests to me that the depression hasn't prevented them putting the claim in, and they could have done it in month two or three.

Gillian Howard

What do employment judges now consider is just and equitable to allow a claim from a claimant where that claim would otherwise be out of time?

Rebecca Tuck

Short delay, with a good reason, where you can show that the respondent has suffered very little prejudice. If they've been investigating it all anyway, because there's been a grievance, then they're going to have difficulty showing that there's prejudice. And if the respondent is saying after month four, well, memories fade, whereas it would all be much fresher at month three, then the claimant's going to be on a good submission there.

Anonymous

If a claimant's still within time limits for submitting a claim, is it better for the claimant to submit a second claim and ask that the claims be joined? Or is it better to submit an application to amend the first claim?

Daniel Barnett

I'm going to add a third option there: Or does it not make the slightest bit of difference?

Rebecca Tuck

When you make the application to amend, the tribunal determine that application on the date that it goes in front of them. Whereas if you put the new claim in, it's on the date that you put the new claim in. So if you've got a choice on the third of March to put in a new claim or to put in an application to amend, if you put in a new claim, you're looking at the three months before the third of March. If you put in an application to amend on the third of March, and it's determined by the tribunal on the third of June, then they'll apply the time limit as of the date of the application, which I think creates some unfairness, particularly with the delays in the tribunal system. But that's what Galilee v Commissioner of Police for The Metropolis (*Galilee v The Commissioner of Police of The Metropolis [2018] ICR 634*) suggests tribunals do. So actually, I think that in many ways, it's more straightforward and you're on firmer ground if you just put the new claim in and then ask for them to be consolidated.

Anonymous
How relevant are gaps in time between acts when trying to establish continuous discrimination?

Daniel Barnett
There's the very nasty judgement of Mr Justice Langstaff in the EAT unlawful deduction from wages claims here, isn't there?

Rebecca Tuck
As a general answer to that, you want as few gaps in time as possible, or you want some kind of regularity to try and show a pattern, to show that it's an act extending over a period, because they are neat for tribunals and lay members to understand. And if you've got massive gaps, then that would suggest that it's not a continuing act. It's a distinct act. But as you've just alluded to, in the context of unlawful deduction from wages, we've still got the judgment of *Bear Scotland*, (*Bear Scotland Ltd v Fulton and another [2015] ICR 221*), which says that if there's been a gap of more than three months, then the previous deductions are going to be out of time, which a lot of people think is problematic and were surprised that that point didn't go further. But I'm sure that that point is going to be raised at the appellate courts at some point.

John Halson
If there's been a dismissal and then an appeal, and both are alleged to be discriminatory, does time run from the dismissal date or the appeal date?

Rebecca Tuck
Well, that is one where you would say that this is a continuing act between the dismissal and the appeal. If both are said to be discriminatory, then I think you've got pretty good grounds for saying that this is an act extending over a period, and you go from the date of the appeal. But with all of these things, if in doubt, take time as running from the earlier act. Quite often though, we look at these issues with hindsight, where we're doing the best we can with the facts that the lay clients presented to us.

Daxa Patel
What type of typical reasons have been accepted for out of time claims in the past?

Daniel Barnett
You don't say whether you're asking in connection with the not reasonably practicable test or the just and equitable test, so I'll throw them both at Rebecca.

Rebecca Tuck
With the practicable test, one jokingly used to say that basically, you've got to have been in a coma in hospital for the whole three months before it was not going to have been reasonably practicable to have put a claim in. So that test is very definitely much tougher. In relation to the just and equitable extension and what reasons have been accepted, I mean, how long is a piece of string? And that's why so many of us love employment law, because the reasons that clients come up with are as wide-ranging and broad as you can possibly imagine. If you can think of any reason for somebody not doing something, it has been before a tribunal at some point.

Mike Clyne
What's the longest time extension you've known, and what were the reasons?

Rebecca Tuck
There is a reported case - and I can't remember what it's called, it's from a few years ago - but somebody was nine years out of time in a discrimination case. And it was because she'd gone for a promotion, and she'd always thought that it was a bit dodgy that the white bloke got it rather than the

black woman. But nine years after the event, she discovered documentation that had been hidden from her deliberately. And when she got that documentation, it made good her claim, and so she brought it, and the appellate court said yes, it's just and equitable to extend that time limit. So nine years. (postscript – see below: (*London Borough of Southwark v Afolabi [2003] EWCA Civ 15*).)

Romana Caneti
If an employer fails to deal with a grievance, does that extend time from the act complained of because the failure to deal with the grievance is another act by the respondent?

Daniel Barnett
Is it that the claimant addresses this as an admission to deal properly with a grievance and the relevant time limit is three months from the date when the employer ought reasonably to have been expected to deal with a grievance because that's how tribunals address time limits for admissions?

Rebecca Tuck
Yes, it is, but also beware because claimants often end up running weaker arguments about there being discrimination from HR and how things have been dealt with, because they're out of time for the real substance of their issue, which is the treatment they have received, for example, from co-workers. So be wary about spoiling really good, strong claims with the weaker claims of it being a conspiracy and everybody's dealing with me in a discriminatory way.

Daniel Barnett
The next two questions are about time limits for lodging ET3 response forms, rather ET1s.

Sam Bearman
In relation to a respondent can the excuse of 'the employment tribunal didn't send the ET1 form to the correct department' be a just and equitable reason for having the claim's ET1 form vacated under Rule 20 of the employment tribunal procedural rules?

Daniel Barnett
Rule 20 is the rule about extending time in employment tribunals. Can Rule 20 be a reason for extending the normal 28-day limit for an ET3 if the employment tribunal sent the ET1 form to the incorrect department?

Rebecca Tuck
The approach that tribunals take to the submissions of ET3s is much more generous than the approach to getting in the ET1. the tribunal have got a great deal more discretion for extending time, and as you've seen, under Rule 20, if the respondent explains the delay, then they will get extra time for putting in the ET3. I've seen quite a lot of this in the last 12 months because people have been instructed to work from home and therefore post in offices hasn't been checked nearly as regularly as it ordinarily would be, or ET envelopes have been going to the wrong part of the business and have taken much longer to feed through because of the COVID restrictions. And tribunals are granting extensions for the presentation of those ET3. If a remedy hearing has been scheduled, because it's been taken that there has been no ET3, you've just got to apply to have the default judgment which has been entered set aside, explain the reasons why you didn't get the ET3 in, attach the draft ET3 to that application and say that a full merits hearing is needed in the case.

Daniel Barnett
Sally Robertson has just commented that the case you mentioned where there was a nine-year delay and time was extended was the case of Afolabi v Southwark London Borough Council (*London Borough of Southwark v Afolabi [2003] EWCA Civ 15*).

Anonymous
What reasons should a respondent give when presenting a response out of time?

Rebecca Tuck
Honest and full reasons. The pandemic has caused a great deal of delay and difficulty in this regard, just because people are quite

rightly not working from their offices. And so that has been relied upon very heavily, quite properly. Also, if a respondent has received the ET1 and it's only three or four days before the deadline, then put in the application to extend time as soon as possible and say, rather than having had this in our possession for 28 days, we've only had it for three days. Can we have an extra two weeks, please?

Su Apps
As an employer, if you need an extension of time to submit a response, how do you deal with the fact that often applications aren't dealt with by tribunals until after the time limit's expired? Is the only option to put in a holding ET3? And if so, do you then need to change the application for an extension of time into an application to amend?

Rebecca Tuck
I think counsel of perfection would say put in the application for additional time and mark it urgent. If you don't get a response by the deadline, then put in the holding ET3 and say: we made an application to extend time. This is the holding ET3. We're investigating it. We are proposing to defend the claims and we'll put in a full response within X days. And then when the tribunal gets the full response, it can say, yes, time was extended in that regard. What the tribunal really wants to see here, in my opinion, is that the respondent is engaging. And that's going to prevent the duty judge who's got a huge pile of files from just issuing default judgments. They want to see engagement.

Adriana Pantaleon
In light of Uber's case *(Uber BV and others v Aslam and others [2021] UKSC 5)*, people in the gig economy industry would like to bring claims, but they're out of time. Because of the judgement, I think they have a reasonable reason for time to be extended. Would it?

Daniel Barnett
She makes the point that claims could be redundancy and unfair dismissal - although I'm

not sure that's right under the Uber judgment - I think the claims are more likely to be minimum wage and holiday pay.

Rebecca Tuck
They are and they are the reasonable practicability tests. I don't know whether the delegates on this call watched the House of Commons emergency question on Uber. I cringed my way through about 20 minutes of it, screaming at the MPs that they really need to know the difference between workers and employees, because they clearly don't! These people haven't got unfair dismissal claims. But the test is reasonable practicability, and our system of common law doesn't change the law, it clarifies what the law has always been. So I think that it's going to be difficult for people who are no longer in those gig economy jobs - and haven't been for three months - to bring claims. If they're still engaged, of course, then there will be ongoing omissions on the parts of those engaging the workers.

Jason Braier
In respect of Equality Act claims, what strategic view do you take on whether to apply for a preliminary hearing - so as to ask the tribunals to decide time issues early - or whether to hold back on time points until the full hearing?

Rebecca Tuck
That's a really good question, and it's always a tricky one. If the time point is going to knock out the need to investigate a whole load of really quite stale stuff, then you want to have a go at it early on. When the tribunal are deciding whether they'll grant you the PH on time, one of the things they'll be balancing is how much time a one-day PH would save off a substantive hearing. So if you can say, well, the substantive hearing will be 10 days, whereas you've got a one day PH, and if successful the final hearing will only be a couple of days, then you're more likely get to get the tribunal to grant that. And the other side of the coin is that if you've got an employer who has dealt impeccably with a whole load of grievances

early on in the chronology, and then it looks like the employer has become exasperated at an employee and they've dealt less well with the later incidents, you might not want the PH on time because you want the tribunal to follow the pattern that the employer has had, and to make all their findings of fact on the beautifully dealt with early chronology and be a bit more forgiving on the later allegations. So, I think you have to really look at the underlying merits and the strength of your evidence for the underlying case in order to make that call.

Peter
Please explain how ACAS can extend early conciliation timeframes and for how long?

Rebecca Tuck
I think that's for Andy Short QC, and I think there's been a change. They've changed it to an automatic six-week conciliation period.

Daniel Barnett
You can no longer get extensions. It used to be four weeks with the possibility of some extra time, now at six weeks with no extension at all. So the answer is they can't.

Julie Norris
For an act to be a continuing act, must there be three months between each act of discrimination in the chain?

Rebecca Tuck
Consider the *Bear Scotland* case. But that's in the context, of course, of a series of unlawful deductions where you might expect some regularity. And I think with discrimination, there is much more flexibility. So for example, if somebody from the US parent company visits once every six months, and every time they visit, they're sexually harassing someone, a tribunal would be very sympathetic in saying that's a course of conduct.

David Curwen
What's the rationale for having two different tests for time limits?

Daniel Barnett
Let's go back and ask Parliament in 1975, shall we?

Rebecca Tuck
We're stuck with what Parliament tell us.

Daniel Barnett
Nobody knows. It's just one of those weird things. It's nothing to do with European law or is it?

Rebecca Tuck
No, I don't think it is. Because we had just and equitable in the original *Sex Discrimination Act 1975*.

Julie Norris
Many employers, especially NHS trusts, can take six months to deal with a grievance on a good day. Given that the parties are encouraged to reduce the burden on tribunals by trying to settle a dispute, shouldn't time limits be reformed so the grievance or an appeal extends time automatically? Because otherwise, delay by a respondent helps the respondents case.

Rebecca Tuck
I think what you often see in these cases is the claimant and putting in the claim and the respondent putting in a response saying can we have a stay until we finish our internal processes? Now query whether - with the time it's taking tribunals to get things on - a formal application for a stay is needed now or whether you just need generous directions before you get to a substantive hearing. But the practical answer to that right now is put your ET1 in and say, but I'm happy for it to be stayed or happy to give them extra time until my internal processes are concluded.

Anonymous
If a sneaky employer decides to add the tribunal time limits into their grievance policy, would that give them a good argument to say claims can't be presented out of time Because

they've made the claimant aware of time limits early?

Rebecca Tuck

It's a relevant factor. Somebody very definitely knowing what the tribunal time limits are is a relevant factor. So I think that that would help employers.

Anonymous

Is it likely to make a difference where the gaps in time are due to the workplace closing for lockdown?

Rebecca Tuck

Yes. That will be a relevant matter. But if somebody has been out of the workplace now for 12 months, that's a very significant gap. I can see litigation coming on this issue, actually. It's an interesting point. I mean, I suppose it's similar to my example of somebody from the parent company coming every six months: the fact is, every time I see this particular person, they harass or discriminate against me. There was a gap because I was working from home where that didn't happen, but it happened before and it happened after. You can see the arguments that are going to be made on both sides of that.

Hannah

How do partisan judges best manage claims involving a long history of complaints?

Daniel Barnett

So I think she's referring to an ET1 that has 755 different allegations of discrimination within it, all over a long period of time.

Rebecca Tuck

Vivienne Gay has now retired. She was my Regional Employment Judge when I first became a fee paid judge. She was a great fan of trying to get claimants to take their six best points. And we've had EAT authority on the extent to which tribunals can case manage, and they can't force this. But I think there's a great deal to be said for Vivienne's approach, because if you're not going to get home on your six best points, you're not going to get home at all. And if you get home on your six best points, then is that not going to get you the remedy that you need? And we do have HHJ Tucker in a recent EAT judgment *(C v D [2020] UKEAT/0132/19)* asking us all to be concise in our pleadings. So as advisors, just take your best points.

Daniel Barnett

Thank you very much, Rebecca Tuck QC.

TRIBUNAL PROCEDURE
JUDE SHEPHERD, 42 BEDFORD ROW

Daniel Barnett

I'm joined today by Jude Shepherd from 42 Bedford Row, and she'll be answering questions on employment tribunal procedure.

Jude Shepherd, good afternoon. A couple of questions from me, if you wouldn't mind. First of all, something that I get asked a lot - and I seem to change my mind every five minutes on this one - can a claimant speak to the press when litigation is going on?

Jude Shepherd

Yes, they can. I suppose the more interesting question is whether it's advisable for them to do so. My experience is that it's rarely a good idea. Given the potential pitfalls, I usually advise clients against it if at all possible. Claimants will often think it's a good idea to try and exert pressure or think they'll get a lot of interest in their side of the story. But obviously, once you speak to a journalist, you then have no control over how the story is portrayed in the media, but there's no rule against speaking to the press.

Particular care needs to be taken about speaking to the press during the currency of an actual hearing, particularly a final hearing when evidence is being given. That's amply demonstrated by what happened to Miss Chidzoy in her claim against the BBC *(Chidzoy v BBC UKEAT/0097/17/BA)*. Miss Chidzoy, who was a journalist herself, was overheard discussing her case with a journalist during a comfort break, despite having been warned - as witnesses always are - before the break by the judge that she shouldn't discuss her evidence

with anybody, not just journalists, because she remained under oath. And unfortunately for her, she was overheard. The BBC brought that to the tribunal's attention and applied for her claim to be struck out. And the tribunal acceded to that application, essentially, finding that she discussed what she'd been asked in cross-examination that morning with the journalist. They effectively found that trust in her was irreparably damaged and that a fair trial was no longer possible. You've got to be very careful about what happens during the course of the hearing. The EAT found that the tribunal were entirely entitled to reach those conclusions. So there's a potentially high price to pay. I always say it's better to keep your powder dry until litigation is over.

Daniel Barnett

While you were talking about that, you actually reminded me of a case we did against each other two or three years ago now in the EAT, where I very embarrassingly had to turn up - I think it was after lunch - and tell the EAT that my client had told me that while we were all having breakfast in Pret a Manger that morning, and I was telling my client about why I thought she had a lousy appeal, one of the wing members was standing right next to us. We were totally unaware it was the wing member. The wing member claimed not to have heard a word that we said.

Jude Shepherd

I do remember that now, yes. Well, there you are. There are pitfalls everywhere.

Daniel Barnett

What about phone recordings? We often have this problem in tribunals. Can a phone recording be used, even if one side didn't tell the other side at the time of the conversation that the call was being recorded?

Jude Shepherd

This is something that comes up a lot more nowadays because it's so easy to make covert recordings. The answer is probably yes. Tribunals do still take a dim view of covert recordings. It's not done, really, to record people without their knowledge. But the reality is that more often than not, tribunals will allow them to be used. So there's no rule that says that evidence that's either been unlawfully or improperly obtained is automatically excluded. There was a civil road traffic claim - the beautifully named Mustard v Flower and others *(Mustard v Flower & Ors [2019] EWHC 2623 (QB))* - where the question of covert recordings was considered. And in that case, the judge said that essentially what's required is that the tribunal, or the court in that case, considers the means that have been employed to obtain the evidence together with its relevance and probative value, and the effect that admitting or not admitting it would have on the fairness of the litigation process. And the tribunal has to balance those factors and consider with regard to the overriding objective whether to admit it or exclude it.

Broadly, if it's really just a case of an employee having recorded a meeting with a manager or something along those lines, more often than not that will be admitted. The position is rather different if a party seeks to covertly record private deliberation. So you sometimes get this situation where somebody will leave their phone in their coat pocket when they're sent out of the room for a disciplinary panel to decide whether they should be dismissed or not. That is rather different because of the public policy considerations as to an adjudicatory panel or body being able to speak freely. So, often you will have more

success excluding that kind of evidence from a hearing. Although often it will depend on what's being said. So if, for example, during that recording, somebody says something discriminatory, or there is clear evidence that there's something fishy going on, that will potentially lead the tribunal to say that it's relevant and probative value outweighs the public policy reasons for excluding it.

Daniel Barnett

When Jude refers to rules during her answers, for anybody who's not familiar with them, she's referring to schedule one of the Employment Tribunals (Constitution and Rules of Procedure) Regulations 2013, in which the majority of the tribunal rules are set out.

Natalie White

What's the most common mistake that employers make when responding to claims?

Jude Shepherd

Gosh, that's an interesting question. I would say respond to the claim that is made. So often what you'll see in ET3s is that respondents don't stick to the point and that they will ramble on about things. What the tribunal wants to see is a response to the claim. Something that's sometimes frustrating for me when acting for respondents is that respondents will anticipate what a claimant might be trying to say or might want to claim and they'll plead to it, even when it isn't pleaded. On behalf of a respondent, you then get to a hearing where there's then a debate about what's pleaded on the claimant's case, whether there's an indirect discrimination claim or something along those lines. And I'll merrily be saying this isn't on the face of the claim form; the claimant would have to amend. To which the judge then says, well, Miss Shepherd, your client's pleaded to it in your ET3, which the client has done as an abundance of caution, but actually, you really don't need to do. It's a bit like exams: look at the question, answer the question and stick to that point. Don't be too verbose because it might actually get you into difficulties later down the line.

Daniel Barnett
That's a good point. There are three others, I come across quite a lot. Failing to take time limit points is quite a common problem employers have; failing to deal with the little claims - so you might stress the unfair dismissal, but you'll forget about the holiday pay or the breach of contract claim - and the biggest, biggest, biggest mistake that employers make is missing the 28-day time limit or forgetting to ask for an extension of time. That can cause all sorts of problems. Jude, do you have any others to add to that list?

Jude Shepherd
The time limit points is a good one. You should forensically look at every aspect of the claim and think, where is my line of attack here? And that often isn't done. Respondents often get hung up on other matters. But you should have a bit of a checklist of looking at time limit points and any points that you can plead to because particularly if you've got litigants in person, it won't always be obvious on the face of the claim form what claims are being made. So, for example, there might be a holiday pay claim just tucked away in the claim there in one line. You need to make sure that you've looked carefully through it before you plead your response.

Penelope Douglass
As I am not a solicitor, I know I can't claim costs in an employment tribunal. But what sort of things can I claim for under a wasted costs order?

Jude Shepherd
You'll see from the rules that the rules relating to wasted costs orders are quite different to the notion of simply a costs order being applied for. So, what you have to have is improper, unreasonable or negligent conduct on the part of a representative on the other side.

You would be making an application for any costs thrown away by that conduct. So it's a very specific situation. It doesn't come up very often. I can probably count on one hand the number of times I've been in a position to make a wasted costs application against a representative on the other side. So it isn't an alternative to a costs application, in that sense. It is very specifically a type of costs order all of its own.

Daniel Barnett
As you were answering that I was wondering whether the question was actually referring to a preparation time order.

Jude Shepherd
I wondered that too.

Daniel Barnett
You can see that at rule 79.

Jude Shepherd
Obviously, if you're conducting a case on your own part and you're not a lawyer, you can, of course, make an application for a preparation time order because you're not incurring legal costs, but you are spending time preparing the claim. That's considered on the same basis as a costs order in respect of legal costs. I think the current limit is something like £33 or £34 an hour for the amount of costs that you might incur. But it's considered on the same basis as a costs order otherwise.

D Ross
Is it possible to observe employment tribunals remotely at the moment?

Jude Shepherd
Yes, very much so. Assuming that it's a public hearing. Obviously, if it's a closed preliminary hearing, you won't be able to. If it's a trial, you can indeed dial in to the hearing and observe it in the same way that you would be able just to pop to the back of a tribunal ordinarily and observe it. I've done many remote hearings where we've just had observers popping in and out of the hearing without difficulty.

Rachel Hancock
Will the UK Supreme Court have the right to depart from European law, such as the working time regulations?

Jude Shepherd
We are still dealing with the European laws that we have. So we will still be applying the working time regulations in respect of holiday pay claims, and so on and so forth, as the law stands at the moment.

Pam Connell
How much leeway do small employers get as respondent in an ET?

Daniel Barnett
I'm not sure whether the question is about leeway in terms of procedure, or leeway in terms of having acted really awfully as an employer.

Jude Shepherd
It does rather depend on the circumstances. So if you're looking, for example, at an unfair dismissal claim, and the process that you might have followed, the tribunal are entitled to look at the size of your organisation and the reasons why you might have followed a slightly different process than if you'd had more extensive resources and human resources, and so on and so forth. So I suppose to that extent, they will take account of the fact that you're a small employer and you've only got a limited amount of resource open to you. But I wouldn't say that they necessarily give you leeway. Certainly, from a procedural point of view, the rules will be applied to small employers as they will be to large employers. It depends on the circumstances and what you'd like leeway on, I suppose, and the reasons behind it. If it is a question of you simply not having the resource to, for example, be able to respond in a timely fashion to a claim that's been brought and seeking an extension, that might be a material reason why the tribunal would give you an extension. But otherwise, unfortunately, as a small employer, you are nevertheless subject to the same rules of procedure as a large employer is.

Toni Evans
If an employee is a repeat offender at bringing claims against their various employers, can you raise this at an employment tribunal?

Jude Shepherd
This is a very interesting question because it is something that comes up in a fair number of claims that I deal with. You will often find that a claimant has indeed brought claims before. You have to tread very carefully. A claimant may well say, well, it's not my fault that I've just had lots of really terrible previous employers. I'm entitled to bring claims and as long as I'm not a vexatious litigant, then what relevance can that possibly have?

So you do need to be careful. Tribunals will not be quick to judge a claimant on previous litigation. Obviously, there are rules and it's very difficult to establish that a litigant is vexatious in the true meaning of the word. But that said, if there are a lot of previous claims brought in a very similar fashion, on similar facts, and you think that the claim brought against your employer is indeed vexatious, then as long as you do it carefully, that may well be evidence that might be helpful to you before the tribunal.

Daniel Barnett
Back in the late 2000s, there was a man - I forget his name - who was reported in the Sunday Times as being a serial age discrimination claimant. He used to apply for jobs where the adverts said things like 'we want someone who's young and vivacious' - whatever the adjectives might be - and then he'd try and extort £2,000 or £3,000 pounds from the company. Someone who did the maths actually worked out that he'd earned about £400,000 through that extortion in the course of about two years. He was slapped with a serial litigant order, which stopped him

doing it. But yeah, I always thought that was a great business idea.

Jude Shepherd
I think there definitely are a few of those litigants out there who might make a bit of a career out of it. They're the exception rather than the norm, I would say, but, yes, it's certainly a thing.

Melanie Pimenta
Do you see hearings becoming heard remotely becoming the norm after COVID 19?

Jude Shepherd
Yes, very much so. I would think that certainly in respect of what we would call fast track hearings - Wages Act claims, things that can be dealt with relatively easily in a short hearing that might have some live evidence, but some fairly straightforward evidence - and certainly for preliminary hearings, both open and closed hearings that might have a limited amount of live evidence. I just don't see how the tribunals can turn away from it now that they've got structure in place. Telephone hearings, for example, have become very popular. When I started in practice, I'd have to schlep up to Leeds for a one-hour hearing. It seems nonsensical. Those days are gone. And CVP has only added to the convenience of that.

That said, I'm sure that once lockdown is over and we go back to some normality, the lengthier hearings, the discrimination claims, which are being done remotely at the moment to some extent, I think they won't stay remote because it's not ideal. It is difficult to cross-examine. There are drawbacks, and there are difficulties with doing those kinds of complex cases remotely. I'm sure that we will see those happen in person, but for other fast track hearings, I think CVP is definitely here to stay.

I like the fact that I don't have to commute and I can wear my slippers during the course of a hearing. I do find them tiring and I'm not massively keen on cross-examining remotely.

I've done a lot of it, but I would prefer to do that in a live tribunal situation. But it's definitely here to stay, I think.

Jamie Feldman
At what stage do the pleadings become publicly available documents? Can a member of the press get a copy of a recently filed ET1?

Jude Shepherd
I don't honestly know the answer to that. I don't think that the press could simply apply to the tribunal to be provided with a copy of the pleadings. But once you get to the hearing stage and there is a copy of the bundle, then they can certainly look at the documents in the bundle. I think the tribunal would be reluctant to provide copies of the pleadings right from the get go. But in all honesty, I don't know the answer to that.

Daniel Barnett
I think the answer actually changed probably about 15 years ago now because the tribunal rules were amended to remove the register so that members of the public couldn't find out who was suing whom and get their details. And the reason for that change was because there was a certain well-known large employment consultancy that was contacting all of the named respondents to any claims that were filed, claiming to be associated with Acas and offering to represent them. The DTI, as it was, thought that was improper, couldn't do much about it, and so just stopped the register, which included the details of the parties, becoming public. And if the register is not public, it follows the ET1 and ET3 aren't.

Jude Shepherd
Yes. Wasn't that around the same time that they required employment consultants to become registered and so on and so forth? There were various measures taken at that point in time, so yes, that rings a bell.

Ed Jenneson
How much detail should a respondent include in the ET3? I'm conscious that it shouldn't

read like a witness statement. What's actually required?

Daniel Barnett
The EAT said something on this recently, didn't they?

Jude Shepherd
Pleadings should be concise. I have to say that I'm a little bit guilty whenever I draft a response of possibly erring on including more rather than less. But it's true to say that it is a pleading, so it shouldn't be a witness statement, it shouldn't contain loads of evidence, it should, as I said earlier, respond to the claim that is made, and put forward the legal defence that you are making. So you shouldn't include a lot of evidence in it and it should be as clear and concise as possible. It's a grey area because it is difficult when we're dealing with employment tribunal claims. The reality is, particularly if you get litigants in person where extensive points are raised in the claim, it's natural for a respondent to want to respond to those points. There's a balance to be struck, I think. You don't want to be too concise because you don't want to be in the position of being told that you haven't pleaded a point later down the line. So, yes, of course, being concise is important, but make sure that you've covered all of the relevant points that are in the claim.

Anonymous
Have you got any experience of judicial assessment? Is it ever used and is it worthwhile?

Daniel Barnett
Just before you answer that question, we do have quite a lot of employment judges watching these webinars, so it might be an employment judge asking you this question.

Jude Shepherd
I don't have a great deal of experience of judicial assessment being used. It's difficult to say because, of course, clearly claims are reviewed at an early stage by employment judges. That is why you often see an element of case management at an early stage, and you'll often see a case being listed relatively early on, for example, for a PH on a jurisdictional point, which has clearly been picked up on the basis of an assessment. Have I ever seen a case being judicially assessed and struck out as a consequence of there being no jurisdiction in the tribunal, or there being poor prospects for success? No. I mean, I simply haven't seen that happen. That might be a measure of the types of work that I do and the types of cases that I'm instructed on. It may well be the case, for example, that there are cases for litigants in person who put in claims that simply don't have any foundation, that are judicially assessed and struck out. But my personal experience is that I don't think it's greatly used in the sense of getting rid of claims. They are certainly assessed in terms of early case management. Again, at the moment, that very much depends on your tribunal, how much resource there is and simply whether or not they have the capacity to be looking at claims in that level of detail to be able to case manage them early on, or whether that's left to the parties to draw things to the tribunal's attention once you get to a PH.

Melanie Bonas
How accommodating are employment tribunal judges when a respondent is defending themselves or acting with HR support when the knowledge of the employer or the HR professional will be far less than that of the solicitor or barrister for the claimant?

Jude Shepherd
My experience is that employment judges are very accommodating and understand that it's not just claimants who appear as litigants in person. Obviously, as a barrister, more often than not my experience - certainly as a member of the bar - is that at least one party is represented. Of course, that's not the majority of claims that tribunals are dealing with. A very large proportion of the claims that tribunals deal with are relatively small

claims, for want of a better word, where both parties are unrepresented. Tribunal judges are well-practiced at dealing with cases in those circumstances and helping both parties navigate their way through the procedure and through the evidence and everything else. So, I wouldn't be concerned that you're not going to get a fair hearing from an employment judge if you're unrepresented as a respondent, because you will.

Mike Clyne

Do you see any indication of tribunals returning to their original aims of being a simple forum to resolve employment disputes?

Jude Shepherd

I think those days are long gone following all of the legislation that we've had in recent years. It is a fact now that employment law is a very complex area of law. And when the tribunals were first brought about, employment law was a lot more simplistic. There were very few specialist employment law practitioners. I don't see a return to that. There's a lot of talk at the moment about reforms and how the tribunal system goes forward. Of course, there's an argument for making things as simple as possible, but I don't think we can, for example, return to the days when it was essentially designed that parties weren't represented. Although, see my response to the last question, which is that nevertheless a lot of the cases that are heard and tribunals are still unrepresented parties, but the complexities of the law are such that we're always going to need a forum that deals with complex claims, it seems to me.

D Ross

If a witness is on annual leave, and not available to attend, can they enforce somebody's attendance? And if not, what happens with the ET dates?

Daniel Barnett

Presumably 'they' means the party or the tribunal.

Jude Shepherd

Yes, they can be forced to attend. So you can apply for a witness order. I mean, obviously, where respondents have got to call employees to give evidence and it clashes with an employee's annual leave, then you would hope that you would know about that at the points at which you were fixing the case for trial. Normally, you'd be able to submit your dates to avoid. The difficulty is that if somebody later then books annual leave having known that they were going to be a witness - or I suppose if you suddenly decide you need somebody as a witness who you hadn't anticipated before, this might come up - that a tribunal will be not terribly sympathetic about taking a lengthy trial out of the list just to accommodate somebody's holiday to Tenerife. So that's a difficult one. It probably wouldn't be grounds for an adjournment of the entire trial. And if your employee's objecting to it, yes, indeed, you could seek a witness order for them. But that's a tricky one to navigate as an employer, as opposed to as a party.

Neil Coombes

Almost all respondents will threaten a claimant with costs at some point, hiding behind without prejudice save as to costs. Is there any way a claimant can argue this is unreasonable conduct in the carrying out of the proceedings?

Jude Shepherd

I would only ever advise my respondent clients to put a claimant on a cost warning if there were indeed good grounds to do so and they were thinking further down the line that they would indeed make an application for costs, rather than it just being an empty threat. But respondents who do make those empty threats and do it in an oppressive way - which is something that you do have to be very careful of with cost warnings, as a respondent - if they cross that line, then there is the potential of arguing that it is unreasonable conduct. And I suppose it depends upon the impact that it has as to where that will take you. I suppose it has to be a fairly oppressive approach and perhaps repeated warnings for you then to make that point before the tribunal in order for it to tip over into an unreasonable conduct is a fairly high bar. But yes, it's not impossible if you've got a particularly aggressive respondent to put them back in their box.

Daniel Barnett

There was once a regional employment judge based out of Bristol, who developed a practice - and all the claimant lawyers knew this - of whenever a claimant wrote in and said, I've received a cost warning from the respondent, he would call that respondent lawyer in front of him and say, prove to me why I shouldn't land you with unreasonable conduct costs for trying to bully the claimant. And it effectively got rid of the practice of doing that in Bristol, which I think was a very smart move.

Jude Shepherd

I know exactly who you're talking about. And that particular regional judge, I think, has had a lasting impact on a number of ways in which lawyers conduct themselves on various issues. So a robust approach it was, but not necessarily a bad one. Yes, it's definitely had a lasting effect, I think.

Nick Hine

If an interim relief application is granted, is there a good argument for an expedited hearing, bearing in mind the fact the ex-employer is continuing to pay salary?

Jude Shepherd

Yes, there is, and tribunals will often try to accommodate hearing the case as soon as possible as a consequence, but it doesn't always happen. It depends upon the complexity of the case and how quickly it can be ready for trial. But yes, there definitely is an argument for that for a respondent. Obviously, it is an onerous thing to be paying a salary, particularly in circumstances where regardless of what the outcome of the trial is, that salary will not be recouped.

Anonymous

Do tribunals dislike subject access requests? Would you advise a claimant to make a subject access request, and if yes, at what stage should they do so?

Jude Shepherd

I wouldn't say that tribunals necessarily dislike SARs. I suspect they dislike so much talk about the ins and outs of the SARs, which you often see nowadays - huge amounts of correspondence and bickering over whether or not the SARs are complied with, and so on and so forth, which is generally just a complete distraction from what the real issues in a case are. So they probably dislike that. A SAR shouldn't be a replacement for the disclosure exercise. SARs have their place: they can be useful for a claimant who may be considering whether or not to bring a claim. But you shouldn't be repeatedly making SARs at the same time as going through a disclosure request as an alternative to that, because that simply shouldn't be necessary.

Anonymous

I have a preliminary hearing on disability status soon where the claimant has no medical evidence, just a disability impact statement. The employment judge has indicated her displeasure at the respondent calling witnesses to challenge the claimants position on disability. Do you have any views on that?

Jude Shepherd

Only that it would be unusual for the respondent to call evidence on a PH about disability, unless it's a slightly unique situation of the respondent having evidence to call into question the credibility of what the claimant says about their disability. Obviously, if that is an issue, and the respondent has evidence about it, then you probably would need to call witness evidence about it. But the judge is probably looking at this from the claimant's perspective. It's the claimant's disability - can she satisfy the relevant test under the

Equality Act? What the respondent may or may not say about it is not going to help the tribunal determine that point, unless they say, for example, she says she can't walk very far, but I have observed her skipping along doing X, Y and Z. So that's probably what the judge has in mind, I would think.

Daniel Barnett

My experience is that when respondents approach me with grainy video footage of somebody leaving their house and walking down to Tesco and coming back with a carrier bag and saying, "Ha! this disproves that they're suffering from depression," It never, ever does because the claimant will say - and a judge will accept - that (a) that was a good day, (b) my GP told me to get out the house if I possibly could. Respondents drastically overestimate the impact of something they might see on Facebook, or social media or anywhere on their ability to challenge the existence of a disability.

Jude Shepherd

I quite agree. I would say it's a very rare case where the respondent would have some relevant evidence to challenge. A claimant will inevitably say that for most disabilities, you're going to have good and bad days and I would say that most tribunals would take a dim view of that kind of evidence. It's probably not the best approach to defending a PH on disability. There are other better points you can probably make.

Daniel Barnett

One of the worst experiences I ever had was with someone who was representing somebody who was claiming to be disabled - claiming to be epileptic. And we were challenging it. It was in the very, very early days of the Disability Discrimination Act. I was cross-examining this claimant and accusing her of faking it, and she actually went into an epileptic fit in the witness box, which was absolutely horrible. We obviously conceded disability after that. Challenging disability

just rarely gets you anywhere I find. Focus on the merits of the case and prove you treated somebody less favourably for a reason not connected with a disability. That's how to win a disability claim.

Sharee Kitley

What's the probability of getting a claim struck out for continued non-compliance with orders? How sympathetic are tribunals towards non-complying parties?

Jude Shepherd

It's going to be very fact-specific. Obviously, it's a very draconian act to strike out for non-compliance of orders, but tribunals will do it if there is repeated non-compliance. As a respondent generally, you probably want to do it in stages. There's no point going in very early and saying they've not complied with the order for disclosure. I've tried to get them to disclose, but it's late, so please strike them out. That's probably not going to happen. But if they have repeatedly said that they won't comply, the best approach is to apply for an 'unless order' first of all. Ask the tribunal to make an unless order, and then you are going to have an easier job of persuading the tribunal. Given that the party knew what the potential consequences were of not complying, you'll have a better chance of striking out. It really will depend on the reasons for the non-compliance. If they really are just not progressing their claim, if they really are just ignoring the orders, then yes, there will come a point where the tribunal will say enough is enough. In my experience, it's rarely that straightforward. There's usually some backstory behind non-compliance and them saying that they have complied and it's you that's not complied, or something along those lines, and there's an argument to be out.

Gillian Howard

What do you need to put in a notice of appeal in order to persuade the EAT that an employment judge's decision is perverse?

Jude Shepherd

As we all know, perversity appeals are very tricky indeed. Again, they are going to be very fact-specific. But you're going to have to have some pretty clear points to be made for you not to get sifted based on them being findings of fact that the tribunal have made and the EAT just aren't going to interfere with them. It has to be that no reasonable tribunal could have reached that conclusion on the facts before them and you want some fairly punchy points as to why you're going to be able to establish that perversity appeal. Waffling on about why you don't agree with the outcome and why it seems jolly unreasonable to you is not going to get you home. But it is going to be very fact-specific. Perversity appeals rarely succeed for that reason. So, yes, be punchy and concise in your notice of appeal, if at all possible.

Daniel Barnett

Jude Shepherd from 42 Bedford Row, thank you.

UNFAIR DISMISSAL: CONDUCT
IMOGEN EGAN, OUTER TEMPLE CHAMBERS

Daniel Barnett

I'm joined by Imogen Egan from Outer Temple Chambers, and she'll be speaking on conduct dismissals.

Daniel Barnett

Imogen Egan, good morning. Let me start by asking you a couple of my own questions about conduct dismissals. A question that crops up from time to time is what happens if somebody has committed an act of misconduct outside of work, but not in the actual workplace. Can an employer fairly dismiss an employee for an act against another employee which takes place outside work if the police don't press charges due to a lack of evidence?

Imogen Egan

I think the answer is yes. But as with most of these questions, it's going to be fact-specific. So the starting point, the basic principle in the Acas code at paragraph 31, is that if an employee is charged with - or in this case, we know charges have been dropped or not pursued - or convicted of a criminal offence, that isn't normally in itself a reason for disciplinary action. You've got to give consideration to what effects this charge or conviction - or in this case, the incident - has on the employee's suitability to do the job and their relationships with their employer, work colleagues and customers. You've got to consider the nature of the offence, or the incident, so was it violent conduct? Was it dishonest? You've got to consider the nature of their work, so do they work in a position

of trust or with vulnerable service users, for example? You've got to consider the extent to which their work involves contact with other employees or the general public. And finally, you've got to consider the status of the employees, so, are they a public figure or particularly senior in the organisation?

Once you've assessed that and decided that you are going to institute formal proceedings, you've got to remember still that you've got to have a fair investigation and you've got to give them an opportunity to respond to the allegations against them at a disciplinary hearing. In this case, I think the fact that the police haven't decided to take it any further due to lack of evidence isn't determinative. It's important not to get too hung up on that because, of course, the standard of proof required is different in criminal proceedings and in workplace or employment law matters. So an employer only has to have a genuine belief in misconduct based on reasonable grounds following a reasonable investigation, rather than proof beyond reasonable doubt, which is required in criminal proceedings.

I think this is, in some ways, analogous to the scenario where an employee is charged but acquitted of an offence. We know from case law that disciplinary proceedings can properly be pursued, even where an employee has been acquitted of a criminal offence. That's the case of Saeed v Greater London Council (*Saeed v Greater London Council [1986] IRLR 23*). I think, really, it's the same kind of scenario here. If it's going to impact their work and their relationship with the employer, then it may be relevant for disciplinary investigation. Another angle is that in this case, it's involving a fellow employee, so you've got to consider their working relationship. Even if there's not provable misconduct, if their relationship has broken down to such an extent and you can't move this employee to another area of work, does it mean that then there's potential for some other substantial reason dismissal if there's a breakdown in the relationship? I think, possibly. So, yes, overall, but always investigate properly.

Daniel Barnett

Let's move to the other end of the spectrum: the director-level conduct issue. Is a failure by a director to disclose a conflict of interest an act of gross misconduct which can result in their service agreement or their employment contract being terminated without notice?

Imogen Egan

Again, it's a matter of specific facts. So I think potentially, yes, the director's statutory duties are set out under s175 Companies Act 2006. And that requires them to disclose any conflict of interest. Assuming that there are no express terms in the contract on this issue, a serious failure might be something which breaches the implied term of fidelity in their employment contract or their fiduciary duty and, as such, it could amount to gross misconduct.

The duty of fidelity, as described by Lord Woolf in Attorney General v Blake (Attorney General v Blake [2000] UKHL 45), is that the employee must act in good faith, he must not make a profit out of his trust, he must not place himself in a position where his duty and his interest may conflict and he may not act for his own benefit or the benefit of a third party without the informed consent of his employer.

Of course, the fiduciary duty is a duty that a director owes to the business, over and above a normal employee, to act in the best interests of the business. However, as I said, it's going

to be fact-specific. The employer might want to consider how serious the conflict of interest is, whether the director ought reasonably to have known that it would be a problem when assessing the seriousness of the director's failure to disclose the conflict. As ever, are there any other mitigating factors? Simply don't resort to dismissal as a knee-jerk reaction.

Su Apps

Can you please talk about the type of circumstances in which multiple allegations of different misconduct under one disciplinary process could provide grounds for summary dismissal, even though each allegation taken alone wouldn't amount to gross misconduct?

Daniel Barnett

So really, this is a question about totting up like for speeding fines or penalty points. Can lots and lots of minor incidents tot up to justify dismissal if there haven't been previous warnings?

Imogen Egan

I can see that that can happen. I think it's important to think about the whole picture and the seriousness overall. Hopefully, this is something that you'll have set out in your disciplinary policy so that employees are aware that this is a possibility, and at each stage, they ought to be warned that dismissal is a possibility, as you're investigating. Regarding the types of circumstances, I'm struggling to think of specific examples where it might happen, but perhaps something which is set out as misconduct in the disciplinary policy- so use of a mobile phone- but not gross misconduct? If you're talking then about multiple incidents back to back to back of using a mobile phone at work, then perhaps it could be, but I struggle to see a scenario where you've got all of these incidents of misconduct - not gross misconduct - and you've not had an opportunity to give them a warning after each one, so that they're all coming together as part of the same investigation.

Daniel Barnett

As a matter of theory, of course, there might be a situation where something cumulatively might make it within the range of reasonable responses to dismiss, which statutory test. But I'm struggling like you to think of anything. So even if you have an employee who was discovered to have used some stamps for personal use, misused mobile phones, been rude to a colleague, failed to clock in properly on one occasion - even if you've got lots of lots of little things, I just don't think a tribunal would say that once someone's accrued two years' employment, you can get rid of them the first time you catch them doing that.

Imogen Egan

David Mackay has asked in the chat: What if they all happen within a couple of days? Again, I think that if this is the same offence repeated multiple times before you've been able to give them a warning, and it's not something that on its own would normally be gross misconduct, then I don't think that would be enough. Give them a warning, keep a record of it and then come back to it.

Daniel Barnett

Paman Singh, who spoke yesterday on individual redundancy, selection and consultation, has referred me to the Mbubaegbu case (*Mbubaegbu v Homerton University Hospital UKEAT/0218/17/JOJ*), which is a very rare example of someone being fairly dismissed under a totting up process where no individual act amounted to gross misconduct.

Su Apps

Please talk us through the interrelationship between misconduct dismissals and some other substantial dismissals based on breakdown of trust and confidence and when it would be appropriate to plead both because, arguably, in almost all gross misconduct dismissals, there will have been a breakdown in trust and confidence.

Imogen Egan

I think, generally, it's better to keep your pleadings as clean and concise as possible. So I know that there is sort of a habit in some quarters of pleading absolutely everything you can and then leaving it to the barristers to narrow it down when they get to tribunal. That, I think, annoys employment judges, so it's not something I'd recommend. If it's really clear that it's a misconduct issue - it's something that is set out in your disciplinary policy and you've gone through the disciplinary process - then I wouldn't plead it as a some other substantial reason dismissal. I think where that's more relevant is where you can't show that there is necessarily misconduct on the part of the employee but circumstances mean that the relationship has otherwise broken down. That's when it's more appropriate to plead some other substantial reason. But as a rule, try and keep it concise and stick to one if you can.

Daniel Barnett

I totally agree. There was some case law years ago. It was Mr Justice Burton when he was president and he said everything can be pleaded in the sense that trust and confidence has broken down because someone's committed an act of misconduct, because someone's not been at work for a long, long time, because, because, because. He said just don't waste time saying the relationship's always broken down. That just goes with the flow. I'd avoid pleading SOSR unless you have to. The principal reason for dismissal is conduct, and that's the end of it.

Hayley

What's the best approach to managing misconduct - poor behaviour - when mental health issues are cited as the reason?

Imogen Egan

That is a good question. I suppose it's important to remember that most employers aren't going to be health professionals or mental health professionals. So you need to seek expert advice. You need to get the employee's permission to refer them to Occupational Health and get a report there. Hopefully, you'll have a good Occupational Health provider and they'll answer your questions when you say: "The employee has explained that, for example, their depression and anxiety have caused them to have these outbursts in the workplace and to use bad language towards their manager. Can you explain whether or not that might be a possibility, and how we can best support them?"

I think once you've done that and you've got evidence that you're reasonably comfortable is sufficiently thorough, and you've put in place measures to support the employee and then the conduct doesn't improve, then you can look at escalating it to the next stage. But I think you're right to be careful that when that reason is given, you need to make sure that you're satisfying your obligations to your employee who's potentially in a difficult place with mental health issues. I think that's right.

Amaya Corcuera
What's your advice on taking into account expired warnings, or similar conduct that hasn't led to a formal warning, in a disciplinary process?

Imogen Egan
I think generally, the principle is that it's unreasonable to rely upon an expired warning in order to dismiss for an offence which wouldn't be gross misconduct normally. But I think there's case law. The case of Airbus UK Limited v Webb (Airbus UK Ltd v Webb [2008] IRLR 309) from 2008, which says that in very limited circumstances, an expired warning can be taken into account when deciding whether or not to afford leniency as to sanction. So I think that's the stage at which you could take it into account, but only in limited circumstances. Generally, if it's expired, it's not going to be relevant.

Natalie White
How wide is the discretion for employers in deciding whether misconduct is gross misconduct, and how is an employer expected to justify that in an employment tribunal?

Imogen Egan
I think it is relatively wide. Of course, it's going to be down to the discretion of the manager who is dealing with it at the disciplinary stage. Hopefully, it will be the kind of conduct that you can see from your disciplinary policy is likely to be something that's gross misconduct. I don't think there's unfettered discretion. So if it's something which most reasonable people applying common sense wouldn't think was gross misconduct, then you're going to have a difficult time justifying it to the tribunal. The best way to justify it is to have a really clear disciplinary policy setting out potential examples. And I suppose to have a clear record of what's happened in similar cases in the past - how you've treated them and how it impacts the business and why this misconduct, in particular, is so fundamental that it goes to the heart of the employment relationship.

Anonymous
If an employee is on bail for grooming and the case won't come to court for seven months, can we suspend for this period on full pay, given the view that there's a risk to the business?

Daniel Barnett
He works on a secure site needing security clearance.

Imogen Egan
I'm trying to think about how grooming relates to the secure site. I suppose that, in theory, yes, when you're suspending someone, you're supposed to do it for the minimum amount of time necessary. That may be where, for example, there are concerns about the employee coming to work in the workplace.

If you can say that the grooming offences are something which really do impact the employee's work on your secure site, for example, they're having to work on a secure site with young or vulnerable people, then, yes, I think it would be possible to justify suspending them for that long. But in general, you should keep it under review and not keep them suspended for any longer than you need to.

Sherry Jacobs
Where a new employee has failed, despite numerous requests, to provide proof of their home address so that an advanced disclosure and barring service check can be undertaken - they're working with children - would the termination of their employment be for conduct, for a breach of a statutory enactment or for SOSR?

Daniel Barnett
I suppose, more fundamentally, does it matter, given that they won't have two years' employment?

Imogen Egan
I think that's right. No unfair dismissal. But if we were talking about someone who had been employed previously and now gone into a role where they needed DBS that they didn't need before, perhaps, then we could be looking at an unfair dismissal. I think if there's a legal obligation on you as a school, as the employer service provider to have members of staff who have DBS, then I think it is an illegality issue, isn't it?

Daniel Barnett
I don't think it matters. It could be conduct not providing it, but it's in reality, I think it's breach of statutory enactment because it is unlawful to continue employing them without the DBS check. If not, it's SOSR. It's unwise to continue employing them without the DBS check.

Su Apps
To what extent would the tribunal consider the extent of potential risk of damage to the employer's reputation when considering the fairness of a dismissal, even if, as a matter of fact, there was no harm done?

Daniel Barnett
I often see "this created major risk to our reputation" in dismissal letters, particularly in social media cases, when, in fact, there was no damage at all. Is that potential risk, a relevant factor for employers to take into account?

Imogen Egan
I think it is. But perhaps I'm wrong on that. The fact that it didn't result in damage is perhaps more by luck than by design. If the misconduct was serious enough that it would have harmed the reputation had other people seen it, then that's important. There's also the difficulty of your reputation internally amongst other employees. If they were to know about the misconduct that this employee had committed and not been dismissed for, then that's going to potentially harm your standing with those other employees as well. It's reputation externally and internally.

Daniel Barnett
I suppose an analogy - and I entirely agree with you - is an employee who takes a Colt 45 revolver, points it into a crowded room, puts a blindfold on and fires and luckily, it doesn't hit anyone. The fact that they were lucky enough not to hit anyone doesn't mean it's not gross misconduct.

Imogen Egan
Absolutely.

Daniel Barnett
It's a slightly silly example, but that's how barristers do it. We just take dramatically exaggerated examples to prove a point.

Anonymous
Is an employee still an employee after they've been dismissed and while they're waiting and appeal?

Imogen Egan
No, I don't think so. I think the contract has been terminated. It's come to an end unless they're reinstated on appeal, in which case,

retrospectively then they'll have back pay and all sorts. But no, they're not an employee if they've been dismissed and not as yet reinstated.

Daniel Barnett

The way that courts and tribunals deal with reinstatement is to say that the successful appeal effectively vanishes the dismissal. I've never been able to get my head around that because, of course, what happened to covenants and fiduciary duties during the intermediary period? Did they exist or didn't they exist? I think that's yet to be solved by the courts properly. But you're absolutely right. They are not employees until an appeal is heard and allowed.

Anonymous

If an employee breaches the government lockdown guidelines, thereby breaking the law, putting themselves at greater risk of contracting COVID and presenting the employer with an enhanced risk when they return to work, would that amount to gross misconduct?

Imogen Egan

I think we might be treading on the toes of Caspar Glyn QC, who covered COVID issues in the workplace last week. I think it would be difficult to say. For starters, are they in breach of the law in the lockdown or just the guidance? How far can an employer control their employees' behaviour outside the workplace? I think you'd be on potentially shaky ground unless it's something that's really obviously wrong, such as hosting a large party in their back garden.

Then I suppose you might also have the question of reputational risk. There was the case of the Chiltern Railways employees who held a baby shower in Patisserie Valerie at Marylebone Station. That was an issue that was reported in the news and it was potentially damaging for Chiltern Railways to have that misconduct reported upon, so I can see how that is relevant. But as a general rule, no,

only as it impacts your employer and your employment.

Daniel Barnett

The other issue, save for the extreme example of holding a rave or something like that, which has reputational issues, I don't think it's within the range of reasonable responses to dismiss. Assuming someone's worked for more than two years, the employer can just spend £17 and give them a rapid flow antigen test and check they haven't got COVID. That, at a stroke, removes the problem of them infecting others in the workplace. So I suspect a tribunal would say it's disproportionate to dismiss.

Sonia Jain

How much weight should be given to the remorsefulness or lack of remorse of an employee during disciplinary action?

Imogen Egan

I think you take this into account after you've assessed the seriousness of the conduct and you're looking at possible sanction. That's my view. I don't think it necessarily affects whether or not it's misconduct or gross misconduct. It's going to vary from employer to employer and from manager to manager because it's something that's subjective. In practice, I think it is something that weighs quite heavily with employers. If you're looking at the extent to which the employment relationship can continue and how you can trust the employee in the future, if they are remorseful and they say they wouldn't do it that way next time, then you're more likely to be able to say: "well, I could trust them to come back to the workplace" and might give them a final written warning for this gross misconduct rather than dismissal, and keep that on their file in case they do it again.

Leszek Werenowski

If an employer dismisses without holding an appeal, where an appeal was requested, but then offers an appeal after it gets the ET1, can that appeal be taken into account when deciding the reasonableness of the dismissal?

Daniel Barnett
I assume implicit in the question is that a very long time gap has passed between when the appeal should have taken place in the ET1 has been lodged.

Imogen Egan
I think it's going to be potentially embarrassing for the respondent turning up at tribunal having to explain (a) the initial refusal and (b) why they've suddenly been prompted, out of the goodness of their heart, to offer this appeal on receipt of an ET1. But I don't see why it couldn't. If you can show that the person dealing with the appeal has done a full rehearing, for example, and that they are someone who had their mind open, they're not previously involved and that reinstatement was a real possibility, then I think you could rely on it. It's going to be really difficult to show that because the motivation at this stage is to try and stymie the claim against them rather than because they actually want to comply with their obligations. I think, in theory, if you employ someone external to hear it rather than someone who was internal, it might have more force. Have you ever come across such a case? I don't think I've had one like that.

Daniel Barnett
No, I haven't, but I agree 100% with what you're saying. I think that's bang on.

Jamie Anderson
How do you deal with someone who has genuine reactive depression in response to a notification of a disciplinary hearing?

Imogen Egan
You need to get expert advice. So perhaps consider asking them for a report from their GP, refer them to Occupational Health to see whether or not they're going to be fit to deal with and respond to the disciplinary allegations. See if there are any measures that could be put in place. Are there any

adjustments that you can make to your policy? For example, you could allow them a trusted friend or companion to support them at their investigatory meeting, which you wouldn't necessarily normally allow under your policy and isn't required by law. I don't think it automatically means that you abandon the process. If the cause of the depression, the stress, is the disciplinary proceedings, then it's not going to improve whilst the disciplinary proceedings are outstanding. You need to find a way to move forward with the employee on the basis of medical advice in a way that will enable them to participate without risking serious harm to their health. I appreciate that that's very hypothetical. It might be difficult on the ground to deal with such a scenario.

Daniel Barnett
Be very careful to say it's genuine reactive depression because it's very, very common for people to go off sick with depression and stress and anxiety once they get the letter invited into a disciplinary hearing. But I think you can never actually prove conclusively as an employer, whether it's genuine or not. What you have to do is act in a way that's within the range of reasonable responses.

I generally think that you're unlikely to run into trouble with a tribunal if you've sent them to Occupational Health, as Imogen suggests and if you've given them at least two - if not three - opportunities to let somebody else make representations on their behalf or to put representations in writing. The fundamental question, of course, is not whether they are suffering from reactive depression, it's whether they are reasonably capable of responding to disciplinary allegations.

Unless the Occupational Health person says that they're not capable of responding to disciplinary allegations, which I think would be quite unusual, you can press ahead with the process. And I generally say, look, give them three opportunities to come along, then make a decision, then give them a right of appeal, and they'll have had four opportunities by that stage. And you'd have to be very, very unlucky for a tribunal to say that falls outside the range of reasonable responses. Do you think that's right or do you think I'm being too gung-ho?

Imogen Egan
No, I think that is right. So I suppose there might be personal injury complications there. I think you have to be very unlucky for a court to think that that was sufficient [to cause personal injury]. I think that has to be right, certainly from an employment tribunals perspective of the fairness of the conduct.

Daniel Barnett
Quentin Colborn has put a message in the chat. In response to Jamie Anderson's question, he says that it's important to keep in mind the responsibility for an employee's health and welfare. This might be best protected by pressing ahead with a disciplinary process, rather than leaving it lingering.

Daniel Barnett
That's a great point. If somebody is suffering from reactive depression, then you've got to do your best to remove the cause of the stress. And if you leave a disciplinary process hanging, the cause of the stress will remain.

Joe
I have a potential disciplinary for someone refusing to conduct COVID tests in a school, claiming it's not part of their terms and conditions. Is the request for them to conduct COVID tests a reasonable and lawful order that could result in disciplinary proceedings if ignored?

Daniel Barnett
I'm assuming that's a teacher or teaching assistant or something like that.

Imogen Egan
The first question is whether there is a contractual right to require that employees carry out the duty. I expect that their contract will have something in it which says 'and such other duties as may be reasonably required by the employer'. I think in the context of the pandemic and the difficulties facing schools, tribunals will be sympathetic to a school employer saying that members of staff have to assist. The other question is whether the reason is just that it's not part of the terms of the employee's contract, or whether there's something more fundamental there, such as a reasonable refusal on the basis of the risk to their health and safety. I think that's going into Caspar Glyn's territory and Gus Baker's as well because he talks about health and safety.

If you're confident that it's a reasonable request, that their refusal is unreasonable, that you've had a discussion with them about their refusal and you're still not satisfied, then I think you can consider instituting the disciplinary procedure against them. I think tribunals would be very sympathetic in the current circumstances. What do you think, Daniel?

Daniel Barnett
I struggle with whether dismissal would be a reasonable response, but I do think it would justify a written warning or something of that nature. Also, if there had been previous things, then it could tot up to dismissal. The only thing that I would be fractionally cautious about is whether there's any belief discrimination going on here - if somebody fundamentally believes that COVID doesn't exist - but that's probably not worthy of respect in a democratic society.

Paman Singh
If you believe that an employee has lied in an investigation or in a disciplinary hearing, can you add that in as a fresh allegation of gross misconduct?

Imogen Egan
I think you could, but you can't just tack it on at the end. You actually have to investigate it and give them an opportunity to respond to it. I don't think that you can present it as a fait accompli at the disciplinary outcome stage.

If it's something you want to rely upon, you might consider that you don't need to rely on it as a separate allegation, then you're going to need to deal with it properly and take it through the stages. It's really important that you can't dismiss an employee on different charges from the ones that have been put to them at the point that they've been invited to a disciplinary hearing.

You may need to have someone different investigating and deciding that charge because, of course, the person who's raising the complaint and saying they think the employee is lying is the person who's making the disciplinary decision, having conducted that disciplinary hearing. So consider whether or not you really need to do that. You could say as part of your reasons that you don't believe their explanation and that on those grounds, you've found them guilty of the misconduct with which they were originally charged, rather than setting it out as a separate charge on its own.

Daniel Barnett

I think it's the flip side of the resource question. It's an exacerbating factor in terms of the sanction that you might apply. But I think that if you try to start a separate, new disciplinary process it almost seems like you're trying to double the penalty, as though you're trying to get two disciplinary strikes out of one incident. I don't think tribunals would like that very much. The only exception to that would be if there's been some level of fraud going beyond just lying. So if an employee had concocted documents or forged documents, I think that could be a separate disciplinary charge that could justify gross misconduct.

Andy Tovey

What can an employee do if they were dismissed for conduct, in that they were set up to fail, but they genuinely believe the real reason for dismissal was redundancy, but the employer wanted to avoid paying a redundancy payment?

Imogen Egan

This is quite a specific scenario. If you bring an unfair dismissal claim to a tribunal, the burden is on the employer to show that the reason was genuine. If we're saying that performance or capability issues have been raised - they've been set up to fail - then think about what kind of evidence you have of that, so that if you went to a tribunal, you could demonstrate that they weren't valid concerns. I think it's going to be very difficult to show, potentially, without really firm evidence. It is a very specific question. I don't think I've seen someone like that. Essentially, bring the unfair dismissal claim, put the onus on your employer to prove that there were genuine capability or conduct concerns, and put forward all of the evidence you have about the redundancy situations. That might be the financial circumstances of the business, insofar as those kinds of records are available. Ask for specific disclosure of those kinds of documents.

Daniel Barnett

I suppose the first question is whether you were replaced or not. If you weren't replaced, that gives rise to a prima facie redundancy situation. It doesn't, of course, mean - as the employer would inevitably argue - that they dismissed you for conduct then realised that you weren't actually doing very much, that you were a big fat waste of space and they didn't need to replace you, which is how the employer would respond. But I guess that would be enough to trigger the tribunal to start thinking about what the real reason for dismissal is here.

JP Choi

If there are several allegations of misconduct, which overall result in dismissal, would you recommend splitting out and reaching an individual conclusion on each allegation as well as an overall sanction?

Imogen Egan

Yes. You need to be able to show that you've got a genuine belief in the misconduct on each point, that you have reasonable grounds for coming to that genuine belief and that each of them has been investigated. So what evidence do you have if you were to get to tribunal?

Daniel Barnett
What about saying in respect of each allegation that if this was the only thing, I would have dismissed you for this allegation, or, I would not have dismissed you for this allegation?

Imogen Egan
That can only be helpful, can't it? Because if there's going to be a challenge, whether it's an appeal or an employment tribunal claim, where some of them are upheld, but not others - so you didn't have a genuine belief or it wasn't formed on reasonable grounds on these five, but on one it was, and the one on its own would have been sufficient to justify dismissal and you've explained how and why it would be, perhaps with reference to disciplinary policy - then that sort of stymies the claim really, doesn't it?

Mel Stacey
If any employee fails to reveal that they were dismissed from a previous role - and it wasn't picked up in references - could the person be dismissed for breach of trust and confidence when this information comes to light?

Daniel Barnett
I doubt it'll arise often in practice because most of the time employees won't pick up two years employment.

Imogen Egan
I think when you say 'fails to reveal that they were dismissed', I suppose the question is did you ask? Is it a requirement to disclose that? I'm not sure that it necessarily is unless you asked them as part of the recruitment procedure, and you know that they've lied to you. If they've lied to you and you've got proof of that, then that's definitely something which you can return to once you become aware

of it. Otherwise, no, I don't think that's in the range of reasonable responses

Daniel Barnett
Agreed. And of course, everyone's dismissed from a previous role unless they resigned. They could be dismissed for redundancy or they could be dismissed for all sorts of other non-sinister reasons.

Katy
How much allowance or latitude would a tribunal expect an employer to give an employee because of the stress of the COVID pandemic? For example, an employee who has repeatedly been very rude and aggressive with colleagues at work argues at the misconduct hearing, 'I'm stressed because of the pandemic'. Neither the employee nor the family have had it, nor are they medically vulnerable.

Imogen Egan
I don't think that's going to carry that much weight. It's a matter for the employer, how much weight they attach to it and can you justify what weight you attach to it? I'd probably think about that. So some mitigation of sanction stage rather than the misconduct itself. It sounds pretty weak, really, on those circumstances. If they're saying they've got a genuine medical condition, be that stress or anxiety, again, get Occupational Health to report on it and whether or not it would be likely to cause that kind of misconduct.

Elizabeth
To what extent is a loss of confidence in a senior executive grounds for dismissal?

Imogen Egan
I suppose it depends on the reasons for the loss of confidence. So are we really talking about a capability issue rather than a conduct issue? I think it could be, but you'd have to give fair warnings, I think. I don't think you could simply say that you've lost confidence in them and dismiss summarily. Of course, it's relevant to say that a senior executive has a lot of weight

on their shoulders and you need to be able to trust them and have confidence in them. But unless we're talking about something like a potential fraud or something like that, I don't think you can jump immediately to dismissal. I think this is a capability issue and you need to explain the problem and manage it properly.

Mel Stacey
What is the current cap on the financial award for an employee in a conduct dismissal case?

Daniel Barnett
I don't know the answer to that off the top of my head. Of course, you've got the cap on a compensatory award of a year's pay. £88,519 pounds is the maximum compensatory award.

Anonymous
Can you take action if it comes to your attention that there's a WhatsApp group with employees that has inappropriate content in it?

Imogen Egan
Yes, I think, potentially, you can, especially as in this context we're not talking about an employee talking with their friends or family privately; we're talking about a group of employees and perhaps there are references to the workplace. I think you can if it's the kind of inappropriate content that is going to go to the trust and confidence in the employee and to the nature of the relationship that you have with them. Also, consider whether or not they're doing it on work equipment. Is this on a work phone during work hours? Yes, I think you can, but it would depend, as with the question about criminal offences, how linked it is to their employment and how serious it is. Again, try to avoid a knee jerk reaction. Don't jump straight to gross misconduct summary dismissal. Investigate it.

Allyn Walton
If an appeal is lodged rather desperately positing a crude conspiracy theory not previously argued by the employee, is it safe for the employer to disregard this conspiracy theory, or should we reopen the investigation altogether?

Daniel Barnett
It's a damned if you do, damned if you don't.

Imogen Egan
I would be tempted to say investigate it but only to the extent that it's reasonable and proportionate to do so. So that doesn't mean that you have to go and interview every single other employee who may possibly have had a grudge against this dismissed employee. But if there are relatively straightforward steps that you can take, such as interviewing the dismissing officer, interviewing the investigating officer and putting that evidence to the employee before the appeal hearing. I think it's going to show willing, at least, for the employment tribunal. It's evidence that, ultimately, you're going to be able to rely on if it gets that far. So I can't see the harm in doing that, bearing in mind resources and time.

Daniel Barnett
I agree. You've got to do something. I would actually go to the employee and say, give me the six questions you want me to ask these four people to prove there's a conspiracy. It throws the ball right back in their court because then you ask their six questions and a tribunal is going to say you've done what you were asked to do.

Kirstie Stuart
What about using demotion as opposed to dismissal for gross misconduct, if it's not an option covered in the disciplinary process?

Daniel Barnett
I think she means it's not an option in the contract of employment.

Imogen Egan
I think that's going to be a breach of contract, isn't it? I'm not sure that's something you want to be doing. Stick to the options that are allowed under the contract and the disciplinary

policy. I expect that's going to be a repudiatory breach on the employer's part.

Daniel Barnett
I think there's a case, isn't there, Hogg v Dover College *(Hogg v Dover College [1990] ICR 39)*, which says that even if somebody takes a demoted job, they can still claim unfair dismissal in respect of the higher job they were sacked from, so don't do it.

That said though, if they do take a demoted job, it massively reduces the compensation because there's much less loss there. So do do it. There we go. Lawyers changing their answer on the toss of a coin.

Anonymous
Is it safe to tell staff that an employee's employment has been terminated during the period between the dismissal and the deadline by which the dismissed employee has been given to appeal?

Daniel Barnett
That's a nasty question.

Imogen Egan
I'm not sure what the legal answer is, but I wouldn't. I think it's opening you up to potential allegations of having pre-determined any potential appeal. If you're saying "they're sacked and they're not coming back", when the round-robin email is disclosed as part of the tribunal proceedings, it's going to make it easy for the claimant's representative to say, "look, you had no intention of allowing them a fair appeal". So I absolutely wouldn't. I'd keep it as neutral as possible that they're not doing work and we're not going to talk about it.

Robert
You mentioned some people putting everything into an ET3 and then leaving it to the barrister to sort out at the tribunal stage. As a barrister, how early do you want to become involved in a case that seems likely to end up in the employment tribunal?

Imogen Egan
That's a really good question. I think probably at the point that the ET1 is received. If you're going to give your barrister the trust and control to advise on strategy throughout, then they don't necessarily have to be the person drafting the pleadings, but you can discuss what's going to go in there. And think about the kind of witnesses and evidence that you need to have on standby from a really early stage. I think that's the gold standard, the best possible option. But, of course, I appreciate it's not always possible with funds, and, of course, you may well prefer to keep it in-house. It's really a matter for you, but that would be my preferred option.

Daniel Barnett
Yes, I think there are a number of factors here. Funds is a very, very obvious one, as you say. There's also the fact that no one ever knows whether the barrister is going to be available for the hearing. So there's no point going to barrister A if you're going to end up using barrister B at a hearing. The other factor is the experience of the solicitor or the HR person doing the instructing. Plainly, an inexperienced person should probably come to a barrister earlier than a very, very experienced person.

Imogen Egan, if somebody does want to come to you as soon as the ET1 arrives, what's the best way to get in touch with you?

Imogen Egan
Go to Outer Temple's website and click to contact my clerks. Alternatively, my email address is imogen.egan@outertemple.com or find me on LinkedIn.

Daniel Barnett
Imogen Egan, thank you very much.

UNFAIR DISMISSAL: ABSENCE
NADIA MOTRAGHI, OLD SQUARE CHAMBERS

Daniel Barnett

I'm joined by Nadia Motraghi of Old Square Chambers for this Q&A on absence dismissals.

Nadia Motraghi, good morning. First of all, a question from me. If you're an employer worried about the authenticity of an employee sickness absence, can you use a private investigator to follow them around and see whether they're secretly moonlighting and working for somebody else?

Nadia Motraghi

I think in the right circumstances you can. An employer does need to tread carefully here. But I think it's going to be a reasonable step for someone to take to retain a private investigator if there's some evidential basis for retaining them. For example, if a colleague has seen the employee in uniform for another employer or at another workplace, or if the employee themselves has orally suggested that they were moonlighting while off sick. What we're looking at here is potentially an issue of fraud, which is obviously very serious, and that could warrant surveillance.

I think it's worth drawing to mind the case of City and County of Swansea v Gayle *(City and County of Swansea v Gayle [2013] IRLR 768)*, a 2013 decision of the EAT. That's the rather colourful case where there was an employee who was going off to play squash on work time while clocked in and then he raised various human rights issues saying that it breached his article eight rights that he had been subject to covert surveillance.

Surprisingly, that was an explanation that was swallowed by the employment tribunal, but ultimately, at the EAT level, they said there was no difficulty in having surveillance in those circumstances where another employee had tipped off the employer that they had seen them playing squash on another occasion and that it wasn't disproportionate to use covert surveillance in those circumstances.

I think what I would add is that it's very important to make sure that you're following ICO guidance when using covert surveillance. There is an Employment Practices Data Protection Code. So you need to look at whether or not it's appropriate and proportionate or whether or not it might prejudice any detection of crime or equivalent malpractice. Then I think added to that, you want to make sure that the PI that you're retaining is themselves doing an appropriate and lawful job. So make sure that you've got some sort of contract with them that specifies that they're acting in compliance with GDPR. And so those are the key considerations that I would have in mind here.

Daniel Barnett

Just one other question for me. Should persistent intermittent absence, be treated as a conduct dismissal, capability dismissal or some other substantial reason dismissal?

Nadia Motraghi

That's a really good question. Depending on the circumstances, it could be any of those. I'm going to put to one side any consideration of disability discrimination. Although, obviously, if you've got a person who may potentially be disabled, then you could be facing disability discrimination complaints, including reasonable adjustments.

I think in the case of genuine absence, that is something that would be dealt with under capability rules. If we're talking about short-term absences that are caused by a number of different and unconnected minor illnesses, then that might not be an incapability reason at all. It could, in fact, be a misconduct issue or an SOSR issue on the basis that they weren't capable of rendering effective service.

If we really are in sick absence territory, then that's going to be a question of fairness, ultimately, under s98.4, has the employer acted reasonably in treating the ill health as sufficient grounds for dismissal, and much there would depend on the procedure that's followed, including, crucially, consultation with the employee and medical advice. It's important to err on the side of caution and in all the most unusual cases, to make sure that you obtain medical advice.

Of course, if you've got suspicions that it could be fraudulent absence, then you've got misconduct rules that apply. And if you think it's persistent short-term absence, then the rules seemed to be a bit of an amalgam of both incapacity and conduct rules. And one case where SOSR was used, the case of Kelly v Royal Mail (Kelly v Royal Mail Group Ltd UKEAT/0262/18/RN), concerned a postman who was dismissed after review of his attendance record. He'd had two operations on top of the poor sickness record and the Royal Mail relied on SOSR. The EAT concluded that labels in this context aren't decisive, but plainly the employer didn't have confidence in that individual's ability to work consistently. So SOSR had been an appropriate reason to rely upon. And interestingly, in that case, the EAT relied specifically on the fact that the policy that

Royal Mail had did refer back to being able to use not only sickness that just occurred but also sickness that went back some time, including following serious operations. So the employee wasn't surprised about that as a potential turn of events and had an opportunity to challenge the employer's case. So depending on the precise circumstances, it could be any one of those three.

Su Apps
There was a suggestion from another fabulous speaker earlier in the series, that a capability dismissal for long-term sickness absence would, though fact-specific, rarely be fair if absence had been for less than 18 to 24 months. We have always advised far more robustly than this, starting formal absence proceedings far earlier if the medical evidence supports it. What's your view of this?

Daniel Barnett
Just before you answer, my recollection is that I had a chat with the speaker on air about that, and I think they dialled her view back a little bit to say 12 months is the general starting point at which a dismissal for absence is reasonable.

Nadia Motraghi
I think I have to agree with Su on this one. I think I would be more robust and start sooner if the medical evidence supported that. If you've got medical evidence that suggests that an individual won't be able to return to work ever, or for a particularly long time, then that is very significant evidence to have. I think, in addition to that, if you are contemplating dismissing - or at least starting the process at a much earlier stage - you perhaps need to rely on some other factors as well. So the size of the organisation may be a significant factor here if it makes it more difficult for the employer to bear the sickness absence of that particular person if it's causing difficulties for colleagues and indeed for the business. So I think, yes, I think I would be a little bit more bullish about that in line with what Sue is saying. In terms of whether a disability changes it, I think a disability always

285

changes these issues and adds another layer of complexity to it. And so there, you're very much going to have to consider reasonable adjustments and what you can do to support the return to work of that individual. And, of course, it's a fairly low bar before you, in fact, need to implement a reasonable adjustment. So you need to be guided by the medical advice on that front.

AJ Fraser
How long is an employer expected to wait before dismissing a long-term sick employee who is awaiting elective surgery that's been postponed indefinitely due to the pandemic?

Nadia Motraghi
Goodness. That, in fact, is the question that the tribunal will be asking, which is, by the time the case comes on at the tribunal, how much longer should an employer have waited in those circumstances. What would have been reasonable? I think it's going to be quite different where you've got somebody who's surgery is planned, but then postponed. So, planned for the next month, but postponed, and then planned for a couple of months later and then postponed, and where you've just got somebody whose surgery is postponed indefinitely. I personally find it difficult to think how an employer is going to retain an employee where there's just a completely open-ended elective surgery that's due to take place. There may be some additional requirement for the employer to consider whether the employee can do anything from home while on sick leave if, for example, you've got somebody who has a mobility issue that wouldn't necessarily preclude them from being able to do office-type work from home. But I don't think there is a hard rule of thumb here. I think it's about making sure that you've gathered as much information as is reasonable to be satisfied that it is an indefinite postponement and that there aren't other things that the employee would be able to do from home.

Daniel Barnett
I suppose with a lot of elective surgery, you'd be fully capable of working anyway, depending on the type of surgery. So if somebody is saying that they're waiting for elective surgery, so they're not coming into work, there may be an issue about whether they're malingering to an extent.

Nadia Motraghi
Yes, that's also correct.

Su Apps
Any tips on how to get the best out of an Occupational Health report?

Nadia Motraghi
I think we've all seen a range of Occupational Health reports, verging from the extremely helpful to the far more common far less than helpful. So I think, really, that a detailed set of instructions, for want of a better word, is needed and a very clear and detailed set of questions. And if you don't get answers to those specific questions, then go back to the Occupational Health advisor. They are there to provide the advice that you want. So if they have provided a report that you think is unsatisfactory because it doesn't cover those questions, go back to them. I have to say I have seen, on a number of occasions, an Occupational Health doctor or advisor who simply provides a one-sentence answer to questions one to five, which isn't acceptable. So I would encourage both clarity and precision in the instructions and going back to the Occupational Health advisor if those questions haven't been properly answered.

Daniel Barnett
Also, refuse to pay the bill. It's almost automatic to just pay an £800 or £1,200 bill when it's sent. But if they haven't provided a proper report, say I'm not paying your bloody bill until you answer these questions I asked you.

Beth Bearder
What's the best way to manage someone with mental health issues who refuses to engage in a sickness absence process?

Nadia Motraghi

That's a difficult question. I think we've all been there in terms of individuals who've got mental health issues, who are not engaging because they may think it's not in their best interest to engage. I would say that the best way to do this is to be absolutely clear and upfront about the importance of engaging with the employer in the sick absence process. That includes the reasons why you want that information, how it aligns with your policy and, indeed, the consequences if they're not able to engage in the sick absence process by way of refusal.

I think you need to be listening to the responses you receive from them and making appropriate attempts to work with the employee to provide the reassurance they need during the course of that sick absence process. So if, for example, they have concerns about seeing a particular Occupational Health advisor, then consider whether or not it's appropriate to send them to a different Occupational Health advisor or a different expert. But I think it's also a question of creating an audit trail so that you can defend your position later, while trying to constructively engage with them so that they understand and are reassured by the process that you're following.

Rebecca

An employee went off sick in January for eight weeks. Our holiday year runs from April to March. During the last 12 months, they've been hesitant to take annual leave, as they're unable to go anywhere, much like everyone else. They've requested all their annual leave remaining to be carried over. They've got 15 days out of 33 days remaining. We only allow five days to be carried over. What should we do with the balance of 10 days?

Daniel Barnett

So they allow five days to be carried over. The employee wants 15 days to be carried over.

Nadia Motraghi

I have to say I take a less charitable view of this than Michael Ford would do. I know Michael Ford thinks that it's important for the employee to have the opportunity to use the holiday leave as they see fit. I may be misattributing this to him. I think he also says there could well be a difference between your working time regulation entitlement and your contractual entitlement. Putting that to one side, in my view, the purpose of holiday pay is not necessarily to take holidays in the sense of somewhere nice in the sun. It's about taking rest and recuperation. It's for a health and safety reason. And if that individual has had in the past 12 months an opportunity to take that time but has chosen not to, then I don't see that simply being off sick for eight weeks allows them to take the entirety of that 15 days balance over into the next holiday year.

Daniel Barnett

I've got some vague recollection of the back of my mind about some regulations that apply at the moment. If you're unable to take your holiday due to coronavirus, then you have a right to carry over up to 20 days for up to two years. Might that be relevant here?

Nadia Motraghi

That may very well be relevant. You will clearly have to look quite carefully at the definitions in those regulations because I think it's if you are prevented from taking those holidays for coronavirus reasons. And that seems to me to be more related to the situation where your employer tells you that they're sorry but you can't take that holiday that you've asked for because they have a need due to COVID for you to continue working, say for an NHS nurse, rather than an individual who thinks they're not going to be able to make best use of their leave at the moment because they can't go to Lanzarote or what have you.

AJ Fraser

If an employee on long-term sick leave receives a government shielding letter, can you proceed with the long-term absence procedure or must you put it on hold?

Nadia Motraghi

I don't think you must put it on hold. In this situation, I think the question is premised on the basis that they would be on long-term sick leave in any event. You may wish to consider whether you wish to discount some periods of their sick leave. But that is just one circumstance for the employer to take into account as part of a multifactorial matrix that they need to consider. I think often there is a view that if it's anything to do with COVID, then everything is completely different than if it was some other sort of illness. There's no hard rule of law that says that. It's part of a situation where you need to consider all factors.

AJ Fraser

When is it appropriate to include periods of long-term sickness absence in your frequent triggers procedure, which may ultimately lead to dismissal?

Nadia Motraghi

Yes. I'm not sure about that one.

AJ Fraser

In frequent absence dismissal cases, what are your top tips for defending indirect discrimination and s15 claims?

Nadia Motraghi

You obviously need to know what the reasons for the absence are. And indeed, you need to make sure that disabled people are not being put to a specific disadvantage as compared with others and indirect discrimination claims. And obviously, if you're trying to justify an indirect discrimination claim, you're looking at the objective justification for the particular policy that you're relying upon. So really, that starts with the employer having a good audit trail and clear thought as to why it is they need to adopt a particular measure.

I infer from this that we're talking about measures in sick absence policies, so it's worth reviewing

whether or not the triggers that you have in your policies are reasonable and defensible. For example, if sick absence in your workplace is actually very low, then do you need to have triggers that kick in after a short amount of time? It may be that you're actually well able to bear that level of sick absence because there isn't a prevalence of sick absence across the workplace. So I think employers sometimes do forget that you need to go back and review your policies. They shouldn't stand there for time immemorial. They should be based on experiences and practices within the workplace.

Glynis LLewelyn

At what point do frequent emails from an employer to an employee who's off work due to stress-related issues, asking about their health and when they might be able to return to work, cease to be supportive emails and become a harassment?

Nadia Motraghi

I think a lot earlier from the perception of an employee than from the perception of an employer. This reminds me of a case I was involved in some years ago, where an employee asked for a period of no contact because he was finding it so distressing to be contacted by the employer at all. The employer agreed that and very shortly afterwards received a call from another employer asking when employee X left their employment, and they said employee X hasn't left their employment; he's on sick. They then found out that, in fact, the employee was working at a different workplace at the same time, so claiming sick pay from one and working at the other. So do just bear that one in mind.

I think it's a good idea to make sure that the person who is corresponding with the employee is someone with whom they have a good or at least a reasonable relationship. If they are corresponding with the person who they have accused of harassment, bullying or discrimination, then that's liable to become a flashpoint a lot earlier. It's good if you have set out in policies that an employee can expect to be contacted at a particular frequency or to be asked about particular matters so that the employee knows that they are not being picked on or treated differently with their particular illness. I have seen that some employers do follow that sort of procedure. Others, of course, don't, particularly smaller employers don't tend to have that degree of specificity.

I think it's also about conveying genuine concern as opposed to it being a tick-box exercise. So if the employee thinks that, in fact, this is just a tick box exercise and that their employer is not really interested in either getting them back to work or supporting them in some other way, then I can understand why an employee may think that it becomes harassment. But of course, in terms of harassment, if we're talking harassment related to disability, then you want to be looking at the definition under s26 of the Equality Act: is this unwanted conduct related to the particular protected characteristic which has the purpose or effect of providing a hostile or degrading intimidating workplace? And all the circumstances of the case have to be taken into account, including an objective view of the situation as opposed to just the subjective view of the individual concerned. I think a tribunal would be very slow to conclude that someone asking factual questions about a person's state of health is in fact harassing an employee.

Daniel Barnett
There's an element here of damned if you do, damned if you don't, isn't there? We sometimes see employees complaining that the employer didn't make contact, didn't invite them to social events, didn't send a Christmas card and didn't ring up to see how they're doing. So it all turns on the range of reasonable responses and pretty much anything an employer does falls within it in this situation.

David Mackay
If an employee uses their exact company sick pay allowance each year, every year,

regardless of how genuine we accept the absences to be, how far back can historic absences be used as part of a fair capability process?

Nadia Motraghi
I think it's about the range of reasonable responses. I think the starting point is going to be what said in the contract and what's said in your policy. Do those indicate how far back you can go? If they don't, then it's simply a question of reasonableness. So long as it's not being used in a way to trap the employee. So for this particular individual, you're going to go back X years, but for individuals who don't have this protected characteristic or even individuals that you like, you don't use this sort of length of time. As long as it's not arbitrary and capricious, then I think that provided the employer can explain why it's using that particular time frame, it's prima facie reasonable.

Jamie Anderson
What's the most effective argument for a dismissed employee to argue that strictly drafted repeat absence criteria are unreasonable?

Daniel Barnett
I suppose this arises most in the context of reasonable adjustments for disabled employees.

Nadia Motraghi
I'm going to infer here that we're talking about situations where the person comes back to work and then faces a return to work meeting or something of that nature and has to go through the reasons for their absence over and over again. I think if it's that circumstance and you've got somebody who has a long-term condition - let's say it's anxiety or depression - and the employer is well aware that coming back and participating in one of those return to work meetings is going to be stressful and upsetting for them and the employer already knows the cause, then I think at the very least,

you could argue for some truncated process where perhaps the individual is simply asked if there is anything this time that's different to the last time and whether there is anything that can be done to support them rather than making it a procedure that involves a long meeting with one or more people in attendance in a formal situation. There could be particular situations where you're asking for certain types of reasonable adjustments to that kind of process. But I just want to make sure that I haven't got the wrong end of the stick in terms of that question.

Jamie's actually put in the chat that it's just about challenging the policy regarding the number of short-term absences. So presumably, you're talking about a policy that says that after X absences, we put you to final warning, etc.

Yes. So in that case, I think you'd be looking for something that's specific about the nature of the person's absence to indicate that for that condition they would be more likely to have repeat absence. So some people might go off once, and it may be for a very long period. For others, the nature of their illness may be something that has an ebb and flow or the need to take sick leave. So I think that educating the employer about that particular condition would be a good way of being able to challenge the repeat absence criteria.

Laura Sheridan

Can an employer refuse to accept a GP's sicknote from an employee? If so, what's the justification and what's the best way for an employee to challenge it?

Daniel Barnett

I've actually asked Laura to join us so that she can explain that one in a little more detail because I think it could be quite fact-sensitive. Laura, why would the employer refuse to accept a GP note? What's suspect about it?

Laura Sheridan

It's actually a colleague of mine that's dealing with this case, but from what I understand, the

employee has had a couple of periods off sick previously, but it's disability-related absence. The most recent sick note that has been sent forward to the employer, the employer has simply said that they're not accepting the sick note, that they're not accepting that it's a valid sick note. I suppose the question is can an employer do that? From my understanding, they can, but they'd have to justify it, surely, and it'd be quite difficult to justify going against a GP's recommendation. It's not one that's come up for us very often, I have to say. It's not something that happens very often, so I was just interested.

Nadia Motraghi

I would tread extremely carefully if I was acting for an employer before refusing to accept a GP sick note. And also, what's the consequences of refusing to accept a sick note? Because in the first seven days of sickness, you self certify anyway. What's the consequence of them not accepting it? Is it that they're now treating the employee as being absent without leave? An unauthorised absence? I think you need to have very good grounds before you don't accept a sick note. For example, somebody says to a fellow employee that they've been to the doctor, told them a pack of lies and now they've got their sick note. Or, indeed, the sick note says the person is immobile and can't get off the sofa, yet you've seen them running around Tesco car park. So I think, absolutely, the employer should be giving a clear justification for not accepting it. And I can't think of any occasion in my career so far where an employer has said they're not accepting set note. I think they could be in very hot water by doing that.

Laura Sheridan

It's definitely the first one that's come up for our team, I have to say, so it's not one that's come up for us before. Obviously, we represent employees so we're supporting the employee to challenge that.

Daniel Barnett

Gillian Howard has popped in the chat that the HMRC guide to employers on statutory sick pay says that a doctor's fit note is strong evidence of sickness and is usually acceptable. The language there says HMRC takes the view that it's not conclusive evidence of sickness, and, of course, that's right. That's not necessarily exactly the same as a s98.4 test, is it?

Nadia Motraghi

No, it isn't. But I think it's certainly very helpful guidance to have and it's worth putting Gillian's points to the employer in the case that Laura just mentioned.

Jeanette Clure

We've got conflicting evidence. An employee has been absent for 18 months because of depression and anxiety. Our Occupational Health report says they're fit to return to work. The employee doesn't agree and continues to be signed off by their GP, but they refuse to give authorisation to write to their GP and they refuse to attend welfare meetings. Is it fair to bring the employment to an end based on absence?

Nadia Motraghi

That's a really tricky question. Jeanette, I don't envy you in this situation. What I would say is that I think you do have good grounds to start the capability process here. I think what we need to bear in mind is that in this area, as with other sorts of dismissal, we aren't looking at the absolute truth of the situation. It's not a criminal trial. We're looking at the information that the employer has and whether it's reasonable in all the circumstances for the employer to bring the employment to an end.

Where the employer has done its level best to obtain appropriate information and to try and be sure of the veracity of the information that it's receiving and the employee is not playing ball, then it needs to fall back on the information that it does have, namely, that the Occupational Health report is saying they're fit to return to work, but the GP is saying that they are not currently fit to return to work. So you don't have any further information about

when, in the employee's view, they're going to be well enough to return and you've got the employee not being willing to attend welfare meetings and, I infer, give further information. The employer needs to use the information that it has.

I think if I was pleading this, ultimately, once a dismissal had taken place - if it was to take place - I would be pleading it as capability as well as some other substantial reason. And depending on the lack of cooperation, you might also want to plead it in a further alternative of conduct if the employee is failing to attend welfare meetings without good reason. So I think those are the sorts of things I had in mind on the unfair dismissal point.

James Fairchild

My client has an employee who rings in sick 30 per cent of the time. It's suggested by colleagues that he is a fan of the bottle. Could the employee argue that alcohol dependency is a disability?

Nadia Motraghi

I think if I remember rightly, that alcoholism, as with other things like wishing to start fires and so on, is one of those illnesses that is treated as not being a disability for the purposes of the Equality Act. Addiction to alcohol, nicotine and other substances is to be treated as not amounting to an impairment. I think the tricky part here is that a savvy employee may say that they're not relying on their alcoholism, they're relying on the surrounding circumstances. So it's very likely that they might also have anxiety, depression, or some other sort of impairment that wraps around that alcoholism.

You may wish to consider whether they are a disabled employee by reason of some other associated condition and then what sort of reasonable adjustments might be made. The answer may be that there aren't really many reasonable adjustments that can be made or that even once taking into account reasonable adjustments - so discounting a certain level of absence or anxiety or depression - that the level of sick absence is still unacceptable.

AJ Fraser

How would you persuade a reluctant or difficult line manager that managing absence properly is a must-do rather than a nice-to-do exercise?

Nadia Motraghi

Well, it's a reasonable instruction to them, isn't it? I think that's very much in the realms of good HR practice rather than strictly speaking and employment law question. A manager needs to manage, and management of sick absence is a very important part of that. Because otherwise, the team is not supported, you don't have effective service from that team and there's also a danger of lack of consistency within the organisation.

If you've got one manager choosing to interpret the rules one way and doing nothing about it and other managers actually taking the steps that they're supposed to take, you could be making yourself vulnerable to other claims in relation to discrimination, for example, if you've got that inconsistent practice. So I think a robust conversation with them bringing these matters to their attention and identifying that failing to participate in that sort of process could itself amount to a form of misconduct on their part if they don't listen the first time around.

Mike Clyne

Do you think the Bradford factor yardstick of absence analysis is useful, wrong, or too blunt an instrument?

Nadia Motraghi

I think it can be useful, but, of course, it doesn't cater for the situations where you have individuals who are disabled. I think in those circumstances, you need to make sure that you're acting in compliance with the Equality Act. In addition, if you are using the Bradford factor, then I think that's something that needs to be identified upfront, included within the policy and reviewed to ensure that it's working in the way that it should.

Rachel Lester

If an employee is on long-term sickness absence and that long-term sickness absence is disability-related, is there a higher threshold for an employer to overcome if they're thinking about dismissal?

Nadia Motraghi

Certainly, if the reason that they are on sick leave is disability-related, you will want to make sure that there aren't any adjustments that could be made to assist the individual to return to work, and you'll want to make sure that you've had clear engagement with the employee and obtained good medical evidence. In summary, yes, I think that, effectively, there is a higher bar because you need to be more careful and make sure that you're acting in accordance with the Equality Act.

Daniel Barnett

Nadia Motraghi from Old Square Chambers, thank you very much.

UNFAIR DISMISSAL: PERFORMANCE

SAUL MARGO, OUTER TEMPLE CHAMBERS

Daniel Barnett

Today's webinar is on performance dismissals with Saul Margo from Outer Temple Chambers.

Good afternoon, Saul Margo. I'm going to start by asking you a couple of questions off my own bat. Can an employer take into account a live conduct warning when issuing a capability warning?

Saul Margo

I think in the vast majority of cases, that would be a mistake. Capability and conduct are both potentially fair reasons for dismissal, but they are distinct concepts under the Employment Rights Act. So capability is defined as meaning capability assessed by reference to skill, aptitude, health, or any other physical or mental quality. So here, obviously, we're talking about performance so that's skill or aptitude. And that is conceptually different from conduct. There can be cases where you could use either label. So, for example, it could be a case where there's a very senior individual who shows a significant level of incompetence when they must or should have known better and that might shade into misconduct, or perhaps cases where the extent of the training that's been given means that a particular failing by an employee feels like misconduct rather than capability.

In the vast majority of cases, I think the conduct and capability processes should be kept separate, with capability focusing on identifying the performance issue, setting clear

goals, providing opportunities to improve over a particular period of time and potentially providing further support or training that's needed. Those steps wouldn't normally be features of a conduct process. I think that underlines the risk of confusing the two. If you do so, if you confuse them by taking into account this live conduct warning you mentioned - a capability process - I just think you risk muddying the waters and making life harder for yourself down the road, particularly if you have to defend the dismissal at an employment tribunal. So I'd advise against it.

Daniel Barnett

What about if the issues are sometimes mushed up? So, for example, the essence of the allegation being brought against the employee is that although they're naturally very good at their job, they're just not doing it because they're being lazy, because they're distracted, because they can't be bothered, or because they're dissatisfied with their pay rise, that sort of thing.

Saul Margo

It's recognised in the case law that sometimes these issues are hard to distinguish. That can be the case sometimes and the distinction can be unclear. Obviously, if you end up at an employment tribunal, the tribunal isn't going to be obsessed with labels, they're going to be looking at the fairness of the dismissal. If the employer has given it the wrong label, they will still look at what the right label is and whether the dismissal is fair. But I think that the problem is that if you put something in the wrong box, then you risk following the wrong procedure. So I certainly think that you might come to a situation where you think, well, we initially gave a conduct warning there, but I think that this isn't just negligence or carelessness from this employee. I think this is actually capability and I want to take that warning into account but go forward with the capability process, I think you can do that. But you just have to have a very clear sight of what it is you're doing and why. And perhaps acknowledge that you actually see it in a different light now

Daniel Barnett
Some employers just take the view that if you've got an underperforming employee - assuming they've got more than two years' employment - the best thing to do is get them to sign a settlement agreement to leave rather than going through performance management. Is that an approach you'd recommend? Does it have pitfalls?

Saul Margo
From an employer's point of view, it's something that's likely to be attractive if they do not want to go through the time and effort of a capability procedure, especially if it's thought that that process is bound to or very likely to fail. The advantage would obviously be to get it done early and avoid that lengthy process. In terms of how it would be done, I would have thought the sensible approach would be to have a pre-termination negotiation that can't be relied on in ordinary unfair dismissal cases - the exception we have now under s111a of the Employment Rights Act. So in principle, you can have those conversations without being worried about constructive dismissal claims in particular. You don't have to be worried that you've undermined trust of confidence somewhere and they've resigned it within that claim.

Saul Margo
I think that real issues can arise if those conversations are had too soon, at a time when it's a complete shock to the employee. In particular, if those managers have been avoiding having those difficult conversations and then suddenly seek to have a conversation about a settlement agreement. The problem that can arise is that there are circumstances in which those negotiations can be relied upon. And that is anything that is not an ordinary unfair dismissal claim. If there's a claim for discrimination or if there's a suggestion of some improper behaviour, the employee can refer to those discussions. It just seems to me that if you move too quickly, then you could encourage the view from the employee that something improper is going on that perhaps isn't actually about their performance, whether that's the case or not.

So I think it's much better, or more appropriate, to move to these pre-termination discussions at a time when those performance concerns have been discussed, you've had those difficult conversations so it's not coming as a shock, but before the formal procedure has been initiated, so you can make those savings of time and expense.

Daniel Barnett
Last question for me. Imagine you're an employer who hires someone to cover a woman who's off on maternity leave. The person filling in comes to you and says look at all these mistakes my predecessor made, and you realise there are real performance issues with the woman who's on maternity leave. How should an employer handle performance issues that they've become aware of during maternity leave?

Saul Margo
Obviously, you should not be initiating any formal capability procedure during the maternity leave. I think the reason for that is quite a practical one: you're not going to be able to assess whether their performance is improving. A fair process is likely to require a chance for you to explore the reasons for the poor performance, set clear goals and

give them a chance to improve. And if they're absent on maternity leave, you're not going to be able to do that. I think that the real issue then becomes whether you bring it to their attention at all while they're out of the office on maternity leave. I would say that on balance, the best approach is not to raise it with them while they're absent on maternity leave because you're not going to be able to follow up on it in any event during the leave.

Apart from those practical considerations, there's obviously the welfare of the individual to think about and the risk of encouraging a potential claim of discrimination under s80 of the Equality Act that you've treated them unfavourably because of pregnancy or maternity leave. You can discipline people during maternity leave, but again, in this situation, they are tactical reasons that would really point against it.

So what should you do? I think that it would at the very least be sensible to capture the information. Make sure that you record the poor performance and that if there's some kind of investigation to carry out at this initial stage, you capture the information so that you can address it, if necessary, when the individual returns. But I don't think, realistically, it would be right or sensible to move forward with it in a procedural way while they're absent.

Natalie White
What considerations should be made when dealing with an employee who claims a disability, despite reasonable adjustments, prevents them from performing well in their role?

Saul Margo
I think, in any situation where there are claims of disability, obviously, Occupational Health advice is going to be absolutely critical. You need to establish whether they are a disabled person and get as much information about that as possible, and you need to establish what possible adjustments can be made to help

them perform their role. Once you have that Occupational Health advice that suggests the adjustments that person needs, then obviously, as a business, you can consider whether those adjustments are, in your view, reasonable and whether you can accommodate them. So I think that, where possible, it should be taken away from the idea of 'What are they paying me? What are they saying?' to 'What is your objective assessment of the position? What impact is their disability having and what can you reasonably do about it?'

Su Apps
Will it always be necessary in performance dismissals to go through a warning, final written warning and dismissal with performance improvement plans, targets, support, etc., each time to improve at each stage?

Daniel Barnett
Can you give any examples of where you could fairly move straight to dismissal for performance reasons?

Saul Margo
I do have the Acas Code here. The Acas Code disciplinary and grievance procedures offer general guidance. The code doesn't actually distinguish or give a totally separate process for performance versus misconduct, which is quite interesting.

So paragraph 19 says: where misconduct is confirmed or the employee is found to be performing unsatisfactory, it is usual to give the employee a written warning. A further act of misconduct or failure to improve performance within a set period would normally result in a final written warning. In paragraph 20 it says: if an employee's first misconduct or satisfactory performance is sufficiently serious, it may be appropriate to move directly to a final written warning. This might occur where the employee's actions had or are liable to have a serious or harmful impact on the organisation. There's also the

Acas guide on disciplinary and grievance procedures from July 2020 that gives you other non-statutory guidance here. What you can see there, in the way the code puts it, is that in a sufficiently serious case, you could move straight to a final written warning. So it's not suggesting that you might move straight to dismissal. I wouldn't rule it out completely; it can sometimes happen. Obviously, what you'd be looking at is a very, very serious act of something probably bordering on gross negligence. Again, it might be one of those cases that actually looks more like this conduct: something where it's so basic, it's so clear, it's so obvious, they've had such complete and full training, that it's just obvious that they are not going to be able to do the job.

Thinking more broadly about capability, I suppose other examples might be where you have a complete inability to do some particular key area of the role. So, let's say, you have to be able to perform control and restraint because you work in a prison, and it's become absolutely clear that you'll never be able to do that, and it's clear that there's no way around it in terms of adjustments - let's say it's disability-related - I suppose, in principle, you can move quickly there. But the answer is that it's going to be very, very rare. I could perhaps be more creative in trying to think of answers, but it'll be very rare.

Daniel Barnett
I think one of my favourite cases from law school - one of the very few cases I always remember - is called Alidair v Taylor (Taylor v Alidair Ltd [1978] IRLR 82), where an airline Alidair flew between Exeter and the Channel Islands.

Saul Margo
This is the negligent pilot, isn't it?

Daniel Barnett
Captain Taylor, on one occasion, had a really hard landing. No one was hurt, but it was

a hard and negligent landing. But he had the misfortune that the wife of the airline's chief executive was on the plane at the time, and he got fired for poor performance. The Court of Appeal basically said that there was no obligation to put him through a first warning, second warning, etc. They said some things are so serious that you just can't allow somebody a chance to develop a track record.

Natalie White
Do you have any general guidance about what a reasonable timeframe is for allowing employees the chance to improve?

Saul Margo
No, I don't. I think the reality is that you've got to look at the particular circumstances of that employment. I'm just trying to think of an example. If somebody's a junior journalist in a paper, and you don't think their writing style is good enough. If you say that by next week it needs to be better, well, that's just not realistic. They're not going to improve their writing style by next week. No employment tribunal is going to look at that and think that it's a realistic or reasonable timeframe; they're going to think it's a stitch-up, that your mind has been made up and that you're just going through the motions.

So I think you need to look at the industry. The manager is going to be given a wide discretion by an employment tribunal in terms of the period in which improvement is feasible. That's really what you're thinking about. What would the tribunal think when looking at this? Would they say that this is just outside the range of reasonable response? Is it just not feasible? Or is this a fair attempt by a manager to give them a chance?

Anonymous
If you can't manage performance because the individual keeps citing stress of performance management and then going off sick and asking for a change of manager over and over again, how long do you have to

wait - how many absences and how many changes of manager - before you can say you're dismissing because it's impossible to performance manage them?

Saul Margo

I suppose the question there would be: are you dismissing them because it's impossible to performance manage them, or is this actually going to be a long-term ill health absence case? I think that if somebody keeps coming back, and then keeps going off on sick leave because of performance management, that is a really difficult situation. My impression of what you're saying is that they come back, you try to manage them, they don't improve and they go off.

I think it's very difficult. I think you'd obviously need to establish whether there's an underlying issue of ill health, you'd obviously want to get any advice you can from Occupational Health about that. Again, I don't think you can say that there is a golden rule about the length of time and I think that in reality, it may not actually fall within a capability process. You could say it's some other substantial reason and there's a different route for the fairness there. One can obviously see that if you have an underperforming employee, you've done what you can support them and there isn't any other disability or ill health reason that you could sort out with an adjustment, I think ultimately, it is going to be fair to dismiss if you can't find another route through. But it might be some other substantial reason.

Daniel Barnett

I agree. It's probably some other substantial reason, and whilst this is only a rule of thumb, I'd probably say that a 'three strikes and you're out' rule applies here, in that if somebody goes off sick, demands another manager to return, falls out with them, goes off sick, demands another manager to return, falls out with them, goes off sick and demands another manager to return, by the time that's happened three times, I think you're in a

pretty strong position. That's leaving aside reasonable adjustments for disability that might require you to go through a fourth cycle.

Saul Margo

I think any tribunal looking at someone that's allowed those three chances is going to see that this is a genuine attempt to deal with an employee and to be reasonable. Again, they'll be looking at the band of reasonable responses, and I think I agree that I can't see that they'd interfere with that decision.

Helen Longton

If an employer has a performance improvement policy which provides that at the final stage, if an employee hasn't achieved the required standards, they can be demoted or redeployed as an alternative to dismissal if they agree, if the employer then tries to demote or redeploy them and the employee refuses, is that a dismissal or a resignation?

Saul Margo

It is an interesting question. I mean, it actually went in a different direction than I expected. But no doubt, that's a sign of a good question. And I think that if you probably end up dismissing them, wouldn't you? In the way you framed your question, they haven't actually resigned. Yeah, they might do that. So I think in the way you framed it, you've offered demotion or redeployment. They've decided they don't want it. Well, I think you would, you would dismiss them, and assuming everything else had been done properly, that'd be a fair dismissal. There is no obligation to offer alternative employment through a capability process. In fact, there is a case of Awojobi v London Borough of Lewisham (*Awojobi v London Borough of Lewisham UKEAT/0243/16/LA*) in the EAT where his honour Judge Richardson says there's no obligation to offer alternative employment or redeployment. So here, you've gone out of your way, I think. To offer a demotion or redeployment is a very reasonable option if you can they can't perform at that level.

They've chosen not to accept it. I think the dismissal would be fair. Alternatively, if they do resign, so if they say that before you dismiss them, they're resigning, I think they'll have a very great difficulty establishing a constructive dismissal claim.

Anonymous
If an employee says they have a disability at the appeal stage, after a performance-related dismissal, what steps should an employer take? Can they proceed with the dismissal?

Daniel Barnett
I think I'll flip that question. Are they obliged to reinstate the employee?

Saul Margo
Well, I wouldn't say they're obliged to reinstate the employee. I think that the difficulty you have is that where disability comes to light at the appeal stage, I think what you can't do is turn a blind eye to it. I mean, ultimately, the appeal stage is there to hopefully correct anything that's that's gone wrong. I say hopefully to correct anything that's gone wrong - that's putting rather an employer-related slant on it. But it's to deal with any issues that haven't been dealt with properly at the original stage, and you need to investigate it. If they've raised it, you need to investigate it. So, is that a disability that they had at the relevant time? If they did, then you may well have been under obligation to make reasonable adjustments, and you've got to take it into account. You're not obliged to reinstate but you need to take it into account at the appeal stage and decide what to do once you've completed a proper investigation.

Melanie Bonas
What pitfalls should an employer be mindful of avoiding when dealing with long-serving employee performance dismissals?

Daniel Barnett
So to rephrase that question slightly, should an employer take a different approach when dismissing a long-term employee for performance as opposed to someone who's just got over two years?

Saul Margo
I think the answer is obviously, yes. The thing about a long-serving employee is it's going to be more difficult on the whole to establish that they're not capable of doing the job. They've been capable of doing it for a long time. What's changed? So I think what you need to be thinking about is the answer that question: What's changed? Very often, it might be something technological. They were able to do this job when it didn't involve all this it in software, but it might be they just simply haven't been able to get to grips with the new software. There, I think it would be a pretty standard process. You'd be seeking to identify what they can't do, provide extra support and training if necessary and monitor what it is they're not doing properly. But it's just about honing in on that specific thing they can't do and why, and being aware that, in general terms, if the job hasn't really changed, then it's going to be harder to show that they are not capable of doing it.

Mike Clyne
To what extent will an employment tribunal take the view that an employee has a responsibility not to be rubbish at their job versus the employer's responsibility to go through the various iterative stages - verbal warning, written warning, etc. - to point out the gap in performance versus expectation?

Daniel Barnett
Nobody could have any idea which side of the employee/employer line Mike sits on!

Saul Margo
Daniel helpfully gave the Alidair case earlier of the rubbish pilot. There are going to be cases where somebody is sufficiently bad at their job or has done something sufficiently negligent or dangerous that you can jump through all the normal processes. But I don't think an employment tribunal would ever look

at it in that way, saying it's the responsibility of the employee not to be rubbish at that job. They're going to be looking at what processes the employer went through. Did they have an honest belief based on reasonable grounds that the employee wasn't able to do their job? It's that general test that drives the need to identify the performance issues, give them a chance to improve and set a time scale and review dates, etc. So I'm afraid to say that as an employer, you're going to have to expect that the tribunal will be looking for those things in most cases.

Hayley

Are there any tips on managing poor performance when the reasons cited are mental health-related? How long can mental health issues or lack of wellbeing be deemed 'acceptable' mitigation if they don't seem to be seeking help?

Saul Margo

I don't want to fall back on saying all the standard things. My impression is that one of the most common things that happens when you raise performance issues is that some kind of stress-related problem is triggered, or the employee claims to have some kind of stress-related problem. You've got to take it seriously, I think is the first thing to say. I think the fact of the matter is, it can be incredibly stressful for an employee to think their livelihood's on the line, a process is started and they're going to be dismissed. I think on the whole, if someone becomes unwell due to stress for that reason, I'd be inclined to think that it may well be real.

Obviously, you would then make suggestions about going to Occupational Health, make suggestions about making use of Employee Assist, etc. If they don't do any of those things, and they're not getting well and they're not going back to work, then you're into not the performance end of capability dismissals, but the ill health dismissal process. I think that's where your mind should turn. If they're not at work and there's no sign of them improving

then you just need to make sure that you have that Occupational Health advice that says they're not currently fit to work, they're not seeking help, they're not going to their GP and there is no prospect of them coming back. And then you need to start thinking in terms of your long-term ill-health processing. Can you wait longer? What's the effect on the business? So I think that's where your mind returns when someone just isn't doing anything to help themselves and isn't coming back to work.

Daniel Barnett

I've actually done a video called 'Top 10 ways to lose an employment tribunal case' (https://www.youtube.com/watch?v=fJMwTOJtbvk). And in one of those top 10 ways, I talk about allowing an employee to derail a performance or disciplinary investigation by going off sick with stress, and I talk about the ways to combat it. It's top tip number six.

Matilda Swanson

Do you have any tips for establishing whether the issue is because somebody can't do something, as opposed to won't do something? For example, if can't do is performance and won't do is conduct.

Saul Margo

I think what you're honing in on there is what we were talking about earlier. There are going to be cases where it's quite hard to tell which is which. I don't think that the employer has to necessarily 100% get it right in the sense of fully getting to the bottom of that question. I think that, ultimately, the tribunal won't be that hung up on the label. The safest thing to assume in those cases is that they can't do it. So the safest thing to do is to go down the capability route, trying to do everything you can to bring that performance up to standard, setting those targets and giving that support. Then, if they don't meet that standard, whether it is 'can't' or 'won't', it's going to be a fair capability dismissal.

The problem with assuming that it's won't too early, is that you aren't thinking in terms of training and support and things like that. You're focused more on a conduct issue, just issuing a warning and moving on. So I think you're much safer to go down the capability route. You might never get to the bottom of which it is, but I think you'll be pretty safe in an employment tribunal.

Daniel Barnett

I think what you said there is the absolute key to it. You can never really find out which one it is because it's impossible to know what's going on in an employee's mind. And employers are often very, very quick to assume that it's 'won't do' but just so often it's not.

Gillian Howard

How far is an employee allowed to disagree with the targets and standards of performance set by the employer under a performance improvement plan?

Daniel Barnett

It has been known for employers to set unrealistic targets as a way of engineering an employee out of a company. Can an employee challenge that?

Saul Margo

What I just glanced rudely across at is the Acas guide on disciplinary and grievances at work. Page 29 has a section on first formal action on satisfactory performance. It talks about an improvement note, and it says the improvement note should set out the performance problem, the improvement required and the timescale etc. I'll just stop there at the improvement required, because that's what we're talking about here. You're going to need to have a meeting with the employee to discuss it. I think the short answer is that you need to have that meeting, you need to have some dialogue about the improvement required, but ultimately, it's the manager's decision.

The employee is allowed to disagree and the employee should have a chance to express their view. That's going to be really important if you ever have to defend this claim. If they express their view and say it can't be done in six weeks and they need eight, then it's really helpful if the manager has engaged with that and given their reasons as to why it's six. A tribunal is never going to go behind that. If sane, sensible reasons are given, they're never going to step into the employer's shoes and say the employer has to give them eight weeks. So, they can disagree, but it's the manager's decision. You just need some cogent reasons. And I think that dialogue is ultimately probably helpful if you ever come to defend the claim.

Daniel Barnett

I suppose, to put it into lawyers' language, it would come down to whether the targets are within the range of reasonable responses that could be set by a reasonable employer when being reasonable on a reasonable Tuesday.

Saul Margo

Yes, exactly.

Victoria Duff

How do you deal with long COVID and the capability process?

Saul Margo

That's an ill health performance question. You deal with it as you would any other ill health issue. I think the issue with long COVID is that you have periods of being productive during the day. As I understand it, you often may be able to be productive in the morning but less so in the afternoon. There might be a question as to whether it's a disability, and I suspect the answer is that it probably isn't. The suggestion is that long COVID would be likely to last a year. I suspect there are different medical views out there.

I think that you would manage it in a normal way. If there are absences from work, then you need to think about your absence management process. If there are intermittent absences, obviously, you'd use your short-term absences process. If it's a long period of time, you'd look at long-term absence. I think you should be very slow in looking at it as a pure performance issue because there's obviously an ill health issue that underlies it. Just purely from my understanding of it, people tend to get over long COVID in maybe a number of months, so that person, hopefully, should be back at full capacity soon. So I would be cautious about treating it as a reason to jump too quickly through any kind of dismissal processes.

Daniel Barnett
I suppose, in certain circumstances, especially given the the lack of medical knowledge at the moment about long COVID, it could be said that once diagnosed with long COVID, it could be something that's likely to last more than 12 months and trigger disability.

Saul Margo
As I said, I imagine there's a difference of medical opinion out there at the moment. But it could be a disability, you certainly want to get some Occupational Health advice about it. I suspect a lot of people would say at the moment that it's not likely to last 12 months. But I don't know. There's probably difference of opinion out there.

Daniel Barnett
On average, where there are no disability issues, how long does it take to performance manage an employee out of the employment?

Saul Margo
On avearge, how long does it take? Four to six months? Three to four months? Four to five? You know, it's very, very hard to say. I would say you should clearly be able to do it in under half a year. It's going to depend on the sector, and it's going to depend on what reasonable periods of improvement are in that particular sector. But I would have thought in most job roles, giving someone a month to improve - so you give your warning, give a month to

improve again, you have your final warning and then another month - that's going to look pretty reasonable in most in most situations. So, that's three months.

Daniel Barnett
I mean, for classic situation such as a salesman on monthly sales figures, the first month will be, "Those were crap figures last month. Get your act in order. This is a telling off". The second time it would be, "You still haven't got your figures up. Unless you get your figures up, you're fired". And the third time it would be, "You're fired". And I think very few tribunals would find that was an unreasonable or unfairly hasty dismissal process.

Anonymous
How can you prove that an employee has poor performance if they don't have a role which has clearly defined targets?

Saul Margo
It's more difficult. Daniel was talking about, the sales role, when you say they've got to make a certain number of sales and that's completely clear. Not all performance is quantifiable in that way. But I think it's going to depend on the job again. Every manager, if they've identified the fact that performance is bad, must have an idea of what good performance you would look like in that particular role. It could be receiving no complaints from customers based on your performance at reception over the month. It could be producing a higher quality of written work. It's vague, it's not clearly target-orientated, but a manager is able to assess it. And if the manager comes back the next month and says, I've been reading these reports that you've written and they're still of a low quality, a tribunal is not going to go behind that. A tribunal is not going to look at it and say that they think it's really good. I think it's unlikely that they would go behind the manager's view. So it's not as easy to target if it's not target orientated, but if you know the performance is bad, you know why it's bad.

And I think you can then identify something that can be done better.

Mike Clyne

What do you think about contractual clauses that withdraw enhanced company sick pay for sickness absence, if there is a performance process in place?

Saul Margo

I'm not sure I've seen clauses like that myself. If you have a contractual clause like that, then that's the clause in your contract. There's obviously a question about how easy it is to apply in process.

Daniel Barnett

So they'd just they normally get enhanced sick pay rather than SSP. But if they're on performance management, at the time of the sickness, then they don't get enhanced sick pay, they just get SSP.

Saul Margo

I'm not sure it's really for me to say what I think about that. If you have that contractual clause, then there we are. If that's the employment contract, that's the contract you apply. I mean, there might be wider questions about how your workforce feels about it and how that helps to recruit or motivate your workforce, but that's not a legal question, I don't think.

Daniel Barnett

I don't think there's any doubt is there that such a clause would be lawful and enforceable.

Saul Margo

As I say, it'd be lawful, it would be enforceable. I don't think it's a legal question. It's a matter for you as an employer, if you want to have something like that in your contract.

Daniel Barnett

Saul Margo, thank you very much.

Daniel Barnett

I'm joined today by Sarah Fraser Butlin who is going to be answering all of your questions on trade union recognition and collective bargaining.

Sarah Fraser Butlin, good morning. I'd like to start by asking you a couple of questions myself. Can an employer allow trade union representatives onto their premises to hand out recruitment leaflets to try to recruit staff into the union?

Sarah Fraser Butlin

This is something that can be very contentious, and it really raises the temperatures in the workplace. Generally, there's no obligation to allow union reps onto premises to recruit staff. But, where a request for recognition has been made and it's got to the formal stage at the Central Arbitration Committee - the CAC - then there are specific provisions that allow the trade union to provide leaflets to those in the bargaining unit, usually via someone appointed as the qualified independent person - that's someone appointed by the CAC. Once there has to be a recognition ballot, then a union must be given reasonable access to the workforce. But on a day-to-day basis, there's no right to attend. The contentious part is that trade union reps will often stand outside the gates of a factory or outside an office block, on public land, and seek to recruit staff on their way in and out of work. My advice to employers is always not to overreact. If the reps are on public land, and there aren't so many of them that they are causing a public

nuisance, then the employer has no right to stop them and they have to let it go. Of course, in most circumstances as well, an employer can't stop a staff member from recruiting other staff to join the union.

Daniel Barnett

When union officials are standing outside an office, trying to recruit people, are they picketing because there are very strict laws on picketing with a code of practice? There's a maximum number of people that can stand outside the building. Does that maximum apply when a union is trying to recruit members?

Sarah Fraser Butlin

My reading is that it's not picketing because it's not a trade dispute. But you could still see whether there's a tort or something like public nuisance, or trespass. But if not, then cool the temperatures in the workplace. Don't cause a problem by having a heavy-handed approach to a union rep standing outside the factory.

Daniel Barnett

That's the most common advice that I give employers when I'm dealing with this sort of thing. Calm the temperature down; don't escalate it. A lot of employers immediately go to chest-thumping and shouting 'We're the employer don't get in our way - we're the big beast here'. And all that does is agitate and make things worse.

Sarah Fraser Butlin

It really does because it makes staff members feel insecure. It makes it feel like they need the support of the union because the employer is becoming a bully. And actually, if the employer is reasonable and rational, very often things calm down quite quickly. You can make a lot of ground, especially with trade unions, by being friendly and positive towards them. A good trade union relationship can make all the difference.

Daniel Barnett
At the moment, we're seeing a lot of redundancy situations and a lot of collective redundancy consultation that goes along with that. Is there a risk that allowing an unrecognised trade union into collective redundancy consultation could be seen as some form of implied recognition of that union?

Sarah Fraser Butlin
Let's first of all think about what recognition is. Recognition is where there's a collective agreement that unions are entitled to conduct collective bargaining. Collective bargaining, as the name suggests, is about unions being entitled to negotiate. Now, although a collective agreement will usually be in writing, and will usually arise from specific discussions and negotiations with the employer, you can have an unwritten implied collective agreement. But there needs to be clear and unequivocal evidence that the employer has habitually treated the union as entitled to negotiate. The law is clear that information and consultation is different to recognition. They have different functions, different purposes and obviously arise from different statutory provisions. Thinking about something like s188 on collective redundancies, you have to consult about ways of avoiding the dismissals, reducing the numbers of employees dismissed, and mitigating the consequences of dismissals. You have to do that with a view to reaching agreement. Now, if the information and consultation stays within those parameters, it's incredibly unlikely that it would amount to recognition. But if the consultation moves to bargaining about the terms and conditions,

and then it starts heading towards more dangerous territory. It's not an altogether clean line, so care is certainly required, and you'd need to really look at the historic position of the union.

Anonymous
Do you have any tips on dealing with difficult union members, especially when dealing with redundancy consultations?

Sarah Fraser Butlin
Absolutely. I think the starting point is always being polite and pleasant and supportive. And that comes as a really counterintuitive position to take when you are dealing with difficult union members. Firstly, just remember that they think they're doing their best for their members and they are trying to defend the position. But being polite, pleasant and nice does go a hugely long way. I also advise that when things get really messy, and the union rep is being incredibly difficult that you seriously consider escalating it through the union structures. If you're dealing with local representatives, it's okay to go up to the regional officer and say, look, this isn't working. We don't quite know why it's not working, but it's not working. Can we have a conversation about this to try and break the deadlock or break the relational difficulties? A lot of the difficulties arise when you've had a bad relationship beforehand. So if the union has battled for recognition, then you're probably going to have a more fractious relationship and you're going to have to build more bridges.

Peter
Who can be a companion to help represent employees in workplace formal processes? And can an employer legally reject a chosen companion?

Sarah Fraser Butlin
The rights of accompaniment are found in s10 of the Employment Relations Act. The person to accompany could be a fellow worker, they could be a trade union official, or they could

be a trade union officer. Remember, of course, that the worker doesn't have to be a trade union member. And the trade union doesn't have to be recognised. Can the employer reject it? No, generally not. Obviously, if there is a specific problem during the accompaniment, like the person becomes violent or is incredibly difficult or aggressive, then of course, you can deal with that. But broadly, the worker gets the choice of companion.

Anonymous

There is some case law that says that as long as a companion is within s10, no matter how mad or militant or unreasonable they are, they have a statutory right to be there. Refusal to have them there can result in the two weeks' pay, which is the penalty for not letting them attend.

Sarah Fraser Butlin

Absolutely. It's a very high bar before you can stop the companion being there. And I'm really talking about situations where they're extraordinarily aggressive or violent or there is some form of harassment of the dismissing officer or the disciplining officer. Absolutely.

Anonymous

A lot of employers take the view that they will only allow a trade union rep or a workplace colleague into grievance and disciplinary proceedings, and in tribunal hearings they say it's not our policy to let anybody else in. When, of course, there's no written policy saying that at all; they've made it up on the spot. What's your view on allowing Mum, Dad or Auntie Flo in as the companion?

Sarah Fraser Butlin

I think it really depends on the case. And I think it depends on what's being discussed. It can be very helpful to keep the temperatures down by having someone accompany who is maybe a little bit more objective. But it's not a legal right. You can't say you're entitled to them. It becomes a very fact-specific decision dealing with what is the grievance? What is

the disciplinary? And you've got to be aware that you have no idea who Auntie Flo is, so you don't really know what they might be like. So it's one to be very careful of.

Liz Burley

When you're looking to change terms and conditions for over 20 employees, at what point are the collective consultation obligations triggered?

Sarah Fraser Butlin

The issue here is what we mean by 'proposing to dismiss as redundant'. Remember that redundancy in s188 doesn't just mean dismissals. It also means where you're making a fundamental change to the terms and conditions. So what do we mean by proposing to dismiss? This is a really difficult and technical area where the law is not entirely clear.

We also have to remember that the Collective Redundancies Directive talks about when collective redundancies are contemplated. We've got UK law as 'proposed' and the directive provides 'contemplated'. So, we end up looking at the case of Akavan (Akavan Erityisalojen Keskusliitto AEK ry and Others v. Fujitsu Siemens Computers Oy, Case No. C-44/08). The court in Akavan held that the obligation to consult arose prior to the employer's decision to terminate employment contracts. Well, when is that? They held that the consultation procedure must be started once a strategic or commercial decision, compelling him to contemplate or to plan for collective redundancies has been taken. Well, it's tricky to think through what the court actually meant in Akavan. The Court of Appeal in USA v Nolan (The United States of America v Nolan [2015] UKSC 63) was certainly not very sure. They referred the question back to the European Court and they asked is consultation required when the employer is proposing but hasn't yet made a strategic business or operational decision that will foreseeably or inevitably lead to collective redundancies? Or is it only when that decision has been made, and the employer is then proposing consequential redundancies? Unfortunately, the European Court declined to determine the issue because in USA v Nolan, it was actually dealing with staff on a military base and article 1.2(b) of the directive expressly excluded the dismissal of staff on a military base.

We're left with this phrase from the European Court of it being once a strategic or commercial decision compelling him to contemplate or to plan for collective redundancies has been taken. And you'd need full facts, a full understanding of what was going on to be able to advise properly on exactly when that is met, but there is certainly still uncertainty on that point.

Anonymous
Do we need to continue to recognise a union if employees TUPE across from a company where recognition is in place?

Sarah Fraser Butlin
TUPE and recognition is really messy. What we have to be really careful of is exactly what has happened. Recognition applies to a bargaining unit. If your bargaining unit retains a distinct identity after the TUPE transfer, and the union is an independent union, and that category of employees goes across in the TUPE transfer, then in those circumstances, the recognition also transfers. The simple answer is yes, you do if the distinct identity of that bargaining unit remains.

Sarah Fraser Butlin
The complicated bit is if the identity is lost because at that point, the Acquired Rights Directive says that the recognition should be maintained for a period to ensure that representation can continue for a period. But TUPE doesn't have equivalent provisions. So under TUPE, if the distinct identity is lost, then the recognition under regulation six doesn't

transfer, but if under the directive, you at least need to keep it for a short period.

One more thing we need to know about TUPE is that, of course, the type of recognition that was in place before the TUPE transfer is the same after the TUPE transfer. So if it was voluntary before, it's still voluntary afterwards. And you can always remove voluntary recognition.

James Fairchild
What's the best way for a small employer to avoid attempts to recognise a union?

Sarah Fraser Butlin
I think you've got to ask why you want to avoid attempts to have a union in your workplace. And that may be because unions can be difficult, and they can ask difficult questions. But first of all, stop and think about why you don't want a union in your workplace. And you may find that actually, unions can have a really beneficial effect on the workplace. How to stop them? Well, as I said before, you can't stop them leafleting outside the premises if they're on public land. And you can't stop a staff member who is a member of the union recruiting, though that comes with a caveat around appropriate time and exactly how they're doing the recruitment.

Sarah Fraser Butlin
The best way to avoid a union is being a good employer. A workplace that is happy generally doesn't say that it needs a union to sort things out. If employees feel like they are being consulted and discussed with, feel that they know what's going on and feel secure, then unions perhaps don't have such a big role to play. Whereas in a workforce where things are more unsettled, or there is great anxiety, or there's a feeling of the management bullying the staff, then you're more likely to see a feeling that they need to have a union in there to help them. It goes back to why we have labour legislation at all. It's all about the unequal bargaining power between the

employer and the staff. And if you have a relationship which is less unequal, then you're less likely to need to have the union there. That's a really woolly answer, but it's the reality of industrial relations.

Robert

I'm a solicitor and I'm also an accredited trade union rep. If I represent an employee at a grievance or disciplinary hearing, can I also represent the employee at the employment tribunal in the same matter?

Sarah Fraser Butlin

My view is that it's really difficult. I think my major concern would be that if you represented the employee at the disciplinary or grievance proceedings, then your conduct as the rep might be challenged by the employer. And as soon as you become a witness yourself, then you've got a real problem in representing them at the ET. I think I'd be very hesitant about doing that. But I'm not a solicitor, so I don't know what the solicitor rules are. I'd probably say you need to be phoning up the SRA to get some advice on that rather than relying on what a barrister would say because our rules are different in relation to witnesses.

Anonymous

Do we have to share our financial records with our trade union when discussing pay or potential redundancies?

Sarah Fraser Butlin

Well, let's talk about pay first, because that would be in a context of collective bargaining about pay and there are specific duties around the information that has to be provided for collective bargaining. The information has to be something without which the trade union would be materially impeded in collective bargaining and information and that would be in accordance with good industrial relations practice to disclose for the purposes of collective bargaining. It's only information - it's not documents. It's only what's in the employer's own possession. Do you have to

provide financial records if you're collectively bargaining about pay? Well, if the trade union can't collectively bargain about pay without knowing the financial situation of the organisation, then yes, you would be required to provide information. But it's a very fact-sensitive question, because it will depend on what you're bargaining about, and what the financial information is. I mean, there's financial information and there's financial information, isn't there? There's the detail of every single pound and penny from the organisation, and there's the broad information that suggests the organisation is in trouble. And don't forget that if a union goes into a collective bargaining scenario and they think the company is doing brilliantly, they're going to ask for a pay rise. And if the reality is that the business is doing really badly, then it's to your advantage to provide them with some financial information that backs up the claim that actually we're doing pretty badly and a pay rise is not on the agenda.

Daniel Barnett

This really all comes down to openness and frankness being the best policies.

Sarah Fraser Butlin

It really does. I love working with employers and with trade unions who have worked hard at building a relationship. In anything to do with trade unions, I always say the first thing is the relationship. And if you can build a relationship with particular officers, officials and reps, then you've made the majority of progress that you need to make in collective labour law, because then when it comes to the crunch of collective redundancies or a TUPE transfer, there's trust. And if there's trust, then the information or consultation is more likely to go smoothly.

Anonymous

When undertaking a membership check in accordance with our recognition agreement, can I ask the union to provide evidence of memberships such as direct debit payments, as we don't have our own means of checking union membership?

Sarah Fraser Butlin
The position when you're dealing with recognition and you're doing membership checks for recognition with the CAC is that the CAC does it, not the employer. Because the employer has no right to know who the union members are or are not in an organisation. This question appears to say that within the recognition agreement, you've agreed that there'll be a regular check of membership. That then comes down to the construction of the recognition agreement, rather than any legal statutory basis for doing that membership check. So I think that's a question of going back to precisely what the recognition agreement says, rather than a statutory provision.

Su Apps
How can you make sure that a collectively agreed policy doesn't become a contractual term of an individual's employment contract?

Sarah Fraser Butlin
A collective agreement only becomes a term in an individual's contract if there's a bridging term and the bridging term is either express or implied. If your individual employment contract refers to the collective agreement, then obviously it's in the individual contract. And the challenge is more often than not about whether there's an implied term that bridges the collective agreement into the individual contract. And my advice would usually be to actually make it abundantly clear and explicit that the collectively agreed policy is not part of the contract of employment. Expressly say there is no bridging term. And, depending on exactly what the factual matrix is, that should avoid it.

Frances McAulay
Can you insist that new trade union reps are given some training before they take up their role as reps?

Daniel Barnett
I assume the question is about whether employers can assist that.

Sarah Fraser Butlin
It's very rare for this to be the problem. My experience is generally that reps want the training and the employer doesn't want to give them the time off to do the training. Can you insist that they are trained? I think, again, that goes back to your good relationship with the regional officer, where you pick up the phone to the regional officer and say you've got a new rep, they haven't been trained, you're nervous and can you get them to have some training?

Could you require them to have the training? That becomes more difficult. I think you could certainly strongly encourage it. Could you stop them being a companion? If they haven't been trained? Obviously, that would be very difficult indeed, because they would be there as a fellow worker if not as a union officer. So I think again, it comes back to that good relationship with the union and saying this person needs some training.

Anonymous
Can an employer reasonably refuse a solicitor from being a companion at a grievance or disciplinary?

Daniel Barnett
I think there's a couple of things to unpick in that question.

Sarah Fraser Butlin
Absolutely. So first of all, you've got to ask who the solicitor is. The right to accompaniment is of a worker, trade union official or a trade union officer. Now, if a solicitor is none of those three things, then there's no statutory right for them to attend, subject to the complication of where the person who's being disciplined is somebody like a doctor or a lawyer and where the outcome of the disciplinary process would result in the loss of their profession. So we go back to the

cases of G v X (R (on the application of G) (Respondent) v The Governors of X School (Appellant) [2011] UKSC 30) and Kulkarni (Kulkarni v Milton Keynes Hospital NHS Foundation Trust & Anor [2009] EWCA Civ 789), where somebody was going to be put on the POCA register - the Protection of Children Act register - and because of that, they'd lose their profession. So if there's a strong link between the disciplinary hearing and some other significant listing or loss of profession, then there is a right to legal representation. But if it's not one of those unusual settings, then the answer is the accompaniment right is limited to fellow worker, trade union official or trade union officer.

Val Stansfield

Have you got any useful tips for trade union reps and officials who are dealing with difficult and intransigent employers?

Sarah Fraser Butlin

It's a two-way street, isn't it? If you've battled to get recognition and then you're having collective bargaining and it's going nowhere, or you're fighting for information for collective bargaining so you can properly deal with it, it's so frustrating and aggravating as a trade union. You want to do the best for your members and you can't. What I often discuss with trade unions is to say what's your power base? Have you got the base in the organisation to make sure that if you want to take any action, you can? Do you have the real support of the members? And if you don't, that's where to start building your support base. After that, it's about increasing the pressure on the employer. There are two ways of doing this. There's the nice approach of saying, look, we're actually quite useful here, we can resolve matters. And sometimes the best thing a union can do is actually get stuck into those situations between an employer and an employee and be particularly proactive at resolving them. It's about getting involved in those sticky situations between a manager and an employee where the relationship is just breaking down and coming to a good resolution for the employer. It's about showing your worth and showing how valuable you are. There's also the nuclear option of saying to the employer we've got the membership base, you're not negotiating and if there's something that would fall into a trade dispute, we'll start looking at industrial action. But that is nuclear. The first one I would be going for is saying how can we add value and prove to the employer that it's worth working with us?

Julie Norris

If you're an employee and a member of a recognised union but you don't have faith in the union's stance on a particular issue, such as redundancy selection criteria, can you leave the union and tell the employer to negotiate with you directly? Or are you stuck with a union representing your interests?

Sarah Fraser Butlin

We need to be a bit careful about what we're talking about here. I'm assuming we're talking about s188 collective redundancies. If you are an employee within the bargaining unit that is recognised by the union, then the union will be the appropriate representatives. So you leaving the union doesn't actually help because if you are in that bargaining unit that is recognised - and again, that's a really fact-specific question, that you have to look at the recognition agreement very carefully and define exactly who's in that bargaining unit - then there's not much value in you leaving the union, unless, of course, a whole bundle of you leave and talk to the employer and say there's a problem here, then they might then consider derecognising the union, and then you'd get some different representatives in the collective redundancies. But the reality is s188 consultation is only for a certain period, so all of that derecognition stuff would take too long. So my advice would be to have a groundswell of members to challenge the union. And if it's only you that doesn't like the selection criteria, then you're probably having a bit more of a difficult time with it.

Mark Irlam

Can a union member insist on their choice of solicitor for a tribunal case, rather than the union's choice, yet require the union to pay the bill?

Sarah Fraser Butlin

This is really messy, isn't it? Quite rightly, the unions have panel solicitors who do the work for them. And there are lots of good reasons for that. And it's a very rare case that a union would agree to a client using their own solicitor. It comes down to the union rulebook and the specific provisions that the union's got in relation to legal representation. But I would be surprised if there's a provision that allowed for that. So probably no.

Daniel Barnett

Jo Hollingsworth has sent a comment: "I would opt to work with trade unions any day. They can be worth their weight in gold if you build honest, open and trusted relationships. I respect the job they do. And I love it when they give me a run for my money".

Val Stansfield has also pointed out that any member that's not satisfied with their representation can stand for election as a rep themselves.

Anonymous

Can a trade union call for industrial action for ballots on something outside of collective bargaining covered in a collective agreement?

Sarah Fraser Butlin

I'm not terribly sure what the question is about. I think what it might be asking is whether it has to be within a matter that's agreed in a collective agreement before it becomes a trade dispute. The answer would be no. A trade dispute is separately defined. It doesn't have to be within the ambit of the recognition agreement. But no, I'm not entirely clear what that question is about.

Anonymous

There's presently a bus drivers' strike in Manchester, and my client company are providing strike-busting services under contract to the bus company, using my client's own drivers and own vehicles. There have been instances of harassment by union members. Are there specific laws preventing an employer from hiring somebody else to do a job when there's an official strike in place?

Sarah Fraser Butlin

Absolutely there are. This is a really messy issue that they've got themselves into. They need very clear legal advice on what they can and can't do. Strike-busting contracts are a no-no. That's not an empty threat from a union. They need some really careful advice, and they need to start extricating themselves as rapidly as possible.

Daniel Barnett

There could be some serious criminal liability in there.

Sarah Fraser Butlin

Yes. That's not just bad; that's really bad. They need to be dealing with that as rapidly as they can.

Anonymous

Can you refuse a trade union representative entry into a meeting if they don't have identification confirming they're a trade union official?

Sarah Fraser Butlin

I worry about questions like this. If you're going to require everyone to ID before turning up to a trade union meeting - especially if you know that they're a trade union officer - what's that doing for the meeting? Imagine for yourself, if you're ID'd as you walk into work because they don't believe you work there, your hackles are going to be raised before you even go. And you're going to have a union who is sitting at the other side of the table ready for a fight. That's not going to be productive.

Equally, if it's someone unexpected - I had someone on a Zoom call the other day and we all said who the heck is that? It was someone entirely random and we'd been Zoom-bombed. Of course, you need to say, "Hang on. I'm so sorry. I wasn't aware you were a union officer. Can I just clarify the position?" There are ways of doing it aren't there? There's "Give me your ID: prove that you are," and there's "I'm so sorry. I'm sure it's my fault, but could you just confirm and clarify? Could the regional office just give me a quick call to confirm that you are now the union officer?"

Anonymous
Following on from the companion question, what if there's a genuine belief on the employer's part that the companion is compromised in the process? For example, the companion might be a witness in the investigation.

Sarah Fraser Butlin
if they are compromised, and there's a concern then of course, you can say please go and find somebody else, especially if it's an investigation into a disciplinary matter. Of course, you can say, please find someone else but the circumstances have to be very clear before doing that.

Anonymous
We are being threatened with strike action because we've dismissed two union reps. One failed a drug test and one was in breach of health and safety rules. The union has asked us to overlook those indiscretions.

Daniel Barnett
There's not a question following that, but I'm guessing the question is: Should we overlook the indiscretions, or are we entitled to dismiss them? There are, of course, specific rules relating to disciplinary matters with union representatives, aren't there?

Sarah Fraser Butlin
Absolutely. You mustn't discipline or dismiss someone because they're participating in union activities or because they're doing their role as a union rep. Absolutely. But if the dismissal is truly because of a failed drug test or a breach of health and safety, then there's no difference between them and another employee. You do need to be conscious that if they're union reps, you should flag it with the union rather than just going ahead with it. But at the end of the day, if they failed a drug test, they failed a drug test. If there is a health and safety issue, there is a health and safety issue. Their union status doesn't stop them from being dismissed for misconduct. The issue arises regarding whether that's the true reason for the dismissal or not.

Fran
Is there a normal process for collective bargaining around pay? And what happens if you can't reach an agreement?

Sarah Fraser Butlin
So, how do you collectively bargain? Well, the first thing you have to remember is that collective bargaining isn't necessarily about achieving a negotiation. A collective agreement is sitting down and talking. So you've got two options. When you recognise the union, you'll have a collective agreement and that will almost certainly set out a method for collective bargaining. That method will set out the information that has to be provided, the meetings that have to be held, who attends the meetings and how things are dealt with. And there's usually an escalation process - a dispute process - so that if things aren't being resolved, it's clear what happens next.

If you can't agree on the method after the union's been recognised, then there is a statutory method for collective bargaining. Schedule A1 TULRCA sets out the six steps of how collective bargaining should be done. That can be imposed on an organisation by the CAC, if necessary. What do you do if you can't reach an agreement on pay? Well, that's the million-dollar question, isn't it? Because we then come to all the inducement cases where employers have thought, "We can't agree; we'll offer a sweetener and try and persuade the individual employees". Kostal v Dunkley *(Kostal UK Ltd v Dunkley and others [2019] EWCA Civ 1009)* is a really interesting case. What happens then? Or ultimately, does the employer have to dismiss and re-employ? Then you're into s188 collective redundancy consultations. It's a really difficult factual scenario. Firstly, look at the method of collective bargaining. Make sure you've followed that. And secondly, if you can't get to an agreement, then you've got to start thinking about what your options are going forward to resolve the problem.

Anonymous
Our trade union has dwindling membership and invisible representatives. How easy is it to derecognise the union?

Sarah Fraser Butlin
Well, you've first of all got to decide what kinds of recognition you've got. If you've got voluntary recognition, then you can derecognise entirely straightforwardly. Just look at the collective agreement, and it'll tell you how to derecognise. If you've got semi-voluntary or involuntary recognition, then the process is slightly different. Now, just to explain for those who aren't so familiar with recognition: semi-voluntary recognition is where the union made an application to the CAC, it was accepted, but before the CAC adjudicated, there was an agreement to recognise the union. In semi-voluntary recognition, you can obtain derecognition three years after the date of recognition. And it's fairly straightforward to do it. If, however, you end up in involuntary recognition, which is where the CAC has formally done the recognition, then you have a three-year limit and you have to go backwards through the recognition process to get the derecognition. There's a formal provision in schedule A1 of how you derecognise a union. There are some brilliant flowcharts from the DTI of how the recognition processes work. And you basically go through the same process, but in relation to derecognition. So first of all, identify what kind of recognition you've got, and then you'll be able to work out what you can do about derecognition. Of course, remember that once you've got them derecognised, the union could always become active again and decide to seek recognition. So be a bit cautious.

Anonymous
Do you have any tips on how best to respond to employees who, despite the pandemic, are being told by their union not to attend disciplinary or grievance meetings, unless they're held face to face?

Sarah Fraser Butlin
I haven't come across that because most union reps don't want to attend face to face either. I suppose it might be a delaying tactic. You'd need to explore with them why they consider it has to be face to face rather than online. Is there a technological difficulty? Do they have the internet provision? How are they dealing with things as it is? I'd start by asking why they want it to be face to face? What's the issue? If it's a union rep who's really just trying to delay things, again, it goes back to that relationship of trust with the unions and going back to them or to their seniors in the union hierarchy to say that this is the advice that's being given and question if it's really sensible. We want to resolve this quickly and properly. So, I'd be asking why, and if there's no good reason not to have it online, on Zoom, and there's no proper obstacle, then I think I'd probably be getting on with it a bit.

Daniel Barnett
Many clients find that the union representative seems to side with the employer. The representative might be worried about their future job prospects. Is this a real conflict of interest and what can be done?

Sarah Fraser Butlin
It's so fact-specific, isn't it? Because if the employee is in the soup, and the trade union

officer is trying to come to some sensible result for them, it may feel like they're siding with the employer when actually they're trying to do the best for the person. Equally, we've all come across a situation where the employee is not in the soup and the trade union officer is too pally with the employer, it's really difficult to get that relationship, right - between the union and the employer, so that the employer doesn't hate the union and the union doesn't hate the employer, but also that they're not in bed together.

There needs to be some independence and some cooperation but also some appropriate challenge by the union. If the employee is unhappy with the accompaniment, they don't have to have a union officer there. They can have a fellow worker there. It comes down to a choice of saying, actually, this isn't the right person to be my companion. Then they can have another companion. But you do need to be a bit careful in case it's a union officer simply trying to get the best for a client when they're in the soup.

Daniel Barnett
Sarah Fraser Butlin, thank you so much for your time.

WHISTLEBLOWING

TOM CROXFORD QC, BLACKSTONE CHAMBERS

Daniel Barnett

I'm joined today by Tom Croxford QC from Blackstone Chambers, and this morning's Q&A session is on whistleblowing.

Tom Croxford, good morning. Let me ask you a couple of questions of my own. Protected disclosures: one of the biggest issues that a lot of people worry about is how they know at the time they get a grievance or a letter or a complaint from an employee whether or not it contains a protected disclosure. How do you tell?

Tom Croxford

Simply put, it's very hard. One can see from the reported cases that it's particularly hard to persuade a judge that's obviously not a protected disclosure. In Babula (*Babula v Waltham Forest College [2007] EWCA Civ 174*) where Mr Babula complained about a fellow teacher in Waltham Forest, and he reported him to the FBI and the CIA, for being a potential terrorist. And in that case, it was found to be a protected disclosure.

So I suppose what you look at is, classically: what information is there? Does the information, in the reasonable belief of the individual making a disclosure, tend to show a relevant failure, a breach of a legal obligation, a criminal offence and so on? And does that employee reasonably believe that the disclosure is in the public interest?

Now, you should be able to get some of that from the document, but the context is

also important. Actually, a very good recent case, Twist DX (*Twist DX Ltd v Armes and ors UKEAT/0030/20/JOJ*), which is a decision of Mr Justice Linden in the EAT, is that often what's important is actually the reasonable belief point because, of course, a disclosure has to be reasonably believed by the employee to tend to show a relevant failure and to be a disclosure in the public interest. And that can often be the turning point.

Daniel Barnett

You've done seven interim relief applications, which is more than most people. What are the pros and cons of making an application for interim relief, and what should an employer do to prepare for one?

Tom Croxford

If like to think of it in a 'Trump and election fraud' way. I always likely to turn to Trump and election fraud in relation to this sort of point. He genuinely believes that the election is stolen. He discloses information saying there was voter fraud and dead voters were voting. Well, you look at the cases, and Kilraine (*Kilraine v London Borough of Wandsworth [2018] ICR 1850*) is the classic one to go back to, that information might well be sufficient. He might well have a subjective belief that there's a breach of election law, that the disclosure is in the public interest - election fraud is innately public interest - but is it a reasonable belief? Well, that's where, I suppose, one would expect that argument to fall down, particularly once enough judges have said there's no evidence of it. And that's where you go back to the information. Is the information of a type that is likely to show in the reasonable belief of anyone that there has been a breach of relevant obligation?

Just to return to the nature of interim relief, which is an important starting point. Interim relief can only be brought within seven days of the effective date of termination. It gets round the ACAS conciliation process. You've got to get your application in within seven days of the dismissal taking effect. The tribunal then has to list the hearing as soon as possible. Adjourning that hearing ought to be next to impossible, though, in practice, it may be a bit easier in some tribunals. You should be in a hearing, within a few weeks of the dismissal. It's the closest you get to an employment tribunal making an injunction. And if the claimant is successful, the claimant carries on being paid all the way through to the substantive hearing. And that money probably can't be clawed back in any way, shape or form. The interim relief hearing is a public hearing and so many claimants think they can force the respondent to the table at an early stage by making an application. The claimant thinks well, this is the point at which the respondent will want to keep the situation out of the public domain and settle the whole case. It's a common belief and I've brought applications from relief for claimants with that view. But my longer experience is that that view is mainly wrong. It is rare for respondents to be able to get their head around settling a case in time before the interim relief hearing is heard. And therefore, actually, that in and of itself makes it less likely to settle. Also, it's the best chance the respondent has of actually winning a hearing in the case itself.

The test for interim relief is a high one. The tribunal has to be satisfied that there is a pretty good chance of success, having taken account of the evidence. And that is not that hard. If you think about how hard it is to win a substantive trial or whistleblowing, it's

never easy and generally turns on causation. Was the reason for the dismissal actually a protected disclosure? Or was it something else? Was it something related but not the protected disclosure itself? This is at a point where there's been no disclosure, and so for a respondent, preparation is key as well. If you know that there is a claimant who's perhaps brought a grievance in relation to whistleblowing already and you, the respondent, probably, not always, know that he's about to be dismissed - it may be a constructive dismissal - then that's the point to start thinking in advance because once the application for interim relief lands, you may only have a couple of weeks, if that, to get everything in order.

Generally, the way they run is with evidence being in a witness statement, but no cross-examination, and extensive citation of authority. I think there were about 30 authorities in the last case I fought for the respondent - we won. It's that preparation, getting ahead of it, working out who you're going to have witness statements from - disciplining officer, quite likely HR, the person who seems to have been key to the decision, and a person who can say what's been going on in the background. They're very tough for employment tribunal judges to deal with. In my experience, it's half a day of frantic reading, sometimes a day and a half of frantic reading, trying to get up to speed with the authorities on interim relief. And then a hard fight between often experienced counsel, hammering it out in front of you for a day. It's a tough case.

Daniel Barnett
I just want to make a comment and ask a question. You said that normally, or rarely can the respondent claw back the interim relief, continuation of employment salary payments. What are the circumstances where they might?

Tom Croxford
The only circumstance I can think of, and the reason they're public hearings, is that in principle, they are not capable of being

clawed back. It is possible that if the claim itself is based upon fraud, i.e. a claimant has deliberately lied and you can show that the claimant has deliberately lied, you might be able to go back and undo the initial decision for interim relief at some later point. I have to say, I've never heard anyone attempt it, I've certainly never seen it done and I think it would be most unlikely to succeed. The reason that they're public hearings is it is the final determination of entitlement to salary for the period from the interim relief hearing through to the substantive hearing.

Daniel Barnett

The observation is simply that these are very peculiar hearings in the sense that often the judge will be deciding fairly fundamental questions between the parties, albeit on a fair degree of certainty as opposed to balance a probability, but doing so without the ET3 because the respondent often won't have got round to lodging their ET3.

Tom Croxford

Indeed. A respondent may have to take a tactical decision as to whether it wants an ET3 on the stocks or not because generally speaking, it will interrupt the preparation of the interim relief hearings to be simultaneously preparing the ET3. So yes, there's often no ET3. In my experience, most of the ET judges I've been in front of on an interim relief hearing have never done an interim relief before. They are not common hearings. And so they're asking their mates in the judiciary what they should do and what the right answer is, looking at their bench book and trying to work it out. And as a result, they're exciting hearings. They're always exciting.

Daniel Barnett

I used to say to people that most barristers and most judges have done none or one interim relief. I'm not sure that's true anymore since we've had the pandemic, but that was certainly true a year ago.

Tom Croxford

I think there are few who've done many of them. They're tricky things to do.

Su Apps

To what extent can a breach of an individual contract or a personal grievance be something that can be reasonably believed to be in the public interest? Can you give any examples of when this will and won't be the case?

Tom Croxford

In principle, if it is simply a breach of your own contract or a personal issue that you have with somebody, that is not in the public interest. The very reason for the government changing the whistleblowing legislation was to stop precisely these arguments coming before the tribunal. I think that you need to take it a bit beyond the mere personal breach of contract and seek, as a claimant, to elevate it into something more structural or fundamental. I still think that one sees it, for example, in relation to discrimination, and I've seen cases - I can't be too specific, because I've got some pending cases where this is raised - saying that a complaint of discrimination against the employer is capable of being a public interest disclosure, because discrimination is bad and wrong. I think that's going to be tricky to persuade any tribunals that it's not fundamentally, at its heart, a private interest which is being addressed rather than something that is a public interest.

Tom Croxford

I can see though, that perhaps if it's a mass equal pay-type argument, it might be much easier to say that that is a public interest disclosure. Some of it may depend upon how the disclosure is made as well, in that if you frame that the disclosure itself as "I'm complaining about systemic discrimination in relation to pay in this, by way of example, public sector organisation", I think that might be much easier to persuade a tribunal of, even though the motivation for making the disclosure - which is, of course, not strictly speaking, relevant - might be private, the interest might be persuadable to be public.

Daniel Barnett
There was a case that was in the EAT, went to the Supreme Court but settled before the Supreme Court hearing that dealt with the four factors that go towards whether a disclosure is in the public interest.

Tom Croxford
Is it Nurmohammed (*Chesterton Global Ltd v Nurmohamed [2017] IRLR 837*)? The Underhill judgment? That, again, received further support in Twist DX. I think Mr Justice Linden cites it with some slight tweaks around the edges, perhaps in relation to meanings. I think it's worth looking at both of those. But yes, fundamentally, it is looking at whether in fact, in truth, it is subjectively believed to be in the public interest and separately, reasonably and objectively believed to be in the public interest.

Daniel Barnett
I just want to add one other thing to that. There could be a technical foul in a tribunal case if the claimant doesn't give evidence that they actually believed the disclosure to be in the public interest. And there's a case called Ibrahim (*Ibrahim v HCA International Ltd [2019] EWCA Civ 2007*), which says that the absence of saying that can cause a claimant to technically lose. Now, there are problems with that case, but that's the law at the moment.

Tom Croxford
There are. It's always worth remembering that, theoretically at least, the claimant has the burden of proving every element of a protected disclosure, and therefore, the claimant has to give evidence as to it. And again, actually, back to this nice new case of Twist DX, the claimant has to give evidence of their subjective belief as to what head of protected disclosures the information tends to show. It's not enough to say it tended to show that there was a breach. They have to show in relation to each of them, separately, why they believe it

tended to show that relevant failure. And that may be more complicated for some claimants who may, perhaps, have burnished their evidence a little as it goes through the process of getting to a substantive hearing.

Natalie White
What's the first thing an employee should do when an employee makes a disclosure?

Daniel Barnett
Not sack the employee, I'd guess.

Tom Croxford
It depends. This is about a person who makes a protected disclosure. I think that in relation to that, largely speaking, investigation is a great start. If you think it might be a protected disclosure, put it through a whistleblowing policy rather than through the disciplinary investigation policy. Certainly, the grievance policy is better than the disciplinary policy. If you have that concern, that is often the case, that it's capable of being both an act of misconduct and a protected disclosure, that raises some very difficult questions. I think that really does depend very precisely on what the contents of the apparent possible protected disclosure and act of misconduct are. But dismissing first and investigating later is a high-risk option in relation to anything that might be protected disclosure.

Natalie White
Can employers discipline an employee who commits misconduct to uncover information that they make a disclosure about, such as accessing private files?

Tom Croxford
In principle, yes. It's not uncommon for this situation to arise. I think that, as ever, one needs to tread with caution. If the employee has in fact discovered something truly awful, then disciplining them as your first step rather than investigating the truly awful thing that they appear to have uncovered, again, might not be the best plan. In principle, yes, of course, if they commit misconduct, and particularly

where that misconduct is not something that also is said to be the protected disclosure, one can - and one generally will - seek to investigate it first. I think that that's another of the examples where it depends a bit on how your disciplinary policies are framed. But being very careful to distinguish between the investigation phase and the discipline phase is perhaps the best approach. And if one first investigates, perhaps more neutrally and then perhaps, again, pushes things down two different routes from then on, if circumstances justified, i.e. one investigation of the internal misconduct that amounts to the protected disclosure, and separately, the disciplinary offence of committing misconduct. Balancing those can be very tricky.

Su Apps
What practical steps can an employer take when taking unrelated disciplinary action against someone who's blown the whistle to limit the risk of successful allegations of automatic unfair dismissal?

Daniel Barnett
So you've got a whistleblower and you've got separate disciplinary allegations. How do you stop a claimant or a tribunal saying causation, not correlation?

Tom Croxford
That's at the heart, I suppose, of almost every whistleblowing trial I've actually fought and I've fought a number of them. In a perfect world, one might have a person determine the disciplinary allegation, who had, at least at the outset, no knowledge of the whistleblowing - the protected disclosure - and therefore, it would make it innately more difficult for that person to dismiss by reason of the protected disclosure itself, albeit that we see in cases like Jhuti (*Royal Mail Group Ltd v Jhuti [2020] ICR 731*) for example, the difficult questions of attribution of the incorrect evidence of one disciplinary officer in relation to the tribunal itself.

If a company relies upon false information that's been deliberately put in front of the company so that the whistleblower gets forced out, then no amount of clever engineering of your disciplinary process and your whistleblowing process is going to get in the way of a finding of automatic unfair dismissal. I think that the key bit is, as ever, careful investigation, careful discipline and making a sensible, right correct decision and reasoning it effectively.

Andy Tovey
If you've got less than two years' service and you raise an allegation of bullying, might you have protection under the whistleblowing rules?

Tom Croxford
Yes. Whistleblowing gets you round all sorts of problems and that's one of them. So yes, is the simple answer. Though the bullying allegation might well not be enough to get over the public interest issue. That's perhaps the point that might be the first step in relation to that.

Melanie Bonas
Do you think employers do enough to promote whistleblowing in the workplace to make sure whistleblowing is as effective as it should be, and what more can employers do?

Daniel Barnett
There's a nice wide-ranging question.

Tom Croxford
If one looks at the very important work done by Protect (formerly known as Public Concern at Work), you can see that many employers do not do nearly enough. And that even when they do things, it is all too often paying lip service to principles, perhaps sometimes from the financial services industry, for example, there is that self-interested concern on the part of some employers that they need to have all the right things in place to make it look pretty, but that doesn't necessarily prevent them from quietly, but effectively getting rid of whistleblowers. I can think of some past clients of mine who fell

into that precise category, though, obviously, we won't name them in these circumstances. But I think that taking whistleblowing seriously as a vehicle for changing institutional behaviour is something which should be taken more seriously in some but not all organisations. But inevitably, any effective whistleblowing policy needs to be capable of distinguishing between the important things that the institution needs to change - with whistleblowing being a route to that - and the many complaints of whistleblowing that are thrown up at companies that are sometimes on the borderline of abusive on the part of some employees. That ability to distinguish them is the hallmark of an effective whistleblowing policy.

Caroline Oliver

Will employers have concerns settling whistleblowing claims? Because a settlement agreement can't prevent an employee or former employee from making a protected disclosure?

Tom Croxford

Yes, they will. But again, in my experience, it is generally speaking, not something that prevents the vast majority of protected disclosure cases from settling in fact, and employers have a habit of persuading themselves that the real risk of the employee continuing to cause trouble post-settlement is relatively low. One sees repeatedly in whistleblowing settlement agreements, provisions such as "the employee warrants that he's not disclosed the information within the whistleblowing complaint to anyone other than the employee", perhaps they could warrant that they will not disclose the information other than by way of a protected disclosure, i.e. you maintain a duty of confidence, albeit recognising carefully, importantly within the settlement agreement, that the agreement does not prevent the employee from making protected disclosures. But it's worth remembering that it's not a protected disclosure unless it is made to, broadly speaking, the employer, or a regulatory body or some other designated body. That should

reduce the risk for most employers of the employee going straight to the press, which is an unusual route to take to still amount to a protected disclosure given the additional requirements for such a disclosure.

Anonymous

If an employee is dismissed for making a protected disclosure and while on garden leave the employer starts digging to find dirt on the employee to reduce a possible settlement, finds the employees committed an act eight months before that constitutes gross misconduct and dismisses him, could the employees still go for interim relief arising from the reason for the first dismissal, as it could be argued that the employer wouldn't have found the misconduct had the employee not made the protected disclosure?

Tom Croxford

I think this means if you dismiss on notice, for a protected disclosure, and then as it were, shorten that notice period by dismissing summarily for misconduct during the notice period. The effective date of termination is in relation to that second action, the disciplinary dismissal, rather than the protected disclosure dismissal. The employee can still go for interim relief by saying the real reason for the eventual dismissal, i.e. the supposed misconduct dismissal, is in fact the earlier protected disclosure. I think if, in fact, in reality, the reason for dismissal is entirely separate misconduct, then it would be surprising for the tribunal to find that the principal reason for dismissal was in fact the earlier protected disclosure. I don't think it'd be impossible, but it's not quite the same.

In discrimination cases - Rees v Apollo watches (*Rees v Apollo Watch Repairs Plc [1996] IRLR 466*) is the classic one in that area - where dismissing someone for things that you discovered when they were away - on maternity leave, in that case - can be attributed to the maternity leave. The test in relation to dismissal is quite a narrow one for unfair dismissal, generally, the principal reason. I think it'd be difficult to get around that one.

Daniel Barnett
Just agreeing with that and adding to it, the employee couldn't argue that the hunting out reasons to dismiss - because there's been a dismissal for a protected disclosure - could itself lead to an interim relief order being made because that is a detriment, not a dismissal, and you can't get interim relief for decades.

Tom Croxford
Correct. But I think that it might well be a detriment that the employer goes hunting for grounds for dismissal because of a protected disclosure. And it will be a tricky question for an employment tribunal dealing with that, to work out precisely the route through the statutory machinery and whether that is an allowable reason for reducing the compensation that would flow from a detriment. And of course, in some cases, the detriment damages can encompass damages flowing from the dismissal that arose by reason of a detriment. But the separate point would be whether there was contributory fault, or just and equitable grounds for bringing that back down again. It's not an easy question.

Mike Clyne
Do you think the UK government will ever introduce whistleblower incentives as can happen in the United States in some cases?

Daniel Barnett
Could you also explain what whistleblower incentives are?

Tom Croxford
In the US, there are a series of schemes run by the SEC and the DOJ and a number of other institutions there as well, whereby if you are the first whistleblower, you can get a massive chunk of, generally speaking, the fine that the SEC then attributes to the employer by reason of the misconduct revealed. And it's worth remembering that it's not just in relation to fully US-domiciled events. So I have been

involved for a claimant and a respondent in cases where the claimant has brought a separate claim under the US schemes for the whistleblower incentives, despite the proper venue for the claim being in an English employment tribunal. So I think they are quite specific to the US in the style of US reward systems. I don't immediately see that happening in the UK, but the FCA may decide that it's worth their while to bring in such a scheme if it enables them to levy even greater fines on companies in the financial services sector for wrongdoing. I don't know of any immediate expectation of that sort of reward scheme being brought in here though.

Anonymous
For a whistleblowing dismissal, if you're acting for the claimant, would you always recommend naming the dismissing manager as second respondent for an Osipov detriment-type claim *(Timis v Osipov [2019] IRLR 52)*?

Daniel Barnett
Could you just explain in one sentence what an Osipov claim is?

Tom Croxford
Yes. So it is bringing a detriment claim effectively for personal damages against the individual for the detriment of having been subjected to something other than dismissal by the employer. If it's a dismissal, the only claim that can be brought in relation to that is directly in relation to the unfair dismissal against the employer, but a detriment claim brought against anybody. It's quite common to see more and more respondents being brought in, in relation to detriment claims.

I'm unconvinced that they always add much. It's become quite common to just add endless individual respondents and that has a habit actually of making the claim more complicated, particularly if the other respondents seek separate representation. You can very easily double the length of the eventual tribunal hearing by the increased complexity, make it more difficult for the tribunal to resolve it and only to a trivial extent get greater damages as a result. But I can see pros and cons both ways and it's more common I find for a claimant to justify bringing some bigwig US manager directly into the purview of the UK employment tribunals, as a way of actually forcing the head office, wherever they may be, to actually focus on what they may have been hoping to think is a trivial case in some godforsaken global backwater.

Julie Davis
How do you distinguish between the mere imparting of information and the raising of a disclosure? Would a manager who's felt to be gossiping about one of his employees be enough to cross that threshold?

Tom Croxford
I think it's important to remember that it's not about what the employer thinks of the disclosure, even if the employer is of the view that it's definitely not a protected disclosure. So what? It doesn't make a difference. The question is firstly what the employee is doing by disclosing information - Is it to the employer? Gossiping may well not be viewed as being disclosure to the employer in that sense. Secondly, does he reasonably believe it tends to show a breach of a relevant obligation? Something that can be described as gossip is rarely going to amount to that. And thirdly, is it reasonable to believe that it (a) discloses relevant information and (b) is in the public interest? Again, "I thought it was in the public interest to gossip" is not a line that I've seen used in a tribunal, but never say never.

Michael Foster
How do you calculate compensation for injury to feelings?

Daniel Barnett
Just to be clear, you can only get compensation for injury to feelings if the claim is for detriment for whistleblowing, but not for dismissal for whistleblowing.

Tom Croxford
In principle, you calculate it just the same as you do in relation to a discrimination case. And again, in principle, it is supposed to depend upon the injury to feelings of the claimant rather than some made up tariff by the EAT. But in reality, if it gets to the stage of actually dealing with a remedy in relation to a whistleblowing detriment claim - and it rarely does - it's going to look at the tariff of other discrimination cases and say, this was bad, very bad or not so bad, and award a number measured in thousands rather than more than that thereafter. It's incredibly rarely a major component of a whistleblowing case.

Daniel Barnett
What's the main case on that?

Tom Croxford
What, on injury to feelings? God only knows.

Daniel Barnett
I assumed you'd be going to Vento (Vento v Chief Constable of West Yorkshire Police [2003] IRLR 102).

Tom Croxford
Yes, I mean, there's a series of other cases as well, but yes. There's actually one on whistleblowing as well, but I'm trying to remember the name of the whistleblowing case. I'll come up with it later.

June Smith
How frequently are interim relief claims successful?

Tom Croxford
We did a Blackstone Chambers webinar recently where I asked the people on the panel whether they had been involved in the case where the claimant had won an interim relief hearing. I was the only one who had, many years back when it was, strictly speaking, a health and safety rather than a protected disclosure case. No one else had been involved in a case where the claimant had, in fact, won

interim relief. Yes, they do win, but it's much more common for the respondents to win.

Daniel Barnett
Well, you've now challenged me to do exactly that, so I'm just making a quick poll for everybody here. Have you been involved in an interim relief case? Yes or no. If yes, did the claimant win? Yes, or no. Let's see what the answers are for that one.

Nineteen percent of people have been involved with an interim relief case and 81% haven't. Ninety-three percent of those who happened to be involved with an interim relief case say that the claimant lost.

Tom Croxford
What it does show effectively is that interim relief hearings are still rare. And they're rare for good reason. It's rarely a good use of the claims money.

Caroline Lewis
How common or successful are claims for detriment that don't lead to dismissal in whistleblowing cases? And is it feasible for an employee who's brought a detriment claim to remain an employee of that employer?

Tom Croxford
For many employees who bring a detriment claim, there ends up being a breakdown in relationship that leads to a whistleblowing unfair dismissal or perhaps constructive dismissal claim as a result. Therefore, it is, in my experience, rare for there to be purely a detriment claim without a dismissal other than in the non-employee claims - the workers, the consultants, the solicitors and members of LLPs, by way of example - those cases are simply detriment cases, and it's much to the advantage, of course, of the individuals in those cases that it is just a detriment case because the threshold for proving causation is lower; see Fecitt (Fecitt & Ors v NHS Manchester UKEAT/0150/10/CEA).

Daniel Barnett
Tom Croxford from Blackstone Chambers, thank you very much.

JOIN DANIEL EVERY SATURDAY EVENING AT
9PM WHEN HE PRESENTS THE ALL-NEW

LBC LEGAL HOUR

— OR CATCH UP VIA THE GLOBAL PLAYER,
AT BIT.LY/LBCLEGALHOUR

SATURDAYS, 9PM

HR INNER CIRCLE

"The HR Inner Circle has improved my life amazingly,

mainly because it means I have to spend less time researching and more time and more time actually doing the work I'm paid for."

Sue Whittle, Employment & Safety Advice LTD

Join to gain access to the monthly HR Inner Circular magazine

jam-packed with amazing information
for ambitious HR professionals

WWW.HRINNERCIRCLE.CO.UK

What do you get?

1 Monthly live online 'Ask Me Anything' sessions: each month, we host an online video webinar, when you can share your HR problems and ask Daniel anything about employment law. You'll also receive a recording and a transcript each month, so you have a permanent record of the session even if you cannot be there.

Please ask your questions now:
1. click 'Raise Hand'; or,
2. type it into the Questions box

> "Daniel Barnett is an inspirational, walking and talking 'how to understand mind-boggling employment law handbook!"

Ellie King, HR Manager, RWE Technology

2 A specially recorded audio seminar every month, with HR shortcuts and workarounds you can't get anywhere else.

WWW.HRINNERCIRCLE.CO.UK

3 The monthly Inner Circular magazine, jam-packed with valuable information for ambitious HR professionals.

4 Access to Daniel's exclusive, private, invitation-only online Inner Circle group, where you get to discuss HR problems with other smart, ambitious professionals and download precedents and policies they have shared.

"It's the support and help that you get, the reassurance that you're talking to people who know what they're talking about rather than people just randomly giving information."

Nicky Jolley, HR2DAY LTD

5 Access to the exclusive HR Inner Circle website which includes a back-catalogue of all the HRIC resources since the launch in 2015.

WWW.HRINNERCIRCLE.CO.UK

Printed in Great Britain
by Amazon